SCORE AND PODIUM

A Complete Guide to Conducting

SCORE AND PODIUM

A Complete Guide to Conducting

FREDERIK PRAUSNITZ

DIRECTOR OF THE CONDUCTING PROGRAMS
THE PEABODY CONSERVATORY OF JOHNS HOPKINS UNIVERSITY

W·W·NORTON & COMPANY
NEW YORK · LONDON

ACKNOWLEDGMENTS

Elliott Carter, *Double Concerto for Harpsichord and Piano.* Copyright © 1962, 1964 by Associated Music Publishers, Inc. Used by permission. p. 373

Aaron Copland, *Appalachian Spring.* © Copyright 1945 by Aaron Copland; Renewed 1972. Reprinted by permission of Aaron Copland, copyright owner, Boosey & Hawkes, Inc., Sole licensees. p. 289

Aaron Copland, *Music for the Theatre.* © Copyright 1932 by Aaron Copland; Renewed 1960. Reprinted by permission of Aaron Copland and Boosey & Hawkes, Inc., Sole licensees. p. 217

Morris Cotel, *Piano Concerto.* Midbar Music Press (ASCAP). Cotel: Piano Concerto (1968) Copyright Morris Cotel 1973. p. 372

Claude Debussy, *Jeux.* Copyright 1914 Durand S. A. Used by permission of the Publisher; Theodore Presser Company, Sole Representative U. S. A. p. 429

Herbert Eimert, "Debussy's 'Jeux'," from *Die Reihe,* Vol. 5 (1961) p. 15. © Copyright 1961 by Universal Edition Publishing, Inc., New Jersey; All rights reserved; Used by permission of European American Music Distributors Corporation, Sole agent for Universal Edition Publishing. p. 429

Charles Ives, *Second Orchestral Set.* © Copyright 1971 by Peer International Corporation. © Copyright 1982 by Peer International Corporation; International Copyright Secured; All Rights Reserved Including the Right of Public Performance for Profit; Used by permission. p. 417

Maurice Ravel, *Ma Mère l'Oye.* Copyright 1912 Durand S.A. Editions Musicales; Editions ARIMA and Durand, S.A. Editions Musicales, Joint Publication, Used by permission of the Publisher; Theodore Presser Company, Sole Representative U. S. A. pp. 200, 215

William Schuman, *New England Triptych.* © 1957 Merion Music Inc. Used by permission. pp. 187, 190, 196, 478

Igor Stravinsky, *Chant du rossignol.* Copyright 1921 by Edition Russe de Musique; Copyright assigned to Boosey and Hawkes, Inc. Reprinted by permission. p. 236

Igor Stravinsky, *Le Sacre du printemps.* Copyright 1921 by Edition Russe de Musique; Copyright assigned 1947 to Boosey and Hawkes, Inc. Reprinted by permission. pp. 438–41

The text of this book is composed in Palatino, with display type set in Delphian. Composition by Vail-Ballou Press. Manufacturing by Maple-Vail Book Manufacturing Group. Book design by Nancy Dale Muldoon.
Drawings and diagrams by Frederik Prausnitz.

First Edition

Library of Congress Cataloging in Publication Data

Prausnitz, Frederik.
Score and podium: a complete guide
to conducting.
Bibliography: p.
Includes index.
1. Conducting. I. Title.
MT85.P72 1983   781.6'35   82-14342
ISBN 0-393-95154-5

W. W. Norton & Company, Inc., 500 Fifth Avenue, New York, N.Y. 10110
W. W. Norton & Company Ltd., 37 Great Russell Street, London WC1B 3NU

1 2 3 4 5 6 7 8 9 0

SCORE

Adieu, dit le renard. Voici mon secret.
Il est très simple: on ne voit bien
qu'avec le coeur. L'essentiel est
invisible pour les yeux.
— Antoine de Saint-Exupéry, *Le Petit Prince*

AND

Yes, it takes intellect to reach the heart.
— William Schuman

PODIUM

Just as there is a difference
between grammar and declamation,
so there is an infinitely greater
one between musical theory and
the art of fine playing.
— François Couperin

Dedicated to the memory of
Norman Lloyd
and
Richard Franko Goldman

CONTENTS

SCORE   PODIUM

PART ONE

SCORE	PODIUM

PART TWO

Transforming the Information

Communicating Musical Ideas

PART THREE

The Image in Mind

The Instrument

CONCLUSION

A Unique Way of being a Musician   513

ACKNOWLEDGMENTS

THIS book is dedicated to the memory of Norman Lloyd and Richard Franko Goldman.

As Director of Education at Juilliard, Norman taught this young staff conductor something of the joy and the mystery of teaching. Later, as Director of the Arts and Humanities Division of the Rockfeller Foundation, he continued the lesson in long discussions which not only enabled me to become a teacher of conductors, but to organize experiences in the professional field into a format suitable for presentation in a textbook.

Richard, during our early years as colleagues on the Juilliard faculty, taught me to value and endure the artist in myself. Many years later, as President of the Peabody Institute in Baltimore, he placed at my disposal a learning environment in which to equip and strengthen the artist in my students. Under his successor Elliott Galkin, the Peabody Conductors' Orchestra was founded, and the program grew.

It was one of my students who decided that I should write this book. Sheldon Morgenstern, founder/director of a national music festival, took matters in his own hands when he suggested the initial funding of such a project to the Rockefeller Foundation. In the fifteen years that followed, and in the course of a professional life that continued to reflect an absorbing interest in the teaching of conductors, I had generous and expert advisors who provided points of view other than my own. For the development of ideas on a firm but flexible basis for instruction, I am indebted to writers on music David Drew, David Hamilton, Donald Mitchell, and Michael Steinberg.

For my strong convictions about a conductor's relationship to the *score* I have to thank a special good fortune that has granted me the friendship of many composers. I have learned about music and musical performance from Elliott Carter, Luigi Dallapiccola, Roberto Gerhard, Alexander Goehr, Karl Amadeus Hartmann, Elisabeth Lutyens, Peter Mennin, Wallingford Riegger, William Schuman, Roger Sessions, and Edgard Varèse. In addition, my thanks are due to three most resourceful champions of the proposition that all music must be related to the musical experience of our own day: Sir William Glock, former Controller of Music for the BBC and, on this side of the Atlantic, Donald Leavitt and Jon Newsom of the Library of Congress in Washington.

What I know about *podium* aspects of conducting I have learned from the orchestras I have conducted. From the violist of the London orchestra who confided over a pint of Worthington's that "our greatest art is to play *between* your beats," to the anonymous player who, during my first visit to Italy, said that "at the first rehearsal the maestro spoke hardly any Italian, but by the dress rehearsal he talked too much": to these and many others I am greatly obliged.

As the materials for this book were pulled together and its outline began to take shape, several generations of conducting students became readers, critics, and, of course, subjects of every fresh effort to organize and present a text that would serve conductors as well as those interested in learning something about conducting. Peter Bay, James Lucas, Louis Stewart, and Marc Tardue were among the first to lend their cheerful assistance.

Conductors Richard Pittman of the New England Conservatory and Paul Vermel of the University of Illinois read the first draft of the manuscript. Their thoughtful criticism served as a point of departure for a process of re-thinking and re-writing which culminated in a final, complete review, with invaluable help from Leo Kraft of Queens College of the City University of New York. Hinda Keller Farber and Kathleen Wilson Spillane provided expert help in preparing the final text. But that this long labor was brought to its eventual conclusion is entirely due to the ever supportive severity of W. W. Norton music editor Claire Brook. For her informed patience, her resourceful encouragement, and her virtuosic lack of sympathy with most of my favorite stylistic indulgencies, many thanks.

Finally I want to express my very real appreciation to Margaret, whose affectionate forbearance never gave up entirely on a husband who would return from long absences on tour only to fill the house with his young conductors, or lock himself into his study to write a book for them.

Frederik Prausnitz

SCORE AND PODIUM

A Complete Guide to Conducting

INTRODUCTION

TWO SIDES OF A COIN

CONDUCTING is a unique way of being a musician. To direct a musical performance at which he is not to play a note, to rehearse the playing of that performance according to an aural image worked out in silent preparation, and to create that image from a musical text whose evidence ranges from the absolute to the ambiguous—these are separate, interacting, equally important aspects of the conductor's role.

Conducting involves practiced skills in three areas: organizing and evaluating information available in the score, transforming that information into a vivid mental image of the performance-to-be, and communicating the essentials of that performance to an orchestra. The exercise of skills in the first two areas preceed that of the third. Thus the conductor's primary musical instrument is his own mind. Work with the orchestra, his other musical instrument, will be effective only to the extent of his success in transforming the evidence of the score into a living musical image, *before* he mounts the podium.

Every conducted performance requires informed, personal involvement in selective aspects of the music. Points of contact might be notions about a curious musical shape, the consequence of characteristic harmonic structures, or even the compelling memory of some extramusical association with some part of the work. Full participation of the performer is as essential as that of the composer, for, as Mahler observed, "the most important things in music cannot be noted in the score."*

*Gustav Mahler: Im eigenen Wort—Im Worte der Freunde (Zürich: Peter Schifferli Verlag, 1958), p. 43.

1

But the personal dimension in working through a score is only partial compensation for the limitations of ambiguities of our system of musical notation. Central to the musical experience itself is the fact that, although a qualified beholder may find beauty in a page of music, his listeners will not see that page, or even have its special qualities pointed out to them; they will hear it performed, the end-product of a lengthy process of preparation and maturation. That product will reflect what the performer's eye beheld, and then heard, imagined, refined, until the composer's score and the performer's perceptions are merged in a unique blend. "I am convinced," said composer Roger Sessions, "that the performer is an essential element in the whole musical picture. . . . There is no such thing as a 'definitive performance' of any work whatsoever. This is true even of performances by the composer himself."*

The process of hearing, imagining and refining begins in quiet concentration on the score, and is likely to continue as long as the work means something to you. Such personal involvement becomes particularly intense on the podium. It is of prime importance, therefore, that you discipline yourself to listen in rehearsal and performance, not only with your physical hearing finely tuned but critically, according to the expectations of your earliest "points of contact" with the music, and the most recent results of your imagining and refining process. The former will monitor what is noted in the score. The latter is a measure of how successfully you are able to represent your own, "essential part in the whole musical picture." Thus your role on the podium must be considered from the same perspective as your work with the score: to insure faithful compliance with the composer's instructions, while your inner vision of the music is continually resubmitted to the test of fresh musical experiences. In fact, score and podium represent aspects of conducting which are but two sides of the same coin.

Like other forms of artistic expression, conducting does not depend entirely on the richness of available resources for its effectiveness in any given circumstance. A flexible beat and sound musical ideas based on a firm grasp of the score will serve a well-planned rehearsal of any instrumental ensemble. But even a world-class orchestra cannot compensate for a conductor's shortcomings in either area, any more than expensive canvas, brushes, and paints would make up for poor draftsmanship or inexpert use of color, in the most nobly conceived painting.

The most important objectives in our study will involve those disciplines which enable you to absorb and work with information available in the score; and the development of simple physical skills which, with a clear understanding of the principles governing the beat, enable conductors to maintain a flow of signals from the podium.

*Roger Sessions, *Questions about Music* (New York: W. W. Norton, 1971), p. 86.

OUTLINE OF CHAPTERS

PART ONE SCORE sections (a) deal with the nature of musical evidence in a score and the extent of additional input required from the conductor; PODIUM sections (b), with basic technical skills of beat and gesture.

SCORE

1A. *Facts and Instructions*
The surface of music is defined and distinctions are drawn between the kinds of evidence to be discovered.

2A. *Organizing the Evidence*
A sequence is established for systematic inspection of all information available on the surface of music.

3A. *Probing: Musical Clues*
We exploit the evidence of a striking rhythmic figure in the third movement of Brahms's *Third Symphony*, and discover a compelling unity of expressive design.

4A. *Probing: Images / Imagination*
The development of an extramusical fantasy about the Andante of Mozart's *Eine kleine Nachtmusik* is pursued, together with a beat-by-beat theoretical examination of the musical text.

5A. *Storing the Information*
A slight textual discrepancy between score and parts to the second movement of Mendelssohn's *Italian Symphony* becomes the point of departure for characterization, organization, and memorization of the music.

PODIUM

1B. *Posture, Pivots, the Arm in Motion*
The conductors feet are put on the podium, his arms in motion.

2B. *The Beat: Qualities and Functions*
The conformation of the beat is analyzed, and the qualities that distinguish one beat from another, as well as some ways in which the active or passive function of beats contributes to the communication of intended musical shapes, or suggested fluctuation of musical tension.

3B. *The Beat: Functions and Plain Patterns*
The examination of beat functions is continued, showing how 2, 3, or 4 beats may be combined into patterns that serve both metric orientation and expressive illustration.

4B. *The Beat: Subdivisions / Compound and Mixed Patterns*
The method is presented of using successive beats of contrasting quality and function for special metric definition or expressive control.

5B. *Beat and Gesture*
An alternative kind of movement to the beat that controls is examined: gesture that suggests.

PART TWO This deals with the transformation of evidence gathered from the musical surface into a vivid inner image and with the technical means of communicating this image to an orchestra.

6. *Points of Contact: The Role of Detail*
(SCORE) Included are examples of the all-important first step *below* the surface of music, with suggestions of a simple method of determining the direction in which to take that step. Score examined: Mussorgsky / Ravel, *Pictures at an Exhibition*.

7. *The Application of the Beat*
(PODIUM) The means of musical communication from the podium are reviewed. As developed in the five opening chapters, the entire range of beats and combinations of beats is applied to various examples of full score, often with possible alternatives. Rules and relevant summaries are repeated verbatim as they appeared in previous chapters; and extensive cross-references indicate earlier, more detailed discussion of the technical principles involved.

8. *Building Blocks: Musical Shapes*
(SCORE) One general approach to learning a score is illustrated, as well as a possible way of establishing contact below the surface of music. Two kinds of small musical shapes are defined; a third, larger kind is suggested. Scores examined: Brahms, *Third Symphony*; Ravel, *La Valse*.

*The complete score appears in this chapter, fully marked with a variety of beats intended to encourage an exchange of musical initiative between orchestral soloists and conductor.

The information contained in Parts I and II is both fundamental and comprehensive, intended to help you cope with musical demands of a score according to the composer's terms and the orchestra's needs. Ability to translate information on a page of music, without recourse to its instrumental equivalent, into a mental image of its performance, and informed proficiency in the use of simple signals to communicate, selectively, relevant features of this image to certain players in the orchestra are aspects of conducting whose usefulness is not limited to future professionals in the field. One's powers of directing musical thought and imagination according to the silent testimony of a score, and confident skills of testing the emerging inner image of the music in the articulate reality of disciplined movement, are bound to enhance any musician's effectiveness as performer, teacher, or composer. The curriculum of a growing number of music schools and music departments reflects the fact that conducting, the youngest of specialized musical performing arts, has become a craft for all seasons, a useful discipline among general music studies designed to open the doors of perception a little wider.

For those who would choose to make the conductor's podium their professional base, however, something more is needed. Part III is devoted to an examination of memory and of ways to deal with the time element in music; to aids in developing a musical perspective that will permit a clear view of our past heritage from a vantage point in the present; and to an exploration of the orchestra itself, as a group of musicians, as an instrument, and as partner in musical performance.

In all three areas, present study can only initiate a life-long process of learning. In matters relating to the orchestra, to conducting rehearsals and performances, the importance of experience is obvious. Of the other two areas, let it be said that they shall involve a search. Mind and memory provide the place and the condition. Transformation will continue to be the object. And your own, fully developed sense of musical perspective shall be the crucible in which the results of your search will first be tested.

The rest is informed and enduring involvement. The Indian poet Rabindranath Tagore told the tale of a foolish seeker who only endured. Many years had he spent in quest of the magic stone whose touch would turn base metal to gold. His ragged figure had become an object of scorn, as he stooped and stumbled one day along the ocean shore. "Hey, crazy man," shouted one among a group of laughing children that followed him at a distance. "Where did you get that golden chain around your waist?" The man looked down and saw that the iron belt against which he had tested tens of thousands of stones had indeed been transformed into gold. And he realized, in despair, that somewhere he must have had in his hand the very stone he sought, that he had passed it against his iron belt in a long familiar gesture of testing its magic, and discarded it in the mindless habit of his search. Without lifting his eyes to see that the setting sun had turned the entire sky to gold, he retraced his tracks to begin the laborious task of searching among the rubble of his past.

A NOTE ON SCORES

The music examples in this book illustrate *the principles of the beat and their application* as described in the text. When *the process of preparing a score* is the subject of discussion, the reader is expected to obtain copies of the works in question. Only a few compositions are analyzed in detail, but they are used repeatedly to illustrate a variety of approaches.

The reader is urged to start a score library as soon as possible. Pocket scores of standard orchestral works and study scores of compositions still under publishers' copyright (usually photographically reduced versions of the large rental scores) have long been the staple of personal score libraries. But inexpensive, full-size editions of works in the public domain have become increasingly available, as well as excellent, albeit much dearer, critical editions. While it is essential that performers acquaint themselves with the results of research into the literature of their field, conductors are advised to buy inexpensive editions of scores rather than to borrow a costly, definitive text. The process of annotating and correcting one's own scores, aided by the best available critical edition borrowed for that purpose, is an excellent way of memorizing relevant detail in a work under study and of adding perspective to the learning process.

A NOTE ON FLOW CHARTS

Two kinds of charts are used throughout this book. One, in diagram form, represents the steps involved in the preparation of a score for performance. The other illustrates the principles governing the conductor's beat and gesture. Both are used as "flow charts" in Part I, showing the areas of study covered in the respective halves of each of the first five chapters, as well as the subjects of further exploration to follow. Charts are also reprinted at the head of Parts II and III. To assist you in keeping track of rules and suggestions presented in Chapters 1 through 5, these latter charts are furnished with an index referring to earlier pages on which particular subjects were first developed in detail. Review Chapter 7 on the application of the beat uses indexed charts throughout.

A NOTE ON ILLUSTRATIONS

Visual communication from the podium may relate to parts of the musical fabric that are inaudible from a player's particular place on stage. The conductor's beat therefore must convey precise and often multiple instructions based on musical intent. In this book, the technical means by which this intent is demonstrated to the orchestra are represented by a set of interrelated graphic symbols. In addition, some line drawings illustrate the variety of signals that serve the simultaneous transmission of musical messages, as described in the text.

In view of this very close interdependence between text and illustrations, the author took it upon himself to provide his own drawings and to devise his own set of graphic equivalents for various beats and their respective functions. He hopes that perceptible connections between verbal explanation and visual illustration will compensate for his technical shortcomings as an illustrator.

PART ONE

SCORE	PODIUM
The Surface of Music	*Principles and Practice of the Beat*

SCORE sections (a) deal with the nature of musical evidence in a score and the extent of additional input required from the conductor; PODIUM sections (b), with basic technical skills of beat and gesture.

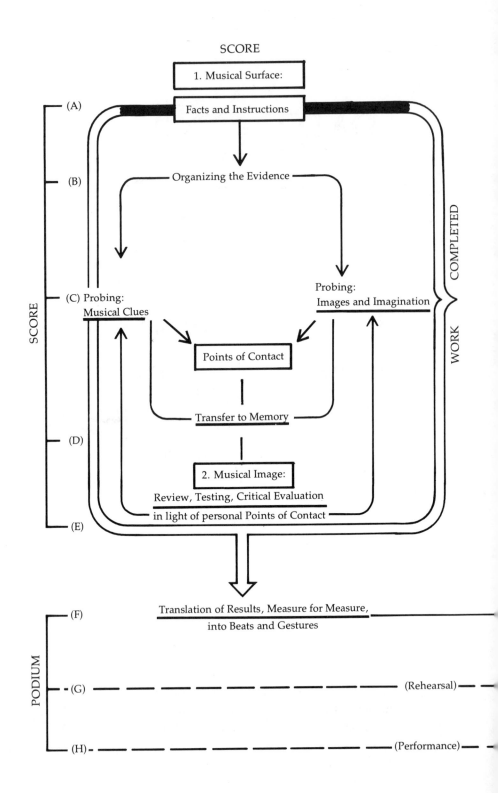

SCORE

1. Musical Surface:

Facts and Instructions

(A)

(B) Organizing the Evidence

SCORE

(C) Probing:
Musical Clues

Probing:
Images and Imagination

COMPLETED

WORK

Points of Contact

Transfer to Memory

(D)

2. Musical Image:

Review, Testing, Critical Evaluation

in light of personal Points of Contact

(E)

(F) Translation of Results, Measure for Measure,
into Beats and Gestures

PODIUM

(G) (Rehearsal)

(H) (Performance)

IA

FACTS AND INSTRUCTIONS

The surface of music is defined and distinctions are drawn between the kinds of
evidence to be discovered.

A score is only the promise of music.
—Count Keyserling

THE conductor's score provides a detailed prospectus of the surface of an orchestral work. We shall call *surface* all those indications and directions which the composer noted, and from which objective conclusions are to be drawn with regard to performance. However, there is more than that to most scores and to their preparation for performance. This is why we should be quite clear about the nature and limitations of this musical surface when we refer to it throughout this book. What kind of information does it contain? What preliminary organization of this information must take place in our minds? In what ways may this information be put to further use as we penetrate below the surface of music?

Our first learning task is to take note of all there is to see on the musical surface, to organize it efficiently, and to remember. Next, we shall try to establish the point at which the composer's work ends and the performer's own contribution must begin.

The system of notation in common use during the years in which the symphony orchestra developed is capable of defining certain aspects of any performances very precisely; other aspects require some flexibility in interpretation; and yet others are left entirely to the discretion of the performer. Your personal, musical image begins to form as soon as you open the score. This should be examined with care as it develops, for it is the source of all the opportunities for discovery once you start to "dig below the surface" of the score. Let it be said at once that the exercise of musical imagination—once the extent of its usefulness has been perceived—should be as disciplined and logical as any other kind of approach to music. But the acceptable range of performer's licence varies greatly from work to work and needs to be weighed carefully, not only with every score to be learned, but every time that score is to be performed again.

A conductor's personal contribution in performance is determined only in part by the extent to which the composer's score does not provide definitive instructions. Pitches, for instance, are fixed and must be accepted as *facts*. An oboe passage is to be played on the oboe, and music for A clarinet will sound a third lower than written. These are also facts. A half note or a quarter will occupy the appropriate length of time that constitutes the indicated fraction of the whole-note value at the given tempo. But the extent of this time may be modified by additional marks in the score (dots or dashes above the note) or be the result of perfectly legitimate interpretive decisions by the performer: a staccato bowing versus legato or détaché will produce notes of varying individual duration. The designated length of a note is a fact which may be modified by composer's instructions or performer's interpretive decisions.

Composer's instructions which require a performer's interpretation include ritardando, accelerando, crescendo, diminuendo (how much?), as well as simple dynamic markings. Forte means loud; but how loud is loud? The composer expects the answer to be implied by the musical context in which such instructions are found. With the passage of time and changing performance practice, however, instructions that would have been obvious in their day require some knowledge of style to be adapted to listening expectations of the present. But when it comes to the "character" of a work, or any section of it, it's every performer for himself. This does not mean that such decisions are arbitrary. We shall devote much time, effort, and practice in searching for clues on the musical surface, recognize their significance in terms of the work itself, and arrive at an appropriate conclusion. And yet, two conductors may well arrive at different interpretations—even if they chose the same data as points of departure. Such is the wonder of music.

It would be difficult to come up with a more basic element of musical performance than tempo. But how fast is "fast"? Since the early nineteenth century, the initial speed of any passage could be stipulated by any composer with an accurate metronome. But the *effect* of that tempo (i.e., whether it "feels" fast or not) will vary greatly, depending on its relation to other main speeds before or after, or on the technical limitations of the orchestra, or on the size of the hall and its reverberation period, or on the way the tempo is introduced by the conductor. Few recorded performances conducted by the composer himself follow metronome markings to the letter. Add to that the individual prerogative of any performer to determine small fluctuations of speed *within* a given tempo, and it will become very apparent that we shall have to rely on informed imagination as well as careful observation of evidence in the score in order to realize the implied and sometimes almost hidden expectations of the music itself.

This, of course, is what Roger Sessions meant when he stated so emphatically that "there is no such thing as a 'definitive performance,'" and what Mahler was talking about, when he claimed that "the most important things in music cannot be noted in the score." We shall distinguish between "facts" and "instructions" when we explore the evidence of a composer's intentions on the musical surface of his score. "Facts" shall include hard, objective information: pitch, meter, instrumentation, etc. "Instructions" will range from dynamics and tempo indications to intangible but nonetheless suggestive musical directions: "espressivo," "schwungvoll," or, as in Stefan Wolpe's symphony, a clarinet solo marked "like a kind greeting." The following outline illustrates this distinction:

Objective facts: clefs, key signatures, meter, pitches, instrumentation
Facts subject to interpretation (in relation to other facts): dynamics, harmonies, tempo markings, textural densities
Instructions (subject to interpretation according to relationships and groupings of evidence left for determination by the performer): harmonic function (if significant), tempo relationships, instrumental balance, dynamic nuance, shapes of phrases, musical "gesture"

Clearly, toward the end of that list, we are already well below the musical surface of a work. Still ahead lie the major problems of how one well-shaped musical event is to follow another so that the cumulative presentation of the music will owe something to every interpretive decision. In order to achieve this, we must learn to "experience" a performance while we are working it out in detail. The process of preparation requires constant overview of the entire work, the way in which a painter steps back from his canvas in order to judge the effect of some new detail in relation to the whole.

Directed imagination is an important working device in gaining perspective on the total effect of a large work in preparation for performance. Nothing is less likely to aid us in bringing the music into sharp focus than drowsy wool gathering while someone else's performance spills from a record player. Only disciplined work on the score will provide a setting in which controlled fantasy and imagination may invest an inner projection of music with some aspects of living reality. A systematic approach to the preparation of scores for performance will be presented in succeeding chapters. A practical illustration of "directed imagination" follows herewith.

Time is one of the "most important things (that) cannot be noted in the score." Music is experienced in terms of its movement in time, much as a dancer's performance is observed in terms of motion in space. Most of us find it easier to imagine the latter than to create a vivid mental equivalent of musical events as they lend their particular qualities to time as it passes. That movement in time can also be imagined at a rate of happening *other* than its normal duration is for most a completely unfamiliar idea. Yet it is not at all difficult to demonstrate. And, with a little practice, it should become possible for you to imagine the passage of musically furnished time (in a single instant), just as you can "hear" the sound of a chord or the timbre of an instrument in the silence of your mind.

The task of transforming the musical surface into a working image of the music, including its extension in time, is basic to the preparation of a conducted performance. The following experiment deals with motion in space; but in its reference to time, it provides a useful illustration of a skill which, in musical terms, should become increasingly important to your work.

The drawing below shows a mountain landscape. Study it until you have a sense of its perspective and of the observation point from which you are about to watch, in imagination, the action.

A person is climbing the central peak from the lower left, then descending on the right. You must decide, first of all, whether you are observing the whole scene (including the central peak) from a distance,

FIGURE 1

another peak perhaps, in which case the climbing figure would remain small and barely defined; or whether you are witnessing the scene from somewhere near the top of the central peak, a helicopter perhaps, in which case the ascending figure should grow larger and more distinct as it approaches, only to diminish as it passes from your view on the lower right. The figure neither stops nor changes pace along the way. You must imagine how it is dressed; how it is lit; what its speed of progress would be, and how that would affect its gait (running, climbing, walking at a leisurely pace); whether it is a man or a woman.

Here you have a visual equivalent to the evidence available in a very simple musical score, and of the problem posed in its transformation into a "working image": the background (a held chord, or a repeating accompaniment) remains the same throughout; the action is vested in a single, moving event (a solo tune); the tempo remains constant. And yet the impact of this representation could vary enormously, because a vital aspect remained unspecified by the composer, and thus was left for you to decide. No, it is not whether the person is man or woman, running or ambling, dressed or naked. It is a question of where *you* are. The person might seem far off, a small, moving speck in an otherwise still and frozen landscape. Or, if you are close by, the person may approach you, recognize you and be recognized, react to that recognition—does he or she smile, speak, ignore or threaten you? And what is the manner of his or her departure? The only information available in this visual "score" is that the speed remains constant.

It will not be hard to memorize the setting, the instructions, and the questions left for you to decide. Now you go to work, as if this were a score, and you the conductor planning its performance. When the whole scene is worked out, and when you are able to see the events you have determined as clearly as possible, try the following:

Think of something else or, if you can, of nothing at all. Then, release the scene you have created in your conscious imagination *all at once*, as with a multiple camera exposure, all on one frame, but without the effect of overlapping figures. Try to get the feeling of a remembered event, something that really took place in time, but is now recalled in a single instance. If there was some kind of confrontation between the figure and yourself, this would be the most likely moment of first recall. Start with that and leave all else to be inferred, but clearly remembered in that instant, and vividly kept in mind until the figure disappears. Or you might be left with a calm, almost lyrical sensation of stillness and loneliness, emphasized by the far-off movement of a barely visible figure. Practice this "performance," including its minimal extension in time. Eventually you will be able to project a musical score into a comparable moment of total concentration before you begin its performance.

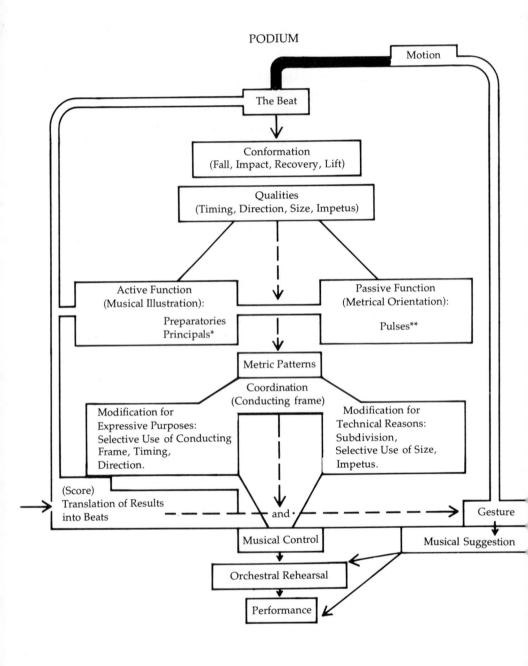

PODIUM

Motion

The Beat

Conformation
(Fall, Impact, Recovery, Lift)

Qualities
(Timing, Direction, Size, Impetus)

Active Function
(Musical Illustration):

Preparatories
Principals*

Passive Function
(Metrical Orientation):

Pulses**

Metric Patterns

Coordination
(Conducting frame)

Modification for
Expressive Purposes:
Selective Use of Conducting
Frame, Timing,
Direction.

Modification for
Technical Reasons:
Subdivision,
Selective Use of Size,
Impetus.

(Score)
Translation of Results
into Beats

and ·

Gesture

Musical Control

Musical Suggestion

Orchestral Rehearsal

Performance

*Exception: *Series* of Principals: (*Passive* Function)   **Exception: *Accented* Pulse: (*Active* Function)

IB

POSTURE, PIVOTS, THE ARM
IN MOTION

> The conductor's feet are put on the po-
> dium, his arms in motion.

THE physical aspect of conducting reflects the flow of musical ideas
in the conductor's mind and controls their implementation by the orchestra. The principal means of implementation and control is the *beat*.
Proficiency, flexibility, and practiced economy in the use of the beat
enable an experienced conductor to suggest subtle differences of stress
and emphasis in a phrase and to insure precision of ensemble, with the
same set of interrelated signals. As we shall see, the simplicity and uniformity of principles governing the theory of the beat is matched by the
range and diversity of its effective application. The beat is the only aspect of conducting that lends itself to systematic analysis. But the beat
is only part of an orchestra's constant perception of the man in motion
on the podium.

POSTURE

The entire body participates in the activity of conducting. A conductor's stance begins at his point of contact with the podium. For all exercises in the podium sections of this and the following chapters you
should designate a definite podium area in which to practice. This
should not exceed three feet square. (Many podiums are smaller.) Imaginary bounderies will do, a marked floor would be better, a real podium
best. Keep in mind, from the start, that the podium is a place in which
to stand, not to walk or to dance. Fancy footwork belongs to the boxing
ring.

Place your feet in such a way that, even with your arms fully extended
in any direction, you have a sense of easy balance and no need for

17

auxiliary shuffles. Your feet should be slightly apart, either parallel (Figure 1a) or with one foot a little forward and to the side (Figure 1b). In the latter case, the forward leg will lead whenever you do have occasion to shift position. Most conductors are distinctly "right- or left-legged," although it appears to be unrelated to their being right- or left-handed. Determine your preference.

Feet too close together provide an insecure base, and require constant adjustments to your stance. Feet too far apart result in an unattractive posture from the audience's point of view, particularly when you bend forward.

Your weight should rest evenly on the balls and heels of your feet. Except for an actual shift of position, both feet should remain firmly planted on the podium. Under no circumstances should you allow yourself to rise on your toes. Actual steps while conducting should be seen as natural movements supporting the requirements of the beat: a dramatic lunge forward could warrant a step in that direction; a sudden *piano*, equally dramatic, might gain additional emphasis if the forward foot is abruptly shifted to the side of the other. In either case the shift in stance lends support to the intended signal of the beat, for whatever you do on the podium becomes part of an overall signal, intentional or not. A conductor lumbering about in a continual shuffle signals aimlessness. *Stand still.*

Next you must decide whether, in your normal conducting position, you will stand straight, lean forward, or lean back. There are three considerations: your comfort, appearance, and eyesight. Do take time and care in selecting your basic posture. An awkward stance can detract from a fine stick technique, a serviceable one can enhance it; there will

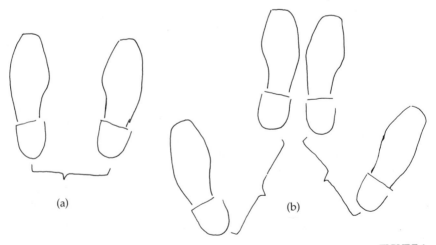

(a)   (b)

FIGURE 1

always be conductors whose looks are very much part of their persuasive powers as performers. Granting that this may not be the most important consideration, the visual impression you make should not speak against you.

But there is yet another point to consider. Leaning back from the waist, even slightly, will remove you quite a bit from the score on your stand. Even though you may conduct a performance from memory, it is important to be able to see the music at rehearsal without changing your basic posture. The following adjustments to your stance on the podium are necessary, depending on whether you wish to conduct leaning forward, standing straight, or leaning back.

Leaning forward, you should stand well back of the conducting stand. That way your eyes can glance at the score whenever you wish, while your face remains directed toward the orchestra. If you stand too close, your face will be over the score, or even in front of it. Having your nose in the score reduces contact with the orchestra for an important reason: next to the beat itself, the conductor's face is his most powerful means of communicating with the orchestra. Eye contact, facial expression, and a mutual sense of sharing are lost every time the conductor is seen to commune with the score. In addition, on most stages, the overhead lighting will put your face in shadow as soon as you look down. Thus you will have lost a large part of your means of communication. Lose that too often, and even the effectiveness of your beat will be impaired.*

Standing straight, or leaning back, you should place your feet close enough to the front edge of the stand so that you can read the music without moving forward (completely altering your stance for no musical reason). This position has the great advantage of allowing you to see score and orchestra from nearly the same angle.

Long before you begin to practice specific motions and beats, it would be worth your while to "conduct" through a fairly familiar work (with a recording, if you wish), using whatever gestures may seem appropriate and natural, and really letting yourself go. You could experiment with a stance that might work for you, particularly if you have a score at hand, so that the angle of reading music and commanding an imaginary orchestra would be compatible. In addition to what has already been said about placement of your feet, however, try to observe the following do's and don'ts:

---

*Those who wear glasses or contact lenses may wish to consider a compromise prescription for conducting. In either of the above positions it will be important to see orchestra and score without changing glasses. Unless your eyesight can be corrected to permit a viewing range from about two feet (over the score) to as much as a hundred (upstage, and more than that in opera), you would be well advised to try a halfway solution in which you can see both a little bit. Bifocals do not work well for most conductors.

Do:

Exercise as vigorously as you like, *above the waist.*

Look at your "orchestra."

Turn your face, or even your shoulders and chest, in the direction of "players" you conduct.

Use a score. Even if it is not the score of the work you are "performing," you will want to make certain that you can read the music before you while you conduct, without changing your stance. Place the score on a table, if you do not have a conducting stand.

Don't:

Move your feet, except to support an occasional, powerful gesture by a small step in its direction.

Bounce on your toes, or bend your knees.

Conduct with your hips.

Have your nose in the score.

Count out loud (or silently but noticeably), either metric pulses or prep-aratory "and's" before (during) an upbeat.

N.B.: Make no attempt to conduct patterns or any other formal appli-cation of the beat. This is to come. Try to find movements that seem natural, comfortable.

Sir Adrian Boult, master conductor and beloved by every orchestra he has directed, was asked what technical skill young conductors should cultivate most of all. "Not to get in the way" was his unhesitating reply. Every orchestral musician performs a variety of musical tasks which owe much of their difficulty to the fact that they are part of a larger, collective effort. Add to the instrumental demands of any orchestral part that it must be played in tune within a harmonic framework provided by a constantly changing, and not always consistent, group of individ-ual players and instrumental sections; that articulation or bowing must match an overall pattern; that phrasing and tempo fluctuations are or-dained from the podium; and that every player's contribution must fit into a rhythmic and metric design of which, depending on his location, he may be unable to hear some significant portions, and therefore be forced to rely entirely on the conductor's visual signals: add all that to a part that's hard to play to begin with, and Sir Adrian's advice will gain considerable force.

Unnecessary and exaggerated movement offers the conductor his or her finest chance to get in the way. Many a fine horn solo has been spoiled due to pyrotechnics on the podium, the shock of which de-stroyed the unsuspecting player's concentration and embouchure. When conductorial frenzy is based on little more than free-flowing adrenalin, and when the maestro's arms are pumping as wildly as his hyperactive heart, his players are likely to react like Richard Strauss, whose verdict was uttered in a clear *sotto voce*, above the orchestral mayhem presided over by a profusely sweating new conductor: "Amateur!" Stand still. Move as needed.

PIVOTS

The conducting arm moves in its shoulder socket rather like a pendulum; and various parts of the arm may articulate its swing with movements of their own, from the elbow, the wrist, even the joints of the fingers that hold the baton. For such motions to become readable signals, they must be seen by those to whom the signals are addressed. The pendulum swing of the arm is therefore moved to the area in front of you, above the music stand, where it commands the best sight-lines. The joints of your arm serve as hinges to keep the arm in position and to insure a smooth flow of controlled movements. The particular joint upon which each movement turns shall be referred to as its pivot.

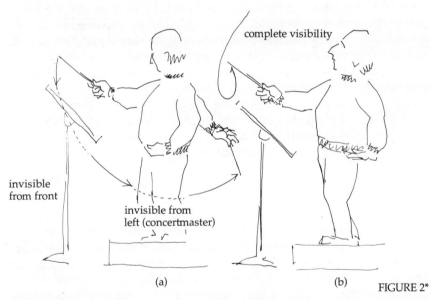

complete visibility

invisible from front

invisible from left (concertmaster)

(a) (b) FIGURE 2*

Shoulder, elbow, wrist, and fingers are the four possible arm locations from which movement may be generated. The pivot of any arm movement is the joint *above* the uppermost part in motion: full-arm

---

*Illustrations in this chapter show conductors *with* baton. The motions described on pp. 23–27 should first be practiced without. After ways of holding the stick have been explored according to suggestions in the second chapter, these same exercises may be repeated with baton in hand.

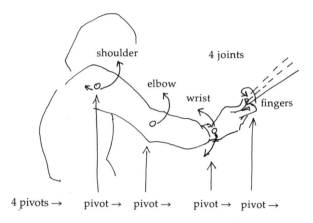

FIGURE 3

motions are generated from the shoulder; the elbow serves as pivot for movements of the lower arm; the hand turns from the wrist. Finger pivots affect only the baton, and will be discussed in Chapter 2.

Our first exercises will involve movements of the entire arm, the lower part of the arm, and the hand, according to certain predetermined conditions. Pivots will be indicated and must be consciously employed. You are urged to execute each exercise exactly as suggested. As with any physical skill intended to serve a purpose decreed by the mind, muscular responses must become accurate and instant.

N.B.: In describing the following exercises the term *motion* will be used rather than *beat*. The latter will be used only when movement with a specific musical function is implied. For now, we are concerned only with the physical aspects of movement as such, i.e. *motions*.

It would be a great mistake, however, to assume that motions involving the conscious use of certain pivots do not in themselves have musical implications. The *choice of such a pivot,* and the motion from the shoulder, from the elbow, or from the wrist would certainly be interpreted by the orchestra as an indication of the conductor's musical intent. Any movement on the podium has a musical effect. This is also true of *the placement of the pivot:* while there is not much you can do about relocating your right shoulder in relation to the rest of your body, the other pivots can have an expressive value according to their position in front of you. For instance, a pianissimo beat from the wrist would normally pivot from a point about a foot or so in front, and slightly below, the conductor's collarbone. But in order to dramatize a sudden pianissimo, he may choose to forego some visibility in order to crouch protectively over a pivot very close to his chest.

FIGURE 4

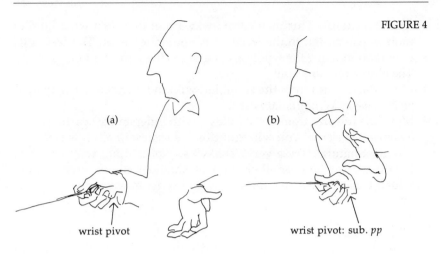

(a)   (b)

wrist pivot   wrist pivot: sub. *pp*

Exercises

THE ARM IN MOTION*

A. Full Arm – Shoulder Pivot

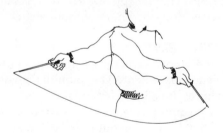

FIGURE 5

1. Move the full arm, from the shoulder in any direction visible to someone seated before you, but keep *all other joints motionless.* The arm must swing freely and may be straight or slightly bent, but the angle at the elbow should not be changed in motion. Take care that immobility at the lower three joints does not result in stiffness at any point. If you feel your muscles tense, make yourself relax at once. If necessary, stop the exercise and shake your arm loosely at your side. Then start again.
2. Move the full arm from the shoulder, adding some independent mo-

*Most conductors use their right hand to conduct. Illustrations in this book are drawn for right-handed conductors. But the author has taught some left-handers. Contrary to early misgivings, a clear and flexible left-handed technique (mirror image of right-handed patterns) causes less confusion in the orchestra than might be the case if a truly left-handed person tried, awkwardly, to conduct with the right hand.

tion *at the wrist.* This may seem awkward at first. Just what kind of motion you assign to the wrist does not matter at all. The feel of its own motion while the whole arm moves is the important thing. *N.B.:* The elbow remains still!

3. Move the full arm from the shoulder, with independent participation *by the elbow.* Wrist remains still.
4. Move the full arm from the shoulder, with independent participation *by wrist and elbow.* You will find this the easiest of all. It is certainly the most natural. Try a very "snaky" sort of motion, with all joints bending a lot, and another kind of shoulder-elbow-wrist motion which barely articulates the elbow and wrist movements. Keep the line fluid.

All these motions can be either large or small, using the full extent of your reach or traveling only a short distance. Compare the feeling of large or small motions of the full arm; the relative fluidity of the motions; and the extent to which you have kept every part of every movement in front of you, and thus visible to an orchestra.

N.B.: Until you have had a chance to examine the proper use of the baton in the next chapter (pp. 42–44), it is recommended that you practice all exercises described here without a stick.

B. Forearm–Elbow Pivot

In using the elbow as pivot for forearm motions we have an additional problem—placement. The shoulder pivot allowed us no choice; but placement of the elbow depends on where it will be of most use as the hinge of a comfortable, visible movement of the lower arm. Take care to place that hinge well out in front and away from the side of your chest.

The cramped position in Figure 6a will feel awkward every time the conductor's beat moves to the left (and bumps into his side). The position of Figure 6b allows much more freedom of motion from the elbow, and it will be even more effective if the pivot remains in a straight line before the point where the elbow would be, were the arm to hang straight down. The elbow should neither "stick out" nor pull the upper

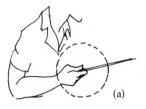
(a)

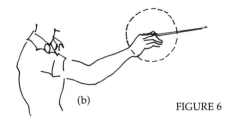
(b)

FIGURE 6

arm to the left across the chest. It should remain quietly in place while the lower arm moves. Until this becomes "second nature," the pivot should always be carefully placed in advance of any exercise, and then maintained in that location.

Try various motions from the elbow, in the same succession as the full-arm gestures: in any direction, large and small, and with selective use of available joints.

C. Hand Motions—Wrist Pivot

For the wrist pivot, also, we must place the arm in a position to insure clear visibility for the orchestra and easy mobility for ourselves. The elbow usually serves as a kind of prop to place the (now motionless) forearm well forward of the body and just under shoulder height. In this way the wrist, which can serve only a very small motion, is the pivot for gestures originating in the hand that will hold the baton: subtle and most likely fast motions, where they can be seen by everybody to best advantage. But, as we pointed out earlier, it is quite possible, and sometimes useful, to place the wrist pivot literally close to the vest for a special effect. In either case, the elbow would remain in its position illustrated by Figure 6b with the forearm bent to the left, so that it could reassume the pivot role without having to be pulled forward again. Try this for yourself:

1. You are conducting with forearm motions. Your elbow pivot is placed as in Figure 6b. In changing to hand motions, you *leave the elbow in position*, as described above, conduct with a wrist pivot somewhat to the left and above its former position, close to the chest. Then reassume forearm motions.
2. Same as above, but in changing to hand motions, you simply draw back your elbow until the upper arm hangs straight from the shoulder and the hand is close to the right side of your chest. Your hand motions will be equally well placed, but the transition to the forearm motions is hampered by your having assumed the position of Figure 6a. And unless there is a lot of room on the stage so that the entire orchestra can sit well in front of you, even your hand motions will be uncomfortably confidential in terms of first violin sight-lines.
3. Once more the same, but this time, instead of leaving the elbow in place or bringing it back, bring it *forward*, almost at full extension of the arm. You will find it comfortable to balance that move by leaning back slightly, particularly with the left shoulder: an excellent position for a dramatic emphasis of small beats, and an easy one from which to move on to other kinds of beats.

If you have held your arm straight in front of you, with the elbow pivot placed foreward and *just* to the right of your chest, you will have made an awkward discovery: one's elbow does not bend outward. The up–down movement will not have been too cumbersome because you are likely to have positioned your elbow somewhat below shoulder height. Thus the upper arm will have pointed in a downward direction; the downswing of your forearm motion will have passed the halfway mark with the arm still slightly bent; and the full extention of the straightened arm should have been enough to allow the complete downward swing of the motion.

For the horizontal swing of the forearm motion there are two possibilities. First, you might position the upper arm at an *outward* as well as *downward* angle from the shoulder. In that case, the full extension of the straightened arm will serve the complete sideways motion, as the full downward extension served the vertical motion when the upper arm was directed not only forward but down from the shoulder. In order to have the downward motion cross the horizontal swing somewhere near its halfway mark, the elbow pivot would have to be placed *well* to the right of your chest. And that is not a good idea: the intersection of the vertical and horizontal planes of the conductor's beat should be in front of the center of his chest, as we shall see. We shall therefore have to adopt another solution for the anatomical limitations of the elbow joint.

This second possibility consists of an anticipatory little hook to the left, during completion of the downward swing (the pendulum described on p. 21) and before you begin the motion to the right. This enables you to move your arm, with its elbow pivot just to the right of the chest, from a position left of center to an equivalent position on the right, *without necessarily extending the lower arm to a complete alignment with the upper part.* Thus the motion to the right was prepared by an anticipatory movement to the left. The concept of peparation for a beat is one of the most important in the theory and practice of the beat, and will occupy us a great deal in the chapters to come. For now, and with this hook to the left well in mind, repeat the exercises recommended for full-arm motions as they apply to motions of the forearm (p. 23; No. 3 does not apply, and 4 is almost another version of 2).

D. Finger Pivots

These have only one function: to enhance movement of the baton itself. Use of the stick will be examined at the beginning of the next chapter. Finger pivots will be explained and practiced along with other exercises in managing the baton.

E. Vertical Sweeps

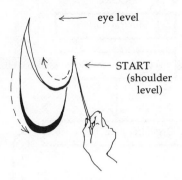

FIGURE 7

Extend your slightly bent right arm fully before you. The palm of your hand faces downward. With a gentle inward curve, raise the arm (shoulder pivot) until the hand is at eye level. Then let the arm swing slowly down and to the right. Complete the swing with a small upward recovery, until you have returned to the starting position. Repeat.

Additional Exercises

Try the same series of motions horizontally—left–right, left–right—with a little "dip" in the course of each beat.

1. Wrist alone, medium speed:
        a. palm turned to the left
        b. palm down
    Forearm and wrist, same speed:
        a. palm turned to the left
        b. palm down
2. Wrist alone, fast small beats (all sideways and "dipping" back and forth):
        a. palm to the left
        b. palm down
    Forearm and wrist, same as above.
3. The entire arm, very slow speed (horizontal sweeps with "dip"):
        a. palm to the left
        b. palm down
        c. palm left on left beat, down and slightly right, on return beat to right

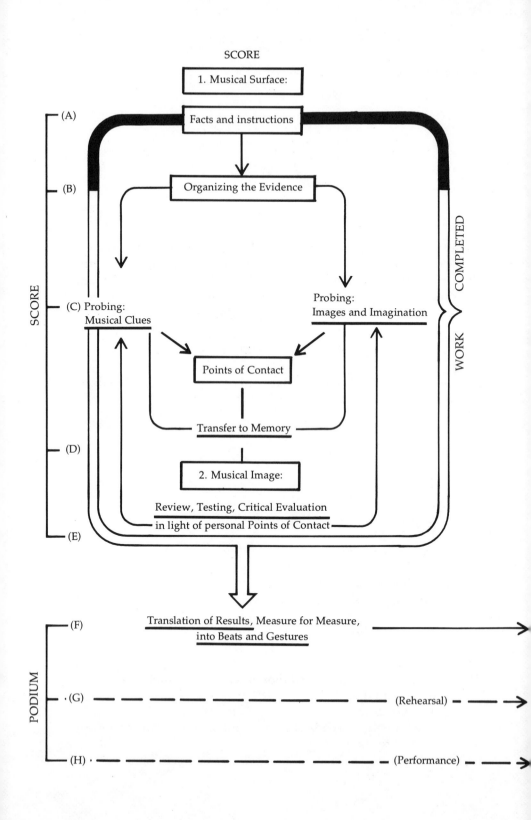

2A

ORGANIZING THE EVIDENCE

A sequence is established for systematic
inspection of all information available on
the surface of music.

THE sum of explicit guidelines for your performance, the musical
facts and instructions which comprise the printed score, has been
defined as the surface of music. This best evidence of the composer's
intent fixes certain aspects of performance with precision. Pitches, key
signatures, meter, and instrumentation are among components of the
musical surface which our system of notation indicates clearly, and
which must remain constant whenever a work is performed. We refer
to these aspects of the musical surface as *facts*.

But the musical surface also features a large number of the composer's
directives which require some latitude of interpretation. Dynamics,
instrumental balances, tempo fluctuations, and harmonic functions are
among the aspects of a composition about which two conductors may
reach different conclusions in performance. To the extent to which they
have taken full account of the perceived musical evidence, both solutions may be representative of the composer's score. This mutability of
musical evidence makes us, as performers, active participants in the
creation of a final product which is fresh and new each time it is heard
in concert. Components of the musical surface subject to a certain range
of legitimate interpretations will be referred to as the composer's
instructions.

The following procedure will help you organize the evidence of a musical surface. It will serve as the framework for a systematic approach
to the preparation of works ranging from simple pieces that may be
more subtle than they seem, to very complex compositions, which become surprisingly tractable once they have been properly mapped out.

Group A: Preliminary Information

1. **Composer:** Call to mind whatever historical, stylistic or anecdotal information you may possess. Except in rare cases, there is no need for further research at this point. Rather, the experience should resemble reading a letter from someone you know. You would instinctively call up an image, an association, the recollection of former dealings. Eventually you will have to address yourself to that person in reply.

2. **Title:** Whether or not a work (or a movement) bears a title is in itself significant. Titles may be self-explanatory in a programmatic sense, or they may suggest structural or stylistic aspects of what is to come. Even the exceptions, the titles considered spurious or irrelevant, may contribute to your knowledge.

3. **Tempo:** The general tempo indication at the beginning of a composition (whether or not it is accompanied by a metronome marking) is your first apparent fact that is really an instruction. Neither time words nor numbers related to a note value can express more than a general suggestion of tempo, from very slow to very fast. Many attempts have been made to provide an objective standard for the definition of tempo, ranging from Galileo's pendulum swings to Maelzel's metronome. In practice these are useful as averages, and to denote tempo *relationships* between sections of a work so marked by the composer. Beyond that we are in the realm of instructions, i.e. we are given evidence on which to base *choices.* At this stage of organizing available information we merely *note the evidence*—time words and / or metronome markings. Choices must await more intimate acquaintance with the music.

4. **Instrumentation:** In contrast to the on-going process of orchestration, instrumentation is a table of contents, usually given on the first full page of score, of the musical instruments used in what is to follow. This list should be carefully read and absorbed. Our initial survey of the musical surface, in search of preliminary data, should also acknowledge transposing instruments. Transpositions may change in the course of a work or a movement. Such changes are scanned right away and, if possible, remembered.

5. **Key Signatures:** Nor should the key signature be noted only at its first appearance. Changes in succeeding movements or in the course of a single one should be fixed in the mind from the start.* If a particular method of organizing materials is also apparent, so much the better. But the momentum of an active, initial survey must not be sacrificed for the sake of premature analysis.

---

*There are of course systems of organizing successive or simultaneous use of tones which do not require key signatures.

6. **Meter:** Like changing tempo markings, transposing instruments, and key signatures, changes of meter must be carefully noted as we map out the surface of music. Like scanning the other variables throughout a composition, looking for meter changes will, if nothing else, give us another reason to turn the pages of the score yet again. This may not result in instant memorization, but it will tend to make some pages look familiar.
7. **Special Notes:** The score of Ravel's *La Valse* has a prefatory note by the composer, stating that the opening music suggests the image of swirling dancers at an Imperial Court Ball, c. 1855. Given the title of the work, an association with Vienna is plausible; *but why 1855?*

N.B.: A whole chapter will be devoted to the vital role of detail in the process of preparing a score for any performance,* whether it be for the first time or *as if* for the first time. Once mastery of the musical surface has been achieved, access to what lies below that surface is most often stimulated by a suggestive detail. This may prompt a fortuitous question which, in turn, may open up unexpected perspectives on the work—musical, associative, or emotional. In a textbook presentation, the learning process must be described and the various aspects of that process need to be organized. Fortuitous questions, however, which play a very important role in the process, are likely to occur to us at any point in our investigation. The question above, "but why 1855," is an example. Since the composer stipulated a date so explicitly and specified an Imperial Court, the statement assumes the nature of *instructions:* we must allow for the implications of "why 1855."

Unless an answer suggests itself spontaneously, we must find out what possible significance an event of about 1855 might have had for Ravel, and what light this might shed on *La Valse.* We shall return to this in the course of this book, as we would during the actual preparation of this score.** The point illustrated is an important one: at any stage of learning a score, we may stumble on an odd detail. In the case of *La Valse*, "why 1855" will turn out to be a most rewarding question. Odd details tend to raise such questions and are to be prized and remembered until we can work out an answer.

At this point, we should also begin to *read* the score, silently, while trying to "hear" it as well. Without forcing it, we should become familiar with the image on the page. And without stopping to assemble chords, note by note, we shall try to remember how they *look* and then, after we have turned away from the printed score, imagine their sound. The "looks" include their placement on the page, i.e. the instrumenta-

---

*Cf. Chapter 6.   **Cf. Chapter 6.

tion. Attempting to hear these sounds in the abstract, or on the piano would involve transcription in the mind and a quite unnecessary impediment to their eventual realization. We shall not be discouraged if, on the whole, we retain only a dim impression. This is normal, and like anything else, will improve impressively with practice. At the very least, however, we shall retain certain information with ease, which we will classify for future use under the three remaining headings.

Group B: The Outline Of Major Divisions

1. **Structural Joints:** If the form of the work falls within easily recognizable structural patterns, there is every reason to take advantage of fitting the material we want to explore into a familiar mold.

   At this early stage, however, it would be a mistake to draw too many conclusions. We shall stake out structural joints and, with luck, discover:

2. **Correspondences:** These are of a structural nature, but do not commit us to any particular structural concept. We simply look for similarity of materials, texture, or rhythmic outlines, and compare the sections in which these appear. In older music we may find that these sections relate to each other in terms of:

3. **Key Changes:** We shall show in a later chapter that pieces can be *about* keys, and that the relationships of the respective tonalities may be more significant than the thematic materials by which these relationships are illustrated. In terms of the large form, as well as the short-term harmonic increase and relaxation of musical expectation, key changes represent the ultimate reference against which such plots are played. A rather sophisticated knowledge of period practice and composer is required, before we can be sensitive to departures from standards which, with luck, will serve as clues to further exploration *beneath* the musical surface.

4. **Divisions other than Tonalities** or Tonal Centers: In some works, the composer's own program indications or tempo changes may well be the best way of keeping a sequence of musical events in mind, and of providing an early and memorable overview of the entire composition. Further examination may then lead to the discovery of a tonal relationship as well.

5. **Rehearsal Numbers:** If all else fails, rehearsal numbers can be a useful framework for a first attempt to organize the evidence of the musical surface. In its noncommittal way, this grid of reference points may even be helpful because one need not take it seriously in terms of structural analysis. For some conductors the association of numerical or alphabetical indicators with simultaneous musical events is an effective mnemonic device, establishing an arbitrary overview of the musical territory to be remembered.

N.B.: While it was once considered the hallmark of the professional conductor to dispense with the score in performance, conducting from memory has today become a matter of personal preference. Orchestras themselves contributed a major impetus for abolishing this particular obsession. Since concerts are not merely vehicles for conductorial display, players had (and have) excellent reason to resent the frequent burden of compensating for lapses of memory on the podium. Some conductors conduct better without a score; others don't.

GROUP C: POSSIBLE OUTLINES OF SUBSECTIONS

1. **Subsections:** With growing familiarity, certain sections will begin to feel like coherent units, subsections of the larger divisions we noted in Group B. These we shall now separate from each other with vertical lines, drawn in pencil (we might change our minds later on!).

   Now, you should *read* the score every day. If that means reading only one line, and *hearing it in your mind,* you have reason to take pleasure in that accomplishment: you will soon be able to hear a good deal more. Next best, in some complex melodic outlines, is awareness of the rhythmic continuity. Pitches will follow at a future attempt, just as facility in playing an intricate instrumental passage comes with practice. Meanwhile you will have the opportunity to deal with your particular learning skills. What kind of musical event do you absorb most readily? Melody? Recurring rhythmic elements? Instrumental color? The important thing is to keep reading, and to keep turning pages as you would in reading a book, without lingering over every real or imagined uncertainty.

   There is no reason whatever why your reading should not be supplemented with listening to recordings of the same works. After listening to a work which you are also reading in silence, your memory will supply many sounds which your imagination could not place before. So much the better!

2. **Periods and Phrases:** If nothing else, the marking of periods and phrases encourages us to sing the tunes. This can be done in silence (as with the daily reading exercise just suggested). But there is something to be said for trying to produce the actual sounds you will expect someone else to play later on. It matters little whether you reproduce these lines in the proper key. But high tessituras should be sung in the appropriate range (male conductors at rehearsal have no compunctions about singing flute lines in improbable falsetto voices) and imagined with proper instrumental color. The same, of course, applies to bass lines. Later two or more simultaneous lines will be "heard" without difficulty.

Periods and phrases are neither facts nor instructions. Their beginnings and ends, to say nothing of the shape in between, are not always easy to determine. For now, we shall make a temporary determination of where an orchestral phrase ends, even if individual melodic lines overlap, like shingles on a roof. Remember, the object of this initial phase of our study is to transfer the musical surface, intact, from score to mind. Revisions of detail are not only inevitable, but must not be precluded by premature classifications. Once the musical surface is available in our imagination, the real task of interpretation will begin.

Periods and phrases shall be separated by short vertical lines *above* the score system.*

3. **Two, plus Three, plus Four:** Units of two-, three-, or four-measure divisions are indicated by the following symbols marked across the top of all score systems on every page. These identify the smallest components of musical flow; and the distinctive patterns of these pencilled brackets provide a powerful stimulus to visual memory. Many conductors use this technique, although their ways of indicating two-, three-, or four-measure units vary.

These are the symbols the author has developed over the years, and found useful:

2 measures =

3 measures =

4 measures =

Larger phrases are usually composites (separated in turn by a vertical line as mentioned above under 2); if not, they are indicated with a number plus an arrow, e.g. 5→. However, even in this instance, the indication of 5→ should be amplified wih a (3 + 2) or (2 + 3) or (4 + 1), etc., depending on the shape of the phrase. Sometimes it is even advantageous to break a symmetrical ⌒⌒⌒ (4), into ⌒⌒⌒, i.e. (4 = 2 + 2), particularly for a long succession of plain four-measure phrases.

4. **Orchestration:** Almost all conductors note special instrumental features in their scores. These may simply be cues to confirm an important entrance, or perhaps visual reminders of some balance problem in rehearsal. Some scores show only the instruments actually playing at any one time on each page of score.

You will certainly evolve your own effective system of marking instruments. Some general suggestions follow:
- select a number of "cues" intended for individual players;
- mark these places in the score as shown in the tables on pp. 36–37;

*Cf. Chapter 8.

- from this moment make a conscious effort to think of all entrances so identified in terms of *players* rather than instruments. *N.B.* Not too many!

There is no reason whatsoever why a conductor should look at an oboe in concert. There are very good reasons why he should exchange glances, from time to time, with an oboist. One valuable result of rehearsals is that players learn, among other things, when to look at the conductor in any given work. In concert they will try again to meet his eyes at the same places in the music—if they get the chance. It is the conductor's business to be ready for that exchange before the player's eyes come up to seek his.

Bringing a score to life in the imagination should include a feeling of players around you. A thousand angels may sit on the head of a pin, but musicians sit to the left, to the right, in front, or upstage of your podium. In order to develop a real "in-the-round" image of an imagined performance, practice is required. A painless way of making this long process of instant association and orientation work for you is to include it, conscientiously, in the constant examinations and reexaminations of a score while you complete the first survey of its musical surface. A sample seating plan of a modern symphony orchestra follows. You are in the center of the bottom line. From now on, your surveys of the score should include the view from the podium.

Some conductors go to greater trouble in marking their scores than others. For those who intend to prepare one large score of the work under study, once and for many years to come, it makes sense to spend time and effort on a multicolored chart which often seems to dominate the printed text: Blue for the winds, red for the brass, green for percussion, and ordinary black pencil for the strings. The author

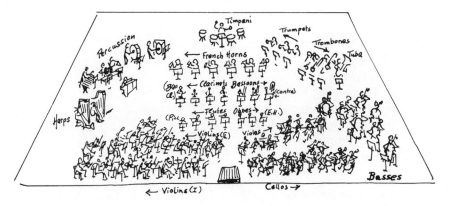

FIGURE 1

prefers to work with a succession of small scores if they are available, a new one for every major restudy of the work. The old ones, of course, are kept for reference, but not consulted until new and fresh impressions of the music have been given a chance to form.

Work with a soft, black pencil (6B, if you can get it).* Even light markings show up well, and erasing is easy. Avoid grease pencils, for they are nearly indelible. Rental libraries (who furnish most contemporary scores) and orchestral librarians hate to see their investments "defaced" permanently, with even the most intelligent and helpful remainders of your findings. This problem will become more acute as you learn to use the score as a kind of diary into which ideas and comments will be crowded, and rehearsal problems recorded with sometimes embarrassing candor.

It is helpful to bracket the left-hand edge of all score systems by instrumental families, in cases where this is not entirely clearly indicated. There is no virtue in denying yourself any visual aids in learning a score.

The following are symbols used by the author (and many others) to draw special attention to certain instruments on the page.

A. All woodwinds are indicated by abbreviations:

Picc.	Piccolo
Fl.	Flute
A. Fl.	Alto Flute
Ob.	Oboe
E.H.	English Horn
Cl.	Clarinet (in B♭ or A)
E♭ (C, D) Cl.	E♭ (C, D) Clarinet
B.Cl.	Bass Clarinet
Bn.	Bassoon
C.Bn.	Contrabassoon

B. Brass and Percussion are shown by symbols:

O — French Horn
+ — Trumpet
č — Cornet
[— All Trombones
↾ ↾̃ — Trombone 1,2
↳ — Trombone 3
T — Tuba

*There is no intrinsic merit in black, of course, except that it is clear and pencils are easily available. The author's teacher used purple. But it is important to get the softest pencil available, for it can be erased most easily.

N.B.: The following percussion symbols may seem fussy and unnecessary. In fact they are of great value if used consistently and, unlike markings for other instrumental families, with prodigal abandon. Complex percussion parts in scores are hard to memorize, but percussion cues must be precise, since the distribution of instruments among the players will vary from one orchestra to the next. The visual impact of these symbols on one's memory helps to condition our reaction.

∪ — Kettledrums

ℚ — Snare Drums

ⓠ — Bass Drum

⊙ — Cymbal (struck)

☆ — Cymbals (crashed)

◎ — Tam Tam

:ö: — Tambourine

△ — Triangle

Glock. — Glockenspiel

∩ — Chimes

Crot. — Antique Cymbals (Crotali)

⦿⦿ — Sleigh Bells

xyl. — Xylophone

▱ — Woodblock

●● — Castanets

T.Bl. — Temple Blocks

⫙ — Harp

Cel. — Celesta

⊐ — Piano

String instruments are marked by groups:

Violins	I	{		V. 1
Viola	II	╱	or separately:	V. 2
	Cello	(		Va.
	Bass			C.
				B.

Before we apply all these suggestions to our preliminary survey of the surface of music, we should examine one more area of classification in this initial process. In contrast to the three groups already outlined, the following is completely unstructured, consciously nondirected, and almost entirely subjective.

GROUP D

This is the Joker in the pack. It includes whatever musical or extra-musical ideas and associations occur in your mind, other than observations in connection with Groups A, B, and C. Group D is not part of any time sequence of study. Ideas may occur to you while you are still exploring the musical surface, or later, as you work with information already organized and assimilated. But they have this in common: they originate in some aspect of visible surface evidence in the score. Some areas in which such ideas may be sparked are listed below. Others, introduced as examples of work *below* the surface of music, are presented in later chapters.

N.B.: Let us be absolutely clear about this: the approach we are suggesting is not a method of *analysis*. It is a means of *organizing information* contained in the score. Analysis (as a basis for decisions concerning performance) follows as a next step. But since the entire process will be part of the preparation for *your* performance, real or imagined, *your* reactions and your own spontaneous associations must be assembled, organized, and remembered together with facts and instructions in the composer's score. The more complete and the more available this two-fold accumulation is from the start, the better the prospects for a genuine fusion of the composer's instructions with "the essential element in the whole thing" which only you can provide.

Some areas in which ideas may be "sparked":

1. **Texture:** Do sections of the work (according to Group B, possibly Group C) strike you as thicker, more soloistic, more contrapuntal, or more antiphonal than others? We determined not to pursue the implications of what we observe, but this is very simple, almost elementary evidence—the kind that will help you remember and identify those sections. Treasure that conscious memory, test it to make certain it remains in place, and let it rest for now.
2. **Shapes:** "Shape" is a spatial concept; when applied to music, it describes events taking place in time. We shall devote a chapter to these all-important building blocks of large musical structures.* On first contact with a score, the eye or the inner ear will sometimes spot significant and characteristic musical shapes. Take care to remember such shapes for possible future consideration. Also take care not to be drawn into further examination, until the entire canvas of available evidence is safely stored *in your mind*.

*Cf. Chapter 8.

3. **Melody:** The *character* of melodic lines may be as memorable as the "tune" itself, and sometimes more so. It may also vary between sections of a work or be especially noticeable in certain parts of the entire musical fabric, e.g. the outer voices or particular instruments. Certain intervals may be favored or avoided. Repetition of notes may be featured or avoided. At this early stage of study, take note, identify the characteristic events with the places in which they occur, and remember.

4. **Rhythm:** Rhythm kindles the fire of many scores. It takes a perceptive and proficient conductor to make a feature of rhythm, so that its fundamental, generating role in the life of a composition is not lost on the attentive listener. Again, the how-to of this task is not yet our concern. But spotting significant rhythms is fairly certain proof that scores are beginning to speak to you.

5. **Dynamics, Articulation:** When articulation becomes characteristic of a particular section, or when a style of bowing is suddenly changed after the ear had become accustomed to it, an immediate impression is created in performance. This impression may be reinforced in the score (composer's instructions) by dynamic indications. What will be obvious to the listener, then, should be noted by the conductor preparing his score at the earliest moment, and remembered.

6. **Program:** You must not feel squeamish about exercising your imagination. While you should not take special pains to endow musical events with extramusical associations, it would be foolish to resist if the music itself happens to intrude on our perception in that way. If something in a score strikes you as funny, perhaps it was intended to be so.

Sometimes the composer will give us a lead, and sometimes we may discover convincing clues to implicit connections between his music and whatever moved him at the time of its composition. But the idea must not take precedence over musical common sense or taste. "Fate knocking at the door," to the rhythm of three eighth notes and one quarter, has no conceivable relevance to the *molto ritenuto* with which it was the custom for many years to begin Beethoven's *Fifth Symphony.*

And then there are independent, often quite irresistible, fantasies as well. They have no rational explanation, nor will they be denied. I own to an image of long standing, which is as real to me as any of the sounds in the Finale of the great C-major symphony of Schubert. Floating over the inexhaustibly dancing triplets at the tips of bows wielded by exhausted violinists, the melody evokes for me the image of a radiant, godlike child in golden light—but only if the performance is good.

PODIUM

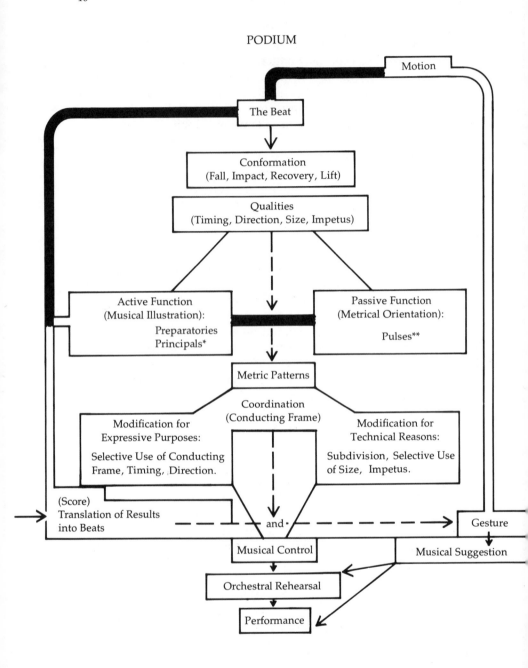

*Exception: *Series* of Principals: (Passive Function)   **Exception: *Accented* Pulse: (Active Function)

2_B

THE BEAT:
QUALITIES AND FUNCTIONS

The conformation of the beat is analysed,
and the qualities which distinguish one
beat from another, as well as some ways
in which the active or passive function of
beats contributes to the communication
of intended musical shapes, or suggested
fluctuation of musical tension.

THE BEAT*

The beat shows when to play,
indicates how to play,
controls the musical shape of individual lines,
coordinates all musical lines in terms of precision and balance,
directs the interchange of musical initiative within the orchestra.

Beats cannot suggest the particular sounds they are to reflect.

But beats can be related to each other so as to match the expressive
relationship of successive sounds according to your prior perception
of the music.

O F the various arm motions described in the Chapter 1b, only a
few would happen to qualify as beats. What distinguishes beats, as the
primary set of conducting signals, is precision and control. The exacti-
tude with which a modern symphony orchestra is able to follow the
directions of its conductor is wonderful to watch. What most of the
audience are likely to see might be the occasional grand gesture, or
perhaps a dramatic change in size or emphasis of the beat. Certainly, it
is difficult to credit the steady flow of carefully articulated "ordinary
beats"—up and down, or sideways—for the ebb and flow of changing
patterns of sound emanating from every part of the stage, now together,

---

*Summaries of principles and practice of the beat, appearing in Chapters 1–5 and reappearing in
different sequence in Chapter 7, are indexed there for convenient review.

now in a finely spun fabric of individual instrumental contributions. Just so miraculous must have seemed the maneuvers of an eighteenth-century naval squadron responding to the string of colorful signals flying from its flagship's masthead.

This nautical comparison is of particular relevance to us. As we embark upon our investigation of the conductor's beat and gain practical expertise in applying technique to music, the single most important fact to remember will be that *metrical and musical definition are vested in the same signal from the podium.* The conductor is not only a communications officer transmitting instructions according to the composer's orders, but also the admiral who determines the extent and the timing of their execution.

The separate but interrelated functions of signals are the essence of the conductor's beat. The very terminology we shall use will reflect its dual role. And we shall take care that, as practical skill develops, this central aspect of the conducting craft will be consciously maintained in practice.

You are now to do two things:

1. Read over, several times, the summaries of qualities and functions of the beat in this chapter. Begin with the definition of what the beat can be expected to do (p. 41), continue with the description of its constituent parts (p. 47), of its properties (p. 58), and of some of its functions (p. 49). Study the illustrations and take note of the technical terms. You may wish to test the "feel" of some beats. Actual practice, however, should be deferred until it is suggested in the text.
2. At the same time, practice the handling of the baton as described below, including the finger pivot (p. 45). Then review all the exercises in Chapter 1b *with* stick in hand (Cf. Exercises, p. 23ff).

Now you are ready to continue with a detailed study of principles and practice of the beat itself, beginning on p. 47. Repeated reference to the summaries of principles, and further practical review of earlier exercises will be useful, not only in connection with this chapter, but also while you work through Chapters 3, 4, and 5.

THE BATON

A useful baton* should be between 12 and 16 inches long, lightly tapered toward the tip, and so weighted that the more than ninety per-cent of its length protruding from your fingers will not overbalance. Nor

---

*Some conductors do not use a stick at all. The technical principles taught in this book may be applied to conducting without a baton; but it will be easier to acquire proficiency in the practice of the beat with the enhanced precision of the baton. For freedom of gesture there is always the left hand.

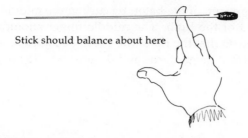

Stick should balance about here

FIGURE 1

should an excessively bulky grip put unnecessary strain on your hand and wrist. Wooden batons balance better than those made of fiberglass.

Many conductors find a small "bulb" at the bottom of the stick useful. A stick without a bulb should be especially light, since it must balance without any counterweight between your fingers.

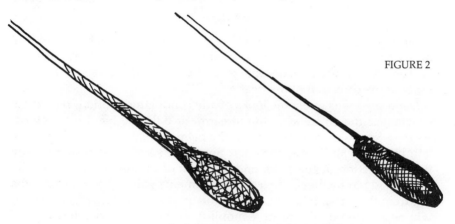

FIGURE 2

actual size of recommended baton bulbs

To test both balance and grip, roll the end of the baton lightly between thumb and forefinger. If this proves awkward, the stick is probably too large and too heavy. Such batons are not only useless, but will seriously impede the development of any kind of serviceable technique.

Pick up the stick with thumb and forefinger (where the finger bends, just below its top joint).

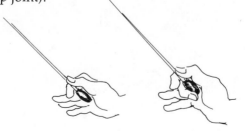

FIGURE 3

Steady the direction of the baton by curling the middle finger (gently!) around the end of the bulb. The middle finger should align forearm, hand, and stick, so that the tip of the baton becomes an extended finger with which to trace the patterns and designs we are about to study.

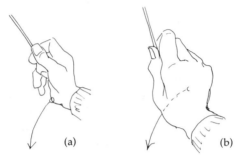

(a)   (b)   FIGURE 4

But first, look at the hand holding the baton. Is the palm or the heel of the hand facing down? In slow, smooth motion it does not matter. Fast and forceful strokes become more "whippy" if the heel of the hand leads in the direction of the beat.

Hand positions affect the looks of any conducting motion, regardless of whether the entire arm, the forearm, or only the hand is involved. As seen from above, in Figure 5a, the palm of the hand is turned to the left; in Figure 5b it faces the floor. Since one's wrist bends more easily in the direction of the palm and the back of the hand, than from the thumb side to the heel, the *feel* of movements will differ accordingly: a flip from the wrist, whether in isolation or at the end of a larger motion, will be affected by the relative mobility of the hand. Try a few flips of the baton, from the wrist, *horizontally*.

Now add this motion to an up-and-down movement (5c) of the entire arm, or the forearm. There should be a little bounce of the wrist at the end of every beat, up or down. It should feel rather like shaking water from your hand (5d).

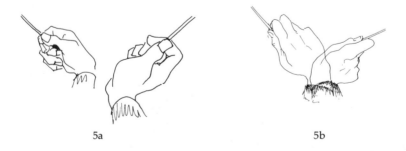

5a   5b

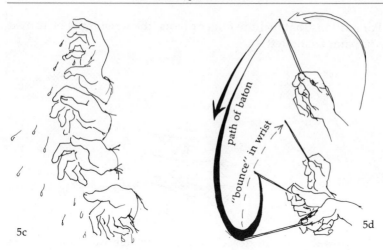

5c

path of baton

"bounce" in wrist

5d

FIGURE 5

FINGER PIVOT

Now what about the "fourth joint" of the conducting arm, the fingers that hold the baton? They are rarely used in the sense of an actual pivot, i.e. as the highest joint from which movement is generated. Since the motion in itself is small and gentle, it is well suited to ticking off silent orchestra measures during an operatic recitative, or silent beats during a solo passage in a concerto. But the undulating motion set off by the finger pivot may contribute greatly to the expressive movement of the other three pivots. It does require a little practice, however.

Take up the stick as usual, and rub the top of the bulb gently between thumb and forefinger (rather like the familiar gesture of "money, money"). When you are able to achieve a rotating motion of the baton tip without losing your firm grip on the bulb, try the same finger motion without the actual rub, moving only the top joints of thumb, forefinger, and middle finger. Either way an independent motion of the baton may be produced in which the tip is seen to rotate.

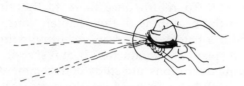

FIGURE 6

Try to produce this rotating motion of the baton, generated by finger pivots, as the natural conclusion of slow sweeps: up–down, left–right, or right–left.

N.B.: For motions that include finger pivots, the wrist must be turned heel down, palm facing left.

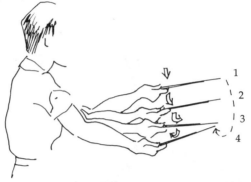

FIGURE 7

Figure 7 shows the arm in descending motion, elbow pivot (i.e. the motion is "from the elbow"). Numbers at the tip of the baton mark four stages of its descent. 1 shows the original position of the arm. At 2, the wrist is seen to bend in a rotating movement that will anticipate the arrival of the arm at its lowest point. The angle of the stick relative to the lower arm has thus far remained the same. At 3, the wrist has passed the lowest point in its rotation, and the rotation from the finger pivot has begun. As a result of the thumb moving forward over the bulb (*try this*), the angle of the baton against the lower arm has changed: its direction points a little more deeply downward, and the tip is dipping in advance of the line normally extending through hand, wrist, and arm. At 4, the forearm has reached its lowest position. Wrist rotation has begun the hand movement upward. The finger pivot has once more aligned the stick with the direction of the hand. The forearm will now be raised, and the same process will be repeated on the next descent. Thus, by extending the arc normally traveled by your baton as a straight extension of your arm, use of the finger pivot adds an elegant, seemingly independent movement to the entire motion.

We have now considered all the *components* of a beat, as parts of motions in general. Some of the motions you practiced may indeed have looked like beats, but they will have lacked at least one distinguishing feature—the message. To return once more to the simile of naval maneuvers used at the beginning of this chapter: your exercises thus far, with or without a baton, hoisted an orchestral equivalent of flag signals at *random* display. The conductor's beat is *specific*.

Read the following definitions and study both commentary and illustrations carefully. With baton in hand, try the beats described, downward, upward, and sideways; slowly and fast; *but always in isolation.* Do not attempt to connect beats, or to "conduct," until you have reached the end of this chapter. Your patience will be rewarded by a clean technique of the beat in a very short time.

Motion vs. Beat

Motions become useful beats if

1. a player can predict, with a safe margin of anticipation, precisely *when* he is to play;
2. a player can predict, with a safe (but in this case more flexible) margin of anticipation, the *type of attack* that will be expected of him (i.e. *how* he is to play his next note);
3. a player can identify the exact moment of the *when* and *how* by *watching the conductor*—without additional recourse to hearing other players, any member of the orchestra should be able to refer to the beat as a visual arbiter of ensemble;
4. a player receives guidance on how to continue, after his entrance (e.g. the shape of the phrase);
5. a player is able to predict, well in advance *when, how,* and, if possible, *to whom* he is to relinquish his temporary initiative.

The beat is a composite motion. Beats differ in the number and proportion of their characteristics according to intended use (function) and the nature of visual features (qualities). The makeup of each individual beat is referred to as its *conformation*.

Conformation of the Beat

A beat may consist of up to four separate elements: fall, impact, recovery, and lift. Of these, the lift may sometimes be used by itself, in place of a complete beat.*

FIGURE 8

The conformation of a beat represents the path outlined by the tip of the baton. Figure 8 shows a preparatory beat (cf. p. 51) the only kind of beat consisting of all four elements. All other complete beats consist of fall, impact, and recovery only.

The thickening of the line of *fall* toward the bottom of the drawing, reflects gathering momentum. *Impact* occurs just before *recovery*, and

*Cf. pp. 239 and 246.

the accumulated momentum decreases. The subsequent *lift* (which is characteristic *only* of the preparatory beat) is a deliberate motion on the conductor's part, increasing momentum in anticipation of the next fall. While the word "fall" seems to suggest a downward motion (and indeed *all beats begin on a downward slant*), the respective gathering and decreasing of momentum is the same with beats in any direction.

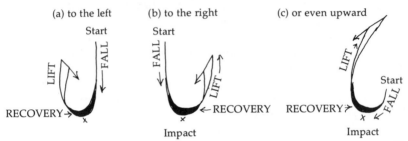

FIGURE 9

Impact always occurs at the bottom of the fall.

Some beats, as in Figure 10, have
only fall and recovery (cf. p. 60).

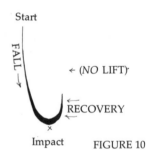

FIGURE 10

One type (cf. p. 56) has so little extension that fall and recovery require the merest flick of the wrist:

FALL→ ⟍⟋ ←RECOVERY

A table of descriptive terms follows, which we shall use in referring to various aspects of the beat and in examining uses of beats in combination. This table is for immediate guidance and for convenient future reference. As the attributes of the beat are further described, examined, and practiced in the technical sections of this book, the specific terms in each of the three categories will always be used as they appear in this table: e.g. "quality" defines a certain aspect of the beat, "function" quite another. They are not interchangeable.

2 possible *functions* of the beat:	active
	passive
3 different *varieties* (types) of beat	preparatory
	principal
	pulsing

4 common *qualities* of all beats
                                       timing
                                         direction
                                         size
                                         impetus

Functions, varieties, and qualities of the beat describe the same motion from different points of view. The natural interdependence of these categories and the conscious use of this built-in interaction gives the conductor a very sophisticated system of controls within a limited framework of movement. Refer to the table above until the descriptive terms and the categories to which they belong are clearly established in your mind.

FUNCTIONS OF THE BEAT

Beats may be arranged to serve either an active or a passive function, depending on the conductor's perception of the expressive relationship between individual sounds of a musical shape.

Active beats accumulate, raise, lower, or release tension. They may anticipate or reflect descriptive, dynamic, or tempo changes. They are explicit technical means to control or repair ensemble.

Passive beats are neutral. They serve neither for expressive illustration nor for the assertion of technical control. A series of passive beats may yield initiative without diminishing established control. Passive beats heighten the expressive effect of active beats which precede or follow.

According to their intended use, active and passive beats can also belong to one of three *varieties*.

Varieties of Beat

The preparatory beat anticipates something of the character of *the next beat:* it accumulates tension, places an entrance, provides additional metric reference if needed. It has *active function* at all times.

The principal beat is the result of preparation. It releases accumulated tension and thus has an *active function.* N.B.: A *succession* of principal beats *without* preparation, (and therefore without tension to release) loses its *active function.*

The neutral pulsing beat neither raises nor lowers tension, is expressively neutral, and serves mainly for metric orientation; it has *passive function.* N.B.: A certain kind of *accented pulsing beat,* whose only function is to generate a sudden increase in tempo, does acquire *active function.*

Preparatory, principal, and pulsing beats are important and distinct types of movement which serve clearly defined musical purposes. They are also very natural motions, familiar to anyone who has ever swung a tennis racket, a golf club, or a baseball bat. As with any of these acquired, physical skills, the common principle of lift-and-strike must be adapted to the practical requirements of our "sport." But once that principle and its application to the theory of the beat are understood, technical proficiency in conducting is only a matter of practice.

The following illustrations show the similarity of the conductor's beat to the technique of playing a children's game called fly-back paddle ball. Each stage of striking the ball is accompanied by the comparable element in the conformation of the beat as shown on p. 47. The player holds a small paddle which has a strong rubber band attached to its center. A ball is suspended from the rubber band, (Figure 11a). When the paddle is lifted, the rubber band is stretched (Figure 11b): *lift,* in the conformation of the beat. As the ball begins to follow upward, the paddle is slapped down sharply (Figure 11c): *fall;* and strikes the ball (Figure 11d): *impact.* The paddle is immediately snapped back (Figure 11c): *recovery;* and lifted again for another strike, while the ball, returning from the farthest downward extension of the rubber band, rises to meet it once more.

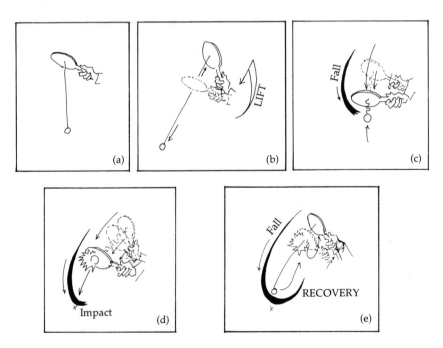

FIGURE 11

The analogy to the conductor's beat is obvious. By gauging the force with which the paddle is lifted and the direction of the downward swing to meet the ball, a skillful player can control the timing of successive strokes, the extent and direction of the ball's trajectory, and the consequent momentum of its flight and return. Lifting the paddle and bringing it down hard to strike the ball are the operative motions, corresponding to the *active functions of the beat: preparatory* (the lift) and *principal* (the strike). A refinement to aid in the timing of strikes is a double rhythm in the right hand: for each flight and return of the ball, there are two motions of the paddle. First the ball is struck as described. Then, halfway between that collision and the next strike, there is an extra flick of the wrist. The little "snap" of the paddle does not affect the flight of the ball, but it helps in the timing of the next strike. This would compare with the *passive function of beats: the pulse*.

The preparatory beat (active function):

It signals *and* characterizes the *following* beat.

Signalling of the following beat (*when* to play) is indicated by the *recovery of the preparatory beat*.

Characterization of the following beat (*how* to play) is the purpose of the *lift of the preparatory beat*.

Preparatories *can be given in any direction:* up, down, left, right. The *direction must be opposite to that of the beat being prepared*.

Preparatories may follow preparatories. In some cases, the cumulative effect may result in an actual crescendo. It will inevitably increase the expressive tension.

In musical examples we shall use the symbol ♪ for preparatories.

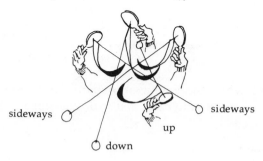

sideways — up — sideways — down

FIGURE 12

Like the ball in the children's game, preparatories may be directed down, up, or sideways, faster or slower, to cover longer or shorter distances depending on the direction and the force with which it is propelled.

These characteristics are signalled by an anticipatory movement of the conducting arm, the more specific and illustrative the better. Force and direction, like the timing of the beat to follow, can be clearly indicated in advance. The baton is lifted and brought down "in time," i.e. each beat anticipates the duration of the next. But the expected momentum of the next attack as well as its place within the measure must also be demonstrated in advance. The direction of preparatory beats should be opposite to that of the beat being prepared. *N.B.:* In Figure 12, preparatories *follow each other*. In music, tension would rise cumulatively, much as it does when you successively hit the ball.

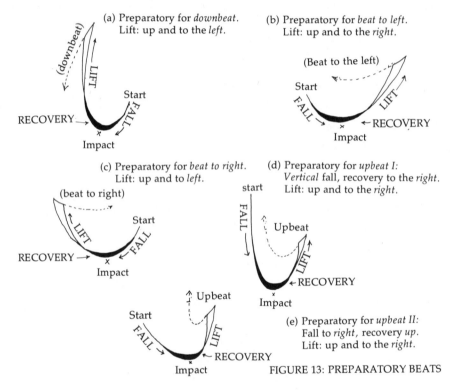

(a) Preparatory for *downbeat.*
Lift: up and to the *left.*

(b) Preparatory for *beat to left.*
Lift: up and to the *right.*

(c) Preparatory for *beat to right.*
Lift: up and to *left.*

(d) Preparatory for *upbeat I:*
Vertical fall, recovery to the *right.*
Lift: up and to the *right.*

(e) Preparatory for *upbeat II:*
Fall to *right,* recovery *up.*
Lift: up and to the *right.*

FIGURE 13: PREPARATORY BEATS

The motion with which the conductor prepares for the next orchestral attack determines not only the exact *timing* of that impact, but also its *force* and its *character.*

Timing becomes an issue when:

1. The attack being prepared is also the opening of a piece or a movement, i.e. no tempo has yet been established. The preparatory (upbeat) is given either at the speed of the beats prescribed in the meter or, if the tempo is slow, at two or three that rate (Figure 13). In

order to effect a smooth connection between the preparatory and beat following, it is important that *the recovery portion of the preparatory bend in the direction opposite to that of the beat being prepared.* If the only aim of the preparatory is a well-timed transition into the first beat, a well-directed recovery is sufficient, (no lift required).
2. The attack being prepared is delayed, i.e. the tempo is being retarded. In that case the preparatory is given in the (gradually) slower tempo.
3. The attack being prepared is to come sooner than the established tempo has led us to expect. This accelerated entrance calls for a preparatory in the new, faster tempo.

Force and character of the orchestral response are *illustrated by the lift* following the recovery portion *of the preparatory beat.* The relative size of the lengthened preparation calls for additional momentum between the end of recovery and the fall of the next beat, or for an accelerated recovery to allow time for a more poised lift. Either way, the *looks* of the lift must indicate the kind of *sound* the beat is intended to prepare: loud, harsh, brisk, heavy, light and feathery, rich and warm. You will exploit this advantage, until experience and practice in applying all three kinds of beat will make you see a preparatory quality in every sort of beat. For music does go on, one event leads to another for which it prepares, and the optimum time to share the anticipation with your players is *before* they are to make something happen: i.e., in your preparation, *con espressione.*

EXAMPLE 1

 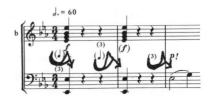

By understanding the principle of preparatory beats, and allowing for ample latitude in their application, we are able to accommodate very different interpretations of the same score with the same set of signals from the podium. To isolate the preparatory beats for the opening of Beethoven's *Eroica Symphony,* we must first have established an "image" of the score. For example, the two great E♭ chords which open the work could be imagined either as broad pillars of sound at the gateway of the symphony, or as sharply defined, whiplash demarcations of its dramatic opening. In Figure 13a, the initial preparation lasts the equivalent of one entire measure $\downarrow. = 60$. Figure 13b allows only one quarter note, $\downarrow = 180$, for the preparatory upbeat.

The first choice would give you an opportunity to demonstrate dramatic tension: find out for yourself how long a full second may seem when all of it must be filled by a single, descriptive upbeat. Start very deliberately, from a central position with your hand in front of and half an arm's length away from your chest. As the slow upbeat comes close to the top of its lift, increase its speed, and reverse suddenly into fall and impact of the downbeat on the first chord. That preparation should inform the orchestra in good time about the powerful release you want. But as a result of your final speed-up, you will also have assured a clean attack.

The second choice, Figure 13b, features a very swift upbeat, $\downarrow = 180$, almost equal to the final speed-up of the first upbeat. The surprise and the suddenness of lashing out like that should result in a much leaner, more explosive orchestral response.

In either case, the downbeat should come to a complete stop on the second quarter of measure 1, lest some players hang on to the opening chord, and its release become ragged. The upbeat on 3 of measure 2 would then have to be brief, as in Figure 13b, but after the fatter sound of the first solution the orchestra would play its second chord just like the first in any case, unless you get in the way. A word of caution: the first two chords are *only* forte, the third is piano!

Preparatory beats are always the most expressive. Since they anticipate the beat being prepared, the orchestra can watch your visual instruction before they must respond. This is not true of principal beats.

The principal beat (active function*):

> The principal beat *releases tension* accumulated by one or more preceding preparatories. *Principals relate to the character of their preparatory beats,* usually in confirmation but sometimes in contrast.
>
> *The character of principles is established in their fall.* There is *no lift* after recovery.

In musical examples we shall use the symbol $\downarrow$ for principals.

---

*A succession of principals, regardless of tempo or dynamics, tends to become heavy and undifferentiated. After prolonged absence of preparatories or pulses between principals, the function of principal beats becomes passive.

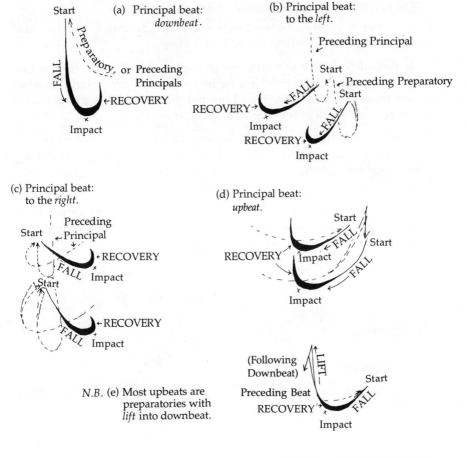

FIGURE 14: PRINCIPAL BEATS

Principal beats are most often associated with the "downbeat" of a measure. But first beats may also be preparatories, as we have already shown, and principals may fall on any other division of the bar, depending on the shape of a musical phrase. The solidity of a phrase, the concrete impression of its shape, is largely the result of placing important principals in their proper places. Naturally, not all principals are accorded equal emphasis, and their preparation will have to take that into account. But they are places of rest within the musical flow, points of reference and sometimes climaxes.

N.B.: *Close proximity of principals* in succession (as in a march) lends a heavy, undifferentiated feeling to music, even in piano passages.

The pulsing beat: neutral (passive function):

The neutral pulsing beat—by far the most commonly used—*marks the passage of time in terms of metric divisions.*

As main divisions of the measure (those specified in the time signature) pulses are characterized by minimum fall and recovery, accurate timing, little impetus, and normal direction. They pass through the center like all other beats.*

As subdivisions (see below), pulses are placed at the end of main division beats, also with minimum fall and recovery and accurate timing, but without passing through the center (they only mark the halfway point of the main beat they subdivide).

Pulses have negative expressive value: neutral in themselves, they throw into relief the expressive value of active beats around them. Thus *they play an important role in clarifying the shapes of phrases.*

In musical examples we use the symbol O for a pulse.

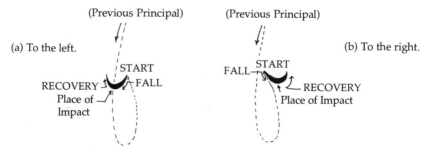

FIGURE 15: PULSING BEATS

Like other kinds of beat, pulses mark the even passage of time according to the speed indicated by the time signature. Unlike other beats, pulses have no other function. In terms of control they are passive beats (i.e. they confirm the "pulse" of the music, but are not useful in enforcing precision of ensemble by clearly defined moments of impact); in terms of expression, they are neutral (i.e. the characteristically small recovery does not lend itself to illustration of the following beat). They do, however, fit smoothly between other beats, principals, preparatories, or pulses. The limitations on control and characterization are most important, albeit negative aspects of pulses. They should not be confused with very small principals or preparatories (which would exhibit characteristically strong fall or recovery according to their respective functions). As soon as pulses become oriented toward mus-

---

*Cf. Chapter 3, p. 86.

ical events to come, they turn (often almost unnoticeably) into progressively aggressive preparatories. Even a very small beat which has a controlling function by virtue of its impact is a principal beat, and must usually be prepared as such.

By far the most interesting use of the pulse is as a point of perspective within a phrase. Because of its expressive neutrality, the active function of surrounding beats is thrown into relief, and the shape of the phrase is clarified. In this way, pulses take on the "color" of their environment. They cannot initiate a sense of rising tension, but would not diminish its established momentum. Similarly, even a very powerful tutti could be continued without resorting to a string of forceful principals (which, as we have observed, tend to become ponderous.)

Example 2 shows possible distributions of active and passive beats, with symbols denoting beat functions as above. Try to "hear" these opening bars of the Minuet from Mozart's G-minor symphony in your imagination, with the respective preparations, principal emphases, and neutral pulses as indicated.

EXAMPLE 2

Although the symbols used to denote respective functions of the beat are part of the "podium" aspect of our study, the decision which their choice is based is essential to the "score" part. The conductor must first examine a phrase, determine its shape, and memorize the result together with the contents of the musical page. Later he will transmit his choice to the orchestra by combining the three kinds of beat appropriately. Thus score and podium, the two sides of the conducting coin, shall become one.

The beat is our chief means of communicating the results of our own work with the score, from the podium, to the players. A continuous flow of musical shapes and images is presented visually by a succession of carefully related kinds of beat. Beats are related to each other in terms of their musical function. This requires that

1. the musical image is clear in the conductor's mind;
2. the function assigned to each beat matches the image;
3. the application of every beat is appropriate to its function.

We have distinguished between active and passive kinds of beat. Beats with active functions may be preparatories or principals; neutral pulses are passive beats. The active part of preparatories is the lift: it describes, times, and controls the following attack. The fall is what distinguishes a principal beat: it may be powerful or gentle, very soft or brutally loud— it may even be a surprise, as when a strong preparation is unexpectedly followed by a weak fulfillment. Even in such a case the effect of the principal *relates* to its preparation. Before we attempt to conduct actual phrases like the several versions of the minuet opening above, we must examine the physical qualities which all active beats have in common (and which, by their absence, indicate a passive beat, or a pulse); and we shall group numbers of beats together according to the metric divisions indicated in the time signature. The patterns usually formed by such groupings will be dealt with in the next two chapters. Individual beats may include the following *qualities:*

Qualities of the Beat

Beats with *active functions* exhibit these four qualities:

1. Timing
2. Direction
3. Size
4. Impulse

Beats with *passive functions* exhibit variable characteristics in terms of the following qualities only:
A. Pulses on main divisions of the measure exhibit
  1. Timing
  2. Direction
    (Size and Impulse are minimal.)
B. Pulses as subdivisions (see Chapter 4b) exhibit only
  Timing
  (Size and Impulse are minimal; Direction follows previous beat.)

Timing

The measured succession (Figure 16a) of metric divisions indicated in the time signature (b) establishes tempo (c).

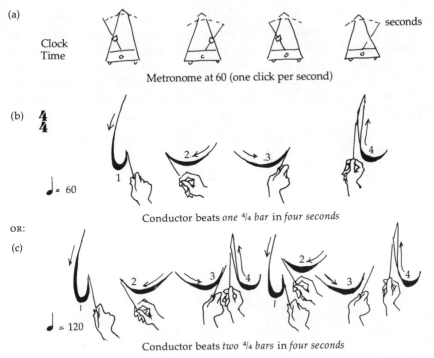

Metronome at 60 (one click per second)

Conductor beats *one* ⁴/₄ *bar in four seconds*

OR:

Conductor beats *two* ⁴/₄ *bars in four seconds*

FIGURE 16

DIRECTION

The path traveled by the *tip* of the baton determines the direction of the beat.* As we have already seen, beats may travel upwards or down, to the left or to the right. Groups of beats forming a pattern according to the prescribed meter of the work being conducted are distinguished by the respective direction of every component beat. Below is a pattern of four, showing beats traveling down (1), left (2), right (3), up (4). Thus the direction of beats serves primarily as a means of metric orientation within each bar: the players see a "picture" of 4 / 4 time.

FIGURE 17

*The metric patterns (the path traveled by the top of the baton) for "plain" meters of 2, 3, or 4 are discussed in Chapter 3.

Size

In conjunction with the three other qualities of a beat, size affects volume, sound quality, and tempo. Variable only with beats serving an active function, size is measured in terms of comparison with the conductor's overall beat dimensions: some prefer a great variation of sizes, others generally large or generally small beats. Small beats are easier to manage.

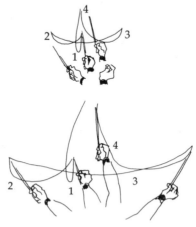

FIGURE 18

Impetus

The comparative speed and power with which the tip of the baton travels and rebounds has an important affect on the musical character of an attack being prepared or given and provides specific information on the desired amount of stress or relaxation for each beat.

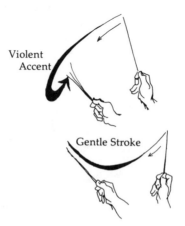

FIGURE 19

SUMMARY

Individual beats can be classified according to

Two Functions:	Active	Preparatory (p. 51ff)
	Passive	{ Principal (p. 54ff) { Pulse (p. 56ff)
Three Varieties:	Preparatory Principal Pulsing	Fall/Impact/Recovery/Lift ⎫ Fall/Impact/Recovery ⎬ (p. 49ff) minimum Fall ⎭ Recovery
Four Qualities:	Timing Direction Size Impetus	Fast–Slow ⎫ up/down/left/right ⎬ (p. 58ff) large–small violent–gentle ⎭

Assignment

Review all motions, and all exercises in connection with motions, discussed in Chapter 1, in terms of the beat according to the summary above. Work through all possibilities from the shoulder, the elbow, the wrist. Place elbow and wrist pivots in different positions before you begin. This review should only involve *single beats* and should be undertaken daily for at least one week.

Combine two beats: preparatory–principal, * also with as many different applications of beat qualities as possible, and with different portions of the arm** in active participation.

To be remembered:

1. The preparatory always precedes the next beat in the *opposite* direction (i.e. down is prepared up, left is prepared right, up is prepared down).
2. Even lateral beats (to left or right) are characterized by the downward "dip" of the fall, and the upward swing of recovery and lift, although their main direction lies along the horizontal axis. These modifications of direction and other beat qualities will be examined in detail in the following chapter.

---

*In that order only, but with variety in terms of timing, direction, size, and impetus of beat.
**Using different combinations of pivots.

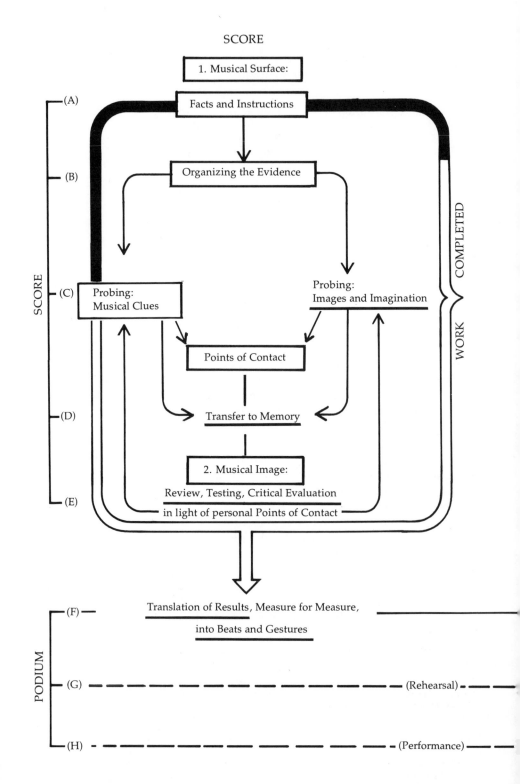

3A

PROBING: MUSICAL CLUES

We exploit the evidence of a striking
rhythmic figure in the third movement of
Brahms's *Third Symphony*, and discover a
compelling unity of expressive design.

BEFORE you begin this chapter, review the method of organizing
the evidence on the surface of an orchestral score as outlined in Chapter
2a (pp. 29–39). Then follow the suggested method of working through
the Scherzo of Brahms's *Third Symphony* on your own. The full score
follows below, already marked according to the categories of Groups B
and C. Your own survey should concentrate on Groups A and D, which
will serve as the basis of a sample analysis beginning on p. 00. Do not
read on until you have finished sifting the available evidence. You
should then be somewhat familiar with the score, and capable of thinking about the information it provides without consulting the musical
text on every page.

We shall then suggest that you look for the "fortuitous detail" which
could serve to establish a point of personal contact with the score. As
the chart at the head of this chapter shows, this may be achieved either
by careful examination of empirical evidence or by the employment of
fantasy and associated images. In this case we are using the former
approach. The results will be outlined in the present chapter, and
developed further in Chapters 6 and 8. In addition, with a flip of the
conducting coin, we shall be able to demonstrate some technical implications of our discovery in Chapter 7.

Here is a work with which you are probably familiar, so that the
tunes and textures come easily to mind as you turn the pages of the
score. As always, begin with a good look at *preliminary information
(Group A)* and take note of random thoughts in passing.*

---

*If some of what comes to mind seems irrelevant, so be it. But to reject even the most fleeting
thought, at this point, would inhibit the flow of further reactions, ideas, reminiscences, and "brain-
waves." You are trying to coax something of your nonrational self into conscious confrontation with
the score.

EXAMPLE 1: Brahms, *Symphony No. 3*, third movement

GROUP A: PRELIMINARY INFORMATION

A1: Composer. Brahms was a nineteenth-century romantic who felt himself "pursued by the heavy tread of the Giant Beethoven," a very difficult giant for lyricist Brahms, late-starter symphonist, to cope with. He maintained a personal/professional relationship with Clara, widow of his generous early supporter, Robert Schumann, and was proclaimed heir apparent to the only true musical tradition as defined by his faithful, anti-Wagnerian, Viennese coterie.

Brahms was a highly acclaimed, very private man in 1883, when he wrote his *Third Symphony*, a work which reflects rather than recaptures the warm and vital élan of some of his earliest music. Outbursts of bright joy, pain, or passion inevitably seem to turn inward and to subside into a wistful sort of sadness. This Scherzo bears such a melancholy mien, resigned, but of great beauty.

A2: Title. None, but see the following:

A3: Tempo. A curious indication, *Poco Allegretto*, a double diminutive. Does it mean "Andante, but a little on the fast side"; or "Allegro, held back—just a little"? In the former sense it woud indicate a slightly slower tempo than the modified Allegro of the latter interpretation. It is too soon to look for answers to questions raised by an ambiguous tempo indication—or is the uncertainty itself a clue? Keep looking.

A4: Instrumentation. Very small—strings, winds, only two of the four French horns available. With only woodwinds to balance chords shared by those horns, the reduction certainly precludes a great range of volume, unless one or both of the horns are in the melodic lead. Expectation: a somewhat subdued movement in which climaxes are likely to be lyrical.

A5: Key. C minor; middle section in A♭. Another perspective: Warmth (mediant relationship), but under the subdued harmonic lighting of a distinctly minor subdominant suggestion, in a piece rooted on the minor dominant of this F-major symphony.

More on tonalities: The preceding movement was in C major, enjoyed a single "outburst of bright joy" (m. 112) after which we experience a sense of harmonic dislocation (mm. 115–21). This leads back to C, but through very weakening allusions to the minor subdominant, ending piano, più piano. The outer movements are in F major, but by m. 5 of first movement, we are in D flat (VI of F *minor*); and of the 309 measures comprising the finale, 266 bear four flats. Is something being revealed?

A6: ⅜ is a triple meter somewhere between a suggested pulse of one and a conducted beat of three. Does this furnish a clue to the question raised by the tempo indication (A3): a sense of moving in *three*, but a little on the fast and restless side; or of a lilting *one* that holds back, reluctantly, in *three*?

GROUP B: MAJOR DIVISIONS

Since our movement is quite simply constructed, there is not a great deal to be discovered under Group B. The *ternary form* of the movement is clearly defined (B1): visually by double bars, thematically by different materials. That this is also a perfect example of correspondences (B2) between main and middle section may not be apparent on first inspection: we shall return to this point when we have found our "clue"; (B3)—key signature and new tonality—have been mentioned above; (B4 and 5) do not apply.

GROUP C: SUBSECTIONS

C1, 2, and 3: Subsections; Periods/Phrases; Two, plus Three, plus Four. The printed score above has already been marked, and further prose description seems unnecessary. More useful will be your own retracing of my progress along the surface of this score in terms of periods, phrases, and smallest (two-, three-, or four-measure) shapelets. If you should disagree with any details of the bracketed outlines, so much the better: substitute your own.

C4: Orchestration emphasizes the differences between main and middle sections, rather than the correspondence we have alluded to. (N.B. If the first hint has made you curious, perhaps you ought to have an exploratory look for yourself—it's all there. In order to mark all the brackets and the various other reminders written into our sample score yourself, you would have turned its pages many more times: and something might well have struck you as "special.") The main sections are indeed melodic lines with accompaniment. The building blocks of the middle section are motivic components—very short—strung together in harmonically determined, larger sequences. Note how in the main section and its return (m. 98) *the melodic lines are solos,* single or doubled as marked, and surrounded by a fine mesh of arpeggiated texture divided among many instruments. Just the reverse happens in the middle section (m. 54): musical continuity is entrusted to a wind *chorus,* against which a *solo counterpoint* in the low strings provides a tenuous counterweight. There are two great swells from *pp* to forte: the first, in the center of the middle section (mm. 70–78), employs the full strings; the second (m. 154 to the end), the entire orchestra.

GROUP D

D1: Compositional texture has been mentioned—melody and accompaniment vs. overall shaping through harmonic control of rhythmic motives. These helped to contrast the outer sections of the movement from its middle part, but are not particularly "special" to this work. In fact we said that we are looking for something which will also be reflected in "correspondences" between sections, not their very apparent contrast. We shall find what we are looking for in examining the next two categories:

D2 and 3: Shapes and rhythm. The rhythm first announced in the cello melody at the opening dominates the main section:

EXAMPLE 2

It is oddly spaced, and stands out in strong relief against the running triplets which form its restless background. As the result of a metric shift from the third beat, the dotted figure assumes two very different meanings: upbeat on three, release on one. Together these two aspects of one rhythm form a cohesive and extraordinarily flexible motif, in which the upbeat tension always appears more powerful than its release.

This effect is enhanced by the harmonic background, coupled with the respective time value of (a) and (b): the upbeat portion (a) of the motive (value = 4 eighth notes) rests on the tonic chord of C minor; the shorter release (b) (value = 2 eighth notes) on a weaker, half-diminished one belonging to the subdominant region. The melodic climax G (m. 2) occurs as a dissonant stress at the very moment of harmonic (and dynamic) letdown. This fundamental "inner" shape is implied in thematic material and harmonic treatment throughout the symphony.*

An example of this establishes the already suggested correspondence between the main and middle sections of the movement. For all their apparent differences in style and texture, the "inner" shape of a strong upbeat finding a comparatively weak release is not only characteristic of the melodic material at the opening and the close. A good look at the middle section confirms a rather striking kinship of harmonic disappointment, underlined by the harmonic nuance right at the beginning of the A♭ major (m. 54):

EXAMPLE 3

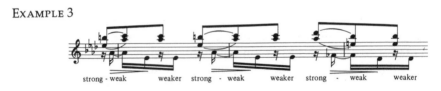

Flutes and clarinets appear to suggest "strong" tonic resolutions on the first downbeats, but these are reversed by the bass motion in bas-

*Cf. Chapter 8, pp. 265–71.

soons and cellos: A♭ upbeat / E♭ downbeat. The prominent emphasis given to that bass line by the single voice in the strings within a choir of winds lends weight to the bass. Add to that the explicit "instruction" of dynamic nuances on every measure, and Brahms might as well have supplied the verbal commentary "strong-weak-weaker," as in Example 3, for this melancholy musical statement.

There are other clues. Note and sing all oboe entrances between m. 54 and the eloquently resigned solo at m. 96: Every one of the strong entrances on A♭ is turned into a weaker release, until the final one, which ends on A♭ (m. 83), as part of three progressively weaker chords. The next entrance (m. 26) anticipates the return of the opening melody, after what is perhaps the most moving example of the autumnal nostalgia of this work: the one passage which did reach a glowing forte climax (mm. 70–78) in the strings was repeated (mm. 87–96) before this last entrance, with a diminuendo from its very beginning.

To discover and to explore this kind of inner relationship between sections of a work which are *not* otherwise variants or developments of related materials is only important to the extent to which your performance will rest on it. True, you cannot determine that extent until you have examined and evaluated every musical lead. Then there are three possibilities: 1) you were wrong—forget it; 2) you were right, but you can't find a way of making your discovery a feature of your performance without doing violence to some other important aspect of the work (performance practice of its period, for instance), so forget it; or, 3) you were right, and you can see how your image of the music could be shared in performance. You have progressed from the question of "what is it?" to knowing the answer to "what does it want of me?". Then your contribution begins.

The learning process leads from "what is it?" to "what does it want of me?". But with every score the process has to be repeated many times. Conclusions must be reviewed, and new discoveries—sometimes after years of confident familiarity with the music—may require new answers. Before you *begin* that process, it is necessary that the musical surface is securely inside your mind.

Let us now examine the first twelve measures of the movement. The two-measure shapes of the main section motive, identical in outline, are repeated twice. But the inherent contrast between strong preparation and weak release is even more marked the second time (mm. 3 and 4) because of the larger melodic leap (a fifth instead of a third) into the accented dissonance at the point of harmonic letdown. Over the next four bars the momentum seems to gather, increasing the expectation of some kind of release in m. 8. It does not come. Instead, this last measure is an elision into a succession of transient chords supporting the twice-repeated "shape" only in the dynamic nuance indicated for the solo voice (mm. 9–12). The effect is a dissipation of intensity. My favorite measure is 12: here we have the final resolution into the tonic—or do we? The "release" is delayed until the second beat, *and* a passing A♮ (viola and flute) prevents the true appearance of a C-minor triad until, once more, it serves as an upbeat measure in the next two-bar shape. Yet Brahms chose to stress the near-resolution on the second beat of m. 12 with a dynamic nuance which, in itself, becomes another unfulfilled musical promise.

So much for "what is it?". Now, "what does it want of us?". Try to hear the effect in your mind. What might have been the tonic in m. 12 strikes me as an *anticipation* of the expressive crescendo to come. In part, that effect is due to the violin upbeat to m. 13, which neutralizes the actual diminuendo still in progress, and prepares for the new twelve-measure shape with its own strong-crescendo/weak-climax pattern. M. 12, final climax of the first twelve-measure phrase, strengthens the preparation of m. 14. By raising the anticipation it serves to emphasize the now-established pattern of harmonic disappointment when it is repeated again. Thus m. 12, far from affording even belated release, binds the next, melancholy effort to the one before, in an elision that becomes in itself an eloquent expression of beautiful futility.

Whether or not you find this way of "hearing" that transition convincing, try to imagine the sound and the feeling of it in your mind. Do not look at the score. You will find that you must first create the sense of *expectation*. The harmonic "disappointment" shall then follow logically. You will be in a position to face a much more difficult assignment: to project that sense of raised and thwarted hope, as a basic and recurring pattern in the musical fabric of this movement, to an audience. Sooner or later, every young conductor faces an orchestra that reads more efficiently than he expected. With some degree of panic, he comes up against the question: "what do I rehearse?". You rehearse *your image of the music;* only you will have to find it first. That way you shall truly become "an essential element in the whole musical picture."

If this movement had ended on the first beat of m. 52, we should have had our ending in C minor after all. Instead, Brahms introduces a foreign chord on the second beat, sustaining it over the next measure as well. It sounds like A♭ minor, but the spelling anticipates its ambivalent function in the middle section which now follows. We must inevitably acknowledge the continued presence of "the shape," as we step over this threshold into the next manifestation of promise and disappointment, transformed from strong-stronger-weak into strong-weak-weaker, "with a wistful sort of sadness."

The task of preparing a score for rehearsal and performance with an orchestra differs radically from the experience of instrumentalists or singers. *As a conductor, your primary musical instrument is your own mind.* Unlike any other performer, you must learn, practice, plan, recreate and preperform music in your imagination before you set foot on the podium for its first rehearsal. You need to imagine sound in terms of melodic and chordal combinations, instrumental timbres, and a dynamic range beyond that of any single orchestral instrument. Even more important, you need to anticipate the *effect* which all these shall produce on the listener. In order to be in control of your imaginary practice, you need to be your own, first listener. We do not learn to *play* the music we conduct, but to *play with it.* Details that a pianist may work out in active dialogue with his piano must be discovered, tried, discarded, or improved in silent concentration, "practiced" in aural imagination, and remembered *without* the aid of the muscular memory on which instrumentalists may rely to a degree. A resourceful imagination is as essential in this as a good ear, flexible stick technique, or knowing how to plan an effective rehearsal. Expressive control through beat and gesture can never be more persuasive than the musical ideas it means to convey.

Method in surveying the surface of a score, and lively curiosity about the possible significance of "fortuitous musical detail" in organizing the evidence of that surface, are complementary aspects of achieving a sense of the total score. The first will provide the framework. The second may achieve unity, and requires imagination, persistence, and luck. The reward is that, at a level well below the surface of the music, you participate as the composer's partner.

In the Brahms, we found such a "fortuitous musical detail" in the form of a two-measure shape. The metric displacement of an otherwise symmetrical rhythmic outline was matched by a harmonic anomaly. Quite unrelated thematic material in the middle section of the movement shared basic characteristics with the "odd" musical shape which appears at the opening. Now we shall persist: do these characteristics answer those questions raised in our initial survey? Are we in a better position, for instance, to form conclusions about aspects of the work *not* related to musical outlines or harmonic functions? Let us test our find in two as yet undetermined areas: tempo and dynamics.

In Group A3 of our survey, we wondered whether the composer's tempo instruction *Poco Allegretto* meant "a little faster than Andante" or "slightly slower than Allegro." In itself, the double diminutive could be interpreted either way. You are now ready to try various sections of this movement in imagination, in the light of whatever comments in

our analysis may appear plausible to you. If none of them do, you will
of course substitute your own interpretation before you come to a determination on the tempo. But based on our comment on m. 12, for
instance, or almost any measure of the middle section as we noted its
"wistful sadness," any tempo *faster* than Allegretto would not work. A
little *slower*, then, somewhere between Allegretto and Andante: we have
found a clue to the "environment of tempo" in the shape of a phrase,
and corroboration in a recurring harmonic feature of this movement.

But as for dynamics, how loud is loud? Even here, the insight we
owe to the discovery of our "odd musical shape," and its reflection in
the general character of this piece, is of very practical value. Measure
150, the beginning of the Coda, recalls the earlier transition into the
middle section of the movement (cf. p. 78). The harmonic resolution
falls on the first beat, but, as before, it is immediately effaced by another,
longer, *dolce* upbeat. We remember the pattern, of course: strong
expectation, fulfilment lacking in strength and satisfaction, resignation
transformed into new expectation. Only this time is the last. Small wonder that the final buildup is so greatly augmented, that its climax is also
the first tutti forte in the entire piece. Music at the close—how loud is
loud at such a moment?

The recurring message of our basic shape is, "I am reaching for something; but what I am able to grasp is always less than the hoped-for
reward of my effort. I will try again." At m. 150 the words might be: "I
shall reach out once more, slowly, with all my strength. Then I shall
stop." The imaginary speaker seems like one who cares without confidence and strives without success, whose reach is strong but whose
grasp is irresolute, whose desire is not to be fulfilled because its object
is not desired. A little farfetched? Look at mm. 154 to end.

The entire orchestra supports a greatly extended first part of our shape,
in a rhythmically unanimous hemiola ascent. In the upper voices this
begins on the *leading note B♮* and moves upwards, scalewise—*to B♭!*
This final lack of fulfilment was preordained in the fourth bar of the
movement, where the seventh step of the suggested C-minor scale is
already flattened to the downward turning minor seventh, B♭. Think,
for a moment, how different the ending would feel, if, at the top of the
final upward rise, there had been a B♮ breaking through, at last, to C
on the following beat. What a heroic last-minute achievement that would
have been—and how vulgar. But our imaginary speaker is neither a
hero nor vulgar. His limits are set in the opening phrase. His musical
identity includes the great urgency of preparatory tension, and the melancholy resignation of a lowered leading tone, from the start. Wistful
and poignant is this movement, to the end. How loud is loud? Not very.

Out of such considerations, a performance image is formed. If you would try to recall your own image of this movement, all at once, in terms of the overall sense and feeling of it, yet with as much concrete detail of the text as you can muster, you should find that you have come a long way toward "transforming a musical surface into a working image of music."

PODIUM

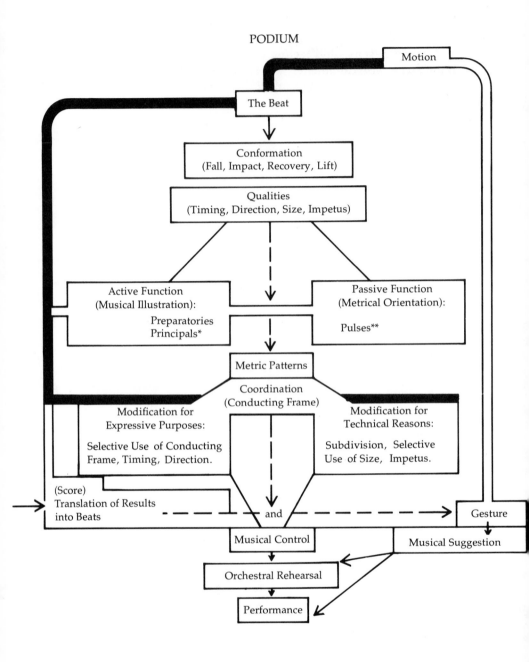

*Exception: *Series* of Principals: (*Passive* Function)

**Exception: *Accented* Pulse: (*Active* Function)

3B

THE BEAT: FUNCTIONS AND PLAIN PATTERNS

The examination of beat functions is continued, showing how 2, 3, or 4 beats may
be combined into patterns that serve both
metric orientation and expressive illustration.

METRIC PATTERNS

Beats are grouped into patterns, according to the number of metric
divisions per measure shown in the time signature.

Patterns of 2, 3, and 4 may be formed entirely of active beats. All
other patterns require the additional use of pulses for clarification
(see Chapter 4). Patterns of 2, 3, and 4 are called *plain patterns*.

The distribution of strong and weak stresses within any pattern
remains variable, according to the conductor's perception of musical
shapes and their reflection in his use of beats with active or passive
function.

W/HILE our *thinking* about music becomes increasingly independent of the chronological sequence of time in which it must be performed, the purpose of our beat is to control musical events in
performance, i.e. in precisely that one-directional sequence of clock time.
In order to simplify the players' perception of these beats, they are
grouped into metric patterns that reflect measures of music in the score,
according to the indicated time signature.

If properly used, beat patterns will fit easily within the requirements
of complete flexibility to allow a wide range of expressive suggestion at
any part of any metric division. The expressive intent of any beat may
modify the basic shape of any pattern, but *does not alter it*. As a system

of metric coordinates, based on the distribution of beats within a framework of specified directions, the respective patterns we are about to demonstrate are absolute and inflexible. A pattern of four will have a recognizable downbeat on 1, every time, regardless of the changing functions of successive downbeats.

With this in mind, we shall enjoy great freedom in using the beat as our primary signal of expressive intent as well. As long as the few principles with regard to "keeping time" are strictly observed, an infinite variety of sophisticated applications of the beat enables us to reflect sudden or subtle changes of articulation, duration, or relative importance in the sounds we invoke from the orchestra. Thus we shall soon begin to see both sides of the "conducting coin."

Simplicity of execution comes with growing proficiency, but it is based on understanding. Beat patterns serve the single purpose of metric coordination. Beats, arranged in accordance with such patterns, serve any purpose of musical communication of the conductor's choosing.

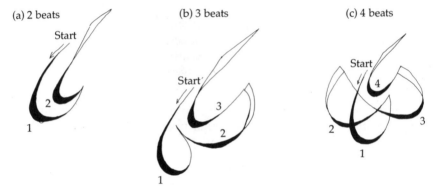

FIGURE 1: PATTERNS OF 2, 3, AND 4 BEATS

The illustrations show beats of equal size in patterns of two, three, and four divisions per measure. Note the graphic symbols* used for the elements forming each beat: a *thickening line* (always curving downward)—the *fall;* at the *maximum extension of the fall—impact* ⊗; the *thickened line thinning* (always curved upward)—*recovery;* another thickening line, *not* filled in (always upward)—*lift*. This last element is part of the conformation of preparatory beats only. In the three illustrations of Figure 1, a) has a preparatory on the second beat, b) on the second and third, c) on the second, third, and fourth beats. in all three, the first beats are principals (no lifts).

Looking more closely at the *downbeats* of the illustrated patterns,

---

*Cf. p. 47: Conformation of the beat.

however, you will note that their direction, instead of following a really vertical downward path, slants vigorously to the left. The reason for this is anatomical: Your right shoulder, the assumed pivot of these beats, is about a foot to the right of center (center being an imaginary point in the middle of your chest). In order to pass in front of that center point, *as all preparatory and principal beats must,* a downbeat hinged on your *shoulder* pivot will slant to the left and recover to the right.

A downbeat hinged on an *elbow* pivot, even with the elbow forward and straight below the right shoulder, may either begin forward of the shoulder and slant to the left on its recovery; or, if the lower arm is already bent slightly inward to the left, it may follow a vertical direction, through center.

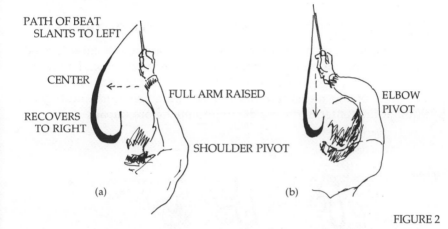

PATH OF BEAT
SLANTS TO LEFT

CENTER

FULL ARM RAISED

ELBOW PIVOT

RECOVERS TO RIGHT

SHOULDER PIVOT

(a)   (b)

FIGURE 2

Try both ways at once, before you read on. Let your physical sense of movement show you why shoulder pivots *must* slant, while others *may.*

Summarizing the overall directions of all beats (including the downbeat) in the three *plain patterns,** we note

two = 1—down; 2—up
three = 1—down; 2—right; 3—up
four = 1—down; 2—left; 3—right; 4—up

The following illustrations show that these directions are indeed approximate. Not only does the downbeat of the full arm slant to the left, as we have seen, but none of the beats move straight in the direction of their eventual destination. The reason for this lies in the natural swing of the arm, the forearm, even the hand alone, on their respective pivots. The slight curve with a "dip," which we observed and practiced

*For mixed and compound patterns, see Chapter 4b.

in the first chapter, will now become the normal path of the beat. This is a most important thing to remember, for modifications in the depth of the "dip" have instant effects on the expressive character of the beat (e.g. the steeper the downward incline of the curve, the more powerful the beat—emphasis in conducting is not necessarily a matter of brute force). More of this presently, but a review of the section in the previous chapter, immediately following the example of the fly-back paddle ball game (pp. 50–51), should demonstrate the vital "dip" (fall-impact-recovery) as a characteristic feature in the conformation of *any* beat.

The illustrations below also show the three demonstrated patterns enclosed in a lopsided square called the *conducting frame*.

The Conducting Frame and the Center of the Beat

All beats, in all metric patterns, move in relation to a cross formed by connecting the four corners of the conducting frame. The intersection of this cross shall be called the *center*. All main beats (i.e. divisions of the measure reflecting the time signature) must pass through the center of the conducting frame before impact.

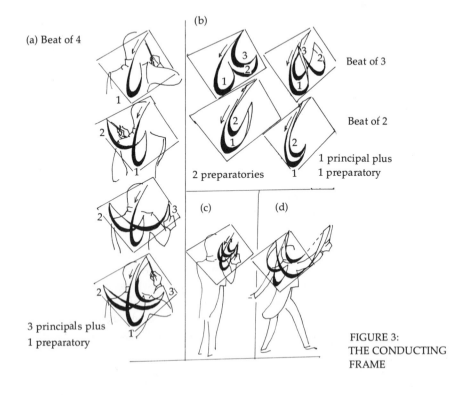

(a) Beat of 4

(b)

3 principals plus 1 preparatory

2 preparatories

Beat of 3

Beat of 2

1 principal plus 1 preparatory

(c)   (d)

FIGURE 3:
THE CONDUCTING FRAME

What is a "normal" conducting frame? The actual size of the area within which the tip of your baton travels depends very much on your physical proportions, your style of gesture (elaborate or understated), and on the music itself. Some conductors (Sir Adrian Boult, Leonard Bernstein) have a "large beat" and others were noted for a minuscule one (Fritz Reiner). On the whole, any beat that requires a shift in your stance, i.e. a movement of the foot to support you at its extremity, is certainly too large in terms of your normal conducting frame. Much more significant, however, are the proportions between one beat and another. The fact that one beat is larger or smaller than another has interpretive significance and will be so understood by the orchestra. Even the proportions between the beat itself and its recovery determine to a large extent what the function of the beat is meant to be. We have already mentioned this in connection with principal and preparatory beats, and Figure 13, on page 52, illustrates the point: if the length of the beat, from its beginning to the impact at the moment of greatest momentum and change of direction, is much larger than its recovery, it will have required greater speed and thus more powerful impetus than its conclusion. Such a beat is clearly designed to emphasize the moment of impact: it is a principal beat—what follows is less important than the moment of attack. By the same token, if the follow-up is larger than the beat (because you need the extra length to demonstrate what is to come) or gathers more momentum because the greater emphasis is to follow, then the beat is a preparatory. In either case, the relative size of *part* of a beat indicated its meaning. Since the effect of preparatories can be culmulative, the difference in size between two or more beats may also indicate an expressive difference. But be careful not to confuse size with dynamics indiscriminately. Here again, impetus is the quality which can prevent a large beat from signaling a loud response, or endow a short but whiplike flick from the wrist with power far beyond its size. *The interaction of beat qualities determines* their message in terms of whatever *function* you have assigned to any beat. *Location in the conducting frame lends precision and flexibility* to your signals.

MODIFICATION OF BEAT SIZE WITHIN THE CONDUCTING FRAME

The respective sizes of beats within the conducting frame, together with their direction and impetus, relate to the musical emphasis to be given on impact.

Beat patterns provide reference points relating beats to the exact moment within each measure to which they are applied. We have looked at patterns of two, three, and four. Double and triple subdivisions will give us patterns of six, eight, twelve, and all the compound and mixed divisions in between (Chapter 4). With our understanding of the nature, qualities, and functions of the beat, and with careful practice as suggested at the end of this chapter, these patterns are not difficult to understand and reproduce, or to use as a framework for shaping music according to its image in your mind.

There are many possible modifications of beat patterns for demonstrating the relative musical importance of successive beats. We have already mentioned modification of the downbeat as a matter of physical expediency, the slant to the left as the full-arm movement whips the baton through the center of the imaginary conducting frame for impact and rebound. An illustrated example of a downbeat modified to prepare an emphasized second beat will follow. But first, take another look at the conducting frame as shown, with an important addition:

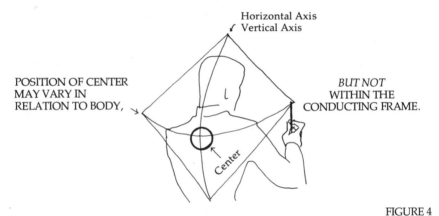

Horizontal Axis
Vertical Axis

POSITION OF CENTER MAY VARY IN RELATION TO BODY,

BUT NOT WITHIN THE CONDUCTING FRAME.

Center

FIGURE 4

The so-called center of the beat is represented by a dotted circle at the intersection of the frame's vertical and horizontal axes. Conscious use and constant awareness of the center as the one *invariable point of orientation* when other aspects of beat patterns are modified may well be the most important part of a flexible but clear stick technique.

The location of the center is not to be modified.

Every beat, on every main division of a metric pattern, must pass *through the center* of the conducting frame *before impact.*

Impact short of the center would in effect shift the frame of reference for all beats: the conducting frame. If, for any reason, this should be *intended* (e.g. a smaller frame, off to the side) then the new center becomes the reference point for all following beats, and the above rule would apply.

With this in mind, we shall address ourselves to the following assignment: to modify the downbeat in a pattern of four, so that it will have the effect of a preparatory to emphasize the second beat.

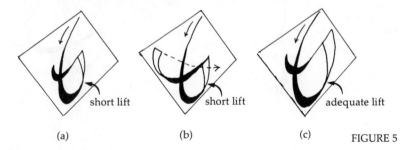

(a)   (b)   (c)   FIGURE 5

The first solution (Figure 5a) shows a downbeat that looks much like the one in the large diagram above (Figure 3c). Although it is intended to prepare a strong second beat, its lift (the thickened line, *not* filled in, which follows recovery) is so small as to be undistinguishable from a normal recovery. The second beat, in this first solution, is very strong but short. The result would be an awkward little push on 2 by the conductor, with no effect on the orchestra.

Solution b begins with the same downbeat, but the second beat extends so far to the left that some belated notice of its intended emphasis is given to the orchestra. The real difficulty in this case would be with the third beat: because the beat has been so far extended on 2, the 3 will have to be large (and consequently just as powerful as 2) in order to pass through center again. What happened here is that the conductor, in effect, gave a *preparatory* beat on 2, by extending it, for belated emphasis, all the way to the edge of the conducting frame. He prepared a powerful 3 instead of a powerful 2.

The third solution (Figure 5c) does treat the downbeat as a preparatory: its recovery is followed by a lift up to the right-hand upper edge of the frame and the second beat is powerfully released into an impact just beyond and below the center. A well-prepared, strong principal beat will have its most forceful, explosive impact at just that location within the frame.

Modification of the beat pattern provides us with an abundant range of possibilities. We have just demonstrated the principles governing modifications of the beat: high elevation of the preparatory lift to provide momentum for the fall of the following beat, and impact which becomes more explosive the closer it is to the center. The same principles govern different *degrees of modification*. This, of course, is where the system becomes capable of projecting a wide range of musical decisions.

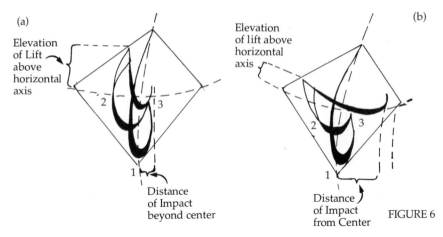

(a)

Elevation of Lift above horizontal axis

2 3

1

Distance of Impact beyond center

(b)

Elevation of lift above horizontal axis

2 3

1

Distance of Impact from Center

FIGURE 6

Suppose the beat signaling a strong emphasis on 3, in a $^4/_4$ measure were to serve a staccato entrance of winds, brass, and percussion, preceded by two pizzicato chords on the first two beats, sempre forte. The diagram (Figure 6a) would look very much like Figure 4c, with the emphasis shifted from the second to the third beat of the measure. Now study Figure 6b: The elevation of the lift on 2 is noticeable, but not dramatic. The third beat itself is longer, i.e. there is actually more time to accumulate momentum. But because the angle of descent from the crest of the lift is less steep, and because the point of impact is a little further beyond the center than in Figure 6a, the result would be a deeper, warmer emphasis, a rich tutti perhaps.

Some things must never change: the location of the center is one. The *direction* of the downbeat and its *extent below center* is another. Thus, "legibility" of your downbeat will be assured even if, for the sake of emphasis, other beats receive upward preparation nearly as high as the first beat of a measure and if the resulting fall of such another beat will appear nearly as steep. Here is the rule:

The fall of the downbeat is not to be modified.

> The first beat, in any metric pattern and regardless of function, is always given in a downward direction, through the center.

> The first beat, in any metric pattern and regardless of function, is the only beat ever to extend substantially below the center before recovery.

N.B.: The first part of this rule does not, of course, invalidate our earlier observation that downbeats, given from the shoulder, *must* slant to the left because your shoulder is to the right of center.

With the exclusion of the fall of the downbeat, the following summarizes modifications of the four elements of the beat.

MODIFICATIONS—BEAT CONFORMATION

Fall: any beat, regardless of its normal direction within a metric pattern, gains in power if its momentum accumulates in a *downward* slanting curve.

In order to *mitigate* the force of impact, after a forceful or expressive preparation, the fall must be *contained*. Its downward slant may be deflected sideways, and/or its size be reduced.

Impact: the more forceful the intended impact, the closer the curve of fall should terminate to the center of the conducting frame.

Lift: preparatories terminate in a lift moving in the *direction opposite to that of the following beat.*

The more powerful the intended impetus of the next beat, the higher the lift of the preparatory connecting with it should be. This is also true of beats preparing for others to be vested with great *expressive* potency.

As soon as you have become familiar with the three plain metric patterns, the practice of modifications should begin. Beyond the elementary level of beating time, conducting music involves constant modifications of the beat to reflect musical shapes, inflections, stresses, and releases, determined in advance according to your image of the score.

It is strongly recommended that before each practice session you write out a brief "score" containing the assignment of technical principles you are planning to apply. A practice score dealing with principal and preparatory beats might look like this:

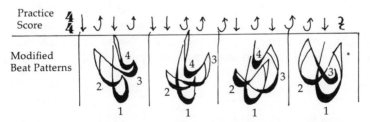

FIGURE 7

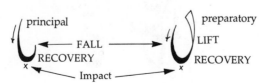

Before you begin, review everything you have read thus far concerning principal and preparatory beats (pp. 51–55). The summaries on the principles governing these beats and their modifications should be reread often and memorized.

The best examples, of course, come from actual scores. Only the musical image itself suggests the many possible ways of shaping even an apparently "simple" phrase requiring modifications of the beat pattern, in terms of direction, impetus, and location of impact. On the other hand, even the most ingeniously contrived exercise combining beat patterns and beat functions is bound to neglect some "side effects" of the combination which, with real music, would immediately become evident. The opening of the Andante movement of Mendelssohn's *Italian Symphony* is a case in point. The unison forte on A must not only be sustained, but should give the listener a sense of tension growing into the second measure. That sounds like a prescription for three successive preparatories on beats 2, 3, and 4 of the first measure, culminating in a principal release on the dotted figure repeated (with an added grace note and therefore a little more important) on the first beat of the second bar.

EXAMPLE 1: Mendelssohn, *Italian Symphony*, second movement

When you try this, and concentrate on the imagined result, it will be evident that what you have achieved is a strong crescendo into the second measure. This could be remedied somewhat by avoiding the powerful impact near the center which the preparatory on 4 should normally produce. Instead, the first beat of bar 2 should "sweep" below center rather than "fall" (as suggested in a comparable example on p. 91), or you might prefer using preparatories which "wrap" themselves around center, on 2 and 3, instead of their normal path.

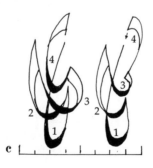

FIGURE 8

We have now reached the last kind of modification within the normal pattern of beats, permitting the use of certain beat functions without the risk of exaggerating the musical result. Here are four possibilities in connection with the downbeat in m. 2 of the Mendelssohn Andante: Give three equally strong preparatory beats (2, 3, 4), leading

1. to a strongly accented principal downbeat,
2. to a strong but unaccented principal downbeat,
3. to a weaker (meno forte or even subito piano) downbeat,
4. to a meno forte downbeat with accent.

The first two solutions resemble what was described above. The third does not follow the score. And the fourth, though interesting and perhaps possible, seems very involved and fussy for an opening which should sound simple and straightforward above all. It will become evident that only one solution will meet the requirements of your musical image. Thus, the beat is always specific.

Modifying the direction of one or all of the preparatories depends on your style. Even at this early stage of your technical development, *you do have a style*. Watch your beat in a mirror: does it employ a big conducting frame? That is not the same as using a big beat. It is a matter of style, and usually a very natural result of your physique and the way you move. Using a small conducting frame, but highly curved beats, may give you the same length of beats as someone else's large frame with straight beats. Beats which "wrap" around the center of a modest size frame are the more effective for the additional "mileage" they afford for expressive purposes along their long, curved path. And a small frame can easily be enlarged if necessary, without becoming unmanageable. Conversely, a conductor with comparatively big, straight beats within a large frame can reduce the size of both frame and beats. What is *not* likely to be effective within the style of this big, straight-beat—large-frame conductor is the florid, curved style of one whose range of motion is more concentrated around the center.

This matter of style which expresses itself in terms of size and range of beats is the natural consequence of a personal sense of movement. The earlier you become conscious of yourself in this regard the better, for this is more than a matter of looks on the podium. We are now at the point where podium and score, the two sides of the conducting coin, are once again very intimately intertwined, and where the score side of our coin is as much a matter of physical preference as of intellectual and emotional penetration. Here is why:

Principals "fall" toward the center. Preparatories "lift" toward the edge of the conducting frame. The conductor who is naturally "centered" in his beat, and tends to work around that magnetic point within the frame, will be inclined to see the score in terms of its principal beats and the musical shapes of that score in terms of their resolutions. His music making will be tight, precise, and disciplined. Toscanini was such a one. Large sweeping movements toward the edges of the frame are for preparatories, rich in characterization and illustration. One could do worse than to divide conductors into "principal" and "preparatory" types.

The difference is profound. That principals aim toward the center (the more so the more powerful the impetus), and that the opposite is true of preparatories is easily verifiable. The word "fall" in connection with the active part of the principal beat, and the "lift" of preparatories away from center, are self-evident. Where the effect becomes mysterious, and where conductors seem to differ musically as well as in movement, is at the point where *tempo* is added to all the aspects we have considered thus far. If principal beats (or pulses) stop, the music stops. But the temporary arrest of a preparatory at its apex has the effect of a gathering charge.

This is where the theory of the beat ends and the art of conducting begins. We shall have many occasions to refer back to the musical opportunities offered by the nature of principal and preparatory beats, opportunities which will tell you quite a lot about the way you move. For now, it will be worth your while to get the "feel" of the difference.

Exercises

1. Beat a slow, calm four. Imagine a rich, softly pulsing musical texture. Somewhere in this context a surprise beat will shatter the calm. Decide in advance on which beat this is to occur, and then allow yourself two measures to establish the mood to be interrupted. On the beat preceding the surprise impact pull away violently from the center—and stop, for a fraction of a second, at the edge of the frame. Then allow the baton to "whip" or "fall" or "travel" or "hammer" or "float" back to center. The effect will be as described, and the force will come from the delayed preparation, compounded from the tension built by a stop.

2. Now try the reverse. Conduct a four in vigorous march tempo, decide where a *subito piano* will take place, stop a normally strong motion on the previous beat just long enough to register the mood of what is to come—and place a very deliberate, soft, principal beat. The interruption can be so brief as to be hardly discernible, but its effect in tempo will be many times that of the most descriptive choreography. The extraordinary thing is that the even and continuous pulse must not falter, or the *music* will stop.

3. Time for review: conscious use of all or parts of available arm's length. Try this first:

> One measure, slow three, using the full arm
> One measure from the elbow
> One measure from the wrist—note how much help an active finger pivot may provide in making a full beat from the wrist appear larger than it is:
> One measure from the elbow
> Repeat

Now change the order:

> Full arm, wrist, elbow, wrist, repeat.

Then, in each measure, the following pattern:

> Down—full arm
> Second beat—wrist
> Third—elbow

Next:

> Down—elbow
> Second beat—wrist
> Third—full arm

Try it now with a pattern of four (either 2nd or 3rd beats might be wrist movements, or both).

Which beats felt like preparatories, which like principals?

N.B.: Remember: Preparatories *away* from center
Principals *toward* center, *regardless of where they occur in the measure.*

Assignment

Work through pp. 181–89 of *Chapter 7*. Study and conduct the Introduction to the third movement (*Chester*) of William Schuman's *New England Triptych*, as illustrated. Observe the accompanying suggestions with care. Practice until all reviewed principles of the beat are consciously and correctly applied.

Chapter 7 is designed to provide a wide variety of practical illustrations, together with instructions for their proper use, measure for measure, to meet requirements of the score excerpts under discussion.

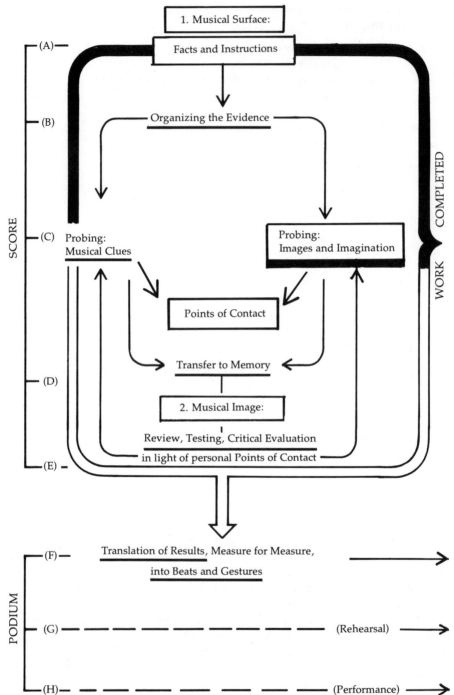

4A

PROBING: IMAGES/IMAGINATION

The development of an extramusical fantasy about the Andante of Mozart's *Eine kleine Nachtmusik* is pursued, together with a beat-by-beat theoretical examination of the musical text.

IMAGINATION, fantasy, and free association may serve as another key to what was revealed by a musical clue in the case of Brahms's *Third Symphony*. The objective is always the same: "ownership" of the score, including answers to certain questions with regard to performance which are *not* provided by explicit evidence on the musical surface of the work.

In this chapter, we shall take a close look at the Andante movement of Mozart's *Eine kleine Nachtmusik*. Work on any score, no matter how familiar through previous study or performance, should always begin with a careful study of facts and instructions. One reason that it is to your advantage to have already accomplished this task is the comparative freedom and the sense of recognition which will mark your second examination of this surface in the following pages. This should be of particular importance since, as an illustration of a different approach to the assimilation of a score, we shall lead you beneath its surface more quickly, and by a less familiar route, than in the case of Brahms.

A capacity to grasp and to hold on to fleeting images and associations, as a means of personal contact with music, is as much part of a conductor's professional endowment as a good ear or a flexible wrist. Like the latter, imagination can be trained and made more effective as a device to get yourself involved with the music you study. Unlike control of an orchestra in rehearsal and performance, your work with the score is a private skill, and whatever may contribute to bringing it to life in your mind is your private affair.

The performer participates in "the whole musical picture" on more than the technical level. In the musical analysis of the Mozart Andante, we shall give examples of the kind of images, feelings, and associations

EXAMPLE 1: Mozart, *Eine kleine Nachtmusik*, second movement, mm. 1–16

which sometimes accompany the performer's learning experience with a score. Since we can neither know in advance whether fruitful questions in connection with a score will arise from intuitive curiosity or as the result of intellectual observation, nor foretell on which of these levels an answer may be found, we must accustom ourselves to keeping track of whatever comes up in the course of study. Having already surveyed the surface of the Mozart work now to be examined, you might have some questions of your own. After many years of working with young conductors whose attitudes to music differed greatly, I am still fascinated by the number of roads which eventually converge at the same destination. You may well find answers to your questions as a result of the exploration to follow, even though its nature is likely to be quite different from the kind of analysis you have employed. If meanwhile you may wish to pursue some other clue or procede with a different type of analysis, do so. But do not sell yourself short by forgetting, let alone rejecting out of hand, either fantasy or image simply because they are not empirical data. They did arise in *your* imagination. Besides, fantasies will help you to remember.

Group A

A1: Composer. Mozart was an eighteenth-century genius with almost unparalleled powers of musical invention, depth of imagination, and prolific creativity, an enigmatic personality, combining childlike pleasure in social activities with stubborn, self-centered arrogance in all matters concerning his music. He was capable of ruthlessness in his relations with those he loved, and irresponsibility with regard to obligations perceived as hindrance to his work. A busy but ineffectual self promoter, he was a sensual person of great charm and vitality.

A2: Title. *Eine kleine Nachtmusik,* meaning *A Little Night Music.* Store in memory whatever that may bring to mind: either an occasion (a festivity, but clearly a fairly intimate one), or a feeling, probably romantic.

Subtitle: *Romanze.* This is either a reference to the occasion which might call for a musical offering, like a serenade (the character of the music could support this) or it tells us something about the structure of the movement: the term *Romanze* describes compositions in extended, double song form with an aba–cdc–aba, or aba–cc$_2$c–aba sequence of sections. This, too, is supported by the musical text.

A3: Tempo. *Andante,* or "walking tempo": how fast? There is another clue: *Alla Breve.* Normally we should note these two items, and leave further explorations for later. But you may already have checked in your earlier survey, and found the following: Joachim Quantz wrote in 1752: "In four-crotchet time it must be carefully observed that when a stroke goes through the C . . . such a stroke signifies, that all the notes, so to speak, become of a different value, and must be played as fast again, than is the case when the C has no stroke through it."* And Leopold Mozart, in 1756: [Alla Breve] "is only the ordinary mathematical division of the bars . . . we have to be able to divine from the music itself whether it needs a slow or somewhat faster speed." Father probably knew best. In any event, the marking suggests a tempo in which the pulse of two can be felt within a meter of four.

A4: Instrumentation—string quintet.

A5: Key signature—C major—C minor—C major.

A6: Meter—Alla Breve (see A3).

A7: Special Notes—none (see A2).

GROUP B

The largest divisions established by key signatures and double bars. Further divisions separate respective middle sections of the C-major and C-minor parts.

GROUP C

In your bracketing according to C3 (Two, plus Three, plus Four), you may have encountered some problems. The retransitions of both the C-major and C-minor sections are more complex than anything we have seen in the Brahms score. At this important stage of *your* work on the Mozart score, it is more important that you arrive at your own decision, than that the decision is theoretically "accurate." *You* must decide where *you* breathe, in imagination. You can always change your mind and no one shall be the wiser. But when you eventually get to the podium, *your* decisions are going to inform the performance, for better or worse. The time to begin worrying about that is now. If you have not already done so, pencil the brackets into the score.

GROUP D

As we said at the first presentation of this checklist, Group D reflects your partnership with the composer. The categories shown in that outline (p. 38) are samples, and some of them will probably overlap with

---

*Quantz used the human pulse as the basis for very general tempo indications. At c. 80 per minute, the pulse beat would measure tempo "averages" within 5 groups ranging from metronome equivalents of ♩ = 160 for the fastest group to ♩ = 20 for the slowest. Andante is listed under the Adagio cantabile group, at around ♩ = 40. At double time, alla breve, this would mean ♩ = c. 80. (Cf. Quantz, *Essay*, Berlin, 1752, ch. XVII, sect. vii, 49 ff.)

earlier headings. For group D, "the joker in the pack," encompasses independent trains of thought which might accompany your reflections in connection with your work with any score.

The pleasure in working through any musical composition is heightened by permitting whatever images, associations, or feelings you may encounter on the fringes of your conscious efforts, to enhance theoretical analysis with an intuitive, free flow of the imagination. In the following description I shall try to show the kind of role spontaneous imagery may play.

A free-association "analysis" of the Andante movement of Mozart's *Eine kleine Nachtmusik* might look like this:

Opening statement of eight measures, four plus four, leading to dominant at halfway point, and returning to tonic at the end. Both halves of this period open with the same melody,	*tutti piano*
but close differently:	*lilting* melody
the first, dominant cadence (mm. 3, 4) uses the dotted, feminine ending of	a curtsy?
the opening measures (m. 2); the second, tonic cadence counters and introduces a sixteenth-note motion which connects the first strain with the second (mm. 7, 8).	a masculine bow? elegant turning of hands?
The *second strain** begins with a pair of two-measure shapelets which lead once more into the G dominant, before a powerful return into C (m. 12).	
*Note: second "shapelet" of second strain (m. 11): crescendo into (m. 12): forte-piano.	*Sempre piano!* Related materials: "turning of hands," a four-bar equivalent of the opening "curtsy" and the "masculine bow" above. But this time there is rather more of the slurred ♩ ♪ ♩ ♪ of m. 3, and only one final recall of the sixteenth-note "elegant turning of hands" (m. 15).

The image of a formal but intimate dance emerges in part of the mind, while the objective analysis continues, and we take careful note of the way in which the composer has furnished the melodic outline just described. *Bass line:*

In the first two measures Mozart
introduces a quarter-note pulse
on repeated C's. This pulse on C   stationary pulse
gives way to lower neighbor B (m. 3)
and to G (m. 4) in the simple tonic
–dominant half-cadence of the third
and fourth measures. Once again
pulses on C in m. 5, and,   stationary pulse
beginning with m. 6,
a I⁶–IV–V–I cadence.   quarter-note pulse

You should try to "hear" everything you read in the score. As an
exercise, associate the right-hand asides and comments with the observations on the left. Most of the time these will be repetitions of descriptive adjectives: this is a part of memorization which we shall examine
in greater detail later in our study. You will find that some of these
adjectives are almost exaggeratedly suggestive. That also is part of a
very old "school of memory" some 2500 years old: the more intense,
extreme, and extravagant one's first impressions, the more memorable
will be the details of which that impression was formed.

Bass, continued:
The *second strain* (mm. 9–12)
recalls the pulses of the opening,
this time on G (mm. 9 and 11), with   Stationary pulses: G.
eighth-note pulses filling out the   Quarters *and* eighths.
very simple harmonic progression.   m. 9: V–I–I; m. 11: V–V⁷–
                                                 I–VI–V (bass always G).

The *return* (m. 13) begins with the
original melody over a secondary
dominant on A, from which the return   Rich, sonorous,
to C in the following measure passes   majestic bass progression.
through II–V⁶₅–I.   *Legato* bass!
In the *final measures* (14–16) the
harmonies *and* the bass quarters   Burst of harmonic color
change on every beat.   and movement, after the
                                                 diffident grounding at
                                                 the start!

Inside voices: second violin moves
in tenths below
the first. When not duplicating
first-violin rhythm, it moves in
legato eighths, outlining chords.
Same in forte repeat (mm. 5–8).
Separate eighth-note pulses, mm. 9 and 11,   *Gentle* pulses.
in middle section:
Secondary dominant on A at return (m. 13)   The most "special" note
is marked by C♯ in second violin   so far: seductive!
followed by G, C♯ again, E of the   Rich chord, and all in
dominant seventh of II.   the second violin: no viola!

Violin:

Enters at the *fifth* measure.	After the initial absence of viola sound, how very beautiful! Unique measure.
Then modest doubling of the bass.	But again an independent figure in penultimate measure of first strain (m. 7).
Second strain: same function as second violins, including support of the only crescendo measure in the piece (m. 11). Next entrance at forte, third beat in measure	After long held G, the independent figure of m. 7 in *melodic* outline. The A, approached from G instead of the previous F, is a quarter note.

The potential significance of "odd details" has been mentioned several times. The two-measure rest in the viola (mm. 12, 13), just when the harmony grows so rich, might strike one as odd. While it does not lead to the dramatic kind of breakthrough we shall observe in some later analyses, the question "what am I being told by the paradox of a thinning texture at the very moment of enriched harmony?" is well worth asking. We are given "instructions" for the execution of the final repeat. The corresponding place in the first strain was a straightforward forte passage complementing the piano first half of the period. Now the piano and forte halves occupy only two measures each of a four-measure phrase; the opening melody returns after a powerful forte-piano climax, but with a harmonic heightening (m. 13). It appears that the viola has been witheld in order to allow for the final intensification still to come: to add the ultimate fullness to the last one-and-a-half (forte) measures. It does seem quite simple and obvious; to make it *sound* natural and inevitable is difficult. But Mozart's piecemeal introduction of that overall crescendo, first by a dramatic reduction in volume (m. 12), then by harmonic enrichment, and finally by fuller texture and volume, prescribes the priorities in its suggested execution.

What, you may ask, was achieved by the second traversal of these 16 measures that the initial survey of the musical surface would not, in good time, have produced as well? The short answer is: there was in fact only one traversal. What was presented in two stages, and at the second in two columns, would in reality have been part of a single approach. From the first contact with the score, the exploration of its surface would have been accompanied by the kind of imagery and fantasy which was suggested by the "curtsies" and "turnings of the hand" in the right-hand column of the page.

But why images at all? Is not the expressive content of the music clear enough without a choreographic outline? Certainly. But we are about to concern ourselves with the most troublesome, albeit the most fundamental aspect of music: time. As a dimension of music in performance, time runs parallel to the pulse by which we live, from one heartbeat to another. And while music is experienced in performance at the same moments in which we may also hear the ticking of a loud wristwatch or periodic coughing in the audience, the *kind* of time represented in the music we experienced is of a very different variety: it can double back on itself, repeat, stretch, or stop. If we are very familiar with a piece, much of it can be so clearly anticipated that the whole of it contracts. And as conductors who explore whole compositions in imagination, with a perspective so total and simultaneous that the entire experience is compressed into an instant, we are able to divest music of its "parallel" clock time. In order to explore widely separated events in a score as if they took place simultaneously—a skill without which mastery of large musical structures would be impossible—we must learn to imagine music without its extension in time.

Mozart himself thought highly of this skill, and was able to visualize large musical structures in one concentrated moment. That this was not the unique achievement of a genius is shown in the following quotation: "If one has mastered a large work in every detail, and from memory, there will be moments when time ceases to exist, and the entire work is present, as if spatially, with complete precision, in one's consciousness, all at once. In such moments one has a true grasp of the work, as if from its inner surface."[*]

The word *spatially* is an important clue; *objects in space* may be perceived whole in an instant. A chair, a book, a house are immediately recognizable for what they are, even though different aspects of each will be seen from different points of view. It is not quite so easy to produce the complete image of a visual *event* (e.g. a ballet) in the mind, without recourse to a proportionate amount of time: physical movement, like music, has duration in time. Most difficult of all, however, is the imagination of music outside its time element. For to the problem it shares with imagined movement is added the need to imagine sound. Theoretical analysis is of no help. Although the time required for recalling aspects of musical construction is bound to be shorter than the performance time of a work, it bears no relation to the time *proportions* of the music in performance.

[*] Alfred Lorenz, *Das Geheimnis der Form bei Richard Wagner*, I: *Der Ring des Nibelungen* (Berlin, 1924), p. 10.

A manageable beginning in developing some proficiency in this area is the combination of conceptual and imaginal recollection of what appeared to present itself naturally in the course of study. What is heard, felt, made conscious, and remembered will be available for recall when we have worked out the concept of structure. And this, again, is more clearly articulated in memory when there are strong associative images. The following is an attempt to provide a visual analogy of the first 16 measures of the *Romanze*.

FIGURE 1: Mozart, *Eine kleine Nachtmusik,* second movement, mm. 1–16, melodic diagram

Measures 1 and 2 begin a pas-de-deux; two dancers bend toward each other. Measures 3 and 4 are the woman's curtsy; 5–6 a repeat of the opening (a little more confident—forte), and 7–8 conclude the first strain with the man's bow. The middle section (9–12) marked by a feminine ending on the first phraselet and a transition instead of the second, is her solo. The return of the opening music (13–14), is richer than before. The visual image is also enlarged in proportion and gesture. The masculine ending of the musical phrase suggests the man's bow.

Look at this composite drawing (Figure 1) for a while, until its outlines become one image. Thus, "frozen" on one page, is an *action* taking place *in time*—translated into available reality *in a single instant*. Furnish the main stages of the dance with their musical equivalents—look up their detailed description in this chapter (pp. 101ff), if you are not sure that you remember. Then fill in the remaining detail: connections, harmonic, turns and the specific uses of instruments at various places. Always try to overlap the image on the page (*not* the sequence of a dance in time!) and the impression of the music. Suddenly you will discover that you cannot only overlap images and impressions, but something you have *heard* as well. That will be a huge step forward, for you will have achieved two rare skills: the ability to "hear" separate events simultaneously and the discovery of practical use for that ancient memory system we have mentioned, in which what is to be remembered is translated into images and distributed among certain memorable places, in sequence.

Our flow chart at the beginning of this chapter has now been completed through Step C. We have not yet come to grips with memorization, however, either with the Brahms movement in Chapter 3a or in the Andante from Mozart's *Eine kleine Nachtmusik*. That will constitute the major portion of the first half of Chapter 5a, and will be based on a *point of contact*, (D) in our chart. Sixteen measures, although a fair sample of the particular approach to the Mozart score they were meant to illustrate, were not quite enough.

Our "conducting coin" is now becoming so thin that what we determine in our imagination with regard to the musical text can be translated into movement, controlling the constant projection of our musical image into a structure of sounds moving in time—a rather extraordinary achievement! When motion and its function as expressed in the beat truly represent what we already know in imagination, and when that prior image truly represents what can be determined from the musical surface, then the score and podium sides of our coin will indeed have become one.

Just as difficult passages on an instrument are best practiced in isolation at first, physical motion with a musical purpose should be

rehearsed quietly, and with constant reference to the image it represents (be that a special kind of shape, as with the Brahms Scherzo, or a
private little fantasy, as with Mozart's *Kleine Nachtmusik*). The shortest
way to technical proficiency is to practice solutions of musical problems
in terms of a disciplined sequence of beats until their functions are clear
and their executions feels easy. The smallest segment should be practiced separately until that point of ease is reached. The long upbeat of
the Brahms, the viola C♯ in the *Romanze*, must be made as real as possible in the imagination and then translated into respective beats that
"feel" the same way. As a control, we already have acquired some basic
understanding of what kind of beat is likely to produce that effect. But
only constant application will make possible the instant response of a
reflex in the true sense of the word: a motion which reflects instantly.
This gestural image of what has reality in your imagination will also
produce, in its turn, an instant response from the orchestra.

This must be practiced in silence. Many students feel uncomfortable
if there is no sound while they conduct. This discomfort comes from
false expectations: it is not the sound coming from the orchestra that
prompts appropriate beats and gestures, but *the "sound" in your imagination*. That sound is for you to provide, *first*, whether you conduct for
a live group, for a teacher, or for yourself. In your mind; you "follow"
the sound image as it connects intimately with all other associations,
discoveries, and determinations you have carfully developed. If that is
the case, and if your technical proficiency is adequate to the task, your
beat and your gestures will have a clear and compelling meaning. A set
of movements that are inspired by what is heard from outside yourself,
from the orchestra or someone playing the score at the pinao, is, at best,
a kind of choreography. It will lack initiative, and you will have for-
feited your "essential role in the whole musical thing."

Once you have marked a score (symbols ♩ , ♪ , and O should be used)
and the functions of the beat correspond to the image of all musical
shapes as marked, the sequence of beats representing these functions
must be practiced: at greater or lesser length; from the shoulder, the
elbow, the wrist; with a large beat, articulating all joints, or with a small
one using all or part of the arm as a single, fairly unmoving unit. A
small beat from the shoulder, for instance, making use of the whole arm
(without undulations), is more visible to an orchestra than equally small,
equally far forward beats from the elbow or the wrist. But only practice
of the same passage in all possible positions will give you the sensation
of the difference. There are also practical considerations: regardless of
whether an elbow or a wrist pivot is to be used, the *placement* of the
elbow in front of you may have to be the same, for reasons of visibility.
Naturally this places a limit on expressive differences, and you might
well be advised to choose the most comfortable way in any case.

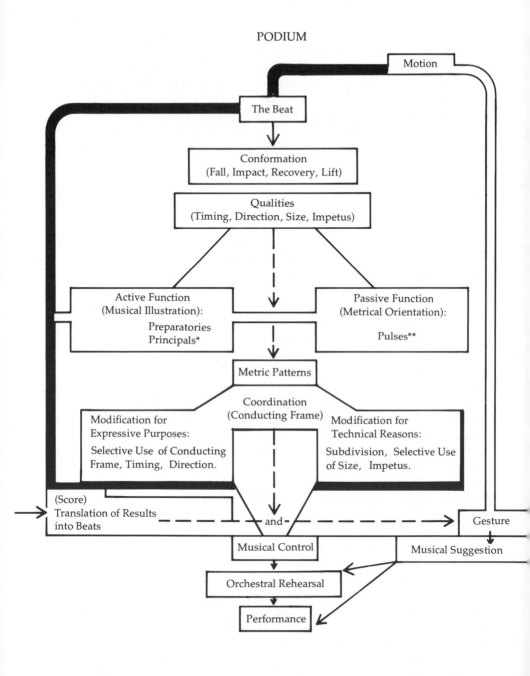

PODIUM

Motion

The Beat

Conformation
(Fall, Impact, Recovery, Lift)

Qualities
(Timing, Direction, Size, Impetus)

Active Function
(Musical Illustration):

Preparatories
Principals*

Passive Function
(Metrical Orientation):

Pulses**

Metric Patterns

Coordination
(Conducting Frame)

Modification for
Expressive Purposes:

Selective Use of Conducting
Frame, Timing, Direction.

Modification for
Technical Reasons:

Subdivision, Selective Use
of Size, Impetus.

(Score)
Translation of Results
into Beats

— and —

Gesture

Musical Control

Musical Suggestion

Orchestral Rehearsal

Performance

*Exception: *Series* of Principals: (*Passive* Function)   **Exception: *Accented* Pulse: (*Active* Function)

4B

THE BEAT: SUBDIVISIONS / COMPOUND AND MIXED PATTERNS

The method is presented of using successive beats of contrasting quality and function for special metric definition or expressive control.

THE PULSING BEAT (PASSIVE FUNCTION)

The pulsing beat, by virtue of its functional neutrality,

helps to define the visual demonstration of musical shapes by separating beats with active function.

provides the conductor with opportunities to employ expressive signals other than, or in addition to, the beat—gesture.*

THE pulse neither prepares nor fulfills, but as a technical device it has a variety of important uses: it serves as a neutral "frame" for *active* beats, setting off their expressive function. Thus it provides a sense of "space" between defining beats, which can also serve as opportunities for expressive signals by the other hand—gestures. It serves to provide additional points of metric reference between very slow beats marking the main divisions of a measure—subdivisions. And it is an indispensable element in the construction of beat patterns which include triple division of each main beat within the measure, e.g. 6/8 (triple-divided two) = 3 + 3; 9/8 (triple-divided three) = 3 + 3 + 3; 12/8 (triple-divided four) = 3 + 3 + 3 + 3. These are compound meters. Combinations of simple (duple) subdivision and triple division make mixed meters, e.g. 5/8 = 2 + 3 or 3 + 2, etc. We shall construct patterns of compound and mixed meters, with the aid of subdivisions, later in this chapter. For now, the following, plain patterns employing pulses should be practiced slowly and carefully, as demonstrations of the use of pulses as passive intervals between beats with active functions.

*For a discussion of *gesture,* rather than the *opportunity* to employ gesture, cf. Chapter 5b. The pulsing beat, as demonstrated in the present chapter, provides such an opportunity.

The pulsing beat

> shares with the other two types of beat (preparatory and principal) their qualities of timing and direction; size and impetus are minimal.

The pattern in Figure 1a represents a series of four beats. The first of these is a principal, the fourth a preparatory, the second and third pulses. Figure 1b represents a pattern of three in which the first and third beats are principal and preparatory respectively, and the second beat is a pulse. In both cases, the only active beats are principal firsts and their upbeat preparations.

In order to appreciate the intensification of these functions as a result of the neutral "middles" of either measure, try a *series* of preparatories instead, beginning with the second beat .

The difference in the effect will be striking. The cumulative preparations throughout each measure will produce a "feeling" of crescendo. Inevitably the downbeat principal, thus prepared, will become the climax of that crescendo. It will feel and look like *an important event in terms of the small musical shape* you have shown: several preparatories released into a principal beat. The same number of beats (as far as their timing and direction are concerned) look and "work" very differently when all but the principal and its preparatory are pulses: *the principal is itself the important event.*

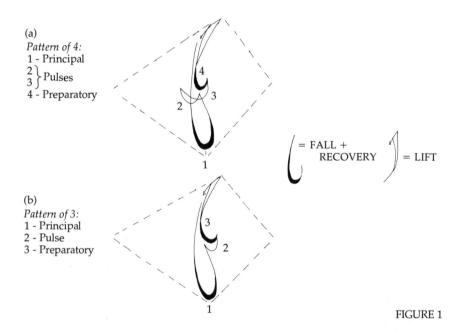

(a)
Pattern of 4:
1 - Principal
2 ⎫
3 ⎬ Pulses
4 - Preparatory

(= FALL +
      RECOVERY   ) = LIFT

(b)
Pattern of 3:
1 - Principal
2 - Pulse
3 - Preparatory

FIGURE 1

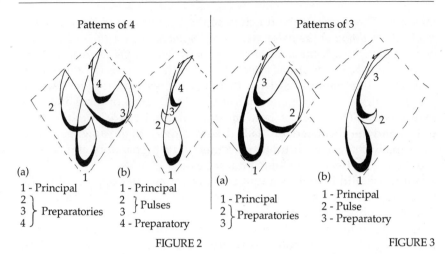

Patterns of 4   Patterns of 3

(a)   (b)   (a)   (b)

1 - Principal   1 - Principal   1 - Principal
2 ⎤   2 ⎤   1 - Principal   2 - Pulse
3 ⎬ Preparatories 3 ⎬ Pulses   2 ⎤ Preparatories 3 - Preparatory
4 ⎦   4 - Preparatory   3 ⎦

FIGURE 2   FIGURE 3

At a glance, Figures 2a and 3a and Figures 2b and 3b look rather more like each other than (a) and (b) respectively of the pattern of four and the pattern of three. Both examples (a) spread themselves, after the initial fall of the principal beat, with quite generous, lifting preparatories to the next downbeat. Even the pattern of three lifts almost as far to the left after recovery of the first beat as did the second beat in the pattern of four. According to the rule that all preparatories lift in the direction opposite to that of the beat prepared, even the principal beat on 1 has thus become a preparatory within a suggested musical shape featuring preparatories. The entire conducting frame is used in both examples (a). Examples (b), again at a glance, look almost like conventional patterns of two, and that is their expressive intent. They feature the respective downbeats in patterns of four and three, and the preparations of these downbeats *only*. In effect, there are two beats per measure, although not in any way the metric equivalent of a two with subdivisions: the pulses divide principal and preparatory unevenly.

What risk is there of actually confusing one of the (a) patterns with a pattern of *two*, since they look so similar? None whatever. What the printed example on the page cannot show is the one beat quality which is common to all preparatories, principals, and pulses: *timing*. Patterns in a diagram, like measures of music on a printed page, are seen all at once, in a single, comprehensive glance. Patterns of actually conducted beats, like the music they control, are understood and related *in time*. A lift at the end of the second beat cannot be mistaken for a lift that is part of the fourth: the recording of time at measured intervals is one of the fundamental qualities of any beat, the only quality which is common to all three varieties of beats.

In the previous chapter we showed how modifications in size and direction of beats, within the context of any pattern, bear an expressive message. They suggest the function of the beat or that of the following beat. *The addition of the pulse, i.e. a beat in which the qualities of size and impetus have been reduced to the minimum, heightens the expressive function of active beats before and after.* On paper the patterns (b) above may look a bit like patterns of two. In practice they feature two beats: a principal first and a preparatory last beat in patterns of three and four respectively. The contrast between the "neutral space" occupied by pulses and the characteristic "fall" (below center!) of the downbeat, and the equally characteristic lift (from center) of its preparatory emphasizes the active function of the first and last beats.

But those middle pulses might provide yet another opportunity: the necessary, neutral background for the use of a *gesture*. Gesture will be the main subject of Chapter 5b; and the passive character of right-hand pulses—relinquishing expressive control while maintaining metric continuity of the beat pattern—will be seen to provide the condition for a left-hand gesture. We shall remember the use of pulses as a very significant opportunity for *substitution of gesture for beat*. In musical terms this will mean the yielding of musical initiative to some degree: while the *beat controls, gesture suggests*. Not all control will be yielded in that way, only the sort which is expressed by *size and impetus*. These, as we have observed, are qualities which, together with modification of *direction*, control expressive function. *Timing* remains, and thus control over tempo is not yielded as long as there is any kind of beat. Under certain circumstances this too may be called for (e.g. with accompanied recitatives, cf. Chapter 11).

The pulsing beat
provides additional metric reference points between main beats of any pattern.

SUBDIVISION

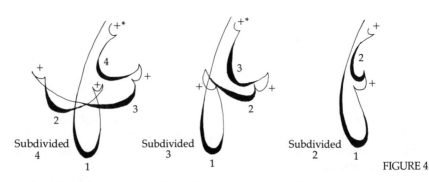

Subdivided 4   Subdivided 3   Subdivided 2   FIGURE 4

*Pulse-subdivision of the *upbeat* is unusual, but should be practiced nevertheless. For upbeat subdivision by preparatory, see Figure 5.

Still another important use of pulses involves subdivision. This may be either a further marking of metric coordinates between slow main beats, for convenient reference of the players, or it may be the means of steadying a shaky ensemble by providing a more compelling grid of divisions within the measure. Either way, subdivisions do not necessarily have expressive functions. In the former instance they should invariably be given as unobtrusive, neutral pulses.

Simple subdivision

is indicated at the halfway point between the count (impact) of main beats.

If the only purpose is enhanced precision of timing, the halfway point is marked by a pulse at the end of a normal recovery of the main beat so divided.

Subdividing pulses are the only beats which *do not pass through center.*

Subdivision by preparatories emphasizes special situations.

Expressive significance of the second half of a slow beat may be illustrated by the lift portion of the first half, bending into a direction exaggerating recovery as any other preparatory.

Expressive reference to a following main beat in slow tempo may be stressed by a preparatory second half of any subdivided beat. In that case, the first half should be kept shorter.

Steadying of orchestral ensemble can often be achieved by one or two sharply accented subdivisions on the second halves of beats not normally subdivided. If the problem requires a slight tightening of tempo, accented pulses will suffice. If a slow tempo must be achieved or maintained, however,the extended sweep of *preparatory lifts* provides a more deliberate application of control. In order to avoid excessive accents on the following attacks (viz.: there is *always* an expressive effect after true preparatories), main beats might be given less forcefully than would normally be the case. In any event, *first* halves of beats subdivided by preparatories should be short.

Subdividing preparatories should originate at or near the center. Beats to be subdivided by a preparatory must therefore recover at or near the center.

Beats subdivided by preparatories are read by the orchestra, within the context of the metric pattern, *in terms of the direction of their fall.* Inasmuch as the fall of any beat assumes greater or lesser downward direction depending on its impetus, the direction is determined by the movement of the baton *in overall relation to the center:* left, right, up, or down.

As with all preparatories, the chief importance of those preparatories that comprise the second half of a subdivided beat lies in their expressive effect on the following beat. But there is also, in this case, some cause for special care in placing the short *first* half of such beats, after clearly establishing their direction, and with a somewhat stronger than usual recovery, at a termination point only *just beyond the center.*

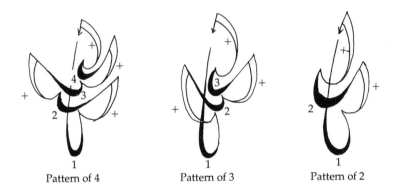

Pattern of 4   Pattern of 3   Pattern of 2

FIGURE 5: Subdivision by Preparatories (added Lifts)

Again, on paper, the strong preparatory subdivisions *in opposite direction to the next main beat* being prepared look like some misdirected main beat: The 1+ of the subdivided pattern of three exends to the left like a second beat in a pattern of four. Now the timing of each part of the pattern is not quite as helpful as with undivided beats, since there are twice as many components in each measure. Even the relative sizes of main beat and subdivision are unpredictable with preparatory subdivisions; unlike pulses, preparatories may be as long as or longer than the main beat they divide.

In practice, however, there will be no danger of confusion, if you make certain that *the first half of each main beat* exhibits the characteristics of a principal. In the illustration above, the preparatory subdivision (second half of beat) is shown by the unfilled outline we have used for

preparatories: ♪ ⅄ ℄ The first half of each beat is represented
                     LIFT

by the bold outline of principals: ⌣ The most striking fea-
                                   FALL RECOVERY

ture of these illustrations, however, is the fact that *fall and recovery* of each beat, and the subsequent *preparatory lift* that completes it, *do not move in the same direction.* Clarity of design, and metric orientation for the player, are assured thus.

Beats subdivided by preparatories

fit into their pattern acording to the *direction of their fall.* Since the fall of any beat may assume a greater or lesser downward slant, the direction is determined by the movement of the baton *in overall relation to the center:* left, right, up, or down.

A timely caution: one good subdivision does not necessarily deserve another. Given the fact that most music is made *between* beats, it follows that the fewer the beats, the more music making can take place.

There must always be a specific musical or technical reason for subdivision. Occasional metric orientation or expressive preparation of certain points of stress within a slow tempo provide a momentary excuse. *When the purpose has been served, stop subdividing.*

Smooth introduction and abandonment of subdivisions within a continuing metric pattern of slow main beats is not an easily acquired skill. The clear distinction between the two alternative kinds of subdivision, pulses and preparatories, must become "second nature" in practice, before one can rely on these technical devices as almost instinctive expressions of musical intent. The following exercises may be varied indefinitely, and should be practiced until some facility has been achieved.

Exercise

Subdivide the beats marked with an *x,* either with a pulse or with a preparatory as indicated.

Pulses	x x	x	x	x x	
1 2 3 4	1 2 3 4	1 2 3 4	1 2 3 4	1 2 3 4	etc.
Preparatories x	x	x			

In the exercise above there is a systematic shift of the group of three subdivisions by one quarter in each succeeding measure. Needless to say this is not necessarily a requirement for such an exercise. You should also invent exercises in patterns of three and two. What is important is that you mark out a design of subdivisions before you begin to beat them. It would also be a good idea to review the simple rules concerning the two kinds of subdivisions several times before practice, and to check yourself carefully with regard to size, centering, and direction of beats and their subdivisions. Clarity of each pattern, as you present it, is very important. Almost equally important is a smooth transition from subdivision to straight beat. Most important is a steady tempo.

Assignment

You may now turn to Chapter 7, p. 190, and complete score excerpts in Reviews I and II. The easier these examples look, the more important it will be to read carefully through the accompanying text, to try alternative suggestions where they are offered (and even where they are not), and to review the summaries where they apply. The more time you are willing to spend on *thinking* through every movement and its musical counterpart as you work your way through these first applications of the theory of the beat to music, the more thorough your understanding of the principles behind the theory should become, and the more assured their future application in your work. *N.B.*: It would not matter in the least if, having considered all the arguments for a certain use of the beat in a given example, you were to disagree with the solution. If you can improve on it with a solution of your own, so much the better. But you must work within the framework of the principles we have outlined.

While you continue your work with the application of the beat to excerpts of full scores in Chapter 7, proceed with the examination of principles governing composite subdivisions, as outlined on the next pages of this chapter. Combinations of double and triple subdivisions form the basis of all compound and mixed metric patterns.

Triple subdivision:*

Subdivision of main beats into three equal metric units requires a combination of pulses and preparatories. As always, the function of each unit determines its type of beat. Clarity of visual design is best served by alternating different kinds of beat.

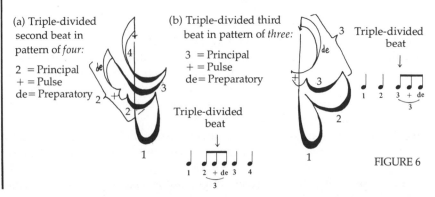

(a) Triple-divided second beat in pattern of *four*:

2 = Principal
+ = Pulse
de = Preparatory

(b) Triple-divided third beat in pattern of *three*:

3 = Principal
+ = Pulse
de = Preparatory

Triple-divided beat

Triple-divided beat

FIGURE 6

*Symbols for triple subdivision include + ("and") for the first and "de" for the second beat between main divisions, i.e. "one-and-de, two-and-de, three-and-de" represents three main beats, triple-divided.

Any beat within any pattern may be subject to simple or triple subdivision. *All compound and mixed meters are thus represented by beat patterns combining either or both forms of subdivision.*

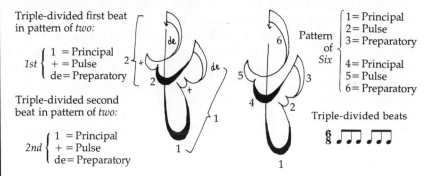

Triple-divided first beat in pattern of *two:*

$$1st \begin{cases} 1 & = \text{Principal} \\ + & = \text{Pulse} \\ de & = \text{Preparatory} \end{cases}$$

Triple-divided second beat in pattern of *two:*

$$2nd \begin{cases} 1 & = \text{Principal} \\ + & = \text{Pulse} \\ de & = \text{Preparatory} \end{cases}$$

$$\text{Pattern of } Six \begin{cases} 1 = \text{Principal} \\ 2 = \text{Pulse} \\ 3 = \text{Preparatory} \\ 4 = \text{Principal} \\ 5 = \text{Pulse} \\ 6 = \text{Preparatory} \end{cases}$$

Triple-divided beats

FIGURE 7: Triple-divided Pattern of Two = Pattern of Six

COMPOUND METERS

Six beats = triple-divided *two* (as above) or, depending on context, simple subdivisions of *three*.

Nine beats = triple-divided *three* or any other combination of principals, pulses, and preparatories, depending on musical context (see below).

FIGURE 8

Twelve beats = triple-divided *four* or any other combination of principals, pulses, and preparatories, depending on musical context (see below).

FIGURE 9

The suggested *variations* of the "basic" patterns of compound meters above are, as we have stressed from the start, the result of expressing the *musical function* of the beat *as well as its metric coordinates within a given measure.* In addition, we shall remind ourselves of the fact that compound meters, being combinations of subdivisions, need not exhibit *all* subdividing beats, *all* the time. Most importantly, *in all compound meters the direction of the main divisions remains constant.*

The opening movement of the Brahms *Third Symphony* (cf. Chapter 7) requires a flexible application of six quarter-note beats, ranging from two to six beats actually given per measure. These changes depend not so much on tempo (a subject covered later in this chapter), but on the musical functions of the beats as determined by the musical shapes they represent. The spelling of such a triple-divided, *slow two* in a variety of ways will nonetheless always look and feel like the same, expressive six *Metric control and orientation is maintained,* as with the simple subdivisions discussed above, *by observing the direction of the fall of main beats in any compound pattern.**

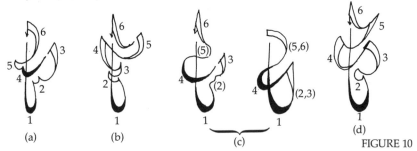

(a)　　　(b)　　　(c)　　　(d)　　　FIGURE 10

Figure 10a shows the basic pattern of six; (b) and (d) are variations reflecting different musical functions of constituent beats. The two patterns in Figure 10c represent degrees of incorporating the subdividing beats 2,3 and 5,6 in the main beats of 1 and 4. The absorption of some or all subdivisions becomes more likely the faster the tempo, and thus the more prominent the underlying "sense" of the two main beats will be.

Likewise the patterns of nine or twelve may reflect musical functions in different combinations of beats, *as long as the direction of the main beats remains constant according to the underlying, subdivided pattern:*

nine = pattern of three:	1—down
	4—right
	7—up / left
twelve = pattern of four:	1—down
	4—left
	7—right
	9—up / right

*This should dispose, for once and all, of an alternative, now obsolete, pattern of six in which the second main beat pointed to the right. It was known as the *German six;* ours is the *French six.*

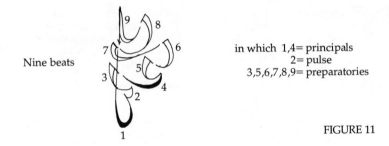

Nine beats

in which 1,4= principals
2= pulse
3,5,6,7,8,9= preparatories

FIGURE 11

This particular sequence of beats represents an intensification of volume and / or expressive tension beginning with the fifth beat.

N.B.: Nine beats can also reflect a mixed pattern of simple and triple subdivisions with *four main beats* (cf. below).

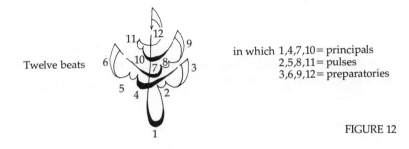

Twelve beats

in which 1,4,7,10= principals
2,5,8,11= pulses
3,6,9,12= preparatories

FIGURE 12

Again, the appearance of this pattern may vary greatly according to the musical function assigned to its beats, but it must never lose the basic outline of a subdivided *four*.

MIXED METERS

Tempo and musical function also determine the distribution of beats in patterns of mixed meters.

Five beats = divided *two* (either 2 + 3 or 3 + 2)

2 + 3

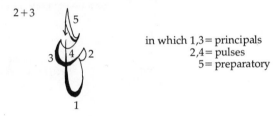

in which 1,3= principals
2,4= pulses
5= preparatory

or (still 2+3)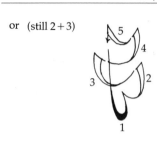

in which   1= principal
                2,3,4,5= preparatories
N.B.: Although the *functions* of
beats 2,3,4,5 are the same,
the *third*, as one of two
main beats, points to the
left with strongest impetus.

or 3+2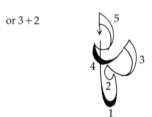

in which 1,4= principals
          2= pulse
        3,5= preparatories

FIGURE 13

Various permutations of functions among 2, 3, 4, 5 are possible, but it
will always be the fourth beat which points to the left, and which is
likely to receive the strongest impetus.

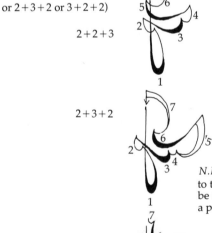

Seven beats =
divided *three* (2+2+3
or 2+3+2 or 3+2+2)

2+2+3

in which principals and pulses
alternate except for 7 (preparatory)

2+3+2

in which principals and pulses
alternate, except for 5 (preparatory)

N.B.: The seventh beat, although the "upbeat"
to the first, does *not* necessarily have to
be a preparatory. In this example, it is
a pulse.

3+2+2

in which principals and pulses
alternate, except for 3 (preparatory)

FIGURE 14

Various redistributions of subdivisions are possible according to musical context. For instance,

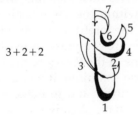

$3 + 2 + 2$

in which 1,4,6 = principals
2,5 = pulses
3,7 = preparatories

FIGURE 15

Eleven beats, thirteen beats, or any other sum of beats not divisible into duples or triplets on every main beat are similarly treated. In most cases, the composer will have indicated the groupings of two or three subdivisions (e.g. $2 + 3 + 3 + 2 + 3$) by numbers or dotted barlines.

Mixed-meter patterns can also result from *uneven division* of even meters. This, also, is most often marked by the composer. For instance, eight beats (normally a subdivided *four*) could be $3 + 3 + 2$: subdivided three, as in Figure 16.

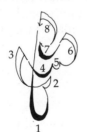

The variable treatment of pulses and preparatories remains, always determined by the musical context. In this case we have shown

1,4,7 = principals
2,5 = pulses
3,6,8 = preparatories

FIGURE 16

N.B.: All our illustrations of compound and mixed meters have one fault in common. In order to keep the outline of illustrated patterns (i.e. the path traveled by the tip of the baton) as devoid of confusing crossings and overlaps *in print*, the center of the beat occupies a larger area than it would in practice. Since the tip of the baton, unlike the drawing pen, does not leave a visible trace, beats that should end or cross *near the center* can safely and advantageously do so. In practice, such an *overlap at the center of the beat* remains one of the basic characteristics of a controlled conducting technique. It serves metric orientation by a clearly defined focus of all main beats. And it aids expressive differentiation by allowing pulses to occupy minimum space either in the center itself or at the end of active beats.

The Importance of Tempo

As we now begin the practice of compound and mixed meters and the
alternation of subdivided and plain beats within the same basic outline, this last observation should be kept in the forefront of self-critical
awareness. The patterns and diagrams above are complex, rather decorative, and intended primarily as illustrations of the *theory* of the beat.
In order to understand the principles of baton technique it will be well
worth your while to retrace them before a mirror and to make every
effort to understand their purpose. But as we have already mentioned,
there will be *modifications in practice* in order to accommodate the real
requirements of constantly changing musical exigencies. *The key to these
is tempo.*

In all these visual blueprints of compound and mixed beat patterns
we have assumed a slow, even tempo. We have distributed subdivisions between main beats, according to their stipulated musical function. The basic outline of all these patterns has been that of their main
beats: an outline of *two* for patterns of five and six; outlines of *three* for
patterns of seven, a mixed eight, and nine; outlines of *four* patterns of
twelve and suggested applications to ten, eleven, thirteen and any other
number of unevenly divided beats.* We shall now retrace the suggested
process in practice, beginning with the underlying, basic patterns in a
moderately fast tempo, and adding subdivisions as we slow down. Then
we shall reverse the procedure.

Exercise A

---

1. Beat a slow *two* ($\frac{6}{4}$ $\downarrow$. = c. 50). Be very conscious of the "feel" and the
   placement of the downbeat as a principal (with a well-defined fall)
   and the upbeat as its preparatory (bending toward center before
   completing the upward lift.
2. While continuing this beat of *two*, count six (aloud!): 1, 2, 3, on the
   downbeat, and 4, 5, 6 on the upbeat.

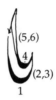

---

*It should be mentioned in passing that evenly divided beats may also be distributed in unusual
ways if the score indicates this: a twelve, instead of 3+3+3+3 (outline of four) could sometimes be
2+2+2+2+2+2 (outline of six). For reasons of clarity, however, most compound and mixed meters
are based on outlines of two, three, and four.

3. Mark in-between beats with pulses or preparatories as follows:

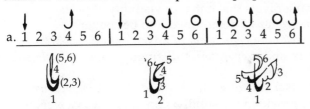

Then the following series of beats:

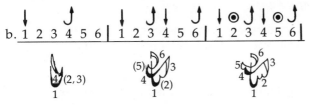

4. Beat a measure of six. Then begin a gradual accelerando like this:

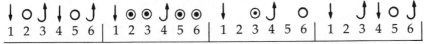

♩ = c. 150 accel. poco a poco .... ♩. = 116

Try to "incorporate" the subdividing beats in the second and third
measures as suggested on p. 118, Figure 10C. *Feel it!*

5. Beat a measure of two, then ritardando as follows:

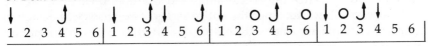

♩. = 116   ritard. poco a poco

Note that in order to "set" the retard, in the second measure, preparatories on beats 3 and 6 acted as a brake. Once the rate of retard is
established these beats may be marked by pulses.

Assignment

You are now prepared to undertake Review III in Chapter 7. While
the summaries following the chart (p. 209) are still fresh in mind, do take
the time to read, think, and work through each one of them—separately!
This is also a good time to review sections of earlier chapters to which
page references with the summaries in Chapter 7 will guide you. You
are bound to read this familiar text with new understanding. Then conduct the score excerpts. Watch yourself critically, and ask yourself questions like these:

(p. 87)   Does my beat remain within the *conducting frame?*
(p. 88)   Does the *fall* of each beat swing through center?

(p. 90) Does my downbeat dip below the horizontal axis?
(p. 23) Am I using pivots that enhance visibility of beats?
(p. 17) Is my stance how I determined it to be? Better?
(p. 113) Is the *direction* of *main beats* in mixed patterns clear?
(p. 116) Are *pulses* and *preparatories* distinguishable in *triple subdivisions?*
(p. 91) Does the *first half* of each subdivided beat *impact just beyond center*, provided the subdivision to follow is a *preparatory?*
(p. 113) Does the subdividing *pulse*, on the other hand, mark the division *at the end of the main beat?*

In this way, each summary becomes a criterion by which you may judge for yourself how well your beat fulfills its requirements.

Subdivision and tempo:

> When a change of tempo is accompanied by a change in the number of subdivisions per measure (including subdividing beats in patterns of compound and mixed meters), *preparatory subdivisions are powerful indicators of a rate of retard.**
>
> *Pulses will not inhibit an increasing rate of speed*, if subdivisions are gradually eliminated.**

This much is obvious from the foregoing exercises, and will *feel* right the more you practice the accelerando and ritardando exercises above and those to follow. But since the entire series of exercises was designed for practice in placing and withholding subdividing beats in compound and mixed meters, it neglects one very important eventuality in connection with tempo changes: the case of a slow *two* followed by an *accelerando.*

Exercise A4 showed an *accelerando following a fast six*. This called for an even faster six (very easy to "read" because of the short time interval between beats) and a gradual elimination of all subdivisions. Exercise A5 showed a *slow two followed by a retard:* as we have seen, preparatory subdivisions not only are useful monitors of the rate of retard, they also serve as a "brake" which produces and controls the retard. But how are we to control an accelerando following such a slow *two?* How, in a complex orchestral ensemble, are the players to respond, instantly and with precision, to an increase in tempo which, because of the relatively long interval between each slow beat, is not easy to "read"?

The answer is subdivision, applied in exactly the same way as in the retard by preparatory subdivisions of Exercise A5, but with *another kind of pulse:*

---

*See Exercise A5.
**See Exercise A4.

THE ACCENTED PULSE

Unlike all other active beats, the accented pulse has no expressive function. It serves to signal and define an unexpected attack, either at the beginning of a piece, after an unmeasured pause, or upon the first noticeable effect of an increase of tempo (i.e. when the following attack is to take place earlier than anticipated, thus establishing a rate of accelerando).

In musical examples we shall use the symbol ◉ for the accented pulse.

The sole purpose of the accented pulse, then, is the control of tempo. And one of its immediate applications, establishment of a rate of increasing speed within patterns of slow beats, will follow this brief description:

The accented pulse shares these characteristics with other pulses:*

Like other pulses, it marks the passage of time—*but this is the passage of time to come.*

Like other pulses, as a subdivision, it is placed at the end of a main division beat, with minimum fall and recovery and sharing its direction—*but with powerful impetus.*

Like other pulses, it has no expressive value—*but also no expressive function.*

Unlike other pulses, it does not clarify the shapes of phrases—*it anticipates tempo.*

Exercise B

1. Beat slow *two* ($\d. =$ c. 50). While beating, count six. After you have established a steady tempo to your satisfaction, introduce a small, powerful subdivision *at the exact moment of the sixth count.* A sharp downward flick of the wrist, at the end of the lift, will be best. The important part is that *this accented pulse must be in the new, faster tempo.*

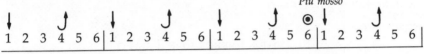

Strictly speaking, the faster tempo marked by the symbol for an accented pulse at the end of the third measure will take effect on the sixth beat: the orchestra's response should be instantaneous. Most *più*

*Cf. pp. 109–12.

mosso markings with upbeat imply such an anticipation of the increase in speed. If the tempo change is to take place exactly on the first beat of the fourth measure, however, the accented pulse—being shorter in duration than previous counts—must be given a little *after* the sixth count: how much after will depend on the new tempo, of course.

One important observation: the accented pulse is given *only once*. Its purpose should then have been achieved, and any repetition would only appear frantic and redundant. Needless to say, ordinary pulses may be used as subdivisions serving to provide additional metric coordinates, if the ensemble is complex.

2. Beat slow two, count six, establish a tempo, as before. Now we shall introduce not only a new, faster tempo, but a new, *progressively faster* tempo. For this we shall indeed employ at least two, possibly more accented pulses. This will indicate to the orchestra not only an initial increase of speed (which may be slight), but *the rate of that increase*, which may be even, in which case two or three accented pulses would be sufficient; or it may come in successive spurts, in which case accented pulses may be needed at the end of every main beat until a steady tempo has again be established. In any case, we shall be able to maintain complete control of tempo.

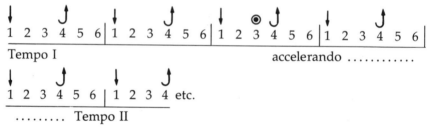

Tempo I   accelerando ....

1 2 3 4 5 6 | 1 2 3 4 etc.

.... Tempo II

You may find that the momentum of increasing speed will need to be checked. This would be the equivalent of Exercise A5: a strong preparatory in the steady, new tempo, just before it is reached will provide the needed brake to control the forward movement.

Practice tempo fluctuations, both sudden and gradual, within a basic pattern of two beats per measure. *Bear in mind that preparatory subdivisions tend to slow down; accented pulses, introduced as subdivisions, are useful in setting a faster pace.*

FURTHER EFFECTS OF TEMPO

Implied in this last sentence, moreover, is one of the most basic aspects of tempo control in general. And we shall take the time to spell it out, and to fix it firmly in our minds before we apply our new skills in placing subdivisions selectively into all patterns of compound and mixed meters at changing speeds. When we talk of preparatory subdivisions helping to slow down, and accented pulses as useful means of increasing tempo, *we are comparing the effect of their respective size* on the flow of music. Preparatories are bigger than pulses. Preparatories inhibit speed, pulses do not and may in fact be used to increase it. There is a functional relationship between size of beat, in general, and tempo:

Tempo and the size of beats:
> Large beats tend to *slow* the musical pace.
>
> In order to *move the tempo forward* with ease, *make the beat smaller.*

No other principle of baton technique is more useful at the right moment—or more frequently violated by inexperienced conductors. Prove it to yourself: As in the previous exercise, count six while you beat 1, 2—principal; 3—preparatory; 4, 5—principal; 6—preparatory. Increase tempo *without* decreasing size of beats (Figure 17a). Then beat 1, 2—principal; 3—pulse; 4, 5—principal; 6—pulse. Keep pulses small (Figure 17b). Increase tempo as you *decrease both principal beats.* Start "driving" with *accented* pulses on 3 and 6. Feel the difference!

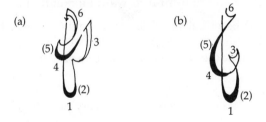

FIGURE 17

The same experiment can be made with any pattern, of course. Decide in advance at what tempo you will start, and how many measures you will spend in order to reach maximum speed. Then there should be a predetermined number of ritardando measures in which to regain the original tempo. Reduction of size and the use of accented pulses will help establish the rate of accelerando. Increase of size and use of preparatories instead of pulses will slow the beat naturally.

There is one other technical device to insure instant compliance with a quickening beat. Figure 18a shows a pattern of *four* consisting of a principal, two pulses, and a preparatory. When the accelerando begins we shall reduce the size of both principal and preparatory, *but we shall increase the size of the recovery of the principal,* so that it will appear bigger than the fall (Figure 18b). At the same time, we shall try to *transform the lift of the preparatory on 4 into another enlarged recovery:* the first and last beats will look very much alike, but *the emphasis on their recoveries will give an upward stress to both* which should aid greatly in the

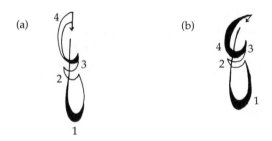

(a)   (b)

FIGURE 18

intended forward movement—particularly if we are careful to *keep the overall pattern small.*

Tempo and modified conformation of the beat:

Special emphasis on the *recovery* portion of the beat, at the expense of the *fall,* encourages *forward movement of the tempo.*

N.B. 1: *Recovery* (natural rebound after impact) must not be confused with *lift* (conscious extension of upward motion beyond recovery, in preparatory beats). Emphasis on the *lift* portion tends to slow movement of the beat and to inhibit forward momentum of tempo.

N.B. 2: The most essential factor in encouraging forward movement of tempo remains the systematic reduction in size of beats. Described above is an additional means, effective only if beats become smaller as well.

To illustrate the special emphasis on the recovery portion of the beat, at the expense of the fall, we shall once more use an analogy involving a rebounding rubber ball. A normal beat could be likened to the natural drop and rebound of a ball, from shoulder height, onto a hard surface. The ball, like the beat, will rebound after impact (Figure 19a). Emphasis on the recovery at the expense of the fall would require hurling the ball against the surface, with special force, and at a close distance (Figure 19b).

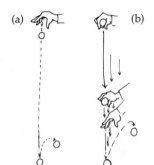

(a)   (b)

The *fall* portion of the ball's path is reduced.
Momentum on *impact* is greater.
Natural length of *rebound* is increased.

FIGURE 19

Applying the same "special force" to the *fall of a principal or prepara-tory* (of reduced size), in order to achieve extra length of natural upward recovery, involves a very similar "whipping" motion as the snaps of the wrist producing *accented pulses*. The result in either case is an instantly detectable driving of the tempo.

Before you try the almost magic effect of such driving, upward recoveries on a forward moving tempo, one distinction must be clearly understood. The difference between increased natural recovery after a forced fall, and the long lift of a preparatory beat (*both* extra upward motions following impact!) is that the first is natural, and is abandoned as soon as all accumulated momentum is released; the second is consciously contrived: natural momentum of the rebound having been spent, the lift now gathers more momentum in preparation for the next beat—and, if anything, tends to lose time in the process. Thus a naturally induced upward leap of recovery presses forward in tempo; a special gathering of power in the preparatory lift holds tempo back.

We are now ready to try all patterns of compound and mixed meters in practice. As with the pattern of *six* (see p. 116), we shall begin with the basic outline of main beats, at a slow, even tempo; we shall count the full number of main and subdividing beats aloud; and we shall fill out the pattern with all in-between beats. This takes us through the equivalent of Exercise A3b on p. 123. We shall begin with a fully articulated pattern and gradually eliminate in-between beats as the accelerando (viz. Exercise A4) permits us to reduce the outline to its basic main beats. Now is the time to try some of our new skills in tempo control and also become thoroughly familiar with complex metric patterns, with their "backbone" of main beats, and with the placement of subdividing beats as they are selectively added or eliminated. As an example, the mixed pattern of 7/8 (2+2+3) would begin like this:

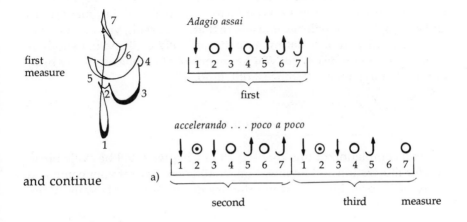

but it might also continue *accelerando molto*

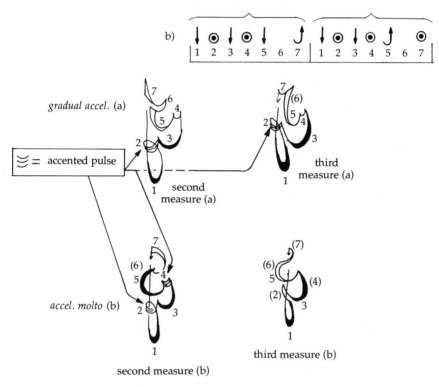

NOTE: Increasingly high rebounds, especially in sequence (b)
      Decreasing size of beats in accel.

FIGURE 20

These exercises must be undertaken daily, for brief periods, but with great concentration. They are a conductor's equivalent of keyboard scales and arpeggios. You will become aware that, as a result, you are not only gaining facility in articulating all patterns, fully or in partial subdivision of their main beats, but you have control of emphasis on any beat, of eventual dynamic differences, of tempo.

Assignment

Upon completion of this chapter, all of Chapter 7 will be available to you for illustration and review. You should now have at your command every basic principle governing the use of the beat. Only painstaking review will assure you of that achievement. As before, you are urged to proceed very slowly, with generous time allowances for reflection and physical experimentation while the theory and practice of the beat becomes a part of you, as natural and individual as your walk.

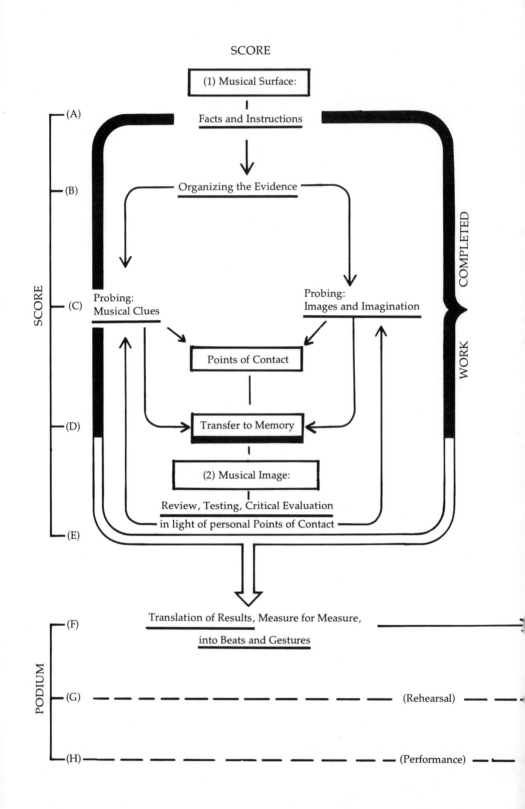

5A

STORING THE INFORMATION

A slight textual discrepancy between
score and parts to the second movement
of Mendelssohn's *Italian Symphony* becomes the point of departure for characterization, organization, and memorization of the music.

MUCH of the emphasis in our work with the score has been on
the transfer of musical evidence from score to mind. The goal being a
memorable image of the work rather than a conceptual analysis, "evidence" was whatever came to mind in the process of organizing the
musical surface. Since the objective is personal—preliminary retention
of music in one person's mind—the road leading to it must accommodate that person's style of getting there. The essential first task is to
become involved.

The following exercise will show how a transfer from score to mind
may be managed, step by step. You are urged to compare every reference with the score, as you examine and assimilate the music. The result
will tell you as much about yourself as about the Andante movement
from Mendelssohn's *Italian Symphony*.

EXAMPLE 1: Mendelssohn, *Italian Symphony*, second movement, mm.
1–2

A two-measure, unison fanfare heads the movement like an insignia.
It consists of two dotted figures—A–Bb–A—at the start of each measure,
connected by three repeated eighth notes A.

The final note A of this insignia is held, at the forte level, while the
rhythmic cell of three eighth notes is reflected in the piano, staccato
upbeat in the cellos and basses, which provides the pattern for an
unfolding bassline to the melody that follows. This transitional bass

link between the opening statement and the melodic section not only takes its rhythmic design from the unison figure which dominates the entire movement, but the terminal notes of each group of four eights (always 3 + 1) outline the dominant chord of A. Each one of these terminal notes is approached from its upper neighbor, another correspondence to the opening statement which serves as the insignia of the movement: this one derived from the repeat of the A–Bb–A figure in the second measure, with upper neighbor C adding poignancy to the Bb, the latter, of course, being upper neighbor to the opening A. The staccato chain of four-note eighths in the bass which leads to the tonic D minor and the unfolding unison melody in viola, oboe, and bassoon (m. 3) will be an almost constant feature throughout this Andante. In the only section in which it does not appear, its absence becomes a powerful characteristic, and, with that, the absence of an ever-present reference to the germinal opening statement, which, because of its ubiquitous nature, we have called the "insignia" this piece. Such nuclear musical ideas are by no means uncommon. Far from being of mostly academic interest, they provide an excellent and very practical means of achieving an intitial grasp of the music.

To return to the beginning of our movement, from m. 3: the unison melody in oboe, bassoon, and viola is marked by two special events of articulation. The first of these is an accent on the half-note A in m. 5; the second a "hairpin" crescendo–decrescendo, stressing Bb after the same half-note A when it is repeated in m. 9.

Following our work pattern of the Mozart and Brahms movements, and according to the suggested system of surveying the musical surface (pp. 29–39), mark off the two opening measures ("insignia") as well as the transitional third. The upbeat to m. 4 through m. 11 shall be bracketed in two four-measure phrases representing the unison melody in oboe, bassoon, and violas; m. 12 begins their repeat in the violins. At this point in our detailed overview of the Andante we come across an unusual compositional detail: in the violin repeat of our opening melody both articulation marks are *missing*.

The omission has in fact been "corrected" in the standard orchestral parts, and on the face of it this would seem a reasonable, minor bit of tidy editing, bound to save the conductor a little trouble in rehearsal. It is also bound to ruin an exceptionally beautiful moment of inspired orchestral imagination. Two flutes fill the space *between* the violins, and above the continuing staccato bass. That instrumental combination, in such an unusual distribution of pitch levels, is of such transparent beauty that Mendelssohn's decision *not* to draw attention away from the flutes, by the mechanical repetition of the earlier inflections, may be interpreted as a very clear signal from the composer to restrain emotion in the melodic line here. The image begins to take form. We have made a little discovery which led to a personal conclusion with regard to the composer's instructions. We are getting involved.

How, and at what stage of our work, an unusual compositional detail becomes evident does not really matter. In the case of the missing articulations this might have happened on comparing the first statement of the melody with its repetition (cf. Correspondences: Group B, p. 32); or one might have been impressed with the unusual scoring of flutes and violins in m. 12, and taken a closer look at the passage as a result. If neither had happened during the preparation of the score, the discrepancy between the violin passage as printed in the score and the "edited" performance played by the section should certainly have provoked a caution from the podium and discovery of the difference in rehearsal. Discovery of this detail, and of countless others that provoke questions leading to *answers not explicitly stated in the score*, depends on our constant readiness to look for just such opportunities beneath the surface of music.

The violin passage is followed by a return of the original trio, viola, oboe, and bassoon, in a continuation of the melody (m. 20). This time, however, there are no mere inflections of the melodic line: a much bigger "hairpin" crescendo–decrescendo is followed by a strong crescendo into sforzato, but then at once interrupted by a dramatic subito piano for the second half of the phrase (m. 24, upbeat). When the flutes and violins repeat this second melodic strain (m. 27), the formerly serene violins show quite a passionate upsurge of emotion, and the flutes, now in their proper pitch relationship, have a crescendo of their own (m. 27). With violas, oboe, and bassoon joining on the piano repeat, there *is* a hairpin on B♭ now; and the flutes have the last word with another little swell. Basses remain piano and staccato throughout. Transition (mm. 35–45): the four-note bass-line upbeat also grows out of the insignia, combining the three eighth notes with the grace-note repeat of the rhythmic figure in m. 2. The entire section is staccato, piano, dominated by the rapid pulse of the bass line. With the end of this section, the pulsing motion of equal eights ceases. It is replaced by yet another element of the opening statement, the "insignia" of this Andante: the grace-note intensification of the sixteenth-note B♭ (m. 2) and the following A become the characteristic melodic pattern of a new and different segment of the piece, introduced by a thus-far unused voice in the orchestra: clarinet (m. 45).

We shall break off here to review, organize, and, if possible, to transform the material we have looked at into memorable images. In order to achieve this, however, we must be very clear about some basic aspects of memorization. Essentially, these concern *why* and *what*.

Why is it necessary to memorize? Because it is not possible to practice a score on its proper instrument, the orchestra, in advance of rehearsal and performance. Decisions about what lies beneath the surface of the music are not taken in isolation. Your overall concept of the work being prepared must be sufficiently detailed to permit your imagination to roam at will over its surface at any time, in order to make decisions, to compare and adjust. Second, your decisions must be *remembered*, because *they shall be as much a part of an eventual performance as the composer's facts and instructions in the score*.

That brings us to the other part of the question: *what shall be remembered?* And by far the most difficult aspect of the answer is the problem of assuring the recall, under the stress of performance, of your own decisions—not only large-scale matters of pacing, but all the many details of shaping, phrasing, and balancing which are your own unique contribution to any score. It could be argued that this part of what is to be remembered constitutes the most important aspect of the "mind image." Whether a note is B♭, a dynamic marking is piano, and this particular sound is entrusted to the oboe can be confirmed, if in doubt, by a glance at the score. Whether this B♭ is the high point of a musical shape, the beginning of a forward move in tempo, the key element in an otherwise ambiguous harmonic fabric, these things are part of your work with the score and must be remembered. Their transfer to mind and memory is an acquired skill. Unrestricted use of that skill is as necessary as the ability to read music. And, in the early stages, it requires practice.

We are now ready for a first exercise in what will be a multistage process of memorization. In the Mendelssohn Andante we have already passed the first stage: an attentive reading of the musical text. In the course of this reading several details appeared to have special significance.* These were marked for further investigation and, equally important, shall now serve to remind us of the subsections in which they were found. As a next step we shall devise a graphic representation of special points of interest.**

MENDELSSOHN, *SYMPHONY NO. 4,* SECOND MOVEMENT

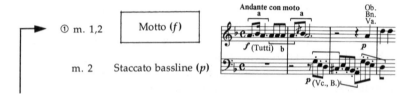

---

*That they consist of one textual and several melodic details is in itself incidental. In earlier perusals of a Brahms and a Mozart movement, musical shape and extramusical images were of initial interest.
**Cf. Chapter 12.

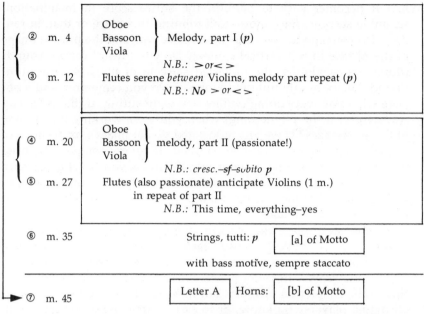

Oboe ⎫
Bassoon ⎬ Melody, part I (*p*)
Viola ⎭

② m. 4

N.B.: >*or*< >

③ m. 12   Flutes serene *between* Violins, melody part repeat (*p*)
N.B.: No > *or* < >

Oboe ⎫
Bassoon ⎬ melody, part II (passionate!)
Viola ⎭

④ m. 20

N.B.: cresc.–sf–subito **p**

⑤ m. 27   Flutes (also passionate) anticipate Violins (1 m.)
in repeat of part II
N.B.: This time, everything–yes

⑥ m. 35   Strings, tutti: *p* | [a] of Motto

with bass motíve, sempre staccato

⑦ m. 45   Letter A | Horns: | [b] of Motto

Clarinets, off-beat entrances and accents

etc.

Look (really look!) at each of these sections of score, remembering its "headline," associating the text above, and adding whatever personal finds you may now discover. They could be anything: another musical detail, an extramusical fantasy, or a feeling suggesting itself with the passage. Then flash the "headlines" (*not* the entire sections) through your mind, in sequence, making sure that what you see / hear is more than purely intellectual recall.

Now scramble the sequence to place repeat orchestrations side by side, rather than repeat phrases in different orchestration as they appear in the score (i.e. No. 2 next to No. 4; No. 3 next to No. 5). Flash "headlines" first, then refer once more to score. Note differences (those already suggested, new discoveries, associations); note similarities (e.g. what is the bass doing, where does it change?—add that to the memory image of that section).

Flash "headlines" once more, and then try to play through this whole beginning of the movement in your mind. If this is not yet possible, *repeat the entire process.* Proficiency in this approach takes as much consistent practice as playing on an instrument. Natural facility is given in greater measure to some than to others—this, in itself, is no indicator at all of future potential. Capacity for practice is.

When it becomes easy to perform the entire score in imagination, scramble sections once more: Call to mind this place or that, at random. Do you tend to "see" the page before you, and the printed image of the phrase in full vertical context? Do you "hear" certain sounds (flutes below violins, the unvaried staccato of the bass, the uninflected, later strongly inflected violins)? Do you remember and associate what you were doing (where you were sitting, if the coffee cup was empty, if the phone rang) when you were working on any one of these passages? Have any associated visual images, or feelings of pleasure, excitement, surprise, startled discovery, or perhaps frustrated puzzlement stuck in your mind? This is your total experience of the score, and it is important to remember how it came to you, in what primary fashion (visual, aural, intellectual), with what simultaneous sensations, images.

One further step: place the work in sequence again, but, as you go through it in your mind, identify each new event in terms of *direction from the podium,* just as if a real orchestra were in front of you. Try to "see" actual players in performance. We shall go into more detail about this in the chapter on memory. For now, it will help either to visualize actual players you know, or to cast an imaginary orchestra with figures of fantasy or history, from Santa Claus to Napoleon, playing whatever instruments or special musical passages seem appropriate to you. This kind of approach works marvelously for some, not at all for others. If you have real problems with it, leave it alone.

We are ready to conduct. A provisional tempo will have established itself. It is likely to reflect the sum of your recollected impressions of the score, and of performances you may remember. This is a perfectly normal point of departure and, for the time being, entirely sufficient.

Now confront your imaginary orchestra (*not* a real ensemble, even if available, and certainly not a recording). "Look" at your imaginary players, seated at an appropriate distance and in a clearly imagined direction from your podium; once more review—but this time the briefest, most simultaneous, image—the "headlines," and associations as they appeared in the graph; and conduct.

These elements of our work with the Andante from Mendelssohn's *Italian Symphony* are part of the process of preparation, transformation, and presentation of the musical surface, *by and for yourself.* This process will eventually take place in your mind. Until you have gained some proficiency at every stage of organizing and storing relevant materials for permanent use, you are urged to follow the scheme suggested below; always conclude by conducting the assimilated passages in silence. The extent to which such a "performance" is real in your imagination is the measure of your success in having transformed the information and the instructions in the score into a useful composite in your mind. Unlike the printed musical surface, this composite is bound to include the reflections of your own involvement with the music. Thus this transformation is the first decisive step. What remains is the critical evaluation of your contribution and a practiced skill in producing the total image of this composite, or any detail of it, instantly and with fully remembered references to your discoveries and associations.

The process involves:

transformation of music from its encoded surface in the score to an organized memory image in the conductor's mind;

preliminary exploration of that image with allowance for unrestricted employment of personal imagination, speculative analysis, or extramusical association;

assembly and temporary reassembly of chosen units within the work under study to provide a practiced sense of identity and continuity for the sections of music which your own involvement has brought to life for you.

Then, having completed the entire exercise, including a "conducted" performance from memory, an evaluation of your results should determine:

1. The most obvious consideration: *were you able to get through all of it?* If not: never mind, real orchestras also break down at first rehearsals. But you must try again.
2. In terms of the step-by-step exploration of musical characteristics of each small segment in our outline, and in terms of the mental preparation that went into putting the segments in an order of form and another order of content, before they were put together again, *how much was reflected in your performance? how much was lost?*
3. *What was lost?* Was it the sense of the whole,
     the "presence" of aural imagination,
     the visual associations of score,
                         performers,
                         images?
4. *What remained intact?*
   What aspects of your preparation seem to hold the most *promise of future usefulness* in your case?
   Where are *your apparent strengths?*

PODIUM

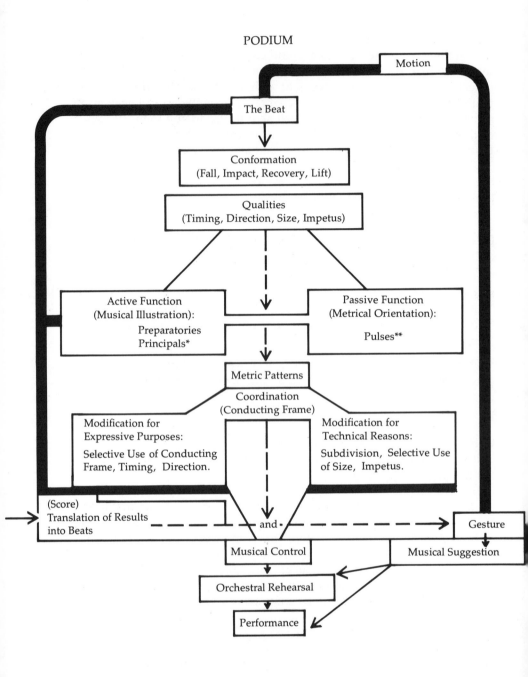

*Exception: *Series* of Principals: (*Passive* Function)   **Exception: *Accented* Pulse: (*Active* Function)

5B

BEAT AND GESTURE

An alternative kind of movement to the beat that controls is examined: gesture that suggests.

THE beat shows when to play and controls the musical shape of individual lines.* The most important alternative to the beat, among the signals from the podium, is the gesture.**

The beat controls, with clarity and precision. *Gesture invites;* because it is *not* precise, it leaves much to the initiative and to the imagination of the player. While it often functions in support of the beat, it is most characteristically an alternative motion: with the beat reduced to mere pulses, the left hand can appeal and suggest with independent, expressive gestures. While these may carry the same kind of message as the familiar functions of the beat, they have the potential for much greater intensity in the range of musical suggestions and for individuality in the invited response. Gesture may also serve to transmit messages *in addition* to those expressed by the beat, neither *supporting* what is already being expressed by the right hand nor functioning as an *alternative means* of signaling musical directions.

For the familiar insignia of the Andante from Mendelssohn's *Italian Symphony* (see p. 142) we prescribed a succession of beats which would

a. signal the initial attack;
b. sustain the forte on 3 and 4 of the first measure;
c. lead into the second measure with appropriate intensity.†

We signaled the attack with a preparatory upbeat, followed by a principal "down" on the orchestra entrance. We sustained the forte of unison A by a succession of preparatories which also provide cumulative power to emphasize the strong repeat of the initial dotted rhythm in

---

*Cf. p. 41.
**Gestures are associated with the left hand, the "poetry hand," in the case of right-handed conductors. In a broader sense, gestures include *any* visual signal other than the beat, e.g. encouraging smile or scowl.
†Cf. p.92.

EXAMPLE 1: Mendelssohn, *Italian Symphony*, second movement, mm. 1–3

the beginning of the second measure. But now we have a problem: the forte A is sustained throughout the second measure, while the basses enter very softly underneath. The beat alone cannot reconcile these contradictory requirements simultaneously. With the aid of gesture, however, there are several quite simple and effective solutions:

1. The right hand could continue to beat a strong series of preparatories until the end of the second measure, with a cutoff on beat 1 of the third m. Tension and volume of the insignia would be maintained to the end, and the beat would also serve the cello and bass entrance after 3. In order to safeguard a very soft attack on this entrance, however, an additional gesture would be required: an admonitory left hand lifted palm forward toward the low strings, or a cautioning finger against the lips. Gestures are subject to personal preference, and reflect the conductor's individuality more directly than beats.
2. The right-hand beat is modified in size and impulse to mark the soft entrance of the basses (by the use of a pulse on beat 2 and a suggestively small preparatory on 3—viz., Figure 7 on p. 91). By way of compensation, the left hand would have to urge upper strings and

winds to maintain full volume and tension to the end of the measure (e.g. a "vibrato" shake from the wrist for the violins, or a forceful lift of the entire left arm to the winds).

Either way, the mere *beginning of the gesture* would improve the overall effect. Once the simultaneous occurance of loud and soft is clear, an occasional reminder should suffice. At the same time, the beat should also remain as unobtrusive as possible, particularly in solution 1. While the dynamic contrast must be expressed, only its first appearance after the third beat is crucial. An exaggerated, prolonged "gesturing" intrudes upon the audience's perception of the music as a dramatic event in itself, and is likely to detract from the very effect it is intended to assist.

N.B.: Visual impressions are heightened when gesture is added to beat, for the audience as well as the orchestra. But the use of choreographic signals must not result in visual overstatements more spectacular than the musical effects.

Solution 1 demonstrates the use of an *independent gesture.*
Solution 2 involves an *alternative gesture.*
Let us examine the first measure once more. Here, too, the volume of unison A needs to be maintained through beats 2 and 3. Some sort of precaution must be taken to avoid an unintentional diminuendo after the second beat. We may support the sustained volume by strong preparatories, as in solution 1; or we could reduce the right-hand motion on beat 2 to a pulse while the left assures the continuing forte, as in solution 2. The latter solution reflects more accurately the inherent shape of the motto: the principal first beat is separated by a neutral pulse from the next preparatory on beat 3. The left hand, in assuming the sustaining role otherwise assigned to continuing strong beats in the right, provides an *alternative gesture.*

3. A third role for gesture is the *supportive* one. Given a straightforward treatment of the first measure by right-hand beats (a principal followed by three preparatories), the left hand could be used to lend additional emphasis to the upbeat of the following bar. It would be raised, in mirror fashion to the right-hand beat 4, so that this third preparatory could be understood as the final, most powerful summons of the release to follow on the next beat—the principal 1 of the second measure.

Independent, alternative, supportive: these are three possible roles for gesture. All three are described in relation to a simultaneous beat. Whether a gesture encourages a different expressive response, provides a temporary substitute of more personal character, or simply lends extra force to the message conveyed by the right hand, the beat remains the determining signal from the podium. It is the continual reference for all other motions. This is because the language of the beat has evolved into a generally accepted and universally understood convention. Allowing for some individual modifications, one conductor's preparatory beats, subdivisions, or basic beat patterns are much like anothers! But gestures are entirely personal.

There is only one rule concerning *expressive gestures: they must stay in motion*. In the case of independent and alternative gestures this means motion other than that of the beat in the right hand. It also means motion of some expressive significance. To develop skill and natural ease with what should be your most individual aspect of conducting, a few preliminary exercises are suggested. These should be carefully worked through before any actual application of gesture to music is attempted. Just as we spent some time examining the steps from motion to beat, we shall now explore similar steps from motion to gesture. Once again a mirror will be of great help to you.

Before we practiced beats, we practiced motions: from the shoulder, from the elbow, from the wrist. Now, before you practice gestures in motion, experiment with various ways of displaying the hand that is to lead the movement. Bear in mind that, for the time being, the term *gesture* will be applied to motions of the left hand only, while the beat remains the business of the right. For practical purposes, this is a fair reflection of the way in which the types of motion we have defined as gesture and beat are employed by most conductors. For purposes of study, this division permits us to *add* the employment of gesture to the practice of the beat, by assigning the development of new skills to the other hand.

Gesture *moves* continuously while the beat monitors metric progress with pulses at regular intervals of time. The role of the beat must be maintained, accurately and sensitively, while an additional, freer, but equally persuasive set of motions amplifies the message to the orchestra. This will require physical independence of your hands, and will test your powers of concentration. With the facility you will have gained with regard to the beat, that concentration may now be directed to the gesture. And the focus of that direction shall be your left hand.

It was the right *arm* that moved the right *hand* that held the stick which gave the beat. That was our approach to right-side motion in the first chapter. Now we shall reverse the process: we shall concentrate on the left *hand* which is to "lead" the left *arm* in smooth, continuous gestures.

Smooth flow of motion is not the only difference between gesture and beat. The very fact that gesture is personal while the beat represents a widely accepted convention of musical signals makes it impossible to prescribe positions, directions, or patterns for the interpretive functions of the beat. Since your body is reasonably symmetrical, the left arm, like the right, hangs from a shoulder and turns on pivots that may be positioned in front of you for movement and visibility. From there on, you are on your own: you *choose* positions, directions, and patterns. Begin with the left hand. And, for the remainder of this chapter, use a mirror.

Hold your left hand in front of you, where you can see both its back, and its reflection in the mirror. Experiment a little: hand open, closed; fingers extended, curved; palm facing up, down, sideways; wrist bent, straight, turning. Whatever position feels good and looks expressive (this is no time to be squeamish) should be studied, remembered for future use. Perhaps, among the alternatives we have listed, you will find another position into which the left hand moves naturally and effectively: open / closed, turning at the wrist until a second, memorable position is reached. Now comes the movement *led* by the hand, the movement of the arm, the gesture itself.

FIGURE 1

Gestures must have a beginning and an ending, *and the movement must not stop from first to last*. Aim for a simple, but complete gesture: a curve rising gently from the center of the conducting frame, up and outward at shoulder height (Figure 1), then down again to near-center. Or the movement could aim forward, then out to the left, and back to center in an horizontal curve. Check yourself in the mirror: does the gesture really look smooth; or is it the sort of start-and-stop motion which is likely to turn into left-hand *beats* as soon as there is music to go with it? Does your arm feel like *your* arm, or more like the loading arm of a crane with a bulky and inert payload at its end? Remember: *your arm should be led by your very much alive left hand.*

N.B.: Practice left-hand gestures (the hand leading the arm) until the entire motion feels and looks natural, *without attempting to add right-hand beats* at the same time. What you are trying to accomplish is not some self-indulgent, extramusical podium display, but a very real, useful mastery of musical signals other than the beat.

A good way to practice this sort of gestural movement is with the aid of recordings, preferably familiar recordings of familiar pieces. The "canned" conductor provides the continuity and control normally vested in your right hand. And every swell, rapid climax or gradually receding musical intensity could serve as background for the practice of truly *unbroken* gestures. Listen carefully to a likely passage and, once you are familiar with its presentation, allow yourself a specific number of appropriately expressive gestures: no more than two or three. Try to begin these gestures between beats and be sure to complete every gesture with the same sense of uninterrupted continuity which should have marked it from first to last. That is the main object of this exercise, and for this you are responsible. Yours is a *commentary* on the music.

As defined above, there are three types of gesture: independent, alternative, supportive. We shall now practice the distinction between them. The third, supportive function is very nearly a duplicate of the right-hand beat, and need not detain us now. The other two, however, should be understood and practiced without music until they not only feel comfortable and natural, but different from each other.

Exercise A

Independent Gesture—Using Both Hands

1. *Right hand:* beat four ($\downarrow$ = c. 72)—principal, pulse, pulse, preparatory. Continue same.

Left hand: 1st measure—hand remains still, fairly close to chest, just to the left of center

2nd measure—hand begins curved motion, forward and up, just after first beat

3rd measure—top of curve is reached at shoulder height, about a foot further forward than at the start; curve continues downward and to the left

4th measure—hand completes curve near point of beginning

N.B.: Try to suggest throughout that the left-hand curve is an expressive gesture (e.g. legato, cantabile), not a dynamic indication.

2. Same with beat of three: principal, pulse, preparatory, etc.
3. Same with beat of two: principal, preparatory, etc.
4. Same with beat of six: principal, pulse, preparatory, principal, pulse, preparatory, etc.

Exercise B

Alternative Gesture

1a. *Right hand only:* beat four (♩ = 60)—principal + 3 preparatories, four measures of crescendo into climax on first beat of m. 5; left hand is not used

1b. *Right and left hand (alternative)*

1st measure:

Right hand	beat four, as above	(principal + 3 preparatories, crescendo begins)
Left hand	remain still	

2nd measure:

Right hand	beat four	2 and 3 are pulses, 4 is a small preparatory.
Left hand		suggest increasing volume, beginning between first and second beat (hand in "grasping" position, or possibly fist; arm moving gradually up and out from "neutral" placing near center, in front of chest)
3rd measure (*left hand*)		increase tension of left hand / arm gesture (possibly begin shaking the hand); continue motion very slowly

4th measure *(left hand)*	continue as above, achieve maximum tension as you lead into the fifth measure

N.B.: The right hand (having served no other function than to keep time in measures two and three) could now be added to take the crescendo "over the top." Whenever the right hand resumes the interpretive initiative, it is perceived as the primary musical indicator. Thus the left hand, completing its gesture as above, would no longer provide an alternative gesture: it would appear to furnish a supportive gesture. The right-hand motion would look like this:

4th measure *(right hand)*	2 is a pulse, three a small preparatory, and 4 a large preparatory into the next measure

2b, 3b, 4b. Same with beats of three, two, and six: Provide an effect of cumulative crescendo over four measures, reducing the function of the beat to the recording of metric pulses, while the left-hand gesture indicates mounting tension. During the fourth measure the right resumes its active role in bringing tension to a climax and release into the next measure, with the left-hand gesture now playing a supporting role.

When we feel comfortable enough with the preliminary exercises to be able to consider left-hand gesture vs. right-hand control as a matter of interpretive choice rather than a technical challenge, we shall be ready to try our options with music. Still before a mirror, and with an imaginary orchestra to conduct, let us work out the opening of the third movement of Brahms's *Third Symphony* as we worked our Exercise B above: first with the resources of the beat alone, and then with alternative gesture.

In Chapter 3a we observed something very remarkable about the start of that movement: the opening figure displays characteristics which, in different ways, dominate the entire piece. As a result of the metric shift of its dotted rhythm in the first two measures, and because of the harmonic underpinnings of this initial musical shape, tension is created which is both longer and stronger than its eventual release on the second measure. This "inner structure" of raised expectations which are never quite fulfilled provides a constant undercurrent of correspondences and relationships that have nothing to do with thematic similarities. This aspect of the opening must be so clearly presented that it will impress itself upon the attentive listener. We now have the technical means to attempt several solutions.

There is, of course, no compulsion to play this phrase in that particular fashion. A simple crescendo on beat 3 of the first measure, arriving at a climax on the following 1, as indicated in the score, certainly meets the composer's dynamic information. What we propose to show, is the relative force of the harmonic background against the printed location of the climax; and the subtle effect of reducing our signal for volume *just* before, to enhance what we may perceive as the composer's overall intent. It could be played either way. Here is how it would look:

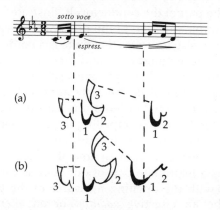

FIGURE 2

Heavy lines indicate the gathering momentum of preparation and its release into the second measure. Solid lines mark undifferentiated beats. Size is relative to size of motion. *Dotted lines connect patterns:* if the music were played, it would "pass" through our conducting frame with the passage of time. In a graphic representation, the frame "passes" the music.

Figure 2 shows a small upbeat, a principal 1, followed by a pulsing 2, and a 3 that increases in dynamic tension until released on the decrescendo 1 of the second measure. There is really no way of controlling the amount of espressivo crescendo or the force of its climax except by rehearsal and a small beat. This is essentially a negative way of conducting this passage: the aim would be to keep a tight rein on the amount of crescendo (and thus the intensity of the espressivo generated in the process) in order to avoid an excessive first climax. The effect of the "harmonic decrescendo" from first to second measure would necessarily have to be left to chance.

Figure 2b, though apparently more complex, leaves the conductor far more in control. Instead of a simple pulse on the second beat of the first measure, we begin the espressivo crescendo. On the third beat this becomes a real, dynamic crescendo, but is *interrupted* just before the following 1. This interruption can take place whenever we feel the maximum level of loudness has been reached. There is no danger of the orchestra's attacking the first beat of the next measure too soon, for we *withhold* the expected strength of that principal beat which would match its preparatory. Instead there is an anticipation of movement by a tiny fraction of a second. But the sudden loss of dynamic tension, and the spent force of a *slow recovery while the first beat is actually being played in the orchestra*, will inevitably, and quite controllably, achieve the effect described above.

This is an example of the so-called delayed response technique, really an anticipation on the part of the conductor. It illustrates the possibility of vesting the descriptive function of the preparatory beat in the anticipated principal beat. It also indicates that there is a border area between gesture and beat, between suggestion and precision, which is rich in expressive possibilities and well worth some experimentation and careful practice. The interaction of deliberately applied beat qualities (in this case timing) and intentional forfeit of the "advantage" of beat over gesture (precision), can be more compelling in performance than much of what passes for choreography on the podium.

But "choreography" exists and, in an area of visual interpretation of musical images, it is a legitimate part of our craft as conductors. Gesture, in connection with the opening measures of the Brahms movement, can either be an effective *addition* or an *alternative* to the expressive function of the beat. In either case we shall have to choose whether the result in performance should sound like Figure 2a or b. However, it is in connection with the latter solution (b), that gesture would provide a less difficult, but equally efficient signal. Instead of introducing the releasing beat itself, just before the barline, and diminishing its strength by the time the first beat of the next measure is actually played, we continue to beat as in Figure 2a; but we blunt the power of the release by a small, cautioning gesture in the left hand, while the preparatory 3 still generates cumulative impulse. The release into beat 1 will be smaller than the preceding third beat, and the effect should be just right.

Further applications of gestures to music are left to your own initiative and taste. There is often a choice between expressive beat and / or expressive gesture. It is very important, for now, that this choice be made consciously and with careful consideration of necessary adjustments: in the foregoing example we *beat* the earlier Figure 2a while a single, small, last-minute gesture helped us to achieve the effect of Figure 2b. Had we merely combined Figure 2b in the beat with that same gesture, the effect would have been too strong—the sort of overdone "choreography" whch defeats its purpose. Another possibility would have been a completely neutral beat, with the entire expressive burden shifted to the left hand. If you try that, you are likely to find that the

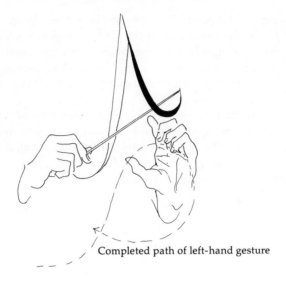

Completed path of left-hand gesture

FIGURE 3

danger of excessive choreography would make the vital effect of strong /
long tension—weak release quite difficult to achieve without exaggeration. By trying more than one solution, and by conscious planning of
alternative possibilities, you will soon gain a sure instinct for the type
of expressive gesture or beat best suited to your developing style.

One very common application of independent gesture is *the cue*. While
this need not necessarily be the special task of the left hand—the right,
even while beating, serves very well, and the eyes better still—the left-
hand gesture of the cue needs to be practiced. It should be small, clear
in direction, and it may well include an expressive suggestion concerning the expected attack. But it must never interfere with the continuing
functions of the beat.

Right handed or left, *the manual cue must be preceded by eye contact
between conductor and player.* If the cue goes to a section rather than an
individual performer, *look at somebody,* preferably in the back of the
section. Principal players in front are likely to participate in your cue
by appropriate motions of the body or the head anyway.

Look at the player well before the cue is actually given. Players are likely
to look at the conductor just in advance of an expected cue. At that
moment the conductor's eyes should already be there, making the
anticipated manual cue a *shared* musical event. In such a case, precision
of timing may well be taken for granted, in favor of a more effective
expressive gesture.

The independent employment of the left hand for expressive suggestion requires some practice, if it is not to jeopardize precision of ensem-

ble, the primary responsibility of the right-hand beat. A distiguished colleague encourages his students to play "independence games" around their homes. The right hand is set in motion with small, precise metric patterns. A metronome may help to monitor the steadiness of that beat. Meanwhile the left is employed in everyday chores (i.e. gestures).

When, a few minutes before his first concert in Europe, the author was trying to screw up his courage to walk from his dressing room to the stage of the Konzerthaus in Vienna, he was startled by the sudden appearance of a distinguished looking face in the crack of the partly open door. The face wore a friendly smile, an appraising look, and introduced its otherwise invisible owner as a music critic with a name as aristocratic as his visage. To complete the total demoralization of one young conductor about to rush a podium which great colleagues had trod at their peril, the face then withdrew with a cheery "I'll be watching your left hand!". Temporary paralysis of the entire left side notwithstanding, I certainly became aware of what was then a fresh dimension of conducting craft. I feel indebted to that critic with the disembodied face. I only wish that his very friendly review had mentioned my left hand.

PART TWO

SCORE	PODIUM
Transforming the Information	*Communicating Musical Ideas*

This deals with the transformation of evidence gathered from the musical surface into a vivid inner image and with the technical means of communicating this image to an orchestra.

SCORE

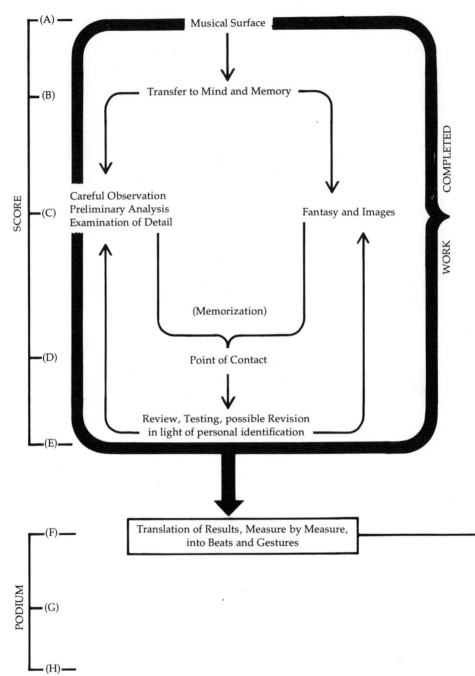

PODIUM

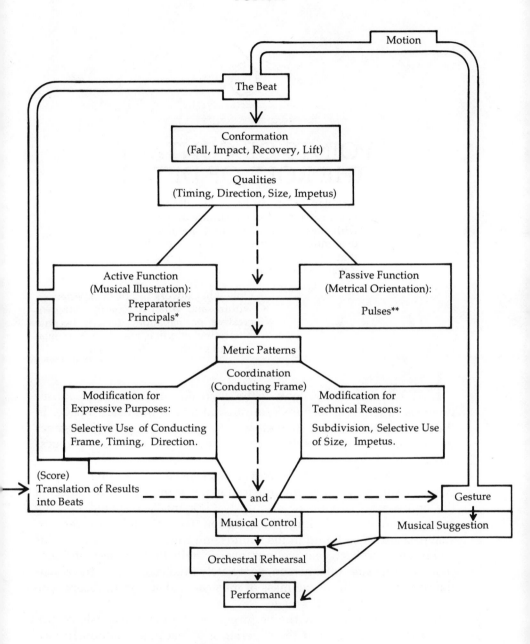

POINTS OF CONTACT:
THE ROLE OF DETAIL

Included are examples of the all-important first step *below* the surface of music,
with suggestions of a simple methods of
determining the direction in which to take
that step. Score examined: Mussorgsky /
Ravel, *Pictures at an Exhibition*

Only when a work has been experienced
within, and when it reflects your own
creative participation, does it become
interesting, effective, and alive. You must
learn to get through to yourself.
—Edwin Fischer

LET us take another look at the chart on which we mapped our
progress in learning to transform musical text into musical image. In
the course of the first five chapters we completed all the precribed stages
but one: translation of results, measure by measure, into beats and gestures.

Personal identification to provide a basis for review, testing and possible revision of an emerging musical image, form the broad subject of
the entire score section of our study. The intellect should be fully
engaged, but so will feelings, imagination, fantasy, and the sheer sensual pleasure to be found in the sounds and rhythms of music. For this
will be *your* intellect, *your* feelings, *your* imagination, fantasy, and sensual pleasure: *your* total person, completely involved. That is the essential condition if, out of the mass of musical evidence in the score, you
are to produce your performance.

It is really strange how the performance of a piece of music is supposed to be exciting, but the experience of learning it is not. In fact,
even an excitingly planned and prepared orchestral performance needs
a lot of help from many players in order to achieve a reasonable measure

of its potential effect. But there is simply no way in which any work may suddenly display qualities in performance that were not part of its preparation in the mind of the conductor. Routine analysis and rote memorization will either result in a routine performance or in mindless, on-the-spot improvisation, exploiting pretty details as arbitrary decorations for an unbeautiful design. True spontaneity in performance is the shared experience of finding oneself beyond the conscious limitations of an already established musical image and finding its essential features revealed in even greater clarity.

There are no arcane mysteries that bar meaningful exploration of a score to all but a chosen few. But neither is it reasonable to assume that putting together the ingredients of a viable performance requires no more than a grasp of compositional conventions, a good ear, and some skill with the baton. Living with a score from first contact to performance is a total experience, and the most vexing problem, more often than not, is how to begin.

At the very center of our chart we note: Points of Contact. We have given some examples of early connections between the learner and the score—a curious musical shape in the third movement of Brahms's *Third Symphony* became a clue (p. 76); a fleeting association of the technical term "feminine ending" in Mozart's *Eine kleine Nachtmusik* was elaborated into a little choreographic fantasy (p. 97); and a textual discrepancy provided some musical insights to the second movement of Mendelssohn's *Fourth Symphony* (p. 133). There are two things that are remarkable about these three approaches: they have nothing in common except their purpose; and, having served their purpose, it wouldn't really matter if, on further reflection, any or all would be rejected as irrelevant or false. What then was their purpose? To help us become involved.

This is not to belittle the value of such devices, or to say that it does not matter whether the points raised are real. It matters very much at the time. And if initial discoveries or personal associations remain valid as your work continues, so much the better. But even if they only serve to get you started, that in itself is of very great importance. One way of climbing the smooth face of a rock is to hammer sturdy spikes into suitable cracks in the sheer wall, use one to support your weight while you place the next, another to secure your rope while you shift your weight. You might have placed those *crampons* a little differently, or another climber might have found another way of getting to the top. But for you those little wedges of steel made the climb possible; even though, once they had served their purpose, you might well have removed some and left others for future use. The method, and the means you chose to use, were yours. So was the risk.

We did suggest a method for the sifting of evidence on the musical surface. And the use of our charts, the steps they describe, the way in which they relate certain aspects of score and podium are also a kind of method. But whatever method you may employ, a work must be discovered afresh, every time. With every piece the transformation of available text into a living image will have to be, for you, a new and different experience. In order to start the process you will need some point of contact. That is the role of detail.

Here is a complete account of such a transformation. Beginning with the accidental discovery of a mildly curious detail that was to become the unsuspected point of contact, I shall then lead you through several levels of subsequent exploration; supply you with all the evidence of review, testing, and possible revision in light of personal identification; and share with you the image that is still stunning to me, so many years after it first emerged. I shall also provide this true story with its rather ironic, but instructive conclusion. This is "The Case of the Missing Promenade."

Modest Mussorgsky's *Pictures at an Exhibition*, a set of piano pieces composed in 1874, was orchestrated by Maurice Ravel in 1922, for Serge Koussevitsky, then conductor of the Boston Symphony. Ravel created a brilliant showpiece for orchestra, so perfectly conceived for a large instrumental ensemble that it is now very difficult to think of the work as anything but what it has become: a staple of the symphonic repertory. Every note seems inevitable, a perfect realization of Mussorgsky's vision. Only one problem: Ravel left out the fifth Promenade.

At a glance, the musical surface of the work confirms the usual program-note analysis: a series of short movements, each depicting in musical terms one of the Russian painter Victor Hartmann's pictures, is framed between "promenades" that are said to represent a visitor walking from picture to picture. The visitor appears before the first three pictures, seems to skip the fourth, and is seen only once more after that. But his walking music turns up in the final picture movement and one other.

Mussorgsky would surely have seen the Hartmann retrospective exhibition, mounted in Moscow in 1873, one year after the painter's death. They had both been members of a group of artists, writers, and composers who had met for some years to share and exchange ideas about what they considered "Russian" in all forms of artistic expression. Ever since Czar Peter the Great had opened their country's "window to the West," Russia's cultural heritage, in their view, was being smothered by "Western" influences. So it is doubtless Mussorgsky himself who walks from picture to picture in promenades that are variations on a theme the composer identifies "nel modo russico."

Having lost him in the crowd after his fourth promenade, we shall take a look at Promenade 5 in Mussorgsky's piano original. It is a slightly fuller, but almost exact, repeat of the very first one.

EXAMPLE 1: Mussorgsky, *Pictures at an Exhibition*, Promenades 1 and 5 (Piano Original)

Perhaps this very repetitiousness disturbed Ravel; perhaps he felt that, after the very taxing solo part of the *Goldenberg and Schmuyle* movement, the first trumpeter deserved a rest; perhaps it was Koussevitsky, far more readily inclined to make short shrift of composers' "faults" than the fastidious Ravel, who insisted on that little cut. The fact remains that in the published score of this famous orchestration one composer of rank "improved" on the work of another.

Leaving questions of conscience aside, does the change matter? Obviously it mattered to Ravel. How the omission affected Mussorgsky's music requires more thought. I became involved with the second question because I was unable to satisfy a mild curiosity about the first. Armed with a brand-new pocket score, I had planned to brush up on memorization of *Pictures* during some tedious hours of travel. The missing promenade was referred to in the preface of my score, the first I knew of Ravel's only willful change in an otherwise scrupulously faithful translation of Mussorgsky's musical text. Although the piano original appeared, measure for measure, below the printed score for comparison, Promenade 5 was not included, nor further information provided. Had the piano score been at hand, curiosity would most likely have been satisfied by one of the guesses above, based on the similarity of promenades 5 and 1. But I was not likely to see a piano score until after I had conducted the piece again. What purpose, besides the programmatic one, was served by these promenades, this series of variations within—it suddenly dawned on me—*another* set of variations? Besides, it seemed a good way to review the score: start with a melodic analysis of the opening trumpet solo, that pentatonic fanfare of the first promenade, and see if something akin to its shape may be found in movements *other* than the promenade variations. Here is what Mussorgsky presents:

EXAMPLE 2

Even at first glance, the theme seems remarkably symmetrical in design. Closer inspection reveals an almost Webernesque construction in which interlocking three-note melodic cells combine intervals of the 2nd the 3rd, and the 4th in five distinctive shapes, including their inversions, retrogrades, and retrograde inversions:

EXAMPLE 3

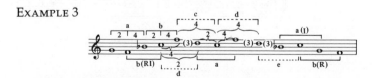

The three-note cells shown in Example 3 appear in the opening statement of the first promenade and in *all* variation movements. They are used *selectively* and characteristically in the picture movements in between. Promenades are variation movements, as are *Cum Mortuis* and *The Great Gate of Kiev*.

The following examples illustrate the selective use of certain three-note cells in melodic material and contours of the picture movements. You are urged to consult a score in order to supplement these suggestions with your own observations.

EXAMPLE 4. Three-Note Cells in *Pictures at an Exhibition*

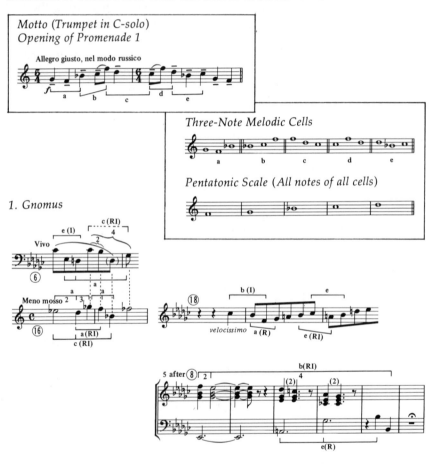

1. Gnomus

2. Il Vecchio Castello

3. Tuileries

4. Bydlo

*Here is a conundrum: These are unquestionably "e" shapes. Because they do not feature a significant three-note outline, however, they don't *feel* like it. Since the object of the exercise is to make *personal* sense of this work, these shapes are not reflected in the summaries.

5. Ballet of the Unhatched Chicks

6. Samuel Goldenberg and Schmuyle

7. Limoges: Le Marché

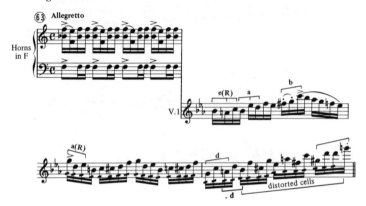

8. Catacombae

Cum Mortuis in Lingua Mortua

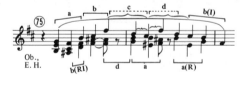

9. The Hut on Fowl's Legs (Baba Yaga)

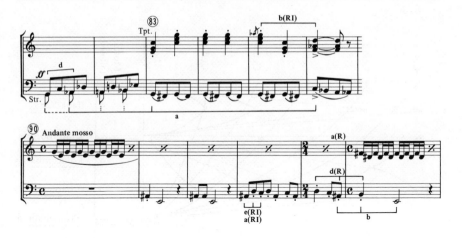

10. *The Great Gate of Kiev*

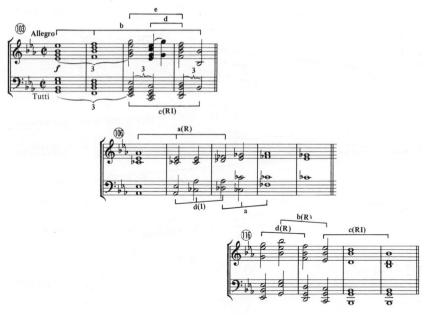

Figure 1 shows the striking symmetry of Mussorgsky's construction. Each picture movement or pair of picture movements is represented by a shape consisting of lines that connect the coordinate points of its melodic cells to respective promenades before and after. The promenades, being variations of the opening theme "nel modo russico," share the "motto" of its trumpet solo, and thus contain all five melodic cells.

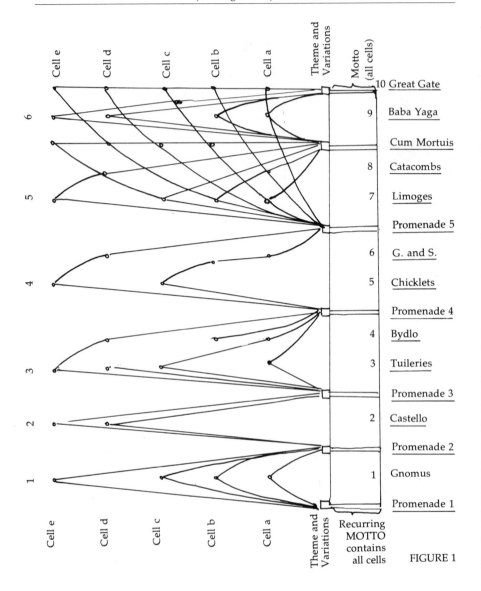

FIGURE 1

In our illustration, the pointed arches of the six picture shapes rest on their supporting promenades, from which spring the contour lines of whatever cells the composer chose to use, and to which they return—either directly or, in the cases of pairs of pictures, through the coordinates of the second picture movement. Thus are created structures which, visually at least, are equally remarkable for their similarities and their differences. Another feature of the diagram reflects the fact that *Cum Mortuis* and *The Great Gate of Kiev* are pictures as well as promenade variations. The five cells of the motto are represented by all five coordinates above their promenade bases. These are connected by lines springing from the promenade preceding *them:* our missing promenade, No. 5.

Granted that some of this visual "evidence" does not necessarily translate into convincing musical argument, it must be remembered that at the time I had no way of knowing what the missing promenade was like. The whole approach as presented thus far was based on two safe assumptions: the placement of No. 5 between *Goldenberg* and *Limoges;* and, as with all other promenades, its use of the motto containing the five melodic cells. But given these reservations and limitations, there was nonetheless cause for some excitement and anticipation: what musical equivalent would the missing promenade provide in its pivotal supporting role for two neighboring arches in my sketch? This was the state of my preliminary analysis by the end of the journey.

Before the conclusion is told, we shall now pause to remind ourselves that the reason for introducing this story is neither Ravel's orchestration of *Pictures at an Exhibition,* nor the dilemma posed by what is beginning to look like a questionable decision to omit one of the promenades. *The story is about the role of detail in the process of transforming musical text into musical image* in the mind of the conductor. Using the account thus far as an illustration of that process, here is a review of some key words and statements found earlier in this chapter. They will be clearer in this freshly remembered context.

"In order to start the process you will need some point of contact. That is the role of detail." (p. 158)

The detail in this case was an obscure reference, in the preface of the score, to one of a "number of small alterations between the original and Ravel's score." Here was a fresh point of contact with a familiar piece. Curiosity and limiting circumstances led to devising a different approach to this work. The process was started. That is the role of detail.

"Whatever method you may employ . . . a work must be discovered afresh, every time." (p. 158)

Here is something to add to that bit of advice. The method must be suited to your point of contact, even if it seems more like a game than a method. This should not in any way diminish the importance of conventional harmonic or structural analysis. The established method was already part of our survey of the musical surface. It will be useful again, once an entirely independent approach has shown us what to use it for.

"These [free] approaches . . . have nothing in common except their purpose . . . what then was their purpose? To help us become involved." (p. 157)

We have already observed that it is unreasonable to expect exciting performances to result from routine preparation. That a sense of excitement can be created in one's work with the score, just as excitement may be created in performance, is a valuable lesson to learn. Gifted students are impatient to "conduct." An almost mystical faith in how much may be accomplished from the podium tempts even very conscientious young conductors to neglect their job of working out, in advance, what they wish to accomplish. In time, one's unwitting temptation is to think more in terms of repeating past successes than of recapturing the frame of mind that produced successes.

Becoming involved, or involved again, with a work is a condition that carries its own reward. The point at which our story was interrupted was one of remembered "excitement and anticipation"—a far cry from brushing up on memorization to while away the tedium of a trans-Atlantic flight. I had become involved.

Having served its purpose, "it wouldn't really matter if, on reflection, [the approach] would be rejected as irrelevant or false." (p. 157)

Suppose that, as our story continues and the piano original of the missing promenade is examined, the evidence did not support the expectations we reflected in the diagram: the promenade did *not* repeat some form of the motto, or its place in the succession of movements was *not* before *Limoges.* The story would have had a different ending, but in no way would I have been able to go back to brushing up on memorization as an adequate way of preparation, no matter how "familiar" the work or how often performed.

"Review, testing and possible revisions in light of personal identification." (Chart p. 154, text p. 156)

"Personal identification" seems to suggest a mysterious condition in which the performer enters into a relationship with the work to be performed, a relationship capable of providing the basis for a range of consistent decisions in review, rehearsal, and performance. *That is exactly what it is intended to suggest.* A demonstration will be provided as we continue.

The piano original of Mussorgsky's *Pictures at an Exhibition* showed Promenade 5 in the expected place and introduced by the expected motto. It also showed that it was an almost exact repeat of Promenade 1, and like its model, was in B♭. *Pictures* is in E♭, with the first promenade appropriately providing an introduction in the dominant. The repeat of that introductory promenade with the first use of the dominant key since the beginning, *followed by the first return to tonic E♭ in Limoges,* strongly suggests, in terms of harmonic structure, the same pivotal role of the fifth promenade that we had suspected on the basis of our sketch: *Pictures* divides into two parts, with the missing fifth promenade marking the return of the Russian theme in its slightly strengthened original setting and in the original key. From there the music branches out into a final part in which promenades become pictures. We recall the lines springing from the dividing promenade into the cell coordinates of *Cum Mortuis* and *The Great Gate of Kiev* in the sketch of the arches.

A chart relating harmonic events to the earlier diagram based on melodic events appears in Figure 2. Retrace functions and relationships in the score, according to this outline. The function of Promenade 5 in

Theme and Variations

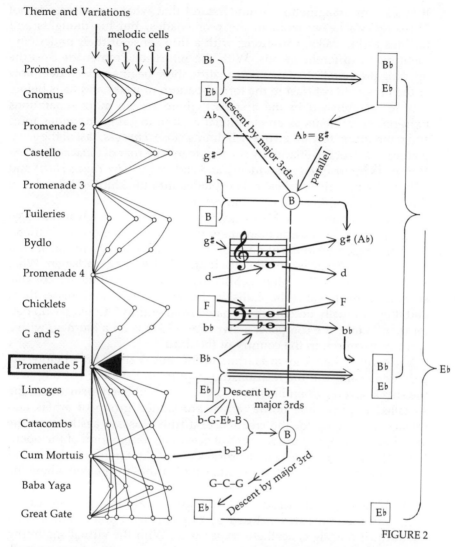

FIGURE 2

redirecting harmonic momentum into tonic E♭ will be confirmed. It divides the first two-thirds of the work from the briefer, more violent close that features a second excursion into the tonal area of the submediant B. The route by which this excursion and the final return to E♭ are accomplished is clearly laid out in the first part. An understanding of what occurs during the final third of *Pictures* must be found on still another level.

According to its published program, *Pictures at an Exhibition* shows a visitor, presumably the composer, walking from painting to painting.

It takes little imagination to understand that what we witness is not Mussorgsky's heavy tread in the promenades, but his thoughts and feelings as he walks: variations, with a firm sense of their underlying identity, in different moods. With the return of Promenade 5 to the opening presentation of that personality, there begins a much freer flow of the music. In contrast to the formal pattern of walks and halts before pictures established in the first part, there are no more separations between movements as an emotional crescendo gains enormous force and momentum toward an overwhelming close. *Limoges,* last of the *genre* pictures, is brutally effaced by the first fearsome roar of *Catacombs; Cum Mortuis* is interrupted as suddenly and rudely by *Baba Yaga's Hut;** and at last, the horrific witches' ride explodes into the shining splendor of the *Great Gate of Kiev.* What is happening?

When Hartmann died, Mussorgsky was already in an advanced stage of alcoholism. The musical monument he created in memory of his friend is a half-crazed vision, but a vision firmly controlled by the structural instinct of a great artist and the discipline of a life-long craftsman. What kind of vision? Of *Cum Mortuis* Mussorgsky said, "Hartmann's creative spirit leads me towards the skulls [in the catacombs]; he addresses them and they gradually become illuminated from within." Could we do better than to take the composer's own words? He is on a journey, with a spirit companion, in the country of the dead.

Mussorgsky had known Hartmann for only a short time before the painter's death, but the relationship appears to have been strong, and the shock severe, when his friend died. Both had been members of the so-called mighty little horde, a self-proclaimed group of artists and musicians striving for the creation of a truly Russian aesthetic in the arts, free of foreign, European influences. The designation of the opening "Allegro giusto, nel modo russico," speaks for itself; the use of Hartmann's artistic legacy as the subject identifies the person whom the composer seeks in the underworld.

The revisiting of the dead artist through his paintings is an evocation which, in the first part (enclosed by Promenades 1 and 5) remains an outward, if nostalgic, aesthetic experience. With the virtual shattering of *Limoges* against *Catacombs,* the personal journey is no longer a walk between paintings. Mussorgsky is drawn through the place where "skulls . . . become illuminated from within," and through a vortex of unbridled, primitive terror, to fulfillment, if not at the Gates of Heaven, then ("nel modo russico") at *The Great Gate of Kiev.*

A transforming, magic journey through the underworld has been the subject of myth and poetry from the *Odyssey* to Dante's *Divine Comedy.*

---

*The rude interruption is directed at the musical protagonist, still agonizing over the final chord of the most moving farewell passage. The *clarinettists need time* to change to B♭ instruments. Fermata!

In 1927, Ezra Pound wrote to his father about his plan for the *Cantos,* his own vast poetic project:

> "Live man goes down into the world of the Dead.
> The 'repeat in history'.
> The 'magic moment' or moment of metamorphosis,
> bust through from quotidien into 'divine or permanent'
> world'. Gods etc."

The description would fit the *Divine Comedy* as well as Mussorgsky's *Pictures.* It also fits something of the role of the artist in general, the performer who would be "an essential part in the whole picture." In the underworld of our imagination, dead guides, shipmates from the past, are waiting to teach us the "moment of metamorphosis." Mussorgsky is with his friend Hartmann now, one of the "skulls illuminated from within."

The excitement of working with a score can be very deep indeed. The excitement of a performance to follow may match it at best, but cannot be expected to exceed it. William Schuman, early in his tenure as president of The Juilliard School, told the students, "When music stops being a romance, get a divorce!" For us as conductors, a small detail, the point of contact—well perceived and properly exploited—is romance indeed. Often unsuspected, sometimes unique, but always tremendously exciting, it allows us to become involved. Henry James called it "the tendency of the artist to vibrate."

An ironic but instructive conclusion was promised as an end to "The Case of the Missing Promenade."

Ironic Conclusion

For all its importance in establishing proper perspective on the work and the pivotal place it occupies within the structure of Mussorgsky's piano original of *Pictures at an Exhibition,* the missing promenade can, of course, in no way be performed as part of Ravel's orchestral setting. There would be no difficulty in matching up the few additional chords with those already existing in the first promenade. (In fact, I have played a private performance of the entire score, including an orchestrated addition of Promenade 5, and everyone present enjoyed it.) But even a successful demonstration of how well it works does not give conductors the right to improve on the clear evidence of the composer's score. The decision to omit the return of the principal promenade was Ravel's, and, in terms of our ground rules concerning the musical surface, that's a fact. It would be one's privilege to do another orchestration, with all promenades in place; or to perform one of several existing efforts by other orchestrators. On balance, however, one is likely to stick with Ravel.

Instructive Conclusion

If Promenade 5 is not played after all, we must ask the question again: does it matter? Yes; but not as much as if we had never tried to find the answer. We became so involved that a new perspective and a sense of personal participation were granted to us. That will not be lost, even if we hear performances without the fifth promenade; and it will most certainly be reflected in any performance we conduct. We shall miss the actual "magic moment" after which the pictures "bust through from quotidien into 'divine or permanent world.' Gods etc." But knowing *that* they do, and *when* they do, one can still infuse that final breakthrough in performance with much of *what* they do.

SUMMARY

1. Point of Contact
2. Working Method appropriate to Point of Contact
3. Personal Involvement

These are the three elements of an approach to the preparation of a score. Prior familiarity with its musical surface is assumed. In the given context of succeeding chapters, other examples of points of contact will be offered. Suitable methods of approach will be suggested but, as we have already emphasized, the proper method depends as much on the conductor as it does on the music. Like excitement, individuality in performance begins with its preparation at home.

Now a word of caution. Odd details and stubborn questions may just as easily point to a flaw in your own perception of a work, as to the magic point of contact and involvement. Knowing this to be so, you will *nonetheless persist*. In the end you shall be answered, quite possibly by the simple question you never thought to ask. Be prepared for uncertainty, frustration, and, occasionally, some unusual modes of resolution.

At the time my father was dying, I was engaged in the final stages of my own preparation for a performance of Mahler's Sixth. On many plane trips to visit my father, the score was always with me. Of many textual problems in that symphony (most of which stem from the *composer's* life-long habit of revising scores every time the *conductor* provided him with new insights),* the two most vexing concern the altered sequence of the two inner movements and the number of hammer strokes in the finale. Originally the Scherzo followed the first movement. The second version was printed with the Andante preceding the Scherzo. And there

---

*Cf. Sessions: "There is no such thing as a definitive performance of any work whatsoever. This is true even of performances by the composer himself." (p. 2)

is reason to believe that Mahler wished the original sequence restored, but this is not certain. The hammer strokes in this highly personal symphony mark highwater marks in the last movement, after which the flood of triumphant music is checked. In Mahler's first version there were three "hammer blows of fate" which felled the fighting hero "like a tree." * After the first performance in 1906 Mahler deleted the third hammer stroke and weakened the original orchestration. According to an unconfirmed report,** Mahler changed his mind four years later. As with the succession of the inner movements, however, every conductor must now decide for himself.

Two or three hammer strokes: that was the question. There is a tradition that Mahler deleted the third hammer stroke out of superstition; that he feared to provoke his own fate by insisting on a third, presumably fatal, blow. To support this thesis, the three blows that life dealt Mahler in the following year—his downfall at the Vienna Opera, the death of his daughter Marie, and the diagnosis of a severe heart condition—are cited, as if Mahler had not been able to mollify an aroused destiny after all. One wonders who is being superstitious. But the fact remains that Mahler altered a perfectly clear first concept—the fighter rising twice to battle on, only to succumb under the third stroke, on the very crest of triumph. By not only eliminating the third hammer blow, but reducing the sonority and power of its instrumental context, he removed the obvious cause for a tragic ending. I could not reconcile this change.

Mundane details: Those hammer strokes also present a difficult technical problem which must be resolved well in advance of the first rehearsal. The composer specifically asks for a "dull" sound (as, presumably, a blow to one's own helmeted head). At the same time that thud must be powerful enough to hush an orchestra in full flood. Many devices have been dreamed up over the years. In our case, we constructed a low kind of scaffold, underneath which was hidden a microphone. Someone had donated a huge wooden mallet that had once been used on railroad ties to drive in the spikes. When the scaffold (in the midst of the orchestra) was struck with that mallet, the sound was amplified by four large theater speakers. Both the visual effect (like a medieval execution) and the audible blow were startling. We spent the better part of an hour, after an evening rehearsal of another program, trying not to make it "ring" too much. I remember going to sleep that night thinking of the surprisingly superficial changes Mahler had made in the orchestration, after deleting the third stroke—and thinking that, given its musical setting, it should probably remain as originally conceived.

*Mahler's own mixed metaphor.
**Redlich, Foreword to the Eulenburg edition of Mahler, *Sixth Symphony*, p. xxxi.

I "awoke" to the noise of many voices, wailing, the rhythmical tramp of military formations passing outside, and the rushing by of large crowds of people. As I struggled to consciousness, I found myself in a small temple, presided over by a woman in plain robes, and opening on a street leading to the Forum. I was in Rome, and all of Rome seemed to be headed for the Forum. Rome was my city then. The woman said: "He is dead. Your father is dead." I pushed my way though the mourners into the square, and saw my father's body stretched on a trestle atop a high scaffold (a very much larger version of the one we had built for our hammer strokes). At this moment of recognition, the A major / A minor harmonic progression, the "seal" of the Mahler Sixth, was not only heard but felt as a searingly intense pain. In a vivid flash of memory, I saw my father at the head of a large number of soldiers on the march, in leather and a steel cuirass, bearing a rough cloak against the driving wind. I heard the fierce beating of a drum in the opening rhythm of the *Sixth*. And my father's life, what I knew of it, unfolded itself before me in an unbroken sequence of images, first in his dream persona of a dead warrior (not his actual life, by the way); then came new and unexpected scenes involving the woman in the temple; then on to a fullfilment that was checked twice by the brutal hammer stroke of my awareness of his death. On each of these occasions a ritual action was expected from me for the benefit of the crowd. But in the end (and this was felt with absolute certainty, in the dream and later on), at the moment which would have marked the third, now eliminated hammer stroke, I found myself alone with my father's body. Nothing was expected of me now, but to experience the fullness of my loss in the privacy of my personal grief. This was the hardest moment to bear, a final great surge of music and feeling, marked not with a blow, but with suddenly mute, ebbing pain.

This remarkably vivid and consistent dream affected the performance in three ways: it removed the question of the third hammer stroke as an issue, as it had been removed from the score; it reversed my planned order of second and third movements as no longer consistent with what I had "experienced"; and it infused every minute of further work on Mahler's *Sixth*, on or off the podium, with a sense of conviction, of having been there.

As an illustration of the way in which answers to stubborn questions are likely to present themselves, the dream is hardly typical. But as an example of the kind of answer I should have sought in the first place, it is perfect. The dream did not address the question I could not resolve—how many hammer strokes?—but the question I had failed to ask—what is happening? Knowing that Mahler had eliminated not only the third "blow of fate," but also enough of the original pungency and power in the orchestra, *at that very spot in the score*, it would not have required a great deal of imagination to ask why. The new ending is at odds with the composer's earlier program. But unlike the missing promenade, the missing hammer stroke was removed by the composer. And there is evidence that Mahler, in some way, modified his image of death at the moment of triumph. It may have been nothing like my dream image, and it certainly was no longer an eyewitness account of the hero's end. But the pain is there. What is happening?

It was Mahler's belief that "since Beethoven, no great music has been written that did not have its inner program." But as a conductor he would have been fully aware of the stifling limitations imposed upon the imagination of other performers or listeners by a published program outline. Whatever the deletion of that third hammer stroke meant to him was his own affair. The fusing of my father's death with that music remains inseparable for me to this day. But if that was my own affair, the ensuing performance was not. I still had to cope with the job of translating what moved me into a performance that would move an audience. Finding personal points of contact is only a first step, but an important one.

The "tendency of the artist to vibrate" is like that of a fine glass: it responds only to a sympathetic pitch. You will want to try your own hand at spotting "vibrant details." Here are four rules which should be helpful in putting you on the track of promising sources for your sympathetic vibrations.

1. *Do look hard.* One good reason for methodical surface examination of every score, every time it is prepared for performance, is that detail—vibrant or otherwise—is only noticed if you respect it. We have already outlined several stages in the preparation of a score, and there are some still to be explored. Finding that "odd" detail that will draw us to where the vibrations start is the best possible beginning. Your first, and often best, opportunity comes in the initial survey. Group D, the "joker in the pack" is the link between the necessary chore of classification and the moment when your performance begins to generate its own momentum. Keep your eyes open.

2. *Do ask simple questions.* This requires practice and concentration. In focusing your attention on a simple problem you define the area to be explored. And since only *you* can determine the questions to which only *you* can provide an answer, this is a way of becoming involved with the music. It is surprisingly difficult to spot some very obvious and, with hindsight, very productive questions. Why *not* the fifth promenade was unanswerable. *Why* the fifth promenade was an obvious second try. Why no accent in the repeat of a phrase in Mendelssohn's *Fourth* was a simple question (p. 134). If you followed the exercise of which the answer was a part, you are not likely to forget that answer, nor the phrase itself in its unusual setting. Another simple question was posed earlier, in connection with Ravel's preface to his choreographic poem *La Valse* (p. 31). The answer will introduce your assignment at the end of this chapter.

3. *Don't pass over the commonplace.* "Nothing up my sleeve" is every magician's claim, and the innocuous details that might prompt a very good question are not likely to appear by magic either. Obviously interesting questions are often the kind for which we are conditioned by our training in conventional analysis. They are also in need of answers, but more often than not the answers end our concern. Whether a five-measure phrase consists of $2+3$ or $3+2$ must be determined at an early stage in the study of a score; whether a harmonic move from one key to another is really a modulation or merely an inflection makes a lot of difference in the way it is to be presented in performance; and whether dynamic nuances edited into a score are in fact stylistic violations sanctioned by long neglect (tradition being, according to Mahler, the sum of bad habits of the past)—all these are important and possibly interesting questions. But they are not likely to establish an absorbing point of contact because we already know how to find the answers. It is the commonplace detail, the one which irritates because it detracts from the grand design, or some celebrated controversy with with regard to the score, that just might get you involved. Magic is not what you see, but what you don't see.

4. *Don't stop.* If a question becomes irritating, boring, and seems stupid, but won't go away, follow it up. The very persistence of a question should signal that, in some way, answers are about to present themselves *to you.* One of the real difficulties in communicating the techniques of solving musical problems is semantic. In music as in life problems are not necessarily solved intellectually. That does not mean that they will disappear if you don't think about them. Or that the results need not be tested by your best thinking. But on the whole it is better to find questions than to pose problems. Don't stop asking.

Assignment

A Comparison of Corresponding Waltzes in Ravel's Choreographic Poem La Valse.

Point of Contact: "Why 1855?"

In his orchestration of Mussorgsky's *Pictures at an Exhibition*, Ravel omitted Promenade 5, which, as part of the original piano version, divides the longer, deliberately paced first part from the intense final third of the work. His own *La Valse* shows a similar dichotomy between a formal succession of exquisitely presented waltzes in the first part and their increasingly frenzied return in the second. The proportions are different: although not all waltzes reappear, the return section of *La Valse* is longer than the first. That in itself is not unusual: the *Emperor Waltzes* of Johann Strauss, at once the archetype and perhaps the finest example of the fully developed Viennese waltz tradition (thirty years prior to *La Valse*), also return in the second half for a leisurely review in different sequence. The full-blown waltz of the late 1880s also features what has been aptly described as a miniature symphonic poem as introduction,* as well as a slow reminiscence of melodic fragments from the first part before the long coda. The introduction of the *Emperor* evokes a glittering image of the Imperial parade ground; *La Valse*, according to the composer himself, is introduced by the image of an Imperial ball, emerging with increasing clarity from a swirling mist of swaying movement at the opening until the scene is in brilliant focus at letter *B*. As is the case in the introductory march of the *Emperor Waltzes, La Valse* features melodic fragments in the opening measures that will become waltzes later on.

In this assignment you will be concerned not with the ways in which *La Valse* conforms to the traditional Viennese waltz at the peak of its development, but with the difference. *La Valse* was commissioned by the powerful Serge Diaghilev of the Ballet Russe in 1919. He asked Ravel to write an apotheosis of the waltz. The result was *La Valse*, a work full of seductive and passionate tunes, in a lush setting. As we have seen, the work is structurally in the mainstream of Viennese tradition at its height. And yet, upon seeing the completed score, Diaghilev thought this "choreographic poem" so unsuitable for his intended ballet celebration of the waltz that he refused to accept it. What happened?

The answer to this "simple question" is part of your assignment. As point of contact you are offered an answer to the earlier question: "why 1855?". The method of developing that contact will be to compare returning waltz themes in the second half of the work, in terms of the "inner meaning" assigned to *La Valse* by the answer. The cumulative evidence of those differences will be an outline of the image into which you are about to transform the musical text.

Why 1855? Here is Ravel's prefatory note:

Between turbulent clouds, by the flicker of lightning, one may catch glimpses of waltzing couples. Gradually the clouds disperse: An immense ballroom is revealed (A), filled by a turning crowd.
The scene becomes brighter. The full radiance of chandeliers bursts forth at the *ff* of (B).
An Imperial Court, around 1855.

*David Hamilton, "The Secret Life of a Waltz," *High Fidelity*, Oct. 1975.

The work was written in 1919. Ravel had volunteered for service in World War I, but was rejected because of his small, slight stature and weak constitution. He tells the story in a touching letter:

Dear friend, as you had foreseen, my adventure finished in the most ridiculous way: I am not wanted because my weight is two kilograms short. Before going to Bayonne [to enlist] I spent one month working from morning to night, without even taking the time to bathe in the sea. I wanted to finish my trio which I have treated as a posthumous work.

At last he managed to get a job driving a lorry, at Verdun, March 1916. While at the front he succumbed to dysentery. Following an operation he was transferred to the automobile park at Châlons-sur-Marne. He was granted compassionate leave in 1917, following the death of his mother; then returned to Châlons. In June he was invalided out and settled in Lyons. He composed *Le Tombeau de Couperin* later in that year; each of its six movements is dedicated to the memory of a friend killed at the front.

"Between turbulent clouds, by the flicker of lightning, one may catch glimpses of waltzing couples"—the clouds must be trailing at ground level. Intermittent flashes of lightning illumine, for an instant, a dark scene in which one may then distinguish movement: It sounds more like the opening of a war film than a ballet celebrating the apotheosis of the waltz; or so Diaghilev must have thought. What then about the "Imperial Court, around 1855"? Surely that would be Vienna, the city of the waltz. There was waltzing at the Imperial Court "around 1855." There was also the gun fire of execution squads with which the House of Hapsburg sealed the bloody suppression of the Hungarian revolt. In the wake of a general uprising which had caused the Imperial family to flee from its capital and forced the permanent exile of the chancellor, Prince Metternich, the restored monarchy took such massive and merciless revenge on the leadership of its Hungarian dominions that even European heads of state, barely recovered from their own difficulties in the 1848 revolutions, tried to intercede. In vain. One probably could not hear the rattle of gun fire over the strains of the waltz, in that immense ballroom, under the full radiance of its chandeliers. But many in that turning crowd would have to waltz harder to shut out the faces of friends before the day's firing squad.

Ravel, in Paris of 1919, would seem to have been unable to shut out the faces of absent friends and scenes where movement was eerily illumunated by the sheet lightning of distant artillery fire. But in Paris of 1919, life sparkled and the scene must have become brighter and brighter as people delivered from a great horror danced harder, until the apotheosis of the dance itself became horrible. *La Valse* ends in a frenzy of celebration, or the paresis of frenzy. You decide. But with his indication of an Imperial Court around 1855, Ravel does seem to be telling us something that is very brilliantly represented in the music of the second half. Your assignment is to trace it.

N.B.: You may wish to use a recording. For the sort of comparison you are to undertake, the sensuous quality of the sounds is as important as their pitches. With the described image of *La Valse* in mind, do choose a performance that seems in accord with the outline we have suggested. Once the recording has served its purpose and you are able to "hear" the sounds in mind, put it aside until you have completed your work.

PODIUM

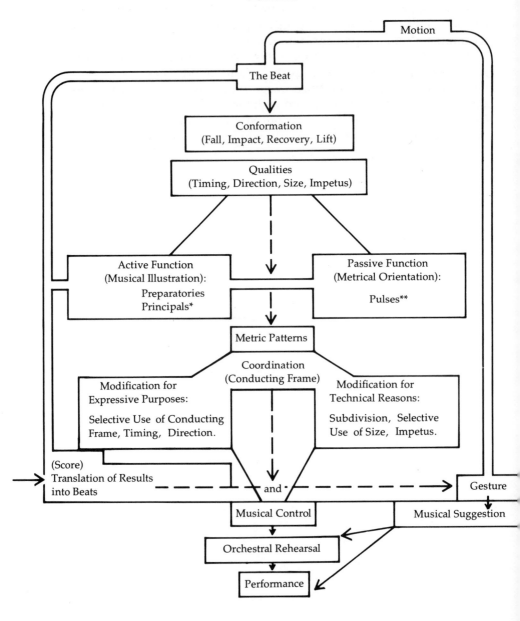

Motion

The Beat

Conformation
(Fall, Impact, Recovery, Lift)

Qualities
(Timing, Direction, Size, Impetus)

Active Function
(Musical Illustration):
Preparatories
Principals*

Passive Function
(Metrical Orientation):

Pulses**

Metric Patterns

Coordination
(Conducting Frame)

Modification for
Expressive Purposes:

Selective Use of Conducting
Frame, Timing, Direction.

Modification for
Technical Reasons:

Subdivision, Selective
Use of Size, Impetus.

(Score)
Translation of Results
into Beats

and

Gesture

Musical Control

Musical Suggestion

Orchestral Rehearsal

Performance

*Exception: *Series* of Principals: (*Passive* Function)   **Exception: *Accented* Pulse: (*Active* Function)

7

THE APPLICATION OF THE BEAT

The means of musical communication
from the podium are reviewed. As developed in the five preceding chapters, the
entire range of beats and combinations of
beats is applied to various examples of full
score, often with possible alternatives.
Rules and relevant summaries are
repeated verbatim as they appeared in
previous chapters; and extensive cross-
references indicate earlier, more detailed
discussion of the technical principles
involved.

THE theory of the conductor's beat, as presented in Part I of this
book, rests upon a set of very simple, interrelated principles. In practice, its application enables the conductor to monitor metric continuity,
to determine and control fluctuations in the musical flow, to assure
ensemble and balance of orchestral performance, and to illustrate
expressive detail. In addition, many of these multipurpose, visual signals need to be determined in instant response to some unexpected con-
tingency, yet must be clearly "legible" without reducing the effectiveness
of other messages to be vested *in the same beat*. It is clear that the application of the set of simple principles that inform the beat requires skills
and judgment of a very high order.

From the start, we have observed the existence of alternatives in the
execution of conducting motions and beats: choice of pivots, choice of
size or momentum of any beat, choice of active or passive function, even
choice of placement and direction of beats within the conducting frame.
Now we shall examine the opportunities offered by the selection of one
combination of beat characteristics over others. Determination of right
or wrong choices can be made only on the basis of the music itself,
hence our continuing occupation with techniques of preparing a score,
i.e. of learning how to use its evidence to form a living musical image.

Communication of the essentials of that image to an orchestra requires a knowledgeable, practiced, clear, and sensitive application of the beat.

We shall now examine a variety of score excerpts in terms of effective uses of appropriate beats. In some cases we shall find ourselves confronted by a possible choice among two or more equally effective ways of beating a passage. We shall then have to consider, for the first time in this text, the final variable in every conductor's decisions: the player.

Since violins, oboes, or trombones do not perform the music we conduct, but rather violinists, oboists, and trombonists, the proficiency and temperament of instrumentalists are factors to be considered, as is the nature of the orchestra in which they play. A group of gifted students in a school orchestra will expect (and require) a more controlling approach to the beat than will a professional orchestra with established traditions of bowing style, a certain brass sound, and, most important, a core of repertory works. Clearly, an experienced conductor might vary his approach to the beat considerably, depending on the expectation of the person on the receiving end of his signal. The necessary flexibility, not only in terms of the score, but also in consideration of the player, can best be developed by a very careful viewing and understanding of alternatives in the application of the beat.

We shall begin by matching *aspects* of the theory of baton technique, as developed in Part I, with opportunities for appropriate application in selected examples of score. These examples will be grouped according to their usefulness as illustrations for principles of the beat that have been examined in Chapters 1–5. Summaries which appeared in the text have been reprinted, together with page references to facilitate more extensive reiew.

The descriptions and commentary which accompany suggested solutions and possible alternatives should be studied with care. Instant and apparently instinctive decisions on the podium are not any less the product of intelligence and understanding for all the need to choose with lightning speed. Over and above their function as practical illustrations, the examples have been chosen for their usefulness in providing the background for considerations and eventual decisions that will be yours to make when printed pages of score pose lively sets of questions and when your answers, in performance, shall depend on your success in clarifying musical intent.

As an aid in maintaining perspective on the overall system of the beat, the Podium charts which headed the second halves of chapters 1–5 are reprinted throughout the text of this chapter. In this sense, we are about to begin a comprehensive review. In another, we are now ready to take the first, and essentially subjective, steps in demonstrating the unity of score and podium, in which musically logical decisions may only be effective to the extent of their complementary reflection in the beat.

PODIUM: REVIEW I

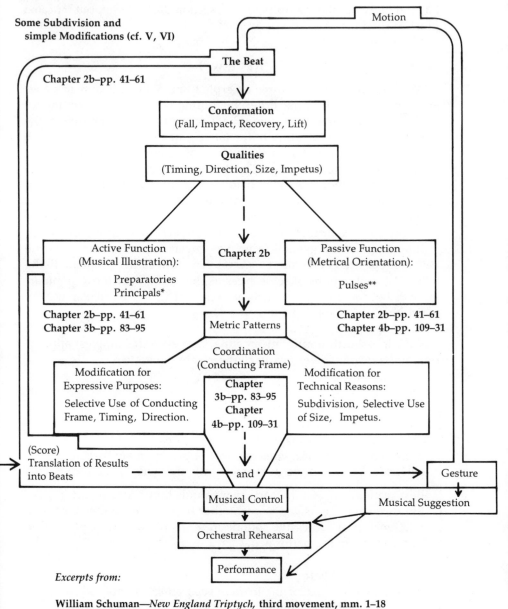

**The Beat and its Conformation
Qualities and Functions
Plain Metric Patterns**

**Some Subdivision and
simple Modifications (cf. V, VI)**

Motion

The Beat

Chapter 2b–pp. 41–61

Conformation
(Fall, Impact, Recovery, Lift)

Qualities
(Timing, Direction, Size, Impetus)

Active Function
(Musical Illustration):

Chapter 2b

Passive Function
(Metrical Orientation):

Preparatories
Principals*

Pulses**

Chapter 2b–pp. 41–61
Chapter 3b–pp. 83–95

Metric Patterns

Chapter 2b–pp. 41–61
Chapter 4b–pp. 109–31

Coordination
(Conducting Frame)

Modification for
Expressive Purposes:

Selective Use of Conducting
Frame, Timing, Direction.

**Chapter
3b–pp. 83–95
Chapter
4b–pp. 109–31**

Modification for
Technical Reasons:

Subdivision, Selective Use
of Size, Impetus.

(Score)
Translation of Results
into Beats

and ·

Gesture

Musical Control

Musical Suggestion

Orchestral Rehearsal

Performance

Excerpts from:

William Schuman—*New England Triptych,* third movement, mm. 1–18
second movement, mm. 28–42
first movement, mm. 152–79

*Exception: *Series* of Principals: (*Passive* Function)   **Exception: *Accented* Pulse: (*Active* Function)

The time you will require to work through this chapter, in relation to the three Score chapters of Part II and the other two dealing with the uses of podium control, is a matter of personal preference and the circumstances of your study. But you are urged to go slowly, to review a lot, and to try out the examples in each section during brief, but repeated practice sessions.

Review I

We shall work through three excerpts from William Schuman's *New England Triptych* in reverse order, beginning with *Chester*, a setting for winds of a William Billings hymn that became the marching song of the American Continental Army in the late eighteenth century, and which serves as Introduction for the third panel of Schuman's triptych.

Even in their studied simplicity these measures require skills of the beat that touch upon more than half the categories on our Podium chart. In addition to general definitions of the beat, its conformation, and its possible qualities, the categories of metric patterns, active and passive functions, and coordination within the conducting frame are involved.

Summaries of the general principles governing these aspects of the beat are reprinted herewith, as they appeared in earlier chapters. In the following explorations of score excerpts, however, only those summaries will be quoted again which are relevant to the particular way in which the beat is applied.

N.B.: It is worth noting, meanwhile, that even the simplest application of the beat involves nearly all there is to the system.

The beat
shows when to play,
indicates how to play,
controls the musical shape of individual lines,
coordinates all musical lines in terms of precision and balance,
determines interchange of musical initiative within the orchestra.

Beats cannot suggest the particular sounds they are to reflect.
But beats may be related to each other so as to match the expressive relationship of successive sounds in terms of your prior perception of the music being performed. (p. 41)

Conformation of the beat:
A beat may consist of up to four separate elements: fall, impact, recovery, and lift. Of these, the lift may sometimes be used by itself, in place of a complete beat. (p. 47)

Qualities of the beat:
Beats may exhibit some or all of the following qualities:

1. Timing
2. Direction
3. Size
4. Impetus

(p. 58)

The four *elements* of which a beat may be formed reflect the *qualities* of that beat in the following manner:

Conformation of the Beat	Timing	Direction	Size	Impetus
Fall	variable	downward, in direction of metric coordinate	variable	variable
Impact	exact (tempo)	none	none	variable
Recovery	variable (relates to *following* beat)	upward	variable, smaller than fall	variable, less than fall
Lift	variable (relates to *following* beat)	upward, and in opposite direction of following beat	variable	variable

N.B. Although this chart contains only information already familiar to us, the import of listing variable qualities of the beat in the context of its conformation becomes quite remarkable when we extrapolate observations like these:

Beat qualities—effect on beat conformation:

Timing — *Only the impact* of fast or slow beats *varies* in exact proportion to the tempo.

Direction — *Except for the impact,* all elements of a beat include either upward or downward movement as a determining feature within their overall *drection*.

Size — *Big or little beats* may vary at the conductor's discretion only in the size of their *fall* or their *lift.*

Impetus — Only the *impetus* may vary in all four elements of a beat. But the *impetus* of the *recovery* portion must be *less than* that of *the fall.*

Metric patterns (plain meters):

> Beats are grouped into patterns, according to the number of metric divisions per measure shown in the time signature.
>
> Patterns of 2, 3, and 4 may be formed entirely of active beats. All other patterns require the additional use of pulses for clarification (viz. Chapter 4).
>
> The distribution of strong and weak stresses according to the conductor's perception of the music remains the *variable* function of beats, regardless of their position within the pattern (p. 83).

Exercise 1.

William Schuman, New England Triptych, *Third Movement*—Chester

The opening of this movement is scored for woodwinds. The beat is a moderate four, mezzoforte without additional dynamic nuances except a general instruction to play legato, dolce. The composer himself has marked equal phrase lengths of four measures each, ending the first three of these on a whole note with a comma for breath. The chorale character of this setting is supported by its texture and by the title *Chester*, a hymn of the American Revolution, presented here in its original harmonization by William Billings.

Thus we have a perfect vehicle for the application of undifferentiated beats, one for each quarter and none particularly in need of expressive preparation or fulfillment. An anthem is not usually conducted with great emotional fervor, and the "religioso" caption, together with a dolce instruction in the opening lines of music, suggest inwardness rather than passion. A plain pattern of four is indicated, with small, even beats, well connected and with little impetus in order to suggest the prescribed legato marking.

In terms of the chart, we are definitely working along the right-hand side of the beat-formation diagram. Well-connected beats need recoveries: thus pulses are excluded, for their recoveries are minimal. Nor will preparatories be required, as we have already determined that our beats shall be devoid of expressive preparation or fulfillment. That leaves principals, which, in absence of preparatories, lose their active function. And having, to the extent of eliminating preparatories and pulses, strayed to the left-hand side of our chart momentarily, we shall remind ourselves of the relevant function of the principal beat.

EXAMPLE 1: William Schuman, *New England Triptych*, third movement—*Chester*

The principal beat: active function:

> A succession of principals, regardless of tempo or dynamics, tends to become undifferentiated. After prolonged absence of preparatories or pulses between principals, the function of principal beats becomes passive. (pp. 49, 54)

That description fits our requirements for the opening of *Chester*. The illustrations on page 55 remind us of the conformation of principal beats. We shall combine them in a pattern of four while we beat *and sing* the excerpt. One more aspect needs to be mentioned—the special characteristic of the downbeat in relation to the conducting frame.

The fall of the downbeat is not to be modified.

> The first beat, in any metric pattern and regardless of function, is always given in a downward direction, through the center.

> The first beat, in any metric pattern and regardless of function, is the only beat ever to extend substantially below the center before recovery. (p. 90)

The object of this exercise is a plain pattern of four, at moderate speed, without expressive illustrations, *with music. You* provide that music: sing, and watch your beat very closely as you conduct.

1. *Pattern of four. Principal beats.* Observe the fall of each beat: gentle impetus (dolce); smooth recovery: impetus dissipating until it disappears completely, just as the next beat is begun (legato, dolce). The conformation of every beat should look exactly like Figure 1. Beats should be small, but big enough to allow for a recovery smaller than the fall, yet large enough to make a smooth connection.

FIGURE 1

2. Now we experiment.

Pattern of four.
Pulses on second
and third beats:

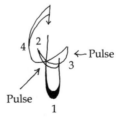

FIGURE 2

The effect of Figure 2 is that of preparatories on four leading to principals on one, connected by two pulses (on two and three). Why preparatories? Why not principals on four, as in the previous pattern? Because the small pulses on the second and third beats would only allow an even smaller recovery, and the fall of four (which may not "extend substantially below the center") is also too small to accommodate a recovery large enough for a normal upbeat *unless it is turned into the lift of a preparatory.* The effect of preparatories on *every* fourth beat is unwanted.

<table>
<tr>
<td>Pattern of four.
Pulses on second
and third beats
of second and fourth
bars only. First and
third bars: principals.</td>
<td>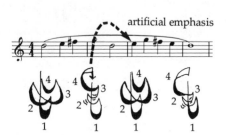</td>
</tr>
</table>

FIGURE 3

The effect of preparatories on four, now in the second and fourth measures only of each phrase, works very well for the final bars (Figure 3), but creates an artificial emphasis for the beginning of the penultimate ones. We conclude:

<table>
<tr>
<td>Pattern of four.
Three measures of
principals, the
fourth consisting
of a principal, two
pulses and a preparatory.</td>
<td></td>
</tr>
</table>

FIGURE 4

Figure 4 will also provide an alternative solution to the comma problem: A fairly strong preparatory, through center,* will mean "breathe."

---

*The illustrations on p. 86 do *not* show a "center" through which all beats cross, since the lines would then blur. Actual beats, however, should swing through a center.

EXAMPLE 2: William Schuman, *New England Triptych*, second movement—*When Jesus Wept*, mm. 28–43

Exercise 2.

William Schuman, New England Triptych, *Second Movement*—When Jesus Wept, *mm. 28–43*

Measures 28–31 of the second movement of Schuman's *New England Triptych,* scored for strings, offer much the same basis for a choice of beat as the opening of the third, except that the meter is in three. But with the upbeat to m. 32 a vast difference in expressive content must find its visual equivalent in the beat we use. The reason is harmonic. If you cannot imagine the sound of the first and third beats of m. 32, play them on the piano, beginning with the G major of m. 31. Clearly we have not shifted to the left-hand side of the beat chart, and shall have to review the expressive potential of preparatories in order to signal before the harmony changes, the sort of effect we are seeking.

Functions of the beat:

Beats may be arranged to serve either an active or a passive function, depending on the conductor's perception of the expressive relationship between individual sounds of a musical shape.

Active beats accumulate, raise, lower or release tension. They may anticipate or reflect descriptive, dynamic, or tempo changes. They are explicit technical means to control or repair ensemble.

Passive beats are neutral. They serve neither for expressive illustration nor for the assertion of technical control. A series of passive beats may yield initiative without diminishing control. Passive beats heighten the expressive effect of active beats which precede or follow.

Active and passive beats are aids to metric orientation; are formed into metric patterns; constitute visual equivalents of the smallest components within a musical phrase. (p. 49)

Varieties of the beat: active and passive varieties of beat

The preparatory beat—active function at all times.

The principal beat—active function except in undifferentiated series.

The pulsing beat—passive function except when accented. (p. 49)

We shall also review the stated functions of the preparatory beat as well as the complete characteristics of the principal beat (partially reprinted with preceding example).

The preparatory beat (active function):

It signals *and* characterizes the following beat.
Characterization of the following beat is the purpose of the *lift of the preparatory beat.*

Preparatories may follow preparatories. In some cases, the cumulative effect may result in an actual crescendo. It will inevitably increase the expressive tension.

In musical examples we shall use the symbol $\int$ for preparatories.
(p. 51)

The principal beat (active function*):

The principal beat *releases tension* accumulated by one or more preceding preparatories. Principals *relate to the character of their preparatory beats,* usually in confirmation but sometimes in contrast.

---

* A succession of principals, regardless of tempo or dynamics, tends to become undifferentiated. After prolonged absence of preparatories or pulses between principals, the function of the principal beats become passive.

> *The character of a principal is established in their fall.* There is *no lift* after recovery.

> In musical examples we use the symbol ↓ for principals.   (p. 54)

Armed with this reminder of the functions of preparatory and principal beats, we return to our excerpt from the second movement of Schuman's *New England Triptych*. Measure 28 through beats one and two of m. 31 will be like the third-movement example above. Before we try a suitable preparatory to the downbeat of m. 32, get the sound of that first chord and its effect after the sustained G major of the preceding measures well into your ear. Then try to hear the harmonic change on beat 3 of m. 32, and finally the whole succession of harmonies, beginning with the G chord. For, as always, *the beat must reflect your experience and your sound image* of this passage. The musical shape which will be heard should˙ then produce a similar experience for the listener.

Taking these two chords and their respective anticipation in isolation, we have two entirely different problems: the preparation of the first beat of m. 32 comes as a new beginning after the phrase begun at m. 28. The composer might well have marked a comma after the second beat of m. 31. The timing of the preparatory and the "when" of the first principal on m. 32 are flexible within fine limits set by the conductor. The same cannot be said of the third beat of m. 32. The sensual appeal of the chord is no less striking than that of the first beat, but the flow of the melody must not be interrupted in midphrase: part of the richness of Schuman's harmonic effects depends on the very simplicity of the melodic pulse. Thus the two D's—the three of m. 31 and the two of m. 32—are both preparatories for unexpected displays of harmonic color, but only the first of these may affect the even tempo.

It would be logical and effective to indicate a slight hesitation on the upbeat D in the first violins which prepares the downbeat of m. 32. The review summary below should be studied with particular care for its important distinction between stress on the recovery vs. stress on the lift portion of the beat to be modified in terms of tempo.

Tempo and modified conformation of the beat:

> Special emphasis on the *recovery* portion of the beat, at the expense of the *fall*, encourages *forward* movement of the tempo.

> *N.B. 1:* Recovery (natural rebound after impact) must not be confused with *lift* (conscious extension of upward motion beyond recovery, in preparatory beats). Emphasis on the *lift* portion tends to slow movement of the beat and to inhibit forward movement of tempo.

> *N.B. 2:* The most essential factor in encouraging forward movement of tempo remains the systematic reduction in *size* of beats.   (p. 128)

N.B. 1 is the relevant passage for the purpose of anticipating m. 32 with a slight hesitation in its upbeat. An emphasis on the lift portion of the upbeat D will be accompanied by just the slight hesitation we wish to employ. The result will not only be a small delay in the attack of m. 32, but also, by comparison with the emphasized lift on the preparatory, an apparent reduction in sound on the principal first beat. If it can be managed, this should suggest the special flavor of that chord, while at the same time guarding against exaggeration by the slight reduction in actual sound when it is attacked. But how is this to be done?

The secret lies in close attention to the center of the conducting frame. As the third beat of m. 31 moves inward and up in preparation for the downbeat on m. 32, it should *remain near the center* until a small upward motion will introduce the next beat at normal speed. *This means a slower speed for the inward motion, toward center, at the beginning of the third beat.*

Practice this a few times with performers actually following your beat. A pianist will do; any combination of singers, string players, or winds would be better. One must learn to *feel* the controlled hesitation of an inward-moving, hesitating preparatory and of the slightly softer attack on the downbeat. Take great care to pass the upbeat *through center* and not in a shorter line upward. The feeling should be one of delaying the actual lift, until the signal for the next attack is actually given. Just how much is enough or too much is a matter of trial and error. And let it be said once again: the judgment of the effect achieved lies in instant comparison with the image in your mind. A glance at our chart will confirm, not only that even with such an apparently simple upbeat problem we are on both sides of the conformation-coordination-control axis, but that we had to work through all aspects of the beat adding up to musical control. At that point, the input on the score side of the "conducting coin" becomes the determining factor: the result of our personal identification with the music—the image.

The third beat of m. 32, another extension of the harmonic framework of this phrase, is prepared by the second beat of that measure. Tempo must remain even, but there is no harm in slightly increased emphasis on beat 3. We can therefore use a normal preparatory, taking care to bring the third beat inward again, through center, because the downbeat of m. 33 should be a pulse. Since the third beat of m. 32 is a releasing principal (i.e. without lift), a slight recovery *from center* is sufficient to connect it to the first-beat pulse of m. 33. There would follow a succession of preparatories, the most difficult of which is the last, the upbeat to m. 35: diminuendo to pianissimo, dolce cantabile. Again, a slowing beat, drawn inward toward the center, should achieve just such a result. You might even draw your hands a little closer to your chest, to dramatize the *diminishing volume at the crest of a cumulative harmonic tension.* *

Measures 36 and 37 will be treated much like mm. 38 and 29, except for the crescendo beginning in the second measure, and perhaps the beginning of a slight forward movement through m. 38: the tensile strength of added octaves makes for cumulative momentum. In m. 41 this momentum is broken, with a diminuendo and simultaneous return to the original tempo. Now is the time to remind ourselves of the technique of applying a brake to gathering speed by subdivision.

Subdivision and tempo:

> When a change of tempo is accompanied by a change in the number of subdivisions per measure . . . *preparatory subdivisions are powerful indicators of a rate of retard.*   (p. 124)

Subdivision by preparatories emphasizes special situations.

> *Expressive significance of the second half* of a slow beat may be illustrated by the lift portion of the first half, bending into a direction exaggerating recovery as any other preparatory.
>
> *Expressive reference to a following main beat* in slow tempo may be stressed by a preparatory second half of any subdivided beat. In that case, the first half should be kept shorter.
>
> *Steadying of orchestral ensemble* can often be achieved by one or two sharply accented subdivisions on the second halves of beats not normally subdivided. If the problem requires a slight tightening of tempo, *accented pulses* will suffice. If a slow tempo must be achieved or maintained, however, the extended sweep of *preparatory lifts* provides a more deliberate application of control. In order to avoid excessive accents on the following attacks (viz.: there is *always* an expressive effect after true preparatories), main beats might be given less forcfully than would normally be the case. In any event, *first* halves of beats subdivided by preparatories should be short.
>
> *Subdividing preparatories should originate at or near the center.* Beats to be subdivided by a preparatory must therefore recover at or near the center.
>
> *Beats subdivided by preparatories are read* by the orchestra, within the context of the metric pattern, *in terms of the direction of their fall.* Inasmuch as the fall of any beat assumes greater or lesser downward direction depending on its impetus, the direction is determined by the movement of the baton *in overall relation to the center:* left, right, up, or down.   (p. 115)

*Cf. pivots, p. 21.

Thus the second beat of m. 41 will have a short first half in order to accommodate a longer, second-half, preparatory subdivision. Well executed, this sudden steadying of the forward movement of tempo by a preparatory will require no more than one subdivision, the two-*and* of m. 41. Once more this is really a matter of "feeling" the beat. The best way of achieving this will be by thorough review of the accelerando and ritardando exercises in the previous chapter. Once established, the tempo should lose further momentum as the volume and intensity diminish during the next two measures.

Exercise 3

William Schuman, *New England Triptych*, first movement—*Be Glad Then, America*, mm. 152–71
The tempo remains constant, at a fast ♩ = 160, in 2 / 4 meter. Dynamic level *p* throughout, except for two *fp* accents to introduce the B pedalpoint endings of the first two phrases. Bracket phrases as marked. Two special problems: a very real need to give cues for all entrances, with minimal motion to avoid premature crescendo (the *p* level will need to be maintained for forty measures!); and every entrance occurs *after* the beat.

The entire passage may be controlled with pulses. We recall that there are two kinds: the neutral and the active, accented. The pulse is an ideal beat when tempo is steady and dynamics remain constant. It is also a remarkably accurate indicator of attacks which must be very carefully timed and executed by players who are not necessarily well placed on stage to hear the preceding "musical" cue very clearly. The visual cue given by the conductor on the rostrum is more often needed for precision in timing than as a reminder of the particular measure in which the entrance is expected.

Our example requires both kinds of cue: the general reminder which is mostly a matter of looking at the player(s) about one measure in advance of attack to confirm the entrance; and the precision of split-second timing which combines eye-contact warning with visual assistance in the actual placing of an attack. Cello cues in mm. 157 and 169 are of the latter kind, as are the viola and the second violin entrances at m. 163, and the first violin entrance at m. 166. All other cues rely on eye contact and on the players' own orientation within the metric framework of a rapid but steady pulse. (*N.B.* A possible exception could be m. 152, in which the string fugato is first introduced, *and the p level set.* The dynamic caution, on which the overall effect of this passage depends, is probably more acutely needed than mere confirmation of the accurate count of measures of rest.)

EXAMPLE 3: William Schuman, *New England Triptych*, first movement—
Be Glad Then, America, mm. 152–80.

The entrances singled out for special attention will be given as *accented pulses*. It will be recalled that this particular beat has a tendency to push the tempo forward.* At every one of the attacks singled out for appli-

*Cf. p. 125.

cation of this beat, there is a danger of slightly delayed entrances after the beat. The small but extraordinarily effective accented pulse is intended to be the proverbial ounce of prevention which may save you many a pound of frustration in rehearsal. Time for review:

The pulsing beat—neutral (passive function):
> The neutral pulsing beat—by far the most commonly used—*marks the passage of time in terms of metric divisions.*
>
> *As main divisions* of the measure (those specified in the time signature), pulses are characterized by minimum fall and recovery, accurate timing, little impetus and normal direction. They do pass through the center like all other beats.
>
> *As subdivisions* (see below), pulses are placed at the end of main division beats, also with minimum fall and recovery and accurate timing, but without passing through the center (they only mark the halfway point of the main beat they subdivide).
>
> *Pulses have negative expressive value:* neutral in themselves, they throw into relief the expressive value of active beats around them. Thus *they play an important role in clarifying the shapes of phrases.*
>
> In musical examples we use the symbol O for a pulse.   (p. 56)

The accented pulse (active function):
> Unlike all other active beats, the accented pulse has no expressive function. It serves to signal and define an unexpected attack, either at the beginning of a piece, after an unmeasured pause, or upon the first noticeable effect of an increase of tempo (i.e. when the following attack is to take place earlier than anticipated, thus establishing a rate of accelerando).

The accented pulse shares these characteristics with other pulses:
> Like other pulses, it marks the passage of time—*but it is the passage of time to come.*
>
> Like other pulses, as a *subdivision,* it is placed at the end of a main division beat, with minimum fall and recovery and sharing its direction—*but with powerful impetus.*
>
> Like other pulses, it has no expressive value—*but also no expressive function* (i.e. effect on the following beat).
>
> *Unlike* other pulses, it does not clarify the shapes of phrases—*it anticipates tempo.*   (p. 125)

Conducting this excerpt from the first movement of *New England Triptych* is, as we have indicated, an exercise in alternating two kinds of pulsing beats to achieve two different kinds of musical control: an unobtrusive succession of *neutral pulses*, with timely warnings to sections about to join the musical flow; and an occasional *accented pulse* to impel an instant response where it is deemed essential.

Before you attempt this passage, memorize the melody, the phrase bracketing, and the way various portions of the single line are distributed among the four string sections. Beginning with m. 153 you will find three two-measure brackets: cello–viola–cello. The last, completing the first phrase on pedal B, is introduced by a *fp* which is to receive the first accented pulse. With the upbeat to m. 160 the same is repeated: two measures of viola, two measures of first violin, and the pedal B, this time in the viola. *But* the new pedal B is not given two measures: instead, the continuation of the phrase (second violin) begins on the very measure of the viola pedal, a risky link in the very fine chain of fast-moving melodic development. Accented pulses on *both* beats of m. 163 should insure unbroken continuity. The second violin upbeat to m. 164 introduces a two-measure statement ending on pedal F♯ in m. 166, over which—at once and with another accented pulse—the first violins are brought in to repeat that statement in an elongated, three-measure version. Finally (m. 169), upon the heels of the first violin's F♯ conclusion, and prodded on by another accented pulse, the cellos introduce what is to become a one-measure "capsule" of the melodic outline just presented by the two violin sections. This is then passed back and forth between the strings with the baffling speed, split-second timing and irresistibly controlled forward movement with which a fine basketball team prepares to score.

Go over the outline, the distribution of voices, and the placing of entrances. Imagine the direction, from your podium, in which cues are to be given. Recall the accented pulses. Conduct.

REVIEW II

EXAMPLES 4, 5, 6, and 8 are the technical equivalents of the third, second, and opening movements of Schuman's *New England Triptych*, in terms of the beat. Ravel's *Enchanted Garden*, the last movement of his *Mother Goose Suite*, opens in much the same serene and deliberate pace as *Chester*; the *Meistersinger* overture requires more alternation between preparatories, principals, and pulses than the Ravel piece, which may be left to develop its own momentum with largely passive beats.

Both works invite some independent experimentation on the part of the student conductor with regard to varieties of the beat. By establishing an even pace, monitored by a series of principal beats, and then

PODIUM: REVIEW II

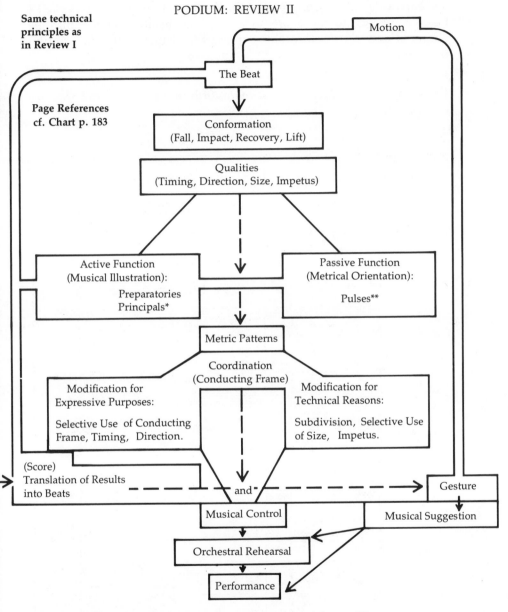

Same technical principles as in Review I

Motion

The Beat

Page References
cf. Chart p. 183

Conformation
(Fall, Impact, Recovery, Lift)

Qualities
(Timing, Direction, Size, Impetus)

Active Function
(Musical Illustration):

Preparatories
Principals*

Passive Function
(Metrical Orientation):

Pulses**

Metric Patterns

Coordination
(Conducting Frame)

Modification for
Expressive Purposes:

Selective Use of Conducting
Frame, Timing, Direction.

Modification for
Technical Reasons:

Subdivision, Selective Use
of Size, Impetus.

(Score)
Translation of Results
into Beats

and

Gesture

Musical Control

Musical Suggestion

Orchestral Rehearsal

Performance

Ravel, *Mother Goose Suite*, V (*The Enchanted Garden*): beat as Schuman III
Wagner, Overture to *Die Meistersinger*,: beat as Schuman III
Mahler, *Symphony No. 4*, m. 2 problem: beat as m. 31, Schuman II
Tchaikovsky, *Symphony No. 4*, Scherzo,: beat as Schuman I

---

*Exception: *Series* of Principals: (*Passive* Function)   **Exception: *Accented* Pulse: (*Active* Function)

systematically altering any part of the conformation of *arbitrarily chosen* beats according to the chart on p. 61, the resulting effects may be observed and *felt:* a self-teaching process for which verbal description is no substitute.

EXAMPLE 4: Ravel, *Mother Goose Suite,* fifth movement—*The Enchanted Garden*

Exercise 4

Ravel, *Mother Goose Suite*, fifth movement—*The Enchanted Garden*

The third beat of the second measure of Ravel's *Enchanted Garden*, for instance, begins a modest crescendo. You have, thus far, been beating small principals. Now you will decide to add a *lift* portion to this third beat of m. 2, making it into a preparatory beat. (Try it!)

The result focuses emphasis on the first beat of m. 3. In order to avoid a heavy stress (clearly not intended by the composer), you have two choices: either you will inhibit that stress by diminishing the *fall* of the first beat (this would result in a special effect, expressive but rather fussy and premature in a movement which features one big crescendo as its overall design); or you will avert the premature release of tension by following the upbeat preparatory with a whole series of preparatories, interrupting the accumulating momentum and volume on the first beat of m. 5, subito piano. (Regardless of how modest your rate of increase might be, the total effect would hardly be *"poco* cresc.")

Next you will try to enlarge the size of the fall of every beat, beginning with the third of m. 2, *without enlarging recovery or increasing impetus.* This results in a very sustained legato series of principals, a very gradual crescendo, and avoids featuring any one beat (provided you do not increase recovery, i.e. run the risk of apparent preparatories). A very good solution.

Now try a completely different approach: at the beginning of the crescendo *reduce* the size of fall and recovery of all beats. As the principals become pulses, the crescendo may be suggested by the left hand. The result is more personal: an intensification of vibrato, for instance, together with the crescendo, would add to the effect—but perhaps too soon. This is not a decision to be made at this time. (It is precisely the kind of decision which may only be made after our work on the score has reached the stage at which its *results* are translated, "measure by measure into beats and gestures."*) But it does illustrate, through observation and by "feel," that there are usually alternative ways of achieving technically satisfactory solutions which, nonetheless, create very different musical effects.

Exercise 5

Wagner, Overture to Die Meistersinger

In terms of the beat, its qualities, and the physical aspects of coordination and control, the opening of Wagner's *Meistersinger* overture

*Cf. Flow chart, beginning of this chapter, stage E.

requires the same skills as the last movement of Ravel's *Mother Goose Suite*. As in the previous example, we are dealing with a moderate, even tempo in plain meter, a homophonic orchestral texture, and a harmonic

EXAMPLE 5: Wagner, Overture to *Die Meistersinger*

progression free of surprises that might have to be stressed or modified by the beat in order to reflect the composer's intention. In some ways, the overture may even appear more straightforward: it is certainly robust, dynamically even, and steady in its marchlike pace. But whether we use an imaginary orchestra or face a real one, there are problems which will affect the beat. The independence of the bass rhythm is one (m. 2—a preparatory for the A octave must be *directed* there), and the series of preparatories beginning with the eighth-note motion in the fourth measure also starts, and must *be* started, with the bass. Less obvious is the implication of the orchestration at the very beginning. *Except* for the bass, continuity in the first measure belongs to the wind and brass. The *sehr kräftig* (very strong) in the bass, and again in all strings in the second measure, must match the *sehr gehalten* (molto sostenuto) of the winds. Too much separation and attack in the strings would produce a false accent on the first beat of m. 2 and would, if continued, make the entire first measure seem weak by comparison. Instead, the sustained, choralelike character we found in the opening of Schuman's *Chester* should realize Wagner's apparent intentions much more successfully than the heavy-handed "march" which is likely to result from thoughtless application of unfocused, large beats (cf. pp. 188–89).

Exercise 6

Mahler, Symphony No. 4, *first movement*
    The opening of Mahler's *Fourth Symphony* looks like another example of neutral and accented pulses. The first upbeat should be a small preparatory, released into a measure of neutral pulses. The second and fourth beats of m. 2 shall be accented pulses to set off the *sf*. But with the violin entrance in m. 3 the entire conducting strategy changes, as does the music. The best way of clarifying the difference is to pretend that the woodwind passage does not exist, so that the movement would begin with the ritardando upbeat in the first violins. Beat the entire third measure with principals at moderate speed, reflecting the music to come. The third beat falls into the category of "subdivision by preparatory to emphasize a special situation" (cf. p. 113), and presents the same problem as m. 41 of the *New England Triptych:* a sudden retard beginning *after* a main beat. As before, we shall show only one subdivision to indicate the rate of retard. The fourth beat will be an undivided preparatory, and the first beat of m. 4 resumes the moderato main tempo (*pp!*) at a slightly more deliberate pace.* Once the woodwinds and

*N.B. The retard at the end of the third measure applies *only* to violins and clarinets. The flutes and sleighbells continue at the original speed.

EXAMPLE 6: Mahler, *Symphony No. 4*, first movement

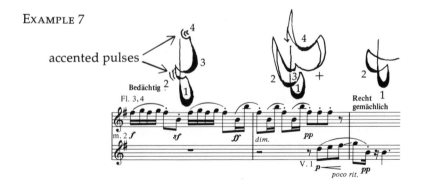

sleighbells are restored to your total image of this opening, you will find that conducting it involves exactly what we have already indicated, including the sudden interruption by an introductory retard into an apparently unrelated, new musical beginning.

EXAMPLE 7

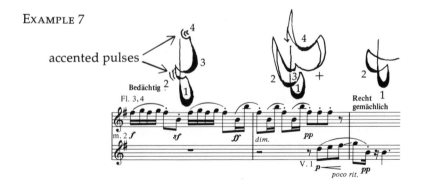

EXAMPLE 8: Tchaikovsky, *Symphony No. 4*, second movement

Exercise 7

Tchaikovsky, Symphony No. 4, *second movement*

The Scherzo movement from Tchaikovsky's *Fourth Symphony (Pizzi-cato Ostinato)* provides marvelous opportunities for practicing neutral and accented pulses, for acquiring a physical sense of the difference, and of the equally important difference between a neutral pulse and a very small, active beat of any kind. You can demonstrate this for your own benefit by beating the piece at a somewhat slower than usual pace ($\.$ = c. 132), and at an imaginary *mf* dynamic level. Increase the tempo gradually to $\.$ =c. 172, rather faster than most performances. Maintain the small beats and the *mf* level until top speed is reached; then reduce the size of the beats until they no longer look and feel as agitated and frantic as even small beats will at such a tempo: suddenly you will be beating pulses. If you repeat this experiment a few times, you will find that you always arrive at the same result: there will not be a gradual transition from small beats to even smaller ones. Suddenly there will be pulses. At that point, beginning with a small preparatory and an initial principal on the first beat of the first measure, beat the entire opening of the Scherzo with pulses, using gesture (left hand) for the crescendo and decrescendo passages. From mm. 17–24 *accented* pulses will provide a useful prod to keep the cellos and basses up to tempo, and to furnish a natural in-between beat from which to develop small principals as the crescendo and the intensity mount. This time the left hand will only be used to signal subito piano before m. 21. The right will resume accented pulses as before. From m. 25 conduct the base line (with *very* light pulses). The afterbeats in the upper voices will follow. From m. 33 you may wish to try accented pulses on every first beat until m. 36, likewise mm. 37–40. After that nearly in *one* until m. 48. Conduct mm. 49–56 like mm. 17–24; then mm. 57–76 virtually in *one*; m. 77 as at the beginning.

Special care must be taken lest, at such a fast tempo, measures beaten in *one* for convenience appear to receive false accents by inadvertence. If a little extra impetus on the first beat is required (e.g. to prod afterbeats), accented pulses in *two* are to be preferred.

REVIEW III: SUBDIVISION AND BEAT PATTERNS OF COMPOUND AND MIXED METERS

In addition to its uses as a beat in itself, the neutral pulse lends perspective to other kinds of beat, in terms of quality (size, impetus: the right-hand side of the beat chart) as well as function (shape of phrase, tension and release: the left-hand side). As part of the former, *the pulse clarifies compound and mixed meter patterns. We have viewed these as combinations of simple and triple subdivisions.*

The pulsing beat

| provides additional metric reference points between main beats of any pattern.

PODIUM: REVIEW III

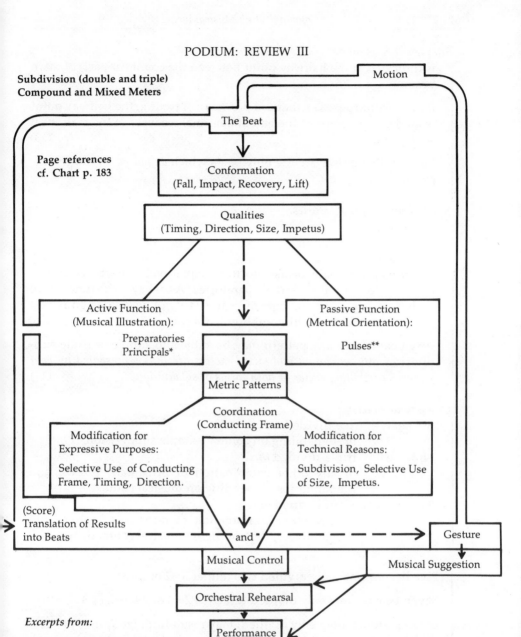

Subdivision (double and triple)
Compound and Mixed Meters

Motion

The Beat

Page references
cf. Chart p. 183

Conformation
(Fall, Impact, Recovery, Lift)

Qualities
(Timing, Direction, Size, Impetus)

Active Function
(Musical Illustration):

Preparatories
Principals*

Passive Function
(Metrical Orientation):

Pulses**

Metric Patterns

Coordination
(Conducting Frame)

Modification for
Expressive Purposes:

Selective Use of Conducting
Frame, Timing, Direction.

Modification for
Technical Reasons:

Subdivision, Selective Use
of Size, Impetus.

(Score)
Translation of Results
into Beats

and

Gesture

Musical Control

Musical Suggestion

Orchestral Rehearsal

Excerpts from:

Performance

Debussy, *Nuages* **mm. 1–4, 11–22**
Ravel, *Mother Goose Suite,* **II—*Tom Thumb,* mm. 1–11**
Copland, *Music for the Theater*

---

*Exception: *Series* of Principals: (*Passive* Function)   **Exception: *Accented* Pulse: (*Active* Function)

Simple subdivision

> is indicated at the halfway point between the count (impact) of main beats.
>
> If the only purpose is enhanced precision of timing, the halfway point is marked by a pulse at the end of a normal recovery of the main beat so divided. (p. 113)
>
> Subdividing pulses are the only beats which *do not pass through center.*

Subdivision by preparatories:

> See p. 194

Triple subdivision:

> Subdivision of main beats into three equal metric units requires a combination of pulses and preparatories. As always, the function of each unit determines its type of beat. Clarity of visual design is best served by alternating different kinds of beat. (p. 116)
>
> Any beat within any pattern may be subject to simple or triple subdivision. *All compound and mixed meters are thus represented by beat patterns combining either or both forms of subdivision.* (p. 117)

Compound meters:

> Six beats = triple-divided *two*
>   or, depending on context, simple subdivision of *three.*
> Nine beats = triple-divided *three*
>   or any other combination of principals, pulses, and preparatories, depending on musical context.
> Twelve beats = triple-divided *four*
>   or any other combination of principals, pulses, and preparatories, depending on musical context.   (p. 117)

Mixed meters:

> Five beats = unevenly divided two (either 3+2 or 2+3)
>
> Seven beats = unevenly divided three (2+2+3 or 2+3+2 or 3+2+2)
>
> Other patterns, unevenly divided, may result from groupings of subdivisions distributed in similar fashion within two, three, or four main beats. This includes uneven division of even meters (e.g. the sum of eight beats need not consist of 2+2+2+2 = simple subdivision of four; it could be 3+3+2, mixed subdivision of three).
>
> Compound and mixed meters may, in themselves, serve as main beats for further subdivision: eleven beats = unevenly divided five.

EXAMPLE 9: Stravinsky, *Rite of Spring*, Part II, 2 after No. 103

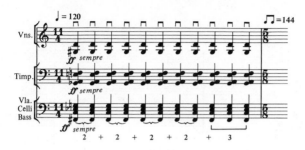

Exercise 8

Debussy, Nocturnes, No. 1—Nuages (*Clouds*), mm. 1–4, 11–21

We have derived beat patterns for all compound and mixed meters from subdivided patterns of plain patterns. In order to distinguish between subdividing beats, pulses as well as preparatories were used. But in order to assure clear legibility of the overall pattern, the direction of main beats (those belonging to the underlying, plain meter) must be maintained. In order to express musical functions vested in these beats according to our perception of the score, the distribution of principals, preparatories, and pulses throughout any compound or mixed beat pattern must reflect the shape of the phrase. Thus, the spelling of a pattern as "a triple-divided, slow *two* in a variety of ways will nonetheless always look and feel like the same, expressive six. *Metric control and orientation is maintained . . . by observing the direction of . . . main beats . . .*" (p. 118).

The first two measures of Debussy's *Nuages* involve two clarinets and two bassoons playing, and between seventy-five and a hundred other instrumentalists counting. *The beat must serve both needs:* the "how to play" of the former, and the "when to play" of the principal oboe, for instance. For the latter, the main outline of a subdivided two is important. For others, with more measures to count, the fact that the downbeat "is the only beat ever to extend substantially below the center before recovery" (p. 90) is even more important: soon, the English horn will play in four over a continuing main pulse of six; and the coinciding first beats of both must be clear and easily distinguishable to all. At the same time, the clarinets and bassoons of the first two measures, and the oboist who joins them in the third, play music that does *not* emphasize downbeats.

A beat of six consisting of a small principal 1, a pulse 2, minimal preparatory 3 and principal 4 (the second main beat, to the left), pulse

EXAMPLE 10: Debussy, *Nocturnes*, No. 1—*Nuages* (*Clouds*)
a. mm. 1–4

b. mm. 11–21

5 and minimal preparatory 6 should fit requirements of the first two measures *provided* that the small downbeat a) clearly extends below the center; and b) all beats have minimum impetus. The third beat, if the shape of the oboe phrase is to be reflected in it, will demonstrate an aspect of the preparatory that will assume increasing importance: it may not only signal *additional* emphasis for the following beat, but with equal persuasiveness *the opposite*. In our case, the C♯ in the oboe is not only the second of three notes introducing a 3 × 2 division of six against the main 2 × 3 pattern, but is also softer than the preceding D, and the final B is softest of all. This will require a preparatory 2 which will establish an even weaker 3 to follow: perhaps again by drawing the small beat against your chest (see figure on the right, p. 23). Beat 3 could be a pulse, with 4, 5, and 6 being principal, preparatory, pulse like 1, 2, 3. As long as beat 1 is a clearly recognizable downbeat and 4 moves noticeably to the left, *metric orientation is assured, while the distribution of principals, preparatories and pulses varies according to their changing musical functions.* This interchangeability of the two sides of our beat chart enables conductors to achieve clarity and considerable musical differentiation with comparatively few, but disciplined, motions.

Measures 11–21 offer comparable opportunities for practice. The shift from 3 × 2 to 2 × 3 occurs several times and must be accomplished without noticeable emphases or accents. The changing *function* of beats clearly replaces a change of *direction:* in a 6/4 meter, i.e. a triple-divided two, preparation of beats 3 and 5 as if they were main beats of a 3/2 pattern, suggests the shift without altering the outline. Needless to say, the smaller the beats, the easier this shift.

Similar treatment is given to music in other compound meters. In order to preserve the clear outline of the basic pattern, however, it will be particularly important to remember the rule concerning the direction of subdividing preparatory beats (p. 114):

> A preparatory beat may precede any main beat or subdivision. *The direction of its lift must be opposite to that of the beat for which it prepares.*   (p. 51)
>
> *Beats subdivided by preparatories are read* by the orchestra, within the context of the metric pattern, *in terms of the direction of their fall.*
>   (p. 113)

The first rule becomes important when the preparatory *is* a subdivision. The second assures clarity of subdivided main beats. According to the first, the direction of subdividing preparatories depends entirely on the natural direction of the beat to follow. The direction of main beats, subdivided or not, never changes: it may be modified for technical or expressive purposes, however (see pp. 91, 128). Changes of main beat direction as a result of changing meter should be indicated by appropriate preparatories, *without* artificial emphasis.* The following example will serve:

EXAMPLE 11: Ravel, *Mother Goose Suite*, second movement—*Tom Thumb*

*Modification of any beat quality, including direction, has expressive effects. When this is not intended, modifications should be as small as possible.

Exercise 9

Ravel, *Mother Goose Suite*, second movement—*Tom Thumb*
Whenever compound or mixed meters alternate with plain ones at a faster tempo than subdivisions would accommodate, only the outline of main beats is indicated. With mixed meters the distribution of main beats (7 = 2+2+3 or 2+3+2 or 3+2+2) is either apparent from the musical context or indicated by the composer. The latter is the case in the following excerpt.

Exercise 10

Copland, *Music for the Theater*
1. Understand clearly what is happening. Mental subdivision of the 7/8 measures is not enough. *Learn* the trumpet melody; add the rhythmic counterpoint; combine.
2. Practice beating the 7/8 measures—3+2+2, 2+3+2, 2+3+2 for the first, 3+2+2 for the single measure at No. 7. Be sure to feel or hum or tap eighth notes while you beat the three main beats.
3. Same as above, while you sing the trumpet line and keep a very clear sense of the rhythmic accompaniment.
4. Practice with addition of 3/4 measures.
5. Practice as if you were conducting an orchestra. The important difference is that in the preliminaries above, you tried to get a physical sense of this passage by singing, tapping, or any other motion which helped you to "feel" the metric shifts and the jazzy accents. Do not try to *help* the orchestra in this fashion. This kind of podium choreography is exciting in performance, if it is natural to the conductor and if the orchestra is sure of its part. In rehearsal, excessive shuffles and shakes on the podium are irritating in direct proportion to the difficulty of achieving a tight ensemble. An absolutely sure beat, with proper preparatories to signal changes, will be welcome because it helps.

EXAMPLE 12: Copland, *Music for the Theater*

PODIUM: REVIEW IV

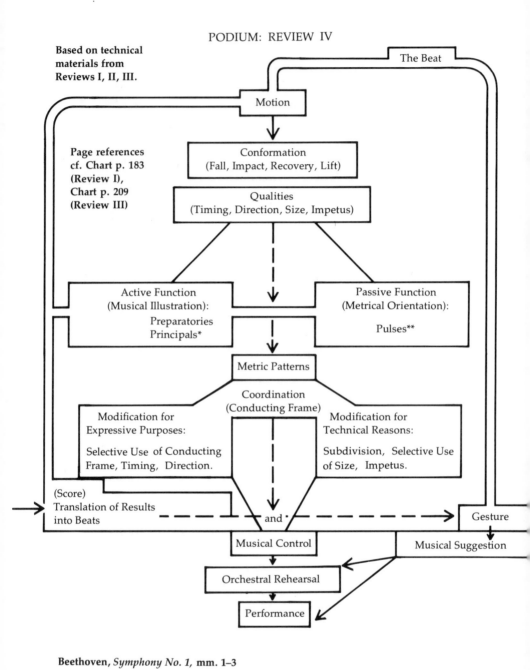

Based on technical materials from Reviews I, II, III.

The Beat

Motion

Page references cf. Chart p. 183 (Review I), Chart p. 209 (Review III)

Conformation
(Fall, Impact, Recovery, Lift)

Qualities
(Timing, Direction, Size, Impetus)

Active Function
(Musical Illustration):

Preparatories
Principals*

Passive Function
(Metrical Orientation):

Pulses**

Metric Patterns

Coordination
(Conducting Frame)

Modification for
Expressive Purposes:

Selective Use of Conducting
Frame, Timing, Direction.

Modification for
Technical Reasons:

Subdivision, Selective Use
of Size, Impetus.

(Score)
Translation of Results
into Beats

and

Gesture

Musical Control

Musical Suggestion

Orchestral Rehearsal

Performance

Beethoven, *Symphony No. 1*, mm. 1–3

---

*Exception: *Series* of Principals: (*Passive* Function)   **Exception: *Accented* Pulse: (*Active* Function)

REVIEW IV

EXAMPLE 13: Beethoven, *Symphony No. 1*, first movement, mm. 1–4

Exercise 11.

Beethoven, Symphony No. 1, *first movement*, mm. 1–4

The metronome marking specifies an eighth note as the basic pulse of the Adagio introduction, but the time signature indicates a four-quarter beat. Practice the following series of beats, with the sound of the music clearly in mind:

Metric Unit		Musical Happening	Beat Variety
4+		upbeat to tutti attack (*fp*)	preparatory for *f*
1	**m. 1**	*fp* in winds, horn; *f* pizz. strings ("wrong" dominant for symphony in C)	principal (*f*)
1+		none	minimal pulse
2		none	minimal principal
2+		upbeat to tutti attack (*p*)	preparatory for *p*
3		*p* release in winds; *p* pizz. strings ("wrong" tonic)	⌈ principal (*p*)
3+		none *	⟨ none
4		none	⌊ none
4+		upbeat to tutti attack (*fp*)	preparatory for *f*
1	**m. 2**	*fp* in winds, horn; *f* pizz. strings ("right" dominant for symphony in C)	principal (*f*)
1+		none	minimal pulse
2		none	minimal principal
2+		upbeat to tutti attack (*p*)	preparatory for *p*
3		*p* release in winds; *p* pizz. strings ("wrong" tonic again)	⌈ principal (p)
3+		none *	⟨ none
4		none	⌊ none
4+		upbeat to tutti attack (*p*)	preparatory for *p*

The final upbeat in the second measure introduces, at last, the "right" dominant, which, in turn, is to resolve to the proper tonic of C. Every beat and subdivision of the preceding measures has reflected its counterpart in the score. The adjectives "right" and "wrong," on the other hand, suggest that there is more to the application of the beat than instant transformation of evidence on the musical surface into visual signals. After five chapters divided into Score and Podium sections, we don't need to be reminded that this present summary, devoted entirely to the podium aspect of the beat, cannot really be considered in isola-

---

*Beat has stopped *near* center (cf. p. 86 and remains *still* until 4+. Although next subdivision follows one full beat later, the rule concerning subdividing preparatories applies just the same.

tion. The example of Beethoven's *First Symphony*, however, makes it almost mandatory that we bear in mind the essential contribution of our work with the score.

The rights and wrongs of the three dominants and their resolutions at the beginning of this symphony are obvious enough; their significance might well occur to us at the beginning of the third measure: why piano? For the author at least, the answer is really very funny. Dominant C to F–wrong: significantly also *fp* to *p*, almost like "that can't be right" (*fp*)–"wrong!" (*p*). Then, second measure, dominant G "could that be it?" (*fp*)–A minor "wrong again" (*p*). Then, with trepidation (*p!*) some overkill: the dominant of the dominant "right! right!" (cresc.) into G, and at last into the tonality of the work: C major.

In what way does such a personal little scenario affect the beat? The left-hand side of our beat chart deals with beat functions, musical illustration, visual phrasing, and modification of the beat for expressive control. The conductor's beat is not only precise; it may also be eloquent. Having acquired the means of being persuasive, we must, however, have some notion of what we wish to express. In the first five measures of this symphony, for instance, there are quite a few *piano* markings. Our chart of suggested beats for the first two measures is adequate in its reflection of all the evidence on the surface of this score. Even the obvious question of how big the crescendo shall be in the third measure (or "how loud is loud" in the fourth) may be answered without having to delve too far: there is a fortissimo, thirty measures later, in the Allegro section for which some power must be held in reserve. But what kind of *p* is to follow in m. 5, and how would it compare to the *p* on the third beats of mm. 1 and 2? Or the onset of m. 3?

It is at this stage that the surface yields no clues, only one piece of further, intriguing evidence: the first violin G, at the top of the *arco* chord in m. 4, is dotted while all other notes in the chord are quarters. Assuming that our whimsical interpretation of the "wrong" dominant sevenths is adopted as a working solution, there would be no problem with the *p* in m. 4. Having reached the "right" dominant, our melodic descent into the proper dominant *seventh* should be one of quiet assurance. The held-over G in the first violins serves as a bridge. Its effect, after the fullness of the *f* chord, will be that of a natural diminuendo into the *p* G sharp, in which the second violin joins.

Now we have something to be eloquent about, and the techniques already reviewed in this chapter should enable you to reflect a tentative beginning, a sense of discovery (mm. 3 and 4) and a warm feeling of being safely and happily home—all in the first five measures of the symphony. There is one additional, technical concern: the transformation of the violin G (m. 4), our initial point of arrival, into the point of departure for the tonal region to which this work really belongs. The succession of happenings in the fourth measure, which includes the first *arco* string chord, could of course be reflected in a principal first beat; a pulse on 1+ to signal cutoff for all but violin I; the (cutoff) principal on two; and a preparatory subdivision on 2+, *p*, which represents the first in a chain of eighth-note upbeats to the dominant G chord of m. 5. But for the occasion, it seems a little pedestrian. Let us recall the final sentence of the very first set of summaries and try to demonstrate a rather elegant, albeit incomplete, beat which may be very useful here. The *isolated lift.*

Conformation of the beat:
> A beat may consist of up to four separate elements: fall, impact, recovery, and lift. *Of these, the lift may sometimes be used by itself, in place of a complete beat.*   (p. 47)

This very special solution, halfway between a beat and a gesture, would accomplish the following: The *arco* chord on the first beat remains a principal as above. But its recovery through 1+ and 2 is suspended by pulses. A subsequent lift on the 2+ *p* will in fact feel more like the completion of a preparatory beat, begun on 1 of the measure, than a separate beat. Ideally, this combination of beats should be tried with an orchestra (both ways); but the way the second solution feels can be experienced by following these instructions carefully, with the underlying expressive purpose clearly in mind. What will be a particularly welcome result is an unavoidable last-moment diminuendo in the first violins, just before the sustained G becomes a *p* G♯. An abrupt subito piano would not produce the sudden sense of wonder and delight which should accompany this harmonic homecoming. To request even a minimal diminuendo, verbally, before the *p* marking, is likely to result in an exaggerated effect. To control the result with a beat which illustrates the conductor's *idea,* without spelling things out in a podium lecture, is always best.

One more example of subdivision and the interchangeability of various types of beat will further illustrate the potential flexibility of our system of the beat. Thus far we have used *pulses* in subdivision for metric orientation, and *preparatories* for expressive purposes and for steadying or slowing the tempo. In the following case, subdivision will be *anchored on a preparatory as the main beat,* with a *principal* as the first *subdividing beat.* Once again the lift portion of preparatories will play an important, almost independent role in setting the stage for this moment.

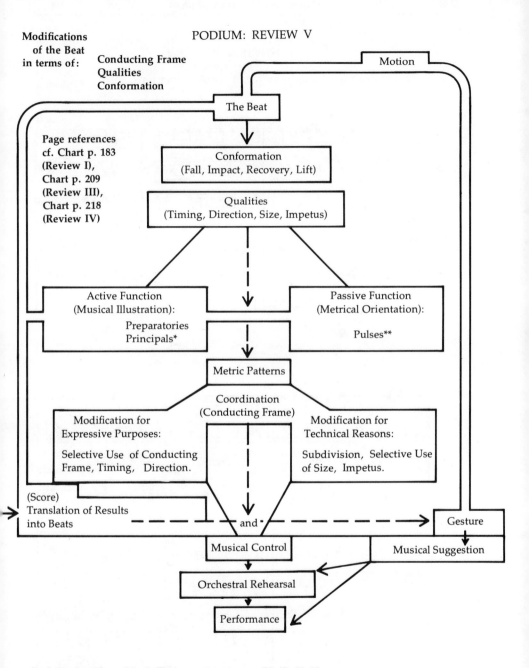

PODIUM: REVIEW V

Modifications of the Beat in terms of: Conducting Frame, Qualities, Conformation

Motion

The Beat

Page references
cf. Chart p. 183 (Review I), Chart p. 209 (Review III), Chart p. 218 (Review IV)

Conformation
(Fall, Impact, Recovery, Lift)

Qualities
(Timing, Direction, Size, Impetus)

Active Function
(Musical Illustration):

Preparatories
Principals*

Passive Function
(Metrical Orientation):

Pulses**

Metric Patterns

Coordination
(Conducting Frame)

Modification for
Expressive Purposes:

Selective Use of Conducting
Frame, Timing, Direction.

Modification for
Technical Reasons:

Subdivision, Selective Use
of Size, Impetus.

(Score)
Translation of Results
into Beats

and

Gesture

Musical Control

Musical Suggestion

Orchestral Rehearsal

Performance

Brahms, *Symphony No. 3*, First movement, mm. 36–45, 83–93

---

*Exception: *Series* of Principals: (*Passive* Function)   **Exception: *Accented* Pulse: (*Active* Function)

Review V

EXAMPLE 14: Brahms, *Symphony No. 3*, first movement, mm. 36–44

EXAMPLE 15: Brahms, *Symphony No. 3*, first movement, mm. 82–96

Exercise 12

Brahms, Symphony No. 3, *first movement, mm. 36–44, 82–96*

First, in order to appreciate the sense of movement in the opening movement of Brahms's *Third Symphony,* imagine the accompaniment figure in strings and flute as realistically as possible. Two things will be apparent: the bass note A occurs only on the first beat of every 9/4 measure; and the C♯ of the A-major chord which completes the harmonic background of the *grazioso mezza voce* melody in clarinet and bassoon does not coincide with this downbeat until the phrase begins its transformation into C♯ major (m. 44). Measures 36–39 are a preparation for this complete A-major chord, as mm. 40–43 are cumulative upbeats to the emergence of C♯ as the goal of this passage (m. 44). And each of these measures is in itself an upbeat, or rather a series of three upbeats to another series of three upbeats. In other words, every beat, from m. 36, is a dotted-half-note preparatory to the following beat, until (with a little swell in the melody) a resolution in m. 40 begins yet another sequence of preparatories into the transformation in m. 44.

Preparatories are characterized by their lifts. An entire passage consisting of preparatories should feature lifts to the extent of almost effacing the fall and impact of the main beats. How is this to be done? By speeding up the fall and, at the same time, minimizing the impetus of each beat before impact. This should place the timing of the beat just *before* the actual moment of attack on every 1, 2, and 3 of mm. 36–39. Try this at once, if only to realize in doing so that what sounds complicated in description is quite natural in execution, *provided the prior image of this musical shape is clear.*

With the abrupt introduction of the C♯-major triad (m. 44) comes a change of direction and shape in the succeeding phrases: from an open series of preparatories, reflecting forward-moving melodic momentum without harmonic motion, the focus shifts to the *second beat of m. 44* and those to follow. The first main beat of this measure lacks the double-bass A of its predecessors, although in other respects it resembles m. 40. The C♯, in the bassoon as before, now becomes both root and pedal point for a measure. In absence of a strong resolution on beat 1 (and still *pp*), 1+ becomes the pivot for a quick tonic–dominant–tonic twist into C♯ major, then to B in the next measure, and back to A in the measure after that. These very important first main beats are to be subdivided in this exercise.

They are unusual among triple divisions in that the first of their subdivisions, the 1+, is treated as a *principal.* 1+de, the next subdivision, will be a *preparatory* and the resolution on 2 another *principal.* This second main beat, as well as the third, immediately show the same open-ended momentum as the beats of preceding measures. The principal second beat therefore ends with a preparatory lift, and that pattern continues. The shape of these measures is bound to recall the shapes we examined in the third movement of this symphony (Chapter 3a).*

With the entire passage from m. 36 to m. 44 consisting almost entirely

---

*For a detailed analysis of this characteristic of *all* musical shapes in this symphony, see chapter 8.

of preparatories, let us consider the modifications which distinguish some of these beats from others, according to their expressive and technical purpose. The following summaries concerning modification of the beat are collected from various parts of the preceding chapters. Every one may be applied to the preparatories of this passage and should help to clarify the choice of appropriate size, direction, timing, and the placement of effective emphasis within beats that appear different but whose function and conformation is nonetheless the same. *All suggestions should be tried at once.*

Modification of beat size within the conducting frame:

> The respective sizes of beats within the conducting frame, together with their direction and impetus, relate to the musical emphasis to be given on impact.   (p. 87)

The operative word is *musical*. This may, but need not, involve loud and forceful attacks. In the case of m. 36–43, the greatest musical emphasis may be on the third beats (cumulative weight of two preceding preparatories), or on the first (the very light, but nevertheless important pizzicato in the double basses). The decision is yours. Whichever it may be, it must be reflected in the beat, in accordance with the suggested modifications.

The location of the center is not to be modified.

> Every modified beat (beats other than the downbeat, which start above their normal height for the sake of added emphasis) must pass through the center of the conducting frame before impact.   (p. 88)

The significance of this rule, as it affects the coordination and legibility of your beats, will already be apparent in connection with the previous exercise. It will become even more evident when we reexamine it in terms of modified fall and lift resulting from changes in direction.

The fall of the downbeat is not to be modified.

> The first beat, in any metric pattern and regardless of function, is the only beat ever to extend substantially below the center before recovery.   (p. 90)

This useful reminder tells us how to make it easy for the orchestra to distinguish a downbeat from other beats which, for the sake of emphasis, have assumed a downward slant. This is particularly important in patterns of *two*, in which both downbeat and upbeat necessarily show a downward fall before impact, and may well be completed with a lift.

Example 16, the *f* equivalent in 6/4 of Example 15 (moving from C♯ minor to A), is a case in point.

On the other hand, "the only beat ever" does not mean the only beat *always* to extend substantially below center. This is a matter of discretion and judgment, and you will have to weigh the relative advantages of extra clarity against the sort of expressive persuasion to be applied in connection with the next two summaries. Both deal with direction and with the consequence of large lifts. Both should be applied to the piano excerpt in *three*, above, as well as to the following forte excerpt in *two*. You will find that the important lift, in the second instance, will have to be mitigated by a very small fall. Clearly, this may not extend below center.

Before we summarize the main modifications of beat qualities for expressive or technical reasons, we should have another look at the chart summarizing the effect of variations of beat qualities on the conformation of the beat (p. 185). The second and third categories are of particular interest:

Direction of *all* beats includes some upward and some downward movement. Except for impact, all elements of all beats exhibit either upward or downward movement *"as a determining feature within their overall direction."*

Size is variable at the conductor's discretion only in the *fall* or the *lift* of a beat. (Impact has no size; recovery is determined in direct ratio to size and impetus of the fall: any modification of recovery should be thought of as a lift.)

Modifications of the beat are adjustments of the proportions of its elements, consciously undertaken by the conductor. It should be understood that this is not an imposed system, agreed upon by conductors, but the result of observed reactions by an orchestra to variations in the perceived beat. No one decided on some gray rehearsal morning that smaller beats mean "play faster." But *experience* has shown that a smaller beat helps to increase tempo; a progressively larger one slows the orchestra down. That this in fact goes against one's instinct in trying to move a tempo, until that instinct is conditioned by training and experience, is part of a conductor's essential understanding of the application of the beat. Which part of a beat may most effectively become larger or smaller, to what purpose, is a further refinement.

Modifications of size or direction of beats are measured within the conducting frame, and in relation to its center through which all beats must pass.

The conducting frame and the center of the beat:

> All beats, in all metric patterns, move in relation to a cross formed by connecting the four corners of the conducting frame. The intersection of this cross shall be called the *center*. All main beats (i.e. divisions of the measure reflecting the time signature) must pass through the center of the conducting frame before impact.
>
> (p. 86)

Modifications—beat qualities:

> Respective *sizes* of beats within the conducting frame, together with their *direction* and *impetus*, relate to the musical emphasis to be given on impact. *Timing* (tempo) may be affected by modification of size or direction of beats before a desired tempo change.   (p. 87)

Modifications—beat conformation:

> *Fall:* any beat, regardless of its normal direction within a metric pattern, gains in power if its momentum accumulates in a *downward* slanting curve.   (p. 90)
>
> In order to mitigate the force of impact, after a forceful or expressive preparation, the fall must be contained. Its downward slant may be deflected sideways, and/or its size be reduced.
>
> *Impact:* the more forceful the intended impact, the closer the curve of fall should terminate at the center of the conducting frame.
>
> *Recovery:* see Tempo

Lift: preparatories terminate in a lift moving in the *direction opposite to that of the following beat.*

The more powerful the intended impetus of the next beat, the higher the lift of the preparatory connecting with it should be. This is also true of beats preparing for another to be vested with great expressive potency.

Before you continue to the most drastic application of beat modifications, those affecting tempo, reread the summaries above, particularly the last, broken down according to *elements* in the conformation of a beat, step by step. First try a few plain patterns of three and four. Observe the *feel* of the results, e.g. an expressive preparatory mitigated before impact of the following beat by a very small fall. Then use the two excerpts from Brahm's *Third Symphony:* nearly every beat has a lift.

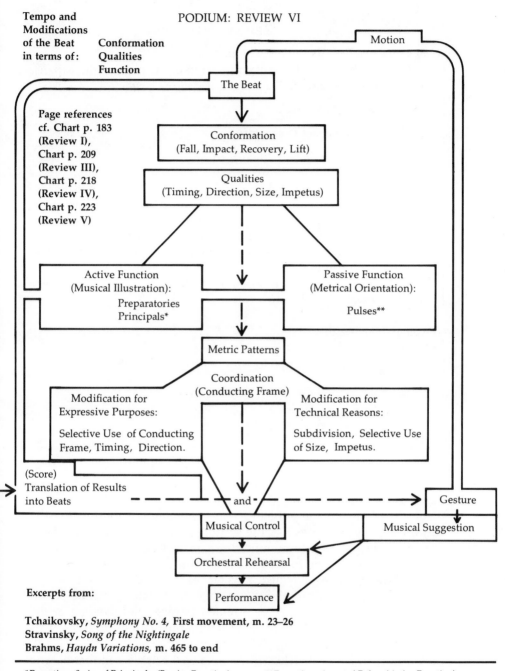

Tempo and
Modifications
of the Beat
in terms of:

Conformation
Qualities
Function

Motion

The Beat

Page references
cf. Chart p. 183
(Review I),
Chart p. 209
(Review III),
Chart p. 218
(Review IV),
Chart p. 223
(Review V)

Conformation
(Fall, Impact, Recovery, Lift)

Qualities
(Timing, Direction, Size, Impetus)

Active Function
(Musical Illustration):

Preparatories
Principals*

Passive Function
(Metrical Orientation):

Pulses**

Metric Patterns

Coordination
(Conducting Frame)

Modification for
Expressive Purposes:

Selective Use of Conducting
Frame, Timing, Direction.

Modification for
Technical Reasons:

Subdivision, Selective Use
of Size, Impetus.

(Score)
Translation of Results
into Beats

and

Gesture

Musical Control

Musical Suggestion

Orchestral Rehearsal

Performance

Excerpts from:

Tchaikovsky, *Symphony No. 4*, First movement, m. 23–26
Stravinsky, *Song of the Nightingale*
Brahms, *Haydn Variations*, m. 465 to end

*Exception: *Series* of Principals: (*Passive* Function)   **Exception: *Accented* Pulse: (*Active* Function)

Review VI

Tempo and modified conformation of the beat:

Special emphasis on the *recovery* portion of the beat, at the expense of the *fall,* encourages *forward movement of the tempo:*

size of the *fall* is reduced;

momentum on *impact* is greater;

natural length of *rebound* is increased.

N.B. 1: *Recovery* (natural rebound after impact) must not be confused with *lift* (conscious extension of upward motion beyond recovery, in preparation beats). Emphasis on the *lift* portion tends to slow movement of the beat and to inhibit forward momentum of tempo.

N.B. 2: The most essential factor in encouraging forward movement of tempo remains the systematic reduction in size of beats. Described above is an additional means, effective only if beats become smaller as well. (p. 128)

Tempo and the size of beats:

Large beats tend to *slow* the musical pace.

In order to move the tempo forward with ease, make the beat *smaller.* (p. 127)

Exercise 13

Tchaikovsky, Symphony No. 4, *first movement, mm. 23–26*

The tempo indication at the beginning of this passage is Moderato assai, quasi Andante. The general tempo marking for the 9/8 movement was Moderato con anima (♩. = in movimento di Valse). In many ways, the passage moves like the section of Brahms's *Third Symphony* discussed above—in a compound three, main beats defined by pizzicato string punctuation. In the present case only the first and last of each group of three is so established. This makes the ensemble a little easier to manage: only the third eighth note of each division must be placed *between* beats, and that may be oriented toward the following or the preceding beats as the flow of slight tempo fluctuation indicates. This also makes it an ideal passage for experimentation.

By m. 23 the lilt of the slow three is so well established that no one will be tempted to subdivide (as was necessary at some junctures in the Brahms excerpt). Still, there should be a little rubato. The *three* eighth notes of which each beat is composed offer an additional point of metric

EXAMPLE 16: Tchaikovsky, *Symphony No. 4*, first movement, mm. 123–28

reference. This will be particularly useful in establishing different proportions in the use of fall, recovery, and lift on each beat, depending on the relative speed with which the baton is made to travel between moments of impact.

Referring back to the summaries, we shall now experiment with small but constantly fluctuating changes of tempo, controlled by *modifications within a single beat.* As outlined above, reduction of size in the fall, accompanied by greater momentum on impact, will produce more rebound on recovery. With this in mind, beat a very gradual accelerando throughout this passage. Then try the same with a more normal beat. The eighths will fall on slightly different parts of the total metric division. This difference will be even more dramatic when we add a conscious lift to each beat and observe the comparative ease or difficulty in trying to achieve an accelerando, a steady tempo or a gradual retard. The larger the lift, the more a slowing up of the tempo will appear (and *feel*) natural. This should be a daily conditioning exercise until the distribution of impetus, speed, and size among elements of the beat *before and after impact* begins to reflect your intention to slow down or increase tempo. N.B. Once more, and with the strongest emphasis, you are reminded that *faster* means a *smaller beat; larger beats* mean *ritardando.*

Once you have achieved a physical sense of the special application of force, delay, and changes in size to respective elements of the beat, and have become accustomed to the natural effects on tempo, your competence and confidence in managing much smaller nuances of phrasing should be vastly increased. You may test your control by identifying certain momentary retards and stresses, and by carrying out these assignments with the same conscious awareness of what you are doing on every part of every beat, as was the case with the gradual changes of tempo before. These modifications should also be applied to other examples in this chapter (second and third movement of Schuman, last movement of Ravel, both examples of Brahms will serve very well) and to any other moderately slow movement. For practice purposes, the adjustments may be arbitrary in nature, but should be *determined in advance.*

Tempo and subdivision:

> When a change of tempo is accompanied by a change in the number of subdivisions per measure (including subdividing beats in patterns of compound and mixed meters), *preparatory subdivisions* are powerful indicators of a *rate of retard.*
>
> *Pulses will not inhibit an increasing rate of speed,* if subdivisions are gradually eliminated. (p. 124)
>
> *The accented pulse* serves to signal and define . . . the first noticeable effect of an increase in tempo . . . *thus establishing a rate of accelerando.* (p. 125)

N.B.: When the rate of retard or acceleration has been established, *subdivision should be discontinued,* unless absolutely essential for further coordination of orchestral ensemble.

We are now reaching the stage in our summing up at which almost every point has already been restated in another context. This was perfectly illustrated in our examination of Brahms's *Third Symphony,* first movement, mm. 36–44 (p. 224) and the subsequent demonstration of an unusual triple subdivision (m. 44) on p. 227. The second movement of William Schuman's *New England Triptych,* m. 41 (p. 190), and m. 3 of Mahler's *Fourth Symphony* (p. 204) are further examples. On the other hand, these examples and others now to follow illustrate a point which is worth making for its own sake:

Subdivisions serve more than one purpose, and are indicated by a variety of beats appropriate to that purpose.

We have listed three kinds of beats that may be associated with subdivisions: preparatories, pulses, and accented pulses. All three, when used to subdivide within a context of plain beats, will produce different results:

> Preparatories will retard.
> Pulses will not affect tempo.
> Accented pulses will accelerate.

Exercise 14

Further examples of the sometimes dramatic rate of sudden retard achievable by determined application of preparatory subdivisions may be found in Stravinsky's *Song of the Nightingale* and Brahms's *Haydn Variations* (pp. 236, 237). The Stravinsky (Molto pesante) is a fine illustration of a sudden retard, controlled by a single subdivision on 1+ of the fourth measure after 17 which, once established, continues at the same slower tempo *without* further subdividing beats, even through the rallentando two measures later. A retard sudden enough to require subdivision is a retard whose rate of slowing must be demonstrated with clear determination. There is nothing subtle about subdivision by preparatory. Give it firmly and with conviction—then, as soon as possible, continue with undivided beats.

EXAMPLE 17: Stravinsky, *Song of the Nightingale*

Quite a different problem is presented by the final ritardando in the *Haydn Variations* of Brahms, which appears first in m. 463 and continues molto ritardando from m. 465 until the sudden *in tempo* from m. 467 to the end. The four-measure retard is accompanied by a metric slowing of sixteenth notes to triplets, then to eighths; by a diminuendo; and by

EXAMPLE 18: Brahms, *Haydn Variations*

a displacement of what appears to be the main beat in the two last scale passages. It is clear that the composer wished this loss of tempo to be accomplished as gradually and without emphasis as possible. A continued beat of *two* during the first ritardando measures 463 and 464 should *allow* the tempo to slow, rather than hold it back by visible effort at any point. The molto ritardando of m. 465 will find the momentum so diminished that the introduction of four beats will seem natural. Beginning with the third beat of that measure the displacement of apparent meter makes the string scales sound as if two 3/4 measures were to follow. Care must be taken not to interfere with that intended impression by giving a strong downbeat on m. 464. As indicated, the feeling should be preparatory on 1 and principal on 2, with two more preparatories to follow. Only the timpani preserves a very soft pulse of the real meter while the dynamic level nears its lowest point.

The same example offers one of the finest illustrations of the use of an accented pulse in order to move tempo forward, suddenly and without the need for an upbeat "in tempo."

The accented pulse
> has no expressive value
> and no expressive function;
> it does not clarify the shapes of phrases
> —*it anticipates tempo.* (p. 125)

> Like other pulses, it marks the passage of time—*but it is the passage of time to come.* (p. 125)

The two statements appear redundant, but they differ in one important respect. The first applies to the accented pulse when it replaces, for reasons of emphasis or clarification of an existing tempo, a neutral pulse. The word *replaces,* in this instance, is to be taken literally: "in the exact, metrically defined, place of." The second summary also refers to a precisely defined place in the musical passage of time, but it is the "passage of time to come."

Problem:
The ending of the Brahms *Haydn Variations* presents an awkward technical problem: the retard from m. 463 continues progressively through m. 466, and there is no chance to insert an upbeat into the final eighth notes of that measure which would anticipate the return to the main tempo at m. 467. Yet that return must be sudden, precise, and— most difficult of all—at a speed which makes an initial beat of four (to establish that tempo) seem frantic and visually disturbing. It would be worth your while to observe even experienced conductors for their technical solution of that problem. Some will rely on the experience of their orchestras and simply give an unprepared, strong downbeat on m. 467 which will be "caught" and incorporated into the faster tempo

on the second main beat of the alla breve movement. This leaves the eight sixteenths in the upper strings, and the second quarter in most of the other instruments, to scramble for themselves; worse, it makes the initial attack of m. 467, which should be as decisive and strong as any in this work, just uncertain enough to take away the edge of conviction. Another, even less effective way, is to lengthen the final eighth note of m. 466 into an upbeat in the next tempo. While the *in tempo* is thus assured, the "inner clock" of the retard is not allowed to run down according to its own rate of release. The unavoidable prolongation of the last eighth, to accommodate an upbeat in the new tempo, spoils the effect.

Solution:

The introduction of an accented pulse *after the final eighth note* of m. 467, and at the upper end of the preparatory marking the revious main (fourth) beat, provides a spectacular solution. Two things are essential: that the accented pulse be given with absolute conviction, and that it be given *as a pulse*. You will be tempted to try a small preparatory, but this would require a full beat in tempo. As it is, the orchestra should have just enough time to attack—and that works out to a fair equivalent of the new quarter note. Measure 467 will be in two as was the entire finale of these variations.

Unlike earlier examples and exercises, the effectiveness of this beat will have to be taken on faith. Nonetheless, you are urged to practice the passage described above until you develop the "feel" of it. Keep in mind that the accented pulse has neither preparation nor appreciable fall or recovery. It is all impetus—a quick jab followed by the sort of principal (or preparatory) which would normally have been prepared by a larger, slower beat. Its consequence is an immediate attack, regardless of the prevailing tempo: hence its usefulness in moving tempo forward.

There are other, equally spectacular and apparently unorthodox uses of the accented pulse. Particularly valuable is a combination of its sudden impetus with the isolated lift of the preparatory.

Conformation of the beat (isolated lift):

consists of up to four separate elements: fall, impact, recovery, and lift. *Of these, the lift may sometimes be used by itself, in place of a complete beat.* (p. 47)

Together with an accented pulse, such a lift becomes a very specialized kind of preparatory beat. The special situation which calls for its use involves opening attacks in which the orchestra is expected to enter strongly, *within* the very first beat given.

PODIUM: REVIEW VII

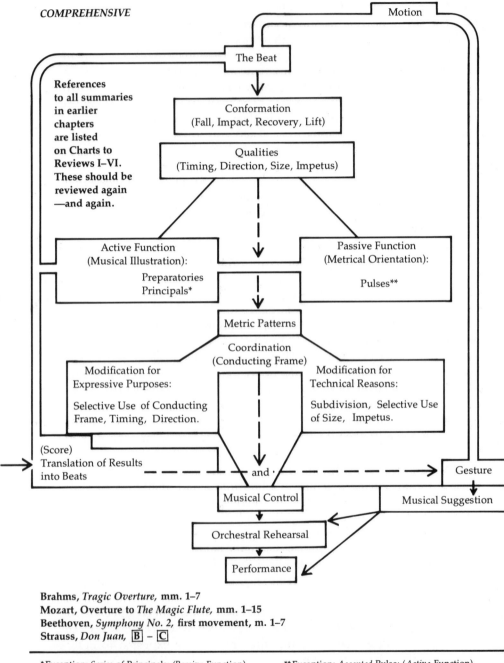

COMPREHENSIVE

Motion

The Beat

**References
to all summaries
in earlier
chapters
are listed
on Charts to
Reviews I–VI.
These should be
reviewed again
—and again.**

Conformation
(Fall, Impact, Recovery, Lift)

Qualities
(Timing, Direction, Size, Impetus)

Active Function
(Musical Illustration):

Preparatories
Principals*

Passive Function
(Metrical Orientation):

Pulses**

Metric Patterns

Coordination
(Conducting Frame)

Modification for
Expressive Purposes:

Selective Use of Conducting
Frame, Timing, Direction.

Modification for
Technical Reasons:

Subdivision, Selective Use
of Size, Impetus.

(Score)
Translation of Results
into Beats

and ·

Gesture

Musical Control

Musical Suggestion

Orchestral Rehearsal

Performance

**Brahms, *Tragic Overture*, mm. 1–7
Mozart, Overture to *The Magic Flute*, mm. 1–15
Beethoven, *Symphony No. 2*, first movement, m. 1–7
Strauss, *Don Juan*, B – C**

*Exception: *Series* of Principals: (*Passive* Function)   **Exception: *Accented* Pulse: (*Active* Function)

REVIEW VII

Example 19: Brahms, *Tragic Overture*, opening measures

Exercise 15

What the opening above has in common with Examples 20, 21, and 24, as far as the combination of an accented pulse and a lift is concerned, are the perfectly acceptable alternatives to its application. In all but one of the examples moreover, it would be fair to add that alternatives would not only be acceptable but preferable unless the orchestra is of professional level. Only in the *Tragic Overture* is the combination beat completely safe with any orchestra capable of coping with the instrumental challenges of the music itself. And that is precisely because the application of that beat concerns the piano, sotto voce upbeat to the *third* measure, with the tempo firmly established by two fortissimo chords of the first. We shall therefore begin with consideration of this example.

The obvious way of beating this opening is with a powerful pair of principals in m. 1, followed by a pulse and a small preparatory on the first and second beats in m. 2. With the possible addition of a cautioning left-hand gesture, the upbeat into the third measure should be as safe and soft as anyone could wish. That is the "acceptable alternative." Why an alternative? Because the safety of this solution does not account for the sotto voce with which the composer qualifies his dynamic instruction. The question "why an alternative?" ought to be "why sotto voce?"—a particularly apt example of the limitations of the musical surface as a source of precise information in terms of performance.

That Brahms had something in mind when he added sotto voce to the dynamic indication of piano is beyond question. What he had in mind is in fact quite clear to anyone who either knows or has taken the trouble to look up what the words mean.* Does it mean pianissimo? Not really, or the score would read that way. There is something tentative and indistinct about the connotation one is likely to associate with the term sotto voce, but no conductor would care to preside over a tentative and indistinct unison attack by the entire string section. Verbal explanations from the podium are more successful as correctives than as primary signals, and even a gesture is likely to cancel out the very quality of understatement which it would seek to convey.

The opening chords having established the tempo, and a very small pulse having marked the first beat of the second measure, it would be unnecessary to furnish further metric coordinates until the upbeat to the third measure itself. But an accented pulse with a brief lift to follow, *after* the expected second beat, will produce an instant and unanimous attack in the strings. The already established tempo should require no more than the merest suggestions of two pulses in the third measure, and the slight stress on the first beat of the fourth will be indicated by a *p* replica of the beat marking the opening measure. In addition to having given a visual equivalent of *sotto voce* in the beat, we have also, by careful use of pulses, called attention to the thematic

---

*Penguin Dictionary of Music: sotto voce (It., under the voice), whispered, barely audible—term used in instrumental as well as vocal music.

significance of the two chords in the first and fourth measures. The musical identity of these should become even more apparent with similar treatment of the repeating phrase culminating in the same chords in m. 6, before the next building block of the structure, introduced by the dotted figure immediately following is presented.

EXAMPLE 20: Mozart, Overture to *The Magic Flute,* opening measures

Exercise 16

Use of the accented pulse with a preparatory lift, after the preceding main beat, but still in a related tempo (the eighth note instead of the quarter) is also relatively safe for the tutti attacks before the second and third measures of the *Magic Flute* Overture. The beat for this introduction is in four. The easiest signal for the sixteenth entrance after the fermatas in the first two measures would be a subdivided fourth beat: a small 4, and a larger, preparatory +. Many conductors will prefer this way of introducing the second chord because it is so clear that a slight extra hesitation over the barline will be safe as well. But with a good orchestra, an accented beat-plus-lift strongly introduced on 4+ (without any motion since the fermata) should stress the unmeasured, elemental quality of this opening without risk to the ensemble. *N.B.* In either event, the three forte chords may, but need not, be held without indicating the second beat. If this is to be shown, however, it should take the form of a preparatory to the cutoff. The upbeat to the fourth measure could either be treated like the previous ones, but piano, or allow its lyrical warmth to flow out of a full-quarter upbeat on the fourth beat.*

Exercise 17

An eighth-note upbeat is also the favorite of many conductors as a signal for the unison D's which open the *Second Symphony* of Beethoven. Some, the author included, will pause momentarily at the crest of that upbeat, expecting that orchestra's attack of the thirty-second note virtually *on* the following downbeat. This assures a safe, unanimous, and powerful attack, while the displacement of the upbeat note cannot be heard anyway: the fermata on the first beat erases effectively any sense of metric pulse. (By the same token, it is best to hold the fermata on 1, prepare the cutoff on 1+, and execute it *on 2*. This will not register as a liberty, since the fermata stretched beyond 2 anyway; but it provides a clean separation of the powerful opening D's from the next entrance, piano, of the oboes and bassoons.) The Introduction is subdivided.

With an experienced and willing orchestra the same opening attack can be introduced by our accented pulse without any lift at all. It will be less safe, and it will lose some of the solemnity of the earlier approach. What would it gain? An element of aggression and surprise which, for some, might be justified by Beethoven's second introduction of the fortissimo tutti, this time as a D-major third. The suddenness of this second fortissimo is certainly a surprise; aggression could be read into the ruthless obliteration of the last woodwind thirds by the tutti D's at the end of the fourth measure, and by the composer's failure to balance the

---

*A good example of the generous but yielding beat described on p. 91: "In order to mitigate the force of impact, after a forceful or *expressive* preparation, the fall (of the following downbeat) must be contained. Its downward slant may be deflected sideways, and / or its size reduced."

EXAMPLE 21: Beethoven, *Symphony No. 2*, opening measures

following D–F♯ in favor of an overpowering octave D on the downbeat of m. 5. The measured value of an accented pulse to set off the opening attack in this case should be a sixteenth.

In order to make quite certain of a unanimous, precise thirty-second-note D at the opening (particularly with an orchestra not familiar with the performance problems of this symphony) a subdivided upbeat—

3+ —is still another way to begin. It may detract a little from the majestic impression achievable by the first solution, or from the explosive intrusion of a column of sound which can provide a very dramatic effect if managed in the second way. But it will sound well. And the orchestra will have time to place the two first D's with great accuracy. In addition to being a matter of technical expediency, however, it is a matter of musical choice. We have almost come full circle again, and a satisfactory solution of podium problems cannot be found without a convincing decision on the score side of the conducting coin.

The accented pulse as well as the isolated lift, separately and in combination, may be used as upbeats to start a movement, *without* necessarily relating to the metric pulse of what is to come. The obvious disadvantage of this is an uncertainty about the tempo we are introducing, an uncertainty which normally is dispelled by a carefully timed upbeat *before* the music begins. In some cases this disadvantage is outweighed by other considerations.

EXAMPLE 22: Beethoven, *Symphony No. 1*, second movement, opening measures

The second movement of Beethoven's *First Symphony* (Example 22) begins with the second violins alone, pianissimo, on the third beat. A small preparatory on the second beat will safely and effectively introduce the string entrance. As an experiment, try the following: Stand in a position of readiness to conduct, but with your right hand still at your side. Raise your right arm easily, lifting it forward and up, slightly to the right, until it has almost reached the position from which—had this been a preparatory *two*—you would have expected the second violins to enter on *three. At that point you increase the momentum of the motion slightly, so that it becomes that of a lift,* completing a normal preparatory beat. A little extra care may be needed on the third beat in order to establish the tempo after the music has already begun, but the move from middle C to F, in a single orchestra section, should not be very difficult to achieve unanimously. The advantage of this beginning is that it produces an unusually smooth start, almost as if, without any particular signal, the players had begun quietly by themselves. Not every conductor feels comfortable with this sort of informality about the opening of a movement, but some works lend themselves to that approach. With a responsive orchestra, the very informality itself becomes part of the musical experience. There is, however, one more rule to remember:

The *accented pulse*, or the *isolated lift*, used as an upbeat unrelated to the metric pulse of the music to come, should always be the continuation of a larger motion already begun.

The reason for this is a very simple one: a surprise signal is much easier to achieve if there has been a previous signal to warn of the imminent surprise, than if the surprise was real. The general movement of the arm is the signal to expect that surprise.

EXAMPLE 23: Beethoven, *Symphony No. 5,* opening measures

The opening of Beethoven's *Fifth Symphony* (Example 23) is quite difficult to beat, unless the conductor "signals the surprise." Take as long as you like on the initial upbeat—it does not need to be in tempo. A very long preparation may suggest gathering power, a very brief one might impress with its ferocity (listeners are able to use their imagination as freely as most conductors). As long as you keep moving, the surprise release into the first beat will work; and the lift, connecting the single beat on m. 1 ($\downarrow$ = 108) to the downbeat on m. 2 will space the three eighth notes accurately. *But you must keep moving.* Just before you are ready to release the first fermata begin a very gradual upward movement of your arm: your warning to the orchestra that the surprise of a sudden downbeat on m. 3 is about to happen. Measure 4 is another powerful downbeat, but the fermata of m. 5 should not be so strong as to be confused with a cutoff. The fermata is released in the same way as the first, with an almost imperceptible rise before the next (*p!*)* downbeat.

Try this with a friend who can sing, play, or pound the table taking the part of the orchestra. You would find it very difficult, as long as you keep moving, to lose your player(s). But stop before any of the surprise signals, and you will find it difficult to be followed.

The principle of movement to connect one beat with the next, to prepare for sudden changes of tempo, or to signal an entrance, is basic to the application of the beat. As long as the baton is seen to move, the conductor's job is merely to control the timing, direction, size, and impetus of that movement in order to produce "legible" beats. Once the beat has stopped (as at the above fermata), it must be put in motion *before* the next, active orchestral response.

---

*While the cutoff of the fortissimo fermata must be strong, the recovery as well as the lift of the beat, also accommodating three *piano* eighth notes in the second violins, should be small and therefore much slower than its fall. Thus the *piano* will be illustrated.

EXAMPLE 24: Richard Strauss, *Don Juan*, B to C

Exercise 18

The opening of Strauss's *Don Juan* (see Example 25) no longer seems as difficult as it once did. Passages about which the composer once comforted members of the Munich Philharmonic ("What one may miss will be managed by another") are standard audition fare today; and young instrumentalists practice them from their excerpt books long before they have a chance to play them in an orchestra. Conducting, too, has become a craft to be practiced like any other musical skill, and the mystery of it is no longer in the exercise of control from the podium, but back in the music where it belongs. You will find that the main difference in the application of the beat to the opening measure of Beethoven's *Fifth Symphony* or Strauss's *Don Juan* (Example 25) is that the latter has two beats per measure while the former takes only one. In principle, the first attack of the Strauss involves the same problem as that of the Beethoven—except that Strauss fits seven sixteenth notes between the first and second beats, to Beethoven's three eighth notes between his first and second measures. And exactly the same solutions apply.

EXAMPLE 25: Strauss, *Don Juan,* opening measures

As always, there are as many ways of applying beats to music as there are ways of thinking about the music: the image comes first, and the results are *translated,* "measure by measure, into beats and gestures." The more flexible our means, the more we need this guide.

Strauss's *Don Juan* begins in the swashbuckling opening tempo (in two) of the tone poem. Two two-measure phrases after B repeat a quickly mounting pyramid on E. On the fourth beat of the fourth measure after B the second pyramid suddenly breaks, the pedal point changes to C, and the volume drops from forte / fortissimo to pianissimo. The same fourth beat also serves as upbeat to an apprehensive little interjection in the strings, lasting one measure and a half. Then a rapid E-major scale, reminiscent of the opening arpeggio, rouses the faltering momentum and restores the pride of the main subject, fortissimo, E major on a B pedal in the bass. By the second measure (three before [C]) the power fades once more, and we hear the sad, pianissimo phrase again, this time *tranquillo* and, for only one measure, on a C-sharp pedal. [C] is like the very first measure, but in G-sharp major, less fully orchestrated, and only *f*.

There is more to be seen, even on the surface of these transitional measures: the E pedal is a tremolo in the middle strings, the C comes in cello triplets, the B in full bass bows, and the C♯ (pedal of the tran-quillo repeat of the pianissimo phrase) sul ponticello—not a very tran-quillo sound. Or compare the two pianissimo sections: the first begins on a fourth beat, the second on the first of the measure; the first is lightened by two triangle strokes, the second expands in a small cre-scendo–decrescendo at the same spot and in the horn connection between string and wind parts of the phrase; the first ends espressivo in the oboe, the second begins and ends *flebile** and has some rather pathetic little accents in harp and all winds. At [C], the tempo is resumed molto vivo but, as we already observed, only forte and with reduced instru-mentation.

For want of a real study of this score, it will be sufficient to trace these surface elements of the example on p. 248. This should give you some notion of the rapidly changing aspects of the music. In order to try an application of the beat to suit the events, it would help to have a good idea of the actual sounds. The simplest way to achieve that is to listen to a recording—an unjustly maligned help in studying a score, which can save time and frustration at the very beginning, and may prove a valuable check on your musical imagination in the end. *N.B.* In between, while you are working your way beneath the surface of a score, some one else's recording—or even a tape of your own, earlier performance—would be disturbing.

Now for the beat. Unavoidably, the following description is the application of certain kinds of beats to this passage according to one conductor's image of the musical and associative events. It must also be remembered that, in trying to describe varieties and functions of beats in some detail, one appears calculating and cerebral about matters which in reality are part of a total performance, involving one's total person. The power of one's inner image of a score is anything but cerebral, and affects the beat as much as the overall pacing of a work one has come to "own." And the discussion of beats to suit a given musical purpose should not really be very different from examining the pros and cons of fingering and bowing certain passages on the violin.

*Tearfully.

Table of beats for RICHARD STRAUSS, *DON JUAN*, [B] to [C]

No. of mm. after [B]	Metric Unit (in 4/4)	Musical Surface	Beat Variety
1	1	*ff* E-major chord, concluding first main section. Tutti.	Alla breve: principal,
	2	*f* only (!), sixteenths pedal in Vln 2, Vla, dotted figure Hrns 3, 4.	adding preparatory lift for
	3, 4	low strings, bns chromatic triplet intro of "pyramid."	*strong* preparatory
2	1	E pedal continues, but *sfz;* bass passes upwards through B♯ to⌐	strong preparatory (but *not too big!*)
	2	C♯ (which remains in bass; winds begin "pyramid" A–E, dotted figure over three octaves, three beats	
	3, 4	continued same	preparatory (easy)
3	1	fourth beat of previous measure held over. E pedal continued (without *sfz*) *f* only.	principal (not as powerful as m. 1)
	2	as in m. 1	add lift
	3, 4	as in m. 1 (but bass going to C♯)	strong preparatory
4	1	as in m. 2, but bass passes through C♯ to⌐	strong preparatory
	2	D♮; wind "pyramid" B–E, three octave	
	3	continued as above	*into center!*
	4	subito pianissimo: C pedal begins (triplets in cello); pyramid stops, but upper strings take up dotted rhythm (*pp*) in "apprehensive" theme*; possibly poco meno mosso. Watch: double bass pizzicato.	subdivision by preparatory, small, clear, close to center.
5	1	apprehensive phrase, dotted rhythm, sempre *pp*, in strings.	*In four:* very small principal
	2	same plus celesta, F major	very small principal

*The technique of associative adjectives, used in earlier chapters (score sections) is carried over here. "Pyramid" is another sample.

	3	same, upper strings held over, celesta	very small principal
	4	strings end, bassoons, horns take over C-major chord (*pp*), flutes imitate last skip of fourth in Vln 1, staccato G to⤵	small preparatory
6	1	C; bassoons, horns hold, pedal stops, sixteenth upbeat in oboe (sempre *pp*) to⤵	pulse
	2	end dotted figure, downward ("reversing pyramid"), *pp!*	small preparatory
	3, 4	E-major scale on 3+, 4, all strings except basses, 16ths, 16th triplets, 32nds, FORTISSIMO!	*Alla breve again* combination beat: accented pulse* plus big lift.
7	1	tutti six-four chord E major (full quarter, accented, while scale disappears on eighth G♯).	principal with *strong* recovery (to clear chord)
	2	everybody off	
	3, 4	tutti six-four chord again, trombones begin diminuendo	principal, generous but deflected *sideways***
8	1	all notes tied over; beginning of quarter-note triplets throughout this measure; six-four E.	(alla breve, continued) *un*accented pulse with lift.
	2	same, triplets continue. diminuendo begins on third triplet, in all instruments.	
	3, 4	same, triplets continue	very gentle preparatory, allow tempo to recede.
9	1	*Flebile:* for two measures. Same figure as in 5 after ☐B☐; tranquillo, this time in *p;* cello pedal on C♯ and sul ponticello, eighth note triplets again. Take note of continuing quarter-note triplets in bassoon, *now.*	*In four again* very small principal
	2	same; place bassoon triplet mentally before you hear it; small crescendo to⤵	small preparatory

*Reminder: accented pulses move tempo forward.
**Cf. p. 91: Modifications—beat conformation, par. 2.

	3	small but warm climax in upper strings (dotted figure *without* a rest) and diminuendo; think of next bassoon triplet; cello pedal begins to fade.	
	4	upper strings end; horns connect as in 5 after B, but con sordino and with a little cresc.–decresc. harp harmonics imitate last skip of the fourth in vln 1, accents, *mf* G♯ to↲	small principal
10	1	C♯; horns hold but fade; flute begins dotted figure, downward E–A (heading for G♯), begins crescendo.	small, unaccented pulse plus lift
	2	wind entrance, *p*, accent (but none yet in flute, *flebile*; all diminuendo except flute.	small preparatory
	3	accent G♯ in flute; other winds hold, diminuendo.	small principal
	4	oboe descends through D♯, diminuendo, to↲	pulse
C	1, 2	C♯, winds off, violins and violas subito forte (but *not* fortissimo) begin same seven-sixteenth-note figure as at opening of tone poem: in G♯.	*Alla breve again.* Accented pulse, with plenty of lift on second beat.

8

BUILDING BLOCKS: MUSICAL SHAPES

One general approach to learning a score is illustrated, as well as a possible way of establishing contact below the surface of music. Two kinds of small musical shapes are defined; a third, larger kind is suggested. *Scores examined:* Brahms, *Third Symphony*; Ravel, *La Valse*.

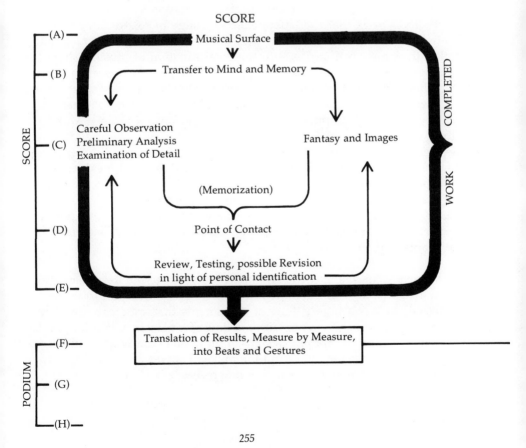

SCORE

(A) — Musical Surface

(B) — Transfer to Mind and Memory

(C) — Careful Observation
Preliminary Analysis
Examination of Detail

Fantasy and Images

(Memorization)

(D) — Point of Contact

Review, Testing, possible Revision
in light of personal identification

(E) —

SCORE

COMPLETED

WORK

Translation of Results, Measure by Measure,
into Beats and Gestures

(F) —

(G)

(H) —

PODIUM

> I have finished my composition, all but
> the themes.
>
> —Ravel

MUSICAL shapes are audible designs. Their size is limited by the length of time during which sounds that have passed can still be related to sounds that are passing. Their contours reflect the performer's conscious control of the way in which successive combinations of sound fulfill, or frustrate, conditioned expectations on the part of the listener. Of all musical concepts that are described in visual terms, shape is likely to be the one most easily misunderstood as a result. Visual shape is perceived all at once, at the moment we look at it. Musical shape is the remembered, cumulative impression of successive moments of perception. Visual shapes may be seen and explored. Musical shapes are created and experienced.

The three-note melodic cells we examined in Mussorgsky's *Pictures at an Exhibition* are not yet musical shapes. The difference between a melodic outline (i.e. identification of a succession of intervals) and a melodic *shape* is that the latter reflects a range of relative importance between constituent sounds, as they are heard or imagined. Elements other than melody contribute to the determination of musical shapes, but the imagined shape must be experienced as music in order to acquire a reality equivalent to seen or imagined visual shapes.

Theoretical analysis of musical evidence (e.g. grouping of intervals) can avail itself of terminology borrowed from a spatial context. Much of this work, in fact, deals with visual verification and interpretation of evidence on the printed page, a two-dimensional space without explicit reference to time. But when it comes to transforming the evidence of that page into the image of a performance, the experience of every aspect of that image must account for the time dimension of music.* At that stage, musical shapes, as very important components of any performance image, must be created from direct and indirect information available in the text.

Musical shapes lend themselves most naturally to the flexible control of a responsive beat. The way in which orchestral performance is directed, by a continuous flow of movements that anticipate, modify, caution, or command events within a flow of music, is particularly well suited to suggest the audible designs of these small components of larger forms. The conductor's beat and the music it serves are locked in step, while musical shapes are created and perceived.

---

*Cf. Chapter 12, *Music and Memory: Time as Rhythm*.

Determination of musical shapes is any performer's privilege, but an absolutely essential part of the conductor's job. The notion that these shapes are already fully accounted for in the score, if one would only take the trouble to look, has some truth to it—wrong side up. It is in the performer's created shapes that the evidence of the score must be accounted for. We discovered at the very beginning of our study that scores are far from being explicit blueprints of the proper execution of music to be performed. However, the legitimate variety of choices available in the determination of musical shapes is mitigated by the fact that they do not appear in isolation. To the extent to which there emerges, from a succession of individual shapes, the sense of an organic musical structure, one performance may carry conviction while another may fail.

RAVEL, *LA VALSE* REEXAMINED*

In this remarkable composition, the materials are presented almost casually in an introductory exposition. There follows (rehearsal figure 18) a series of waltzes, the tunes of which can all be traced to the deceptively simple stuff with which the piece began. After the last of these dances has been heard, a shortened version of the exposition reviews the materials once more (rehearsal figure 54) and is followed by a fantastic reappearance, in altered sequence and form, of most of the waltz tunes. The gathering momentum of reckless abandon and almost lascivious expressivity hurtles the work to one of the most extraordinary and truly shattering climaxes in the literature.

Even this thumbnail sketch of the curious structure of *La Valse* should show how much the impact of the music must depend on a clear and convincing delineation of themes which, in essence, are not only related but somehow subservient to previously presented materials. One of the most powerful common factors in all of them emerges from the very first melodic entrance in the piece, the bassoon phrase at rehearsal figure 1 :

EXAMPLE 1

Practically all of what follows is related to rhythmic or melodic aspects of those few measures. What is more important to us as performers, however, is the introduction here of a metric shift in the second half of

*For this discussion of *La Valse* a full score should be used.

the phrase which, by inference now, and by conscious exploitation later on, establishes two "speeds": A basic waltz tempo at first and a slower three, superimposed on alternate beats after m. 5. In several of the succeeding waltzes, this dual pace creates the dichotomy which, in the end helps to tear the music apart. In the meantime, it governs the essential rubato within many phrases. We shall take note of this element of metric mutability and look more closely at one of its melodic manifestations, the second half of the waltz tune No. 1 ([18]) as it is presented independently at [22].

EXAMPLE 2

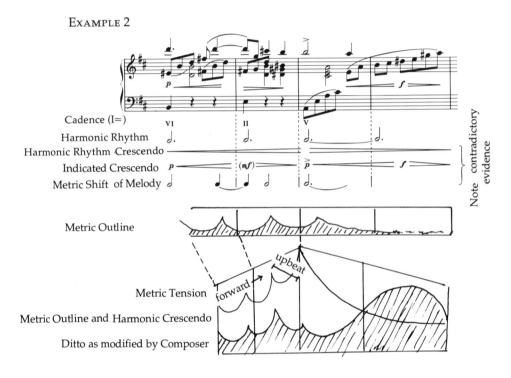

The orchestral texture of Example 2 is light and transparent, with woodwinds on the melody and a pizzicato bass in the lower strings. The ripple of eighth notes is begun in the first violins and later shared between strings and winds. It is worth noting that the dynamic climax in the arpeggio figure is not supported by the doubling violas, after the oboes and flutes have taken over the English horn crescendo. Instead there is a string diminuendo as the arpeggio is relinquished to the winds—not enough to vitiate the second-beat climax in the fourth measure, but enough to make it a gently rounded one, a force spent before it crests. A really affirmative *forte* only occurs on the third repetition of the phrase, in which the whole orchestra reaches a point of dynamic and harmonic fullfilment on the third measure—but that becomes then quite another musical shape.

The captions on the left-hand side of the example show important aspects of the musical shape. The harmonic progression (on its way from B minor to D major) is: VI–II–V, with one measure given to each change and an extra one added to the semicadence. The harmonic crescendo follows the harmonic rhythm. But the composer complicates matters by a very different dynamic articulation of the phrase: a small crescendo at first; a *decrescendo* into the third-measure resolution, landing on an accented piano at the point where we expect the emphatic climax; and a belated expansion of the dynamic range to forte when the force of the cadence has been completely spent. Add to this, then, the already mentioned metric shift from $2 \times 3/4$ to $3 \times 1/2$ in the first two measures compounded with a duple motion suggested by the dotted-quarter phrasing in the arpeggio, and a solid three-quarter oriented bass, and you have a problem with an elegantly supplied solution.

The tension implied in the harmonic cadence is clearly frustrated by the unexpected piano at the point of release (m. 3 of Example 2). The metric displacement in the first two measures not only permits, but almost suggests a relaxation of speed before the onset of the third, with the eighth-note motion coming to a significantly convenient stop as well; while the expansive if belated crescendo to forte in the fourth measure is enhanced and eased by permitting that slight retard to play itself out. We thus have an initial forward movement; a conscious holding back in the two-quarter upbeat to the measure; and a luxurious loss of momentum in the third and fourth measures, before the process begins again. The shaded portion of the second illustration in our example, and the relative length of the spaces allotted to each measure, should give some graphic indication of the modification of musical shape which has thus been imposed on this phrase.

The *extent* of this modification is another matter. The answer partly depends on the place and significance of the phrase in a larger pattern of phrases. But it will ultimately be determined by the performer's decision. Let it be a choice, therefore, which will give him personal pleasure and satisfaction. There is no way in which a conductor's musical responsibility can be shifted to a canon of common consent. But there is some observable ground to be explored, and his first task is to become familiar with this ground. His next and equally important task is the evaluation of evidence, and its imaginative, idiomatic use in creating a performance image with clearly perceived musical shapes. This will involve other aspects of what lies "below the surface" of music, aspects which are discussed in the chapter on time as rhythm. The reader may therefore wish to reread the present chapter and the succeeding one on

EXAMPLE 3

the function of harmony after completing an initial survey of all three. He will be concerned with what they are about for the rest of his professional life.

Example 3 poses far more complex problems. The harmonic background for this phrase (rehearsal figure 50 of *La Valse*) seems to be one of preparation and *non*release, with the first six measures following the upbeat measure rather like sniffs before a sneeze that never comes. Instead the music recovers, breathing deeply: out–in–out, until the process repeats itself. Foreshortened sequels of the phrase eventually lurch into a confused return of the exposition (rehearsal no. 54 which soon reveals that something has gone wrong in an idyllic world swirling to three-quarter time. *But unless this last, transitional waltz can suggest something other than a comic turn, the remainder of the work may appear farcical and grotesque.* Here, then, is an instance where the shape of a single phrase, pivotally placed, has a decisive effect on the musical impact of an entire composition. Clearly, a clownish effect is not what the composer had in mind. We must find a more appropriate solution— but appropriate to what, and on what evidence?

The surface evidence is less helpful than in the previous example. There is one superficial resemblance: The last two measures (6, 7 in Example 3) before the abortive sneeze show a surprising diminuendo where the opposite would seem to be called for. This is followed by a very large and, if played in tempo, very vulgar, heavy wave of sound which rises on a mighty harp glissando, crests in a fortissimo French horn trill, and descends into the trough of another low E to begin again. To play these three measures in an arbitrarily slower tempo (as is often done), hardly adds conviction to an obstinately awkward passage.

Now we may recall the "slowing" of metric pulse built into the second half of the bassoon melody at the very opening of the piece (Example 1). We claimed then that here was germinal material which, in the words of the composer himself, took precedence over the actual fashioning of "themes." Those themes are based on that material, not only in outline but in characteristic behavior. Metric mutability is very much part of this behavior, and our solution lies in recognizing and using that fact. By indicating a diminuendo over mm. 6 and 7 of Example 3 the composer signals that, for practical purposes, these are not two measures of three with attractively syncopated offbeats in the melody, but one "measure" of three half notes, decaying in volume from its "heavy" beat on m. 6. This is followed by an even slower three consisting of the next three measures, each of which becomes one "beat." Naturally, there will have to be a slight but steady retard throughout, so that the transition from three-quarter to three-half to three-dotted-half will not occur too abruptly. In the end, the effect will be that the phrase gathers momentum quickly and spends it completely in the course of a large final wave. That process is repeated, once more subsiding almost to a stop, and then, after a succession of the early, momentum-gathering measures which culminate in an actual accelerando, logically and consistently loses drive (once more in a three-dotted-half slowing "measure") to return at last to the tempo of the exposition, at rehearsal figure 54 .

"How much?" is once more an important but personal decision. Enough to define the shape and, as we have just seen, the function of the phrase. The question of what is enough shall be deferred for later, more complete, consideration. However, it may be added here that the return to Tempo I is not, in the author's view, a binding commitment to precisely the same speed as in the opening measures of the work. Rather, it refers to the general "area" of the opening tempo—and we have just observed how much variation is possible within the general tempo of a single phrase. The tempo of the "return" should probably be a little faster than the opening measures of *La Valse*.

The following illustrations should help to clarify the effect of even a slight modification on the shape of a phrase. The first drawing shows a graph of the phrase at a steady pace. In the second, the contraction and expansion of the spaces representing barlines indicate the increase and relaxation of tempo before and after the first metric shift from 2×3 to 3×2. Thus the latter comprises two measures that become a single unit of three (at ♩. quasi ♩), and eventually the momentum subsides to three measures representing a single unit of a still slower three (at ♩ quasi ♩). It was the unmotivated dynamic thrust of these last three measures *played in tempo* which made us seek a way to allow them a longer, deeper swell; and the metric shift in the two preceding measures gave us the chance. A very carefully calculated and controlled retard ought to accomplish it ("resist" on the upbeat to measure 5, lose tempo as shown).

Very little in the preparation of a score for its first rehearsal takes place in the abstract. We have made it a point, in all that has gone

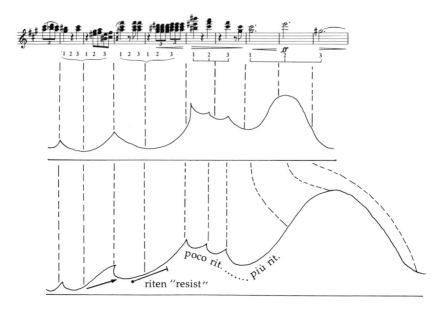

FIGURE 1

before, to present the personal, participatory element of study together with the step-by-step exploration of its analytical and strictly procedural aspects. And we shall continue to explore, as fully as possible, how imagination feeds on apparently fortuitous visual, auditory, and emotional associations suggested by the music. These little incentives to our curiosity are tempered and controlled by our increasing knowledge and mastery of the materials from which they were culled. Unlike singers and instrumentalists, conductors alone among re-creative artists must deal with the whole learning process in silence. Small wonder then, that aural imagination sparks visual and feeling reactions which, properly managed, may well lead to deeper insights, stronger retentive memory controls, and even more convincing technical execution, when it comes to playing the music.

The little sketch of a seascape below, shares an outline of waves with the second curve above. Our earlier reference to a "longer, deeper swell" conjured up the image. When such a little vision flashes across the mind, it makes its own impact on the learning process. In this case, timing the slow heave of a huge visible wave after a series of lesser splashes could be as helpful in getting the "feel" of a reasonable retard as that earlier fancy of an aborted sneeze was discouraging and prompted us to think again! The point is not whether the image is beautiful, or even apposite, but whether, being there, it can be of use. Needless to say, even a successful association may or may not carry over into per-

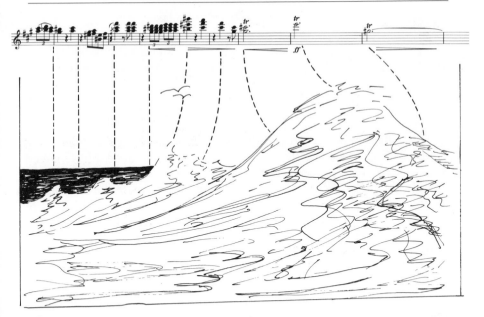

FIGURE 2

formance, and should certainly be abandoned as soon as its suggestive power fades.

"Sneeze" or "wave," it is clear that in the latter case a *very* different musical shape was created than that of the progressive retard, initiated by a marginally slower upbeat. Either way of playing the passage would be acceptable, but the result, as demonstrated in the "wave" version of the phrase ending, argues strongly against the simplistic advice: "If in doubt, play it like it is." The composer is served no better by default on the imaginatively critical side of performers' responsibility, than by arbitrary disregard of textual evidence. Pianist, composer, and teacher Arthur Schnabel put it this way: "The performer does not underline anything which the composer has already made obvious. He has to take care of whatever the composer has left for him to take care of." The defining of musical shapes—involving, as we have seen, choices left for us "to take care of"—is a good place to begin.

Our choice resulted in a modification of tempo. That choice of the "wave" over the "sneeze" was based on the assumption that a 3/2 meter was temporarily superimposed on the flowing 3/4 pulse of the piece. Thus, we achieved a loss of momentum which allowed for a substantially and progressively slower tempo in the last three measures. In discussing the opening bassoon statement (p. 257), we had already pointed out the same kind of metric shift. But there we *would not choose* to let it affect *tempo*. Instead, it should result in a most important *dynamic nuance:*

EXAMPLE 4

The 3/2 effect of the bracketed measures implies a *quasi diminuendo* from what is, in essence, the first ("heavy") beat of two measures merged into one.* While the bass pulse of 3/4 continues throughout that potentially significant little event, the French horn entrance on the last quarter of this elongated bassoon measure adds an accented premonition of musical and expressive crosscurrents to come. The composer has provided a neat foil for this complex phrase ending by indicating a crescendo in the corresponding, very much 3/4, first half of the statement.

In our daily practice of the techniques and progressive skills of auditory imagination, the above example of the opening statement of *La Valse* provides a simple but useful opportunity to examine, at leisure, a characteristic and important musical shape both with and without suggested amplification of the printed text. It is equally important that, with increasing proficiency in "hearing" with our minds, we also develop auditory imagination and judgment with regard to what is not to *be* heard. Trying to "hear," for instance, the first cello entrance (three measures before figure 1) would be futile, for if it were actually heard in performance, it would sound like a badly spliced electronic tape. Here is an event which, if necessary, we shall be prepared *to suppress* in rehearsal. If truth be told, orchestral players don't play every note in every score. Conductors certainly don't want to hear all the ones that are played. And notes both played and heard must often be subordinated according to their function, or suppressed. This too contributes to the "shape" of what is actually experienced in performance and, before that, in the mind.

The matter of the inaudible cello entrance is such an obvious example that we might be tempted to underestimate the problem of deciding what is *not* to be heard. Right at the beginning of the score, however, the composer also presents us with a more subtle decision: How audible are the minor seconds in the bass to be? These repeated quarter-note pulses of E–F have an obvious rhythmic function in that the

---

*Having chosen to shape a phrase in a way *not* apparent to the players from the page before them, the conductor must, of course, indicate from the podium and rehearse the diminuendo which is the key. But musical intent must be absolutely clear in the conductor's mind before he may presume to transmit it to those who must translate his gesture into sound.

accented E helps maintain the feeling of 3/4 even when an apparent 3/2 metre is superimposed. But in a work so overladen with chromaticism, are these minor seconds merely supporting the captioned program in which dissipating patches of cloud will gradually reveal ballroom and dancers? The low, close, muted strings should easily furnish such an effect. Not necessarily so the third beats (E–F sounded together) in the harp. They would be quite definite and distinct in audible pitch, just when an A♭ is added at [1], and the accented E in the bass begins to feel like a leading tone to F. The bassoon figure features C and D (immediately reflected in the middle and upper strings). *Question:* at the risk of losing something of the "cloudy" effect the composer prescribes, should one try to bring out these pitches clearly enough so that, from the very opening measure, a murky pyramid of distinguishable, close intervals becomes an important shape in itself, without metric definition, or a feeling of tempo? Or should the accented E have a preeminent place of its own, while the rest remains cloudy and indistinct? Here we find ourselves at the borderline between determining individual musical shapes and considering a larger structure yet to emerge. We touched on that problem at the beginning of this chapter and will address it again in the next. Meanwhile, here is one conductor's decision on the question raised: *feature the accented E in the third division of basses.* The E becomes a pedal point which, after some forty measures, suddenly "drops" into the main key of *La Valse,* D major, [5], with the first glimpse of a real waltz theme. Only five measures later the pedal point resumes on E for another sixteen measures, before we reach the beginning of a long D major cadence [9] introduced over alternating dominant–tonic basses A–D–A–D. This is also the rehearsal letter (A) at which, according to the composer's program, we are shown the ballroom and the "turning crowd" for the first time. Conclusion: there are no single-issue answers in music. However, we shall now continue to examine the nature of questions concerning musical shapes and what the answers may involve.

BRAHMS, *SYMPHONY No. 3* REEXAMINED*

In Chapter 3a (p. 76) we came across the curious musical shape which opens, and dominates, the third movement of Brahms's *Third Symphony.* What attracted our attention was a metric shift, the displacement across the barline of the rhythmic pattern of this melody:

---

*For this discussion of Brahms's *Third Symphony,* a full score should be used.

EXAMPLE 5

Brahms was fond of asymmetric phrases. The cumulative tension of these long upbeats is released into much weaker, shorter resolutions. This characteristic of the very first shape in the movement became a characteristic of the whole movement, including the middle section, which is constructed of entirely different thematic materials. The matrix of tension and release, the design of a shape *as such*, was the "odd detail" which, once discovered, became a point of contact from which the inner unity of the work would be revealed.

We shall now attempt to use our "Ur-shape" as a means of testing the surface evidence along the entire range of the symphony for clues to the possible extension of this inner unity underneath a wider area of the surface. In a symphony which begins Allegro con brio but ends un poco sostenuto, this may not be an unprofitable undertaking.

The pitches F–A♭–F outline the top of the first three chords in the opening Allegro. They recur immediately in the bass (mm. 3–5). This minor third within an octave is woven into the fabric of the symphony in so many ways, that it becomes a kind of motto which not only dominates the music when it is present, but literally haunts it when it is not. The melodic outline of the cello melody which opens the third movement, for instance, features the minor third at once, but we seek in vain for its completion in the upper octave. So does the music, up to the final augmented scale in C minor which, as we have seen (p. 78), founders and turns back on B♭. Throughout the movement this melody strains upward without ever achieving the fulfillment of a melodic outline established and repeated in various ways since the beginning of the work. The "haunting" presence of this melodic outline contributes to the sense of melancholy which permeates the movement. The feeling-shape of strong-tension—weak-release is enforced by the melodic incompatibility between the cello theme that embodies the essence of musical frustration and the symphony's motto, which combines the opening interval of that melody with its unreachable goal.

Please note that we are not seeking to establish relationships based on thematic materials. The concept of a musical shape as an *audible design* does not require any particular musical content as the means by which a recognizable design may be expressed. If we are to presume that such an imminent shape informs the Brahms *Third* throughout, we shall require evidence that there *is* such an ubiquitous design, that it does *not* depend on related musical materials, and that it can be *heard* in performance. If musical shapes are to be treated as audible designs, whatever cannot be so presented and perceived in performance is useless. Once you have established the shape in your own mind, as part of your performance image, failure to realize it in the orchestral presentation is quite as serious as failure to observe composer's instructions on tempo or dynamics.

The shapes we examined in *La Valse* were dissimilar, in spite of close melodic relationships. They consisted of small musical statements whose message was expressive and immediate: "this theme is nostalgic and beautiful," "this theme has been pulled *out of shape*, and it has become frenzied and ugly." Now we shall be dealing with shapes that are similar, despite different thematic material, because metric and harmonic characteristics remain the same, albeit in context of quite unrelated musical environments: the opening of Brahms's *Third* with its powerful contrasts, or the gently subdued third movement with its "wistful sort of sadness."

We shall distinguish between two kinds of shapes: *independent shapes*, in which harmonic and melodic characteristics serve an immediate, expressive purpose and may, in fact, be modified by contradictory dynamic markings to emphasize the unique and singular appearance of that musical statement (cf. *La Valse*, Ex. 2, p. 258); and *shapes as prototypes*, which provide a matrix for most musical statements in a work, regardless of their individual thematic dissimilarities. Harmony and prominently featured intervals in certain combinations are both means for making such shapes work, and instantly recognizable.

The opening of Brahms's *Third* suggests such a shape. The three-note cell F–Ab–F (above) in the upper winds rests upon a distinctive and memorable harmonic pattern: strong–weak–strong, with the last chord (m. 3) becoming the first of another overlapping three-measure pattern built on a reappearance of the three-note melodic cell in the bass. This pattern dominates the first 30 measures of the symphony, not only by its constant and prominently featured recurrence, but also by the way it *shapes* thematically independent materials like the powerful first theme (m. 3). We shall refer to this pattern as the *motto* of Brahms's *Third*.

A glance at the score will show that, in mm. 1–3, the melodic cell F–Ab–F tops three chords: tonic F major, a half-diminished 7th, and another F major. This last rests on the bass F which begins another three-note cell, whose upper F supports the first inversion of a Db-major chord in m. 5.

In mm. 7 and 8 the three-note motto seems to have become a four-note shape, and so it will finally emerge, independently, as we shall see. But for now, while thematic material is being prominently introduced, the alteration of the third (E♭–E♮) and the same in mm. 9 and 10 (A♭–A♮) does not really extend the cell; rather it attests to another significant feature of the symphony, the minor / major mode mixture which informs the work until this ambiguity is accepted, rather than resolved, at the close of the finale.

With the aid of the chart opposite, you may observe the reflection of this in the first section of the opening movement. Only two phrases, of four measures each (mm. 15–18 and 23–26), are not part of the motto. In a work as meticulously constructed as this symphony, it is doubtful that these two corresponding passages were left out of the overall design inadvertantly. As always, in noting an "odd" detail, we shall reserve consideration of the missing motto in these two phrases, on the chance that an explanation will come to mind in the course of further study. But we shall also guard this compositional incongruity closely so that it can leap forth at the first opportunity. We shall not have long to wait.

Instead of the distinctive intervallic skips of a rising minor third and major sixth, both phrases are characterized by upward, stepwise progressions, and by the sustained roots, F and D♭, of their tonalities. The five measures connecting the final appearance of the motto in this section with the A major 9/4 section to come (mm. 31–35), also have the root of their opening chord sustained. Look in the score.

The beginnings of the wind arpeggios in these five measures are derived from the motto; and the most noticeable movement in the strings, the downward motion by a third in the violas, should sound prominent enough to be understood as an inversion of the third with which the motto begins. In either case, what had been established as a melodic matrix appears to be on the point of dissolving for the time being. The main interest in these five measures lies in the fact that the tempo slows down, and that from the slow pulse of two established throughout the movement thus far, the music changes to a pulse of three in the final two measures (34 and 35).

These two measures are the augmented equivalent of m. 32. To the listener, this must be perceptible as the winds begin their arpeggio in quarters instead of eights. The last measure before the 9/4 corresponds to the second *half* of its model (m. 32), and must therefore reflect the division in three. The many hemiolas of the entire opening section notwithstanding, this is the first time that an actual shift of metric pulse has taken place.

Only once more in the first unfolding of the symphony does the "motto" appear in its radiant *four-note* version. Here are those two wonderful measures (49 and 50), just before the transition to a vigorous closing section of the exposition:

BRAHMS, SYMPHONY Nº. 3, 1st movement, three-note "Motto," mm. 1–31

Measures	Motto: Melodic Cell	Movement: Metric Values	Instrumentation	Context: Harmonic	Dynamic
1–3	(music)	𝅗𝅥. 𝅗𝅥. in 6/4	Flute I, Oboe I, (Horn I) *Texture (Other than Motto):* Winds, Horns, Trumpets	F major/Half-Diminished 7th/F major	f
3–5	(music)	𝅗𝅥. 𝅗𝅥. in 6/4	C.Bn., Trbn. III, D. Bass Cello Trbns., Tym. Strings	F major / f minor / Db major⁶ (I⁶ off)	f
7, 8	(music)	𝅗𝅥. in 6/4	Clar. Horns I, II Strings, Bn.	C⁶major/Diminished 7th/Diminished 7th/C⁶₄	f ⟨ ⟩
9, 10	(music)	𝅗𝅥. in 6/4	Flute, Oboe, (Horn III), Tpt I Winds, Horns, Tpt, Strings	F⁶major/Diminished 7th/Diminished 7th/F⁶₄	f cresc.
11, 12	(music)	(♩) 3× 𝅗𝅥. ♩ / ♪ 𝅘𝅥. in 6/4	Cl. I, Bn. I, Horn I Cl., Bn., Horns, Strings	Bb major/Gb major/Diminished C²	f
13, 14	(music)	𝅗𝅥.♩♩(♩) in / ♩♩ 𝅗𝅥.(♩) 6/4	C.Bn., Cello, Bass Winds, Horn, Tpt., Strings	F⁶/ F ⁶₄ / F⁶/ F ⁶₄	f ⟩
15–18				F major	p ⟩
19–20 (21)	(music)	𝅗𝅥. 𝅗𝅥. in 6/4	C.Bn., Bn., Trbn III, Cello, Bass Tbns, Strings	F⁶/ C⁷ / (F⁶)	f
21–22 (23)	(music)	𝅗𝅥. 𝅗𝅥. in 6/4	Flute I, Oboe I, (Horn I) Winds, Horns, Tpts., Strings	F⁶/ Ab⁷/ (Db)	f (fp)
23–26	(music)			Db major	fp ⟨ p
27–28 (29)	(music)	𝅗𝅥. 𝅗𝅥. in 6/4	Bn. II, Horn IV Fl., Cl., Bn., Horn, Strings	Db⁶/ Ab⁷/ (Db)	p ⟨ ⟩
29–30 (31)	(music)	𝅗𝅥. 𝅗𝅥. in 6/4	Flute II, Oboe I, Winds, Horns, Strings	Db / E⁷/ (A)	p ⟨⟩ ⟩

EXAMPLE 6

Even a brief glance at the lilting 9/4 section that lies in between will reveal much that seems familiar. The stepwise fashion with which the new theme opens in the clarinet (m. 36) is reminiscent of the two four-measure phrases in the first section that did *not* display the motto. Only the position of the outer voices of that passage have been reversed. And while in the two previous passages only the root of F major and of Db major was sustained, in this A-major section root and fifth permeate the entire instrumental texture in a shimmering continuity within which the two moving voices are confined.

If that fails to give an odd sense of recognition to anyone who has worked through the third movement of this symphony (Chapter 3a), then perhaps the coincidence of dynamic indications for the melody will provide a clue: mezza voce, *p* grazioso—and surely "with a wistful sort of sadness." The tonal ground from which the ascending melody of the third movement could not rise to reach the upward resolution of its gentle thrust clings even more firmly here. In upward thrusts of their own, the chain of repeated fifths virtually envelop the moving voices which rarely even emerge above the texture of A and E. A different kind of tension is implied in this passage, in the absence of a suggested release. It merely comes to an end (m. 46). Then, after a quarter rest, this eloquent and moving event in the strings follows (mm. 47–48):

EXAMPLE 7

The A-major theme rises to meet its mirror image descending from above, in a soft but full-throated pleading, that loses itself at the end of two measures in a *pp* return to the motto (p. 265). The reappearance of this ubiquitous shape in its four-chord version is exquisite in its poignant anticipation of the symphony's end.

You are urged to continue the search for the motto and the shape. The entire closing section and transition into the development section (mm. 49–72) is a demonstration of powerful upbeats and anticipations that accumulate propulsive energy because the successive releases are weak. But is this not a contrary result of the strong–weak pattern from that in the third movement? Indeed yes, the only common characteristics seem to be that "something happens" whenever the pattern is at work. Also, the basic shape appears to depend on recurring harmonic events in which the stronger is followed by a weaker. The fact is, the "motto" itself falls into that pattern. Resignation, as a feeling associated with any of the music in the first movement, is suggested only by its ending. Having studied the entire third movement, you will recognize a connection.

EXAMPLE 8

Unlike the independent, "local" shapes we examined in *La Valse*, shapes that function as prototypes within an entire movement or a whole work have an expressive effect on their musical environment. It is the composer, of course, who vests a recognizable melodic fragment or the rhythmic contour of a phrase with affective meaning. Increasingly, throughout the nineteenth century, this became the assigned role of harmony, a subject we shall explore in some detail in the next score chapter. What distinguishes the prototypical shape is that its association with a particular expressive content, once established, colors all further appearances of that shape, whether or not the harmonic environment is the same.

The expressive climate of a work can be established and maintained by various compositional means. That certain musical shapes may be invested with such a function, and that the "meaning" of a shape may then assume a significance quite independent of a given musical environment, will not appear entirely surprising when we remind ourselves of the role of the leitmotif in Wagner's late operas. But the usefulness of this device has been recognized by composers from Bach to Sessions. And it is up to the conductor, once he has determined the significance of certain shapes within the overall musical structure, to stress that aspect in performance, so that its affect will not be lost on the listener.

REVIEW

1. *Individual shapes* are determined by a combination of melodic, harmonic, rhythmic, and dynamic elements. The mixture and its possible effect on tempo and musical momentum must be determined by the conductor. Expressive considerations are likely to be a factor, possibly the main factor in that decision.
2. *General shapes* serve as matrix for any kind of thematic materials or expressive purposes. These have an expressive function and are most likely to be established by harmonic events. The conductor has some choice in determining degrees of emphasis within the shape, but none with regard to elements affecting the characteristics of the shape itself.

There is a third kind of musical shape. It is too large to be perceived by the ear without clear points of orientation within the period of its duration in time. To distinguish this large, articulated shape from those discussed above, we shall use the term *structure* for it. It should be remembered, however, that except for its size and the need to define its passage in time with additional means of aural clarification, a structure is subject to the same requirements of interpretive reconstruction as any other shape. Definition of such structures was, for nearly two hundred years, the primary function of harmony.

Assignment

A. Work through the entire score of Brahms's *Third Symphony*, according to the outline of study which is by now familiar.

1. Survey of the *musical surface.* Use the chart in Chapter 2 until you are quite confident that you are not missing anything.*
2. If you can establish *points of contact, make notes.* Test according to the particular nature of what you found.
3. *Musical shapes* that inform an entire symphony are valuable points of contact. Use the strong–weak shape, as well as the motto, in a review of all four movements in order to determine its distribution, manner of application, and effect. Mark your score accordingly.

---

*Group B2, *Correspondences:* points of contact and musical shapes may indicate very important Correspondences within a work. When you have reviewed any score according to these categories, or those examined in the following chapters, do review your survey according to correspondences. Mark your score.

B. Analyze and mark musical shapes in *La Valse*, using the process illustrated on p. 257. Imagine the result as realistically as possible. Make appropriate use of decisions you will have taken already, concerning the respective character of corresponding waltzes. Test your decisions for possible effect on tempo.

PODIUM

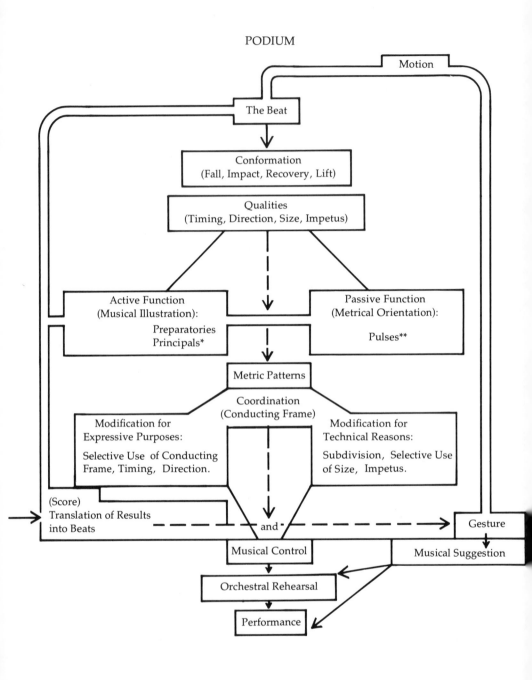

Motion

The Beat

Conformation
(Fall, Impact, Recovery, Lift)

Qualities
(Timing, Direction, Size, Impetus)

Active Function
(Musical Illustration):

Preparatories
Principals*

Passive Function
(Metrical Orientation):

Pulses**

Metric Patterns

Coordination
(Conducting Frame)

Modification for
Expressive Purposes:

Selective Use of Conducting
Frame, Timing, Direction.

Modification for
Technical Reasons:

Subdivision, Selective Use
of Size, Impetus.

(Score)
Translation of Results
into Beats

and

Gesture

Musical Control

Musical Suggestion

Orchestral Rehearsal

Performance

*Exception: *Series* of Principals: (*Passive* Function)   **Exception: *Accented* Pulse: (*Active* Function)

9

CONDUCTING: VARIETIES OF CONTROL

> Continuing where Chapter 7 left off, this chapter addresses the additional problem of directed give and take of musical initiative within the orchestra. Complete score worked through: Debussy, *The Afternoon of a Faun*.

WITH the ease and confidence gained in the practice of the beat as summarized in Chapter 7, you will have made a good start toward achieving the sort of flexible and effective baton technique which modern orchestras have come to require of their conductors. Expectations of technical competence, whether in the case of apprentice conductors or of newly engaged players serving their probationary year, have risen as rehearsal time has shrunk. The ability to communicate clearly, in the language of the stick, is high on the priority list of your future employers. It is equally high on the list of qualifications that the members of an orchestra find impressive in the person on the podium.

The grammar and syntax governing the signals of the beat are based on a comprehensive system that is simple enough in principle and practice. However, it becomes extraordinarily complex in the varieties of control which conductors may wield or yield. The "give and take" in the exercise of control from the podium is a matter of musical judgment and technical proficiency, the two sides of our conducting coin which, at this stage, have become twin facets of a single achievement.

The question of "whose musical initiative?" is basic to all musical ensemble playing, from string quartet to opera. Along with the biblical injunction that it is better to give than to receive (spoken from every conductor's heart!) should go the warning that giving, in our profession, is the more difficult of these alternatives. We shall begin this chapter with further exploration of the varieties of technical control over the means of orchestral performance. As soon as we become involved with complete works, however, it will be aparent that "give and take,"in terms of musical initiative, are two distinct aspects of a conductor's podium craft, as score and podium are both dimensions of his overall professional concern. The aspect of "taking," i.e. the yielding of initiative, without loss of control, will be dealt with later.

In the review chapter on the application of the beat (7) we examined the use of *accented pulse* and *isolated lift* "as upbeats to start a movement *without* necessarily relating to the metric pulse of what is to come."* In the execution of these beats we learned that

> "the accented pulse, or the isolated lift, used as an upbeat unrelated to the metric pulse of the music to come, should always be the continuation of a larger motion already begun."**

Beats that do "not necessarily relate to the metric pulse of what is to come" provide an important illustration of the border area between beat and gesture, control and yielding of control. As long as it was taken for granted that beats would always reflect the metric pulse of the music being played, varieties of control remained qualitative: the beat was either descriptive in terms of expression, articulation, and relative emphasis within the phrase, or its function was passive. Even the last implied precise metric definition. With some of the upbeats demonstrated on pp. 246ff this was not the case.

Nor was it the case in earlier examples and exercises of accelerandos and retards, in which compound meters were gradually reduced to their underlying plain beat patterns, or subdivisions were added to control the rate of retard from plain meters to their compound equivalents. At some point, the change in musical flow had to be entrusted to the shared perception of players and conductor. Beat-by-beat metric control was suspended. But this did not imply that the conductors yielded expressive control.

As we now turn our attention from brief orchestral excerpts to conducting whole movements or works, we shall have to recognize that varieties of control extend over metric as well as expressive initiative. Among the essential skills in the application of the beat, flexibility in the exercise of control is as helpful to the orchestra as it is apparent to an audience. The pejorative term "time beater" does not describe a conductor whose beat is metrically precise, but one who never ceases being metrically precise. Indiscriminately precise beats can be inhibiting to a good player. Naturally, what may seem pedantic and fussy with one orchestra might well be absolutely necessary to keep a less experienced

*P. 246.
**P. 247.

group together. Flexibility in the exercise of control is also a matter of practical judgment on the conductor's part. between rehersal and performance some controls might be eliminated, or need to be more strictly imposed.

Experience will be your best teacher in acquiring a sense of what may be possible and effective in terms of control, or appropriate to the continually changing musical and techical demands of a score in performance. But an understanding of the principles, and an awareness of the opportunities inherent in a constant shift of musical initiative between player and conductor, will set you on the road to gaining that experience.

EXAMPLE 1: Mozart, *Eine kleine Nachtmusik,* second movement—*Romanze*

As always, we begin with the score. The opening phrase of the Andante movement from Mozart's *Eine kleine Nachtmusik* will recall our analysis on pp. 97ff. Review your own notes on that chapter and refresh your memory of whatever results of your work on that score you put in writing.

Next, you will use the table of data (p. 101) to determine a clear shape for this phrase. A clear hope, in this case, is one you perceive so vividly in your imagination that its high and low points are not only understood, on the strength of harmonic and melodic evidence, but also transformed into parts of a solid memory image. At will, you should not only be able to recall the printed image of this opening, but to hear an imaginary transcription of its musical surface. Your image of this simple phrase should include your decisions, the reasons for your decisions, thoughts and feelings which accompanied your arrival at these decisions, and whatever associations seemed memorable.

Why? Because we shall now ask an odd question: What is it that we shall *choose* to control at the opening of this phrase, and again on the third beat of the second full measure? In order to acquire "a *sense* of what may be possible and effective in terms of control, and appropriate to the continually changing musical and technical demands of a score in performance," we shall begin by cultivating an understanding of the *varieties* of control we may exercise by varying the *amount* of control we impose.

The following three solutions are based on three quite different answers to the question of what we may choose to control. Try all three. As soon as you have felt the physical sensation of reflecting subtle matters of phrasing by a beat of *deliberately modified precision,* you will have

EXAMPLE 2

crossed the last dividing line between your own image of the score and the players' need for direction from the podium.

In Example 2, the upbeat to beat 3 is an accented pulse. Its time value would be about one sixteenth. The string attack follows at once. Before the actual upbeat the right arm is already in motion, so that the accented pulse amounts to no more than a twitch in the course of this motion. Neither the speed, the timing, the size, nor the direction of that "background motion" are of any significance. Therefore it is not in itself a beat, and you must take care that its indeterminate quality is maintained until the start of the music. Like all pulses, this accented pulse is very small.

What does it achieve? In the absence of any preparatory element (lift), there will be no sense of fulfilment on the first attack. If we wish to think of the first one and one half measures as preparation for the first beat of the second full measure (as marked in the example above), this opening, followed by a series of preparatories, is ideal. The upbeat to the second half of the phrase, beginning on the third beat of the second measure, would be a strong preparatory. The high C would become, literally, the highpoint of a progressively weakening shape, with its feminine ending as the weakest point, corresponding to the earlier climax: a rather fine symmetry of rhythmic look-alikes with quite different musical functions.

EXAMPLE 3

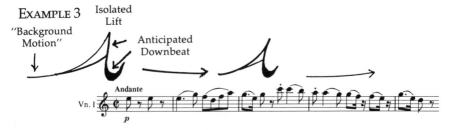

Beginning with the same kind of "background motion," the upbeat to beat 3 in Example 3 is here an *isolated lift*. Its time value may be either shorter or longer than a quarter. In order to avoid the impression of a regular preparatory upbeat (cf. Example 4 below), do *not* try to signal the coming tempo at all. The longer the duration of the lift, the greater will be the accumulated tension released into the attack on the third beat. In order not to allow this tension to reflect on the dynamic level of the opening, the downbeat on 3 must be very small, and timed just *before* the intended attack.*

What is achieved? A very different melodic shape from that described earlier: because of the soft beginning, the first notes are charged with energy. The energy of the lift has not been released. Instead it will be felt through the first beat of the first full measure, after which you should allow it to subside into the first beat of the next. The second half of the phrase, as indicated in Example 3, has the same shape, requiring, before the high C, a deliberately indistinct second beat allowing for another isolated lift. This version of the opening would suggest an underlying passion, propelling the music forward into a climax on the second high C (m. 7). A faster tempo would certainly be indicated. The range of choice, according to eighteenth-century performance practice, is wide (p. 99, Group A3). The basis for choice, within that range, includes the musical shape you have determined.

EXAMPLE 4

The upbeat to beat 3 in Example 4 is a "normal" preparatory, timed to the quarter beat of the music to come. No matter how expressive, this exact preview of the tempo is provided at the price of musical projection. A left-hand gesture, not timed to the movement of the right, could compensate, of course. But we are now concerned with varieties of control, i.e. varieties of precision, and the inhibiting quality of "indiscriminately precise beats" as illustrated in this example: even in an upbeat, before the music begins, precision for its own sake is not a musical virtue.

EXAMPLE 5: Schubert, *Symphony No. 4*, Menuetto

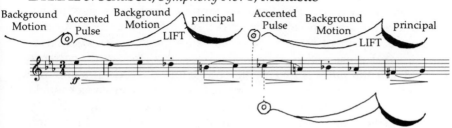

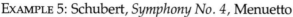

---

*Cf. the anticipated ("delayed") downbeat for Brahms's *Third Symphony*, third movement, p. 149, Figure 2b.

The opening of the Minuet from Schubert's *Fourth Symphony* presents an unusual problem, for the only way to represent the composer's instructions effectively is to use four distinct motions for every pair of 3/4 measures. Only one of these falls on a first beat. The fascination of this unison passage is its tonal and metric ambiguity. In the course of the movement the initial uncertainty in both areas is resolved; but even then the two-measure motive persists as an obdurate, off-beat shape over oom-pa-pa accompaniments or within complex contrapuntal textures. Neither its shape nor its off-beat character is apparent at the start. And that is where the difficulty lies in performance, and where the conductor's beat must not get in the way.

In the absence of any metric or harmonic indicators, listeners are likely to hear the passage as if it were:

EXAMPLE 6

Only at the end of the first part of the main section do the basses reveal downbeats on fast 3/4 measures, as part of a harmonized cadence into B♭ (the actual key of E♭ is withheld until the coda of the return). The composer's instructions clearly require maintaining this mystification as part of the capricious good humor of this piece. Too fast to be beaten in three, the menuet presents a problem. Beaten in one, it will inevitably be played like this:

EXAMPLE 7

Complicated as it may seem, the outline of beats suggested in the Example 5 works. There is no need to explain what is being beaten. Again we begin with a "background motion"; to be *seen* moving not only draws the attention of every player, but makes the slightest acceleration of movement into the accented pulse much easier to observe. The accented pulse will be followed at once by a strong tutti entrance on beat 3. If the pulse is given with conviction, the orchestra entrance will be clean and unanimous, every time. Under no circumstances should the 1 of the first measure be indicated. The pulse was succeeded by another background motion which, in the course of the first measure, develops into a lift. This, in turn, resolves powerfully into the first beat of m. 2. The C♭ at the end of m. 2 is either anticipated by another accented pulse, or (as shown below the staff) the pulse may this time coincide with the third quarter. In either case the even flow of rapid quarter notes would proceed uninterrupted.

To the demonstrated potential of expressive control inherent in temporary renunciation of explicit metric control, we may now add an observation which applies to all kinds of beat.

The intended signal of any beat or gesture is more readily perceived as *change of a movement in progress* than as initiation of movement from immobility.

It follows from this that:

The less precise either the preparation or the actual timing of a beat, for whatever reason, the more important becomes its clear definition as *perceptible change from ongoing motion.*

When we speak of varieties of control, we also speak of the unvariable requirement of a flow of motion. There is no control without motion.

To satisfy this requirement, we introduced the concept of *background motion.* In the absence of meaningful beat or gesture, this is a kind of even movement whose only function is to represent motion against which the smallest, most subtle change can be perceived instantly. The most obvious occasion for this is the moment before the music starts. There are others. Before we attempt to collect all our separate skills in the application of the beat to an orchestral work demanding an advanced and sensitive baton technique, we shall explore briefly the question of flexible control when the metric flow of music is to be interrupted or abruptly changed.

Interruptions are part of the music in which they occur. From a technical point of view, we have learned that the closer we find ourselves to the center of the beat, the easier it is to start again. If the interruption of the musical flow is in fact the end of the piece, we have other choices: we can dramatize a powerful final chord or allow a gentle last note to expire into silence without any terminating motion at all. For once, we may enjoy the luxury of being left physically off balance. But the kind of stop which implies only a temporary freezing of the musical continuity should find us in the best possible position for a suitable start of the music to come.

The finale of Beethoven's *First Symphony* offers several difficult examples of stops, holds, and, in particular, the soft start following the big tutti fermatas near the end.

EXAMPLE 8: Beethoven, *Symphony No. 1*, fourth movement

The transition from the first fermata to the chord that follows should not present a problem even if, for the sake of dramatic effect, you had frozen in a stance resembling the Statue of Liberty. A preparatory upbeat, slashing downward and to the left, through center, is in fact the beat we would expect to give (cf. p. 86). Or we might have chosen to cut off the first fermata, with a fast counterclockwise motion, coming to a stop near center. After a silence to let the *ff* reverberations die, this would have been followed by a normal upbeat for the next *ff* chord.

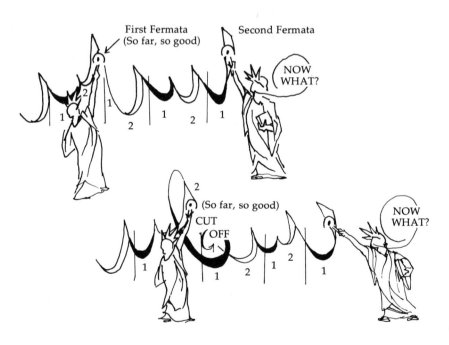

FIGURE 1

The same choice is not available for the second fermata. This equally strong tutti chord is held also. But, unlike the first, it yields to a piano entrance in the second violins alone. It is essential that the second fermata be *held* near the center. For, unless we want to cancel the big, reverberating tutti sound with yet another cutoff to *return* us to center— and spoil the drama of the sudden piano entrance by another theatrical wait—we shall do better to play for safety, and at the same time reflect the wonderful deadpan humor of the passage.

The second fermata should be terminated with a full, *a tempo* measure (in 2) in a brisk, very small beat. This, in effect, adds one measure of silence while the *ff* sound of the tutti chord disappears. It also provides a precise indication of the tempo to come—quite an important consideration if the straightfaced, but really very funny, coda is to make its point before the exuberant conclusion of the symphony.

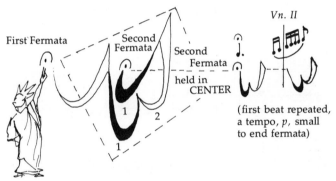

FIGURE 2

Since the start of motion is more easily perceived as change of ongoing motion than as change from immobility to motion, the important corollary in connection with stops and interruptions of motion would be:

> *The interruption of motion,* either a complete stop or a stop involving the transformation into a different mode of motion, *is effective to the extent of the conductor's complete immobility.*

By this we are not referring to the dramatic effect of "freezing" in the pose of the sustained gesture while musical continuity is suspended (although the show-business aspect of conducting is considerably enhanced by appropriate visual drama). If, in the case of the fermatas of the Beethoven finale, the conductor remains motionless until he is ready to begin the preparation of his next signal, the forte will be sustained, strings can change bows if necessary, winds can stagger breathing. If he moves before the next attack, he will risk a slackening of tension. When it becomes necessary to shake a fist to sustain sound, he will most likely have erred already and spoiled the composer's intended effect.

Thus the need to keep absolutely still once the temporary stop has taken place becomes an embarrassment if the pose you have struck leaves you "off base." The possible involvement of the left hand can be of help in making the connection, but it does not absolve the conductor from the requirement of complete immobility while the temporary stop lasts. You are well advised to seek the security of the center if in doubt.

Consider the wonderful moment at the end of Beethoven's *Eroica Symphony*, when the forward momentum of the Allegro molto is transformed into a serene eulogy begun, con espressione, by one of the most beautiful oboe solos in the literature.

EXAMPLE 8: Beethoven, *Symphony No. 3*, fourth movement, mm. 345–55

The *ff* hold could well be "illustrated" by the conductor's freezing in an imperious gesture, with the baton pointing heavenward. But the need to make way for the piano upbeat following the fermata, for the gentle introduction of one musical experience growing out of another, argues for technical wisdom at the expense of visual drama. The holding point of the *ff* chord must be as near to the inconspicuous upbeat-to-come for the oboe entrance as possible. Even if the left hand were to be used for a cutoff of the fermata, a perfectly plausible way of managing this transformation, the right hand ought to be ready to take over from where it already *is:* near center.

More difficult are the following abrupt interruptions of tempo in Mahler's *Fourth Symphony*, third movement:

EXAMPLE 9: mm. 234–44

EXAMPLE 10: mm. 259–66

EXAMPLE 11: mm. 270–81

EXAMPLE 12: mm. 282–86

It is quite surprising how much control is required to achieve a tempo change that cannot be prepared before it is to happen. Example 9 includes meticulous instructions by the composer: mm. 236–37 "Nicht rit.," i.e. don't slow up *before* the change of tempo; m. 238, "Allegretto subito (*Nicht eilen*)," the Allegretto at once (!), *don't rush*; and lest there be any doubt: "Ohne die geringste Vermittlung das neue Tempo," without the slightest concession to the new tempo.

Having examined several ways to start a movement without an upbeat in strict tempo (i.e. by an accented pulse or an isolated lift, neither of which relate to tempo), we already have some experience with apparently spontaneous establishment of tempo. These transformations in Mahler's *Fourth* will demonstrate the principle involved. *Instead of establishing the tempo before the first beat, by a strictly timed upbeat, it is determined between the first and second beats, by a particularly careful downbeat.*

Since there is no chance of suggesting the tempo of the 3/8 measure with the upbeat on the second quarter of the previous 2/4 measure, we must establish the faster beat by a fast recovery and lift on the first beat of m. 238. In other words, *the downbeat of the first 3/8 measure becomes a preparatory for the second beat.* The glissando in Violins 2 makes that a little easier: the second beat will in effect have an accent on it, into which the preparatory on the first should lead quite naturally. The continued pianissimo reinforces the rule that *an increase in tempo calls for a decrease in size of the beat.* Resist the temptation to "flail your arms" in order to move the tempo.

Example 10 involves almost identical problems with the same caveats by the composer: "Streng im Tempo; Allegro subito; der Tempwechsel vollzieht sich ebenso *plötzlich* und *überraschend* wie vorhin"* (the underlining of the words "sudden" and "surprising" is by Mahler himself). It is important that the necessarily brisk beat at m. 265 does not encourage a string dynamic of more than *pp* (up from *ppp*), or wind entrances of more than *p* or *pp* respectively.

The situation in Example 11 is still more difficult; to the questions already discussed is added the abrupt transition from *ff* to *pp*. Once again the center of the beat will prove a panacea for conducting problems. Turn the second beat of m. 27 resolutely *toward center*, without the slightest weakening until just before the next downbeat. There could even be a downward angle to that second beat to account for the sforzato in the horns. The diminuendo in the second violins must be managed by the left hand. Needless to say, the last-moment recovery of this upbeat is minimal. The fall of the m. 278 downbeat is also very small, its lift relatively large (making this beat into a preparatory for the following 2). The elevation of these soft beats will remain high until the crescendo in m. 280.

The most dramatic, and also the easiest, transformation of tempo takes place at m. 283 (Example 12). Mahler, himself a seasoned conductor by this time, shows us just what to do: the quasi fermata (only in the horns) allows time for a clear preparation of the second beat, as well as an expressive left-hand gesture to characterize the suddenly changed expressive climate (cf. p. 145). Such a gesture might begin with an illustration of the string pianissimo and the reduction of volume in all instruments except the horns (which diminish from the second beat).

---

*Translation: Strictly in tempo; Allegro subito; change of tempo takes place as suddenly and surprisingly as before.

The "quasi fermata" says: in tempo but not unyielding. Your beat shall begin to say the same.

EXAMPLE 13: Copland, *Appalachian Spring*

Needless to say, a competent conductor must be *able* to exercise very rigid control over any aspect of orchestral performance when the occasion demands it; and no musical situation requires more "unyielding" control than an abrupt shift of tempo. But this is merely a *technical* problem. Example 13, from Copland's *Appalachian Spring*, is remarkable in that it does *not* insist on "strict tempo and sudden transformation": that is taken for granted. Technically, as with the first three Mahler excerpts, the first beat of m. 28 becomes the preparatory in a suddenly slower tempo, determined by the timing of the second beat which is being prepared. The normal combination of upbeat and preparatory functions at the beginning of a new tempo is split in two: placement of the first chord of m. 28 is still taken care of in the old, faster tempo; placement of the second beat is controlled at the new "more deliberate" speed, with the first beat, slowed by a large lift, defining the difference.

Nowhere is a sense of firm but flexible control, of readiness to yield initiative and instant capacity to reassume technical and musical command, more evident than in the effective alternation of slow, undifferentiated beats with subdivided groupings of pulses in a fluctuating flow of tempo. This is particularly true of works in which the interplay of solo instruments and the interchange of plain and compound meters call for a lively ensemble among some participants while colleagues count, and while the conductor directs, follows, and keeps track. Claude Debussy's *Prelude to "The Afternoon of a Faun"* is such a work.

ONE POSSIBLE OUTLINE OF BEATS
FOR CLAUDE DEBUSSY'S
Prelude to "The Afternoon of a Faun"

Beat Symbols:

$\downarrow$　　—principal beat

$\int$　　—preparatory beat

$\overset{\uparrow}{\circ}$　　—isolated lift

$\bigcirc$　　—neutral pulse

$\bullet$　　—accented pulse

N.B. The metric value of each beat appears directly above its symbol.

EXAMPLE 14: Debussy, *Prelude to "The Afternoon of a Faun"*

Note: No beats are given for the flute solo. Symbols in parentheses could be small gestures, a principal to start, an isolated lift to show the step from C♯ to B, and thus the tempo. Beats begin with fourth measure.

Hold still during the measure rest. Upbeat for following violin and harp entrance occurs on beat 6.

Throughout, principals and preparatories match the phrase, not necessarily "heavy beats" in a pattern.

In the measure of ⊡ and the next, the beats of the opening flute solo are actually given. Tempo fluctuates constantly. In the fifth measure of ⊡ a forward moving tempo, as well as a simple rhythmic texture, is represented by an unsubdivided, flowing beat.

Keep beats small. In the third measure before ☐2 the fall of every beat is minimal, the lift large for the sake of dynamic nuance.

Don't rush. First harp leads on beats 1 and 2, you control the second harp.

A very careful preparatory is needed to insure the *pp* (!) entrance of 2nd violins and violas.

The tempo relaxes throughout the fifth measure of ⟨2⟩ on the first beat only the lower flute C controls the beginning rit. (viz. isolated lift); on the second you take charge (three beats!) also to prepare the *pp* pizz. in the strings. On the third the flute completes it alone (isolated lift).

Previous measure: cresc. only to *mp*, and small accel.

The 9/8 measure above is a fine sample of adjustment of beat pattern according to beat function. Practice the diagram on the right. Note that the *direction of main beats is unchanged* (1, 4, 7).

Practice the suggested patterns and varieties of beats in the three measures before ⟨3⟩. The respective functions must be clear, first. Remember that 12/8 = plain 4, 9/8 = plain 3, subdivided.

At ⟨3⟩ the tempo suddenly quickens: therefore the suggestion of accented pulses. Note bass pizz.

Transition into 3/4 in flowing beat of three was aided by isolated lift at end of previous 12/8, preparatory on first beat above.

Last beat of second 3/4 measure should be held (in center, *not* at top of pattern) to slow for second quasi più mosso at three before 4 .

Note bass pizz. on *second* beat, change in pattern.

From two before 4 little overt control needs to be exercised in the beat. The motion is generally forward, except for the beat before 4 : the transition into the "sweet and expressive" oboe solo suggests that you allow the flute to take time on its trill (hold, very slightly, *near center*).

All entrances are *piano;* the crescendo itself only goes to *mf,* then tutti diminuendo to piano in *one* measure.

Because it looks (and to the players feels) easy, take care that this "animant" section does not run away out of control. Speed can be curbed in diminuendo measure.

Top speed is reached during the passage after ⑤ . The two previous 3/4 measures, with their subito *p* first beats, are held slightly on their respective third beats: *beat to center* and don't lift baton to top until ready to prepare the next downbeat. But don't stop the movement!

Hold the tempo at the speed reached in the third measure of ⑤. The isolated lift on its first beat and that of the next will signal that.

During the retard in the two measures before ⑥ subdivisions are used only when more than one players need to know the rate of slowing down *between main divisions* of the measure, i.e. the flutes and 2nd harp in the measure before ⑥. At ⑥ the clarinet, playing alone between beats, may be given the initiative: you remain in actual control with the second beat.

Isolated lifts in the third and fourth measure of 6 serve only to provide visual evidence of dynamic nuances in conjunction with left-hand gestures. Setting new tempo at change of key is done with full preparatory.

Two classic examples of the need to bring the final beat of any pattern to center before bringing it up: Third measure of ⑦, because of slight stretch of that beat; fourth of ⑦, because of subito *pp* to come.

Throughout the entire passage of wind triplets, it is absolutely essential that the timing of your beat remain *rock steady*. Whatever expressive initiative you will wish to take with the strings must be entrusted to the left hand. Keep the beat small!

You may find it difficult to "hear" in your mind the triplets against the main melodic line, or to control the expressive tension in the strings at the same time. Memorize the triplet line and concentrate on it. The rest will take care of itself.

With the cessation of the triplet figure on the first and third beats of eight before 8 comes your chance to rein in your tempo. The third beat of that measure, subdivided, may serve two purposes: to check the momentum, and to use the subdividing preparatory to control a sudden dynamic drop from above forte to Subito *mf* on the first beat of the next measure.

Two more examples of when (and when not) to subdivide. The second and third beats of six before ⑧ are subdivided, the second because of the harp on beat 3, and the third because it is the last chance to establish the slow tempo of five before ⑧. But the following measures, though very slow, are not subdivided. The horn leads, then the oboe, etc. (Isolated lifts are *not* subdivisions)

If a slight hesitation is wanted on the upbeat to ⑧, be sure that the subdividing preparatory goes through center. ⑧ will be *a tempo*.

More about subdivisions: the first beat of the fifth of ⑧ is subdivided, the second (although the oboe now has *sfz*) is not. The subdivision was not a matter of emphasis, but of tempo: an accented pulse moves tempo forward. More than one such "push," however, would be unnecessary.

By the same token, the corresponding subdivision on the first beat of two before ⑨ is now also unnecessary. But the fourth beats of this measure and the next are divided: the former because of the subito *pp* on the next downbeat, the latter to slow tempo.

N.B.: The fact that exact repetition, for once in this work, makes further comment unnecessary regarding the next few measures is in itself of significance to you as a performer. Familiar materials to return, but not quite in the same way. This kind of musical structure, in which coherence is greatly indebted to a constant process of change, becomes important in the work of many twentieth-century composers cf. Chapter 13).

The subdivision on the downbeat of two before 10 follows a pattern of two-to-the-beat which has been established since the end of the triplet cross rhythm before 8 . In spite of the clarinet triplets on the third and fourth beats here, we continue to hear the sixteenth triplets as 2 × 3.

Beginning with the third beat of the measure before 10 *think* 3 × 2; on the fourth, *beat* 3 × 2. The retard into 10 must be controlled by the conductor.

10 will "feel" like the 12/8 it was earlier, but the duple meter must be clearly subdivided in the second measure of 10.

While triple and duple divisions of each count coincide, keep the beat small, clear, and in four. The dynamic nuances clarify the texture. This is a job for the left hand.

The isolated lift, three before 11, announces a retard, the preparatory on 4+ controls it.

Two before 11: there is no need to subdivide for a solo harp, but flute and solo cello can coordinate only through your beat. On the third beat they will hear the harp; on the fourth they will depend on visual control from the podium.

With very subtle and important nuances to manage in 11, a small, steady, triple-divided beat will leave the left hand free to define shapes and shadings.

Four after 11: On the first and last beats of this measure, the maximum number of coordinates will best control the ensemble. Therefore triple-division is suggested, although most play duples.

[12], ironically, is in eight, for the harps. The second measure of twelve, on beats 2 and 4, requires very clear triple division. If the violins and horns play as softly as they should, they will not be able to hear each other.

Penultimate measure: do let the flute reassume its initiative in placing the G♯.

The following examples from the first scene of Stravinsky's *Petrushka* (1947 version) must be conducted from memory. There just isn't time to follow the rapid changes of meter, translate the information into beats, and control the orchestra without involuntarily adding to the problem. Even a world-class orchestra would find it very difficult to maintain a light, steady pulse *against* a conductor who "gets in the way" by delays of even a minute fraction of a second, the inevitable time lag when beats need to be confirmed by a visual check of the score.

In order to facilitate visual memory of such a passage, the author uses these symbols in marking the top of his score,

$$(\downarrow) = | \qquad \text{and} \qquad (\downarrow.) = \triangle$$

arranged in appropriate patterns to show time signatures of the measures below. Thus

$$\triangle = 3/4 \qquad || = 2/4 \qquad \triangle = 3/8 \text{ and } |\triangle = 5/8.$$

A glance at the phrase outlines tells us that two metric patterns make up *all* the sequences. The most important appears at once: I of Example 15, 13 to 14, consisting of a 3/8, a 3/4, and a 5/8. It appears again in II, 19 to 20; III, 31 to 32 and 32 to 33; IV, 42 to 43; and V, 46 to 47. The metric pattern, with melodic additions, recurs also from 48 to 49 and from 49 to 50. In other words, learning and placing this three-measure pattern is nearly half the battle in memorizing this phrase outline.

The other pattern involves twice-repeated eighth-note triads moving up and down by a fourth—D minor and G major (up), D major and A minor (down). D remains constant in the bass. II, 20 to 21, is the same as V, 47 to 48; IV, 44 to 45, equals V, 51 to 52.

EXAMPLE 15

What kind of beat will be best for these passages? Try the following combination: principal beats or accented pulses for all quarter-length divisions; preparatories for three-eighths, either as full measures or as the "long" beat of mixed meter measures. Here is the suggested scheme:

♩ = *principal beat*, with the following exception:

♩ = *accented pulse* when:
    a. preceded by a quarter, *and*
    b. followed by a 3/8 division.

♩. = *preparatory beat*, regardless of position in measure or the number of articulated pulses within its length.

This sounds much more complicated than it is. Write the appropriate symbols into your score (this is just to get the "feeling" for it, since you will not be using the score to conduct). Then try it. You will find that the *lift of preparatories* supports the extra length of 3/8 beats quite naturally; and that the tendency of *accented pulses* to impel the tempo forward underlines the brevity of quarters against the dotted quarter to follow.

With both basic motivic patterns well in mind and securely fitted into the five passages from the first scene of *Petrushka*, take note of the missing links in between—at first analytically, then by repeated, mechanical repetition, then from memory, passage by passage. *Stay with it, on the first try, until you can do it.* Within a short time, you should know these passages well. By the time you have also memorized orchestration and dynamics you will be able to beat them with ease (small beats, well centered!) and with a good deal of physical pleasure.

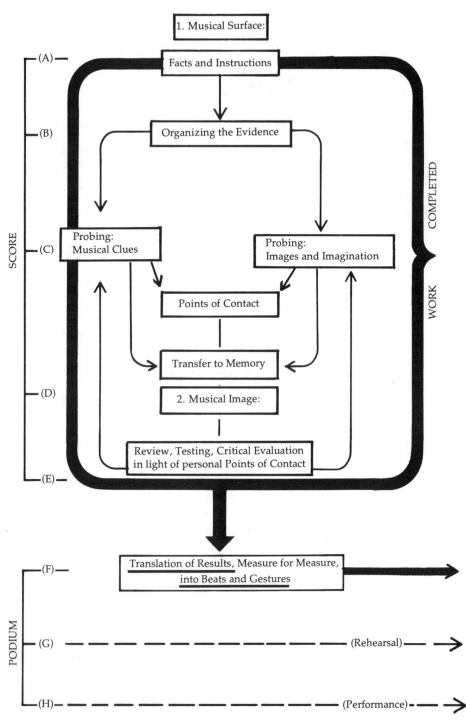

10

STRESSES AND STRUCTURES: THE HARMONIC FUNCTION

Examined are forces that generate musical movement in time and the balance of stresses that is perceived as musical structure. How the containment of such structures was once the exclusive function of harmony, and why this shaping gradually became the function of diverse alternative forces, provides a useful perspective on orchestral music from the eighteenth century to the present. Scores examined: Beethoven, *Seventh Symphony;* Wagner, *Parsifal.*

If melody were all of music, what would be prize in the various forces that make up the immense work of Beethoven, in which melody is assuredly the last?
—STRAVINSKY

Tension is but the vigor of the Mind.
—YEATS

MUSICAL shapes are experienced by the listener as brief, but distinctive, events within the passage of music in time. A series of musical shapes, sharing certain characteristics, may also be heard as one composite part of some larger structure. But in order to create a sense of movement among shapes, or of tension and release within, we need a means of propulsion that has highly responsive thrust, as well as the capacity to reflect degrees of force in the attraction of one group of sounds toward another. For some two hundred years, albeit at a presently diminishing rate, that has been the function of harmony.

The harmonic function defines interdependence of sounds in terms of its own gravitating force, and the consequent significance of musical events in the simultaneous viewing of a structure that, in performance, can only be revealed in increments of time. We have compared musical shapes to the physical contour of a terrain over which we are to walk, and the conductor's beats to steps, carefully matched to the uneven ground. The truly invaluable contribution of harmony is a panoramic view of the entire terrain that may also be focused for close-ups wherever the footing seems doubtful.

For music composed during the hundred years preceding World War I, harmony is a most important key to structure. Earlier still, in music of the Classical style, harmony *was* the structure. In our own century, alternative means of organizing musical materials have gradually gained acceptance, and the music of our time requires conductors able to think and communicate in many different modes of musical expression. None of these, however, has preempted the place of harmony as the common basis of musical logic. And while the harmonic function is no longer the sole gauge of thrust, attraction, and release within the forcefield of a musical structure, the *conventions* of harmony, reflected in the great majority of works in the orchestral repertory, are the more important to present day performers, as "a way of giving significance to sound."*

That harmony has been a variable convention, a once-pervasive force now nearly spent, comes to most of us as a belated discovery, difficult to accept. Far from being solely determined by the accoustical properties of sound, harmonic events are at once the application of choices made by the composer and, within the boundaries of style, a powerful basis for directed expressivity in performance.

Boundaries of style, in this connection, should be equated with the musical expectations of a cultivated contemporary audience, rather than the compositional "style" of any composer, or the historial perspective acquired in a class in "style analysis." Most composers shared musical expectations and conventions with their contemporaries. They made use of them, strained at them, broke them, but they needed to be aware of them in order to do all that.

By beginning his *First Symphony*, with the "wrong" dominant resolving into the "wrong" tonic, Beethoven was able to count on the shocked attention of his audience, because he shared with them the harmonic expectation he violated. Within the boundaries of style, a powerful *basis* for directed expressivity was available to him, in performance. It is doubtful if any listener today, hearing this symphony for the first time, would find anything unusual in the fact that three dominant sevenths have to be resolved in succession before the "right" dominant of C major is reached. That fact must be taken as evidence of a dilemma: as performers, we are expected to conduct a large part of our repertory according to expressive guidelines in the music that are as valid now as they were nearly two centuries ago; but the means with which the effect

---

*Charles Rosen, *Schoenberg* (London: Fontana, 1975), p. 34.

was once achieved will no longer command the intended reaction from present-day listeners.

The choice is between playing it "straight," in faithful observance of the performance practice of its day; or adding touches to achieve the expressive intent in some other way: a slight exaggeration of the wind *fp*s, and a near pianissimo for the piano resolutions in the first two measures of the Introduction, perhaps. But even in this description, the danger of achieving a slapstick effect instead of the intended humor is evident. But the alternative would be to forfeit the endearing character of the opening, and be left with structural significance of a once-pervasive force now nearly spent. As we shall now demonstrate, the spontaneous perception of structural reference in terms of the harmonic function, by a modern audience, requires the same degree of selective emphasis from the conductor as any expressive effects. We have stressed the interpretive, creative role of the performer from the beginning of our study. Now we have reached a point when it should become evident why that role has become more essential than ever, for some of the most important things *in* the score are no longer intelligible to listeners unless the composer receives informed support from the podium. Nothing in the score of a work in the classical style could be more important to its successful realization in performance than to show how, out of harmonic stress, there emerges a unique inner shape. With the introduction of two "foreign" tonalities within a harmonic context of A major, Beethoven created such a shape in his *Seventh Symphony*.

Harmonic stress first appears in Beethoven's A-major symphony in most disarming guise. Soon after an opening that seems to have no other function than to establish the fact that this is indeed going to be a piece in A major, a rather uncommitted, formal, but relentlessly affirmative presentation of the tonic in triads and rising scales, gives way. Volume suddenly diminishes, orchestral color changes, and a lovely, lyrical melody is introduced—in C major (m. 23).

Why C major? By any standards this is a remote key. It was reached, not by an explicit modulation that might disguise the fact that we are now in very diffierent harmonic territory, but by an almost abrupt shift; not by a gradual change of mood, or even a sudden interruption, but simply by reducing volume and texture. It might be an entirely different piece. And it is in C major. Why? The formal presentation of cadences in triads and scales begins again, and is once more transformed into the little melodic alternative, this time in F (m. 42). We are nearly at the *Vivace* main section of the opening movement now. Why F?

Those shifting tonalities must be important: *Music in the classical style is about tonalities*. Well then, we are being told that this symphony is going to be about the keys of A, C, and F. Now take your score and follow the Tale of Three Tonalities as we outline its plot.

Introduction: A-major opening as described. But in mm. 8–10 there is an important discovery to be made. What seemed merely a harmonic enrichment of the initial tonic–dominant (m. 10)—tonic (m. 15) demonstration of tonality is nothing of the sort: both C-major and F-major triads are introduced here, the former on the second beat of m. 8, the latter on the downbeat of m. 9, with an immediate diminuendo to pianissimo. The effect of the resolution into C on the weak part of the measure and the coincidence of F with the first dynamic shading, after the stark contrasts of forte and piano at the opening, is to hide what is really happening here: the two "foreign" tonalities are already part of this very first statement. By the time they are prominently displayed in mm. 23 and 42 respectively, they should still be perceived as *foreign in terms of harmonic convention;* but *in terms of the organic structure* of this particular symphony, they are not.

The expressive diminuendo was to balance an event that previews the harmonic structure of the entire symphony (harmony *is* the structure). It also detracts from the almost furtive introduction of C and F. Yet there is something else being introduced in the F major m. 9: the quivering sixteenth-note pattern. Why sixteenth notes? Like the diminuendo in the same measure, this is a new and different effect. Are these only expressive screens behind which two "foreign" keys have been smuggled into the A-major environment of this opening? In that case, why not diminuendo and sixteenth notes in m. 8, where the intrusion actually takes place? What is happening?

The half-tone step from F to E is underlined by the paradoxical twin effect of diminuendo and fast pulse (mm. 9–10). As with the introduction of C and F, *the expressive commentary can either hide or emphasize something very important.* The half step from F to E in the bass supports an F-major chord going to E unison / pedal point / dominant of main tonality A. It is also the last of six downward half steps in the bass, since the beginning of the Introduction. As such it might escape notice in spite of its harmonic significance. As the single most important interval in the symphony, its significance is revealed (or concealed) by the harmonic import of mm. 9–10.

Now we shall call a momentary halt for reflection on the entire Introduction. We have seen that what appeared to be a very condensed preview of the harmonic confrontation to come, in sixty-two brief introductory measures, does indeed take place in the first ten measures. We may also conclude that, as heir to an eighteenth-century musical consciousness that stipulated a dominant–tonic relationship as the foundation of musical structure, Beethoven is working with full regard for musical expectations which his harmonic plot of A major, C, and F will either frustrate or fulfill, but without which there would be no plot.

His covert introduction of these keys in the opening phrase, and his overt display of their difference within the context of A major, in mm. 23 and 42, are clear indications that he unfolds his harmonic drama against the background of a harmonic convention he shares with his contemporaries. In performing this work we can hardly do less, but in the absence of this shared background with *our* contemporary audience, what does it mean for us?

1. We now have an *image,* not only of what is noted in the score, but also of some very *special events, within the first ten measures, that are not noted in the score:*
   a. This music is about *A, C,* and *F.*
   b. *A* is introduced in the first measure, reintroduced by dominant *E* pedal point and scale in m. 10;

      C and *F* triads are introduced in mm. 8 and 9.
   c. Special events occur in mm. 8, 9, and 10:

      the introduction of *F* (m. 10) is accompanied by *diminuendo to pianissimo;* and the beginning of sixteenth figure.
   d. All harmonic movement is supported by a bass line descending in *half steps;*

      harmonic movement increases: (at A-major opening, chords = ♩♪); at m. 7, chord = 𝅝 ; at m. 8, chords = ♩ ; harmonic movement decreases in dim. / sixteenth notes m. 9: chord = 𝅝 .
   e. *N.B.:* the D-major first inversion chord of m. 7* seems to be attended by special events as well (*viz. above*). Also, the quarter-note chords beginning with the piano repetition of D^6 on the second half of m. 7 are long now (espressivo?).
2. With this image clearly in mind, we have *guidelines for interpretive decisions:*
   a. All appearances of A, C, or F are important: this importance must be demonstrated in performance.
   b. Between tonic A, forte, and dominant E in m. 10, pianissimo, lies a dynamic range which must accommodate the problematic harmonic and expressive events of the first ten measures. *N.B.:* while the pianissimo may be played as softly as you like, the forte opening shall have to be exceeded by a fortissimo when the E pedal resolves into the return of A, m. 15.
   c. The diminuendo serves a purpose. Since that harmonic purpose may not be self-evident to an audience, its effect should ˙be the more apparent: lots of diminuendo into a very soft pianissimo.

      The nervous excitement of the sixteenth figure (also the more important because a spontaneous appreciation of the harmonic event cannot be assumed) will be enhanced by using it as your best opportunity to dramatize the diminuendo and by keeping the level of pianissimo on the E pedal at minimum until the crescendo into fortissimo A major.

d. In view of its demonstrated importance the bass line should probably be stressed in balancing the chords it supports.

The preview of structural elements of great significance (chords of C and F) should be marked by giving maximum expressive value to the long piano quarters in the strings, beginning m. 7. Because of the increased harmonic rhythm in m. 8, the danger of a crescendo impression is real and should be avoided.

Long piano quarters will also provide an opportunity to start the diminuendo of m. 9 on the first beat; but the first sixteenth on beat 4 must not be louder than the end of the first beat.

We are now in a much better position to determine "how loud is loud" and many other questions that cannot be noted in the score. The sum of available information on performance practice of any period will not provide the only, or even the most important, yardstick with which to measure questions about presenting old music to modern audiences. What we have described with regard to the first ten measures of this symphony is a process of translation. The first requirement in producing a good translation is knowledge of the original text. The next is that the translation account as closely as possible for the meaning of that text. And finally, the translation must not only be understandable but, as nearly as possible, should have an effect comparable to that of the original, including feeling. This is a central point in our presentation of how to prepare a score:

> Careful examination and classification of structural characteristics is an essential part of your work with the evidence on the musical surface of a composition. The results will bear on your performance to the degree of your personal involvement in this process. If, in your best judgement, those results should be insufficient—i.e., they fail to excite you or move you—then, no matter how impressively clever your analysis may be, you shall have to continue to work.

At the close of the *Introduction* (m. 53) the half step from F in the bass to unison E, tutti, is precisely the same as the one with which Beethoven's first preview of the harmonic plot ended in m. 10. When that E reveals itself at the beginning of the *Vivace* (mm. 66–67) as the dominant of the principal key of A, it is as if we had already returned "home" from far away harmonic regions. Once again, the unexpected is experienced as something gentle, almost familiar, and so it should be: we have been there before.

Twice more in this A-major movement the keys representing "harmonic stress" are introduced almost tenderly, their far-off gravitational pull notwithstanding—at the opening of the development section, m. 181 (C major, *pp!*), and at the mysteriously calm eye of the storm in the center of the development, m. 222 (F major). We shall do well to fix such "correspondences" firmly in mind at the outset of our study, particularly since they do not always occupy comparable spots in the formal structure of this movement. There is a transcending force field of three tonalities that warrants close observation. The appearances of C and F as part of the sonata structure in this A-major movement are quite different: abrupt, sometimes brutal, and certainly spectacular (cf. m. 136— C major replacing dominant E in the exposition; m. 358 replacing the expected F major counterpart in the recapitulation). But we had best take these in order.

The exposition unfolds in A. However, just when we expected to arrive in well-prepared E, we are violently and memorably pitched into C major (m. 137). A long, laborious haul back to E; C major again at the beginning of the development; and (after another brief reference to E) on to F, pianissimo, the mysterious "eye of the storm." On the face of it, there is nothing very remarkable about the fact that the subsequent return to A major then passes through D minor; but there is something special about this key which will not be revealed until the Scherzo. The incessant rhythmic pounding on the lower minor second (cf. pp. 332– 33) has settled, for unmistakable emphasis, on the now-established bass-note shift of D and C sharp (m. 254). The coda features D and its lower neighbor further, as a stubborn pedal point (m. 401), after an introduction from the furthest remove in tonalities (A♭). The first movement reveals one more point of major harmonic interest in this connection: In the recapitulation, at the place where we were so rudely pitched into C major during the exposition, we are now flung, with equal violence into F (m. 348).

The second movement is steeped in A: A minor, then A major, and then a first return to A minor through suddenly enriched, almost Schubertian, chromatic harmonies hovering for a bit on the now-inverted half step of C♯–D in the bass and culminating in a fleeting but extraordinary breakout into C major (m. 123). Once more A minor, then A major until, just before the end, we are poised again, briefly but powerfully, on C (m. 247). But there is to be only the protest of a single two-measure restatement before the music is drawn irretrievably into a melancholy, fragmented ending on A minor. Even without alluding to the thematic structure of the piece, the use of tonalities provides not only the form, but furnishes us with clues to the character as well.

In limiting our survey of the *Seventh Symphony*'s surface to the evidence of a three-tonality plot, we are obviously leaving out other aspects of equal importance to actual performance. In the context of the preceding chapter, for instance, we might have made much of the single reversal of thematic shape at the end of this Allegretto movement. For once, and with a bitter effect that complements the harmonic frustration we have just described, the two eighth notes which for some two hundred measures have trailed the "heavy" first quarter, appear *on* the beat at the end, as pathetic, passing dissonances. The heretofore single upbeat measure of the recurring motif has been tripled to increase the effect. And to seal the sense of hopelessness which attends this outburst, it is presented as a *déjà vu:* the woodwind chord which in identical spacing was heard at the beginning confirms that we have come full circle in this movement.

The "tonality plot" reveals an aspect of musical shapes that was not covered in the preceding chapter. It is a very important one, particularly for those of us today who no longer claim the securely conditioned sensibility to large-scale harmonic happenings which seems to have informed the eighteenth-century listener and, to some extent, the nineteenth-century public schooled in that tradition. Such large-scale harmonic shapes, interior to the work they support, can only be grasped by us as performers in concentrated auditory imagination. Individual and general shapes, smaller in scale and far easier to imagine and define, relate to this underlying musical topography rather like trees, houses, and loose rocks on a mountain side. The example of our "plot of three tonalities" in the Beethoven *Seventh* will make this analogy seem less farfetched the further we allow a real sense of its "inner" shape to contribute to our total image of this work.

This is not necessarily a solemn matter. Although we are not primarily concerned now with expressive content, there are questions which might nonetheless come to mind. For instance, is the majestic music for the D-major Trio sections of the Scherzo to be completely triumphant, heroic, and perhaps even a little pompous; or is there a hidden suggestion of spoof somewhere in all that repeated splendor? Even the question itself is a personal one, of course (one does not *have* to ask it), but having been asked, it begs guidance from the score.

One "thematic" tonality was neglected in the preceding Allegretto movement. F major is the last key of the harmonic triumvirate as originally introduced, and the Scherzo is in F—but even the first repeat ends in A! From there, through C (m. 41) to B♭ and back to F—clearly the plot continues. At m. 118 we are in C again and this time we close in F. The middle section is in D. It is not likely that the composer has abandoned his tonal scheme at this late stage; rather, this "new" key* heightens one's awareness of the other three. Lest we forget that in this F-major Scherzo with a D-major Trio we inhabit an A-major environment, an extraordinary pedal point of A is sounded throughout the entire D-major section. Both times it appears, and again at the end. There are other aspects of consistency: the falling minor second, an important feature in the entire movement, really blossoms in the Trio. It is by far the most important interval now, and the transitions from Trio to main section place it where in fact it had been from the first: on D and C♯ in the bass. The coda provides the clue: the pedal A introduces the "strange" D major yet again (m. 641). Still another Trio repeat? No, but something rather like the composer's own joke: the answer to the first two D-major measures is in D *minor*—and then the whole Scherzo closes abruptly with a five-measure presto cadence in F.

Why is that funny? It depends on one's musical sense of humor, of course, but the sudden revelation of the Trio tonality as a D-major disguise of the one chord common to *all three* keys concerned in this symphony appears to me as if the "real" D peeped very briefly and impishly around an unexpected corner and produced, with the rapid succession of final chords, the relieving outburst of laughter following the incongruous but illuminating solution of a joke. That this is an interpretation which may carry conviction for only one conductor is not the point. Nor is it important whether the sudden D minor, as common denominator of A, C, and F, is acceptable as further "proof" of Beethoven's master plan. What is inescapable however, is that such a notion, once perceived, affects one's thinking and feeling about the piece in ways that really matter to its eventual performance. In this case, if only for this conductor, it not only flavors the end of the Scherzo, but lends a delightfully fanciful air to the Trio. And in its moments of conspicuous triumph the possible presence of a little tongue-in-cheek, as was suggested before, would seem a very likely addition to the intended sparkle of the occasion.

With the Finale, another aspect of harmonic "shape" must now be mentioned which will receive further and more detailed attention in Chapter 12. The relative duration, in time, of any musical event measured against another, is one of its basic sources of effectiveness. What strikes one immediately about the last movement of Beethoven's *Seventh Symphony* is the inordinate length of harmonic tension in phrase after phrase before each final release. At the opening there are seven measures of intaken breath before we are able to exhale on the eighth. The effect is greatly enhanced by offbeat accents throughout these seven measures, accents on every second beat which are shifted to the first only on the ultimate resolution in the tonic. The element of tempo, so

---

*N.B.: D major, as a VI⁶ of A, introduced C and F in the ten-measure preview at the opening of the first movement.

far missing from our discussion, may be the final arbiter in determining a heard musical shape. Chapter 12 will be devoted to the time dimension of music.

On the basis of the foregoing, the reader is now urged to follow, for himself, the final confrontations of A, C, and F in the Finale. As a single instance, we shall here point to the beginning of the development as a particularly striking example (m. 125). Appearing to aim at F major, the harmonic direction is deflected (by the now familiar half step down) back to E, on to A minor and settles at last on C. Before the recapitulation another abortive approach to F (m. 198) slips down into E, as the dominant to A major. The relationship of the F tonality as parallel major to the minor subdominant of A (hinted, as we suggested, at the end of the Scherzo) is fully displayed and affirmed before the coda (m. 342) where the most powerful reiterations of F major and its dominant C are finally turned into A major and its dominant E, for the ultimate apotheosis of the main key.

The often-mentioned repeated half-step motion also comes to its last fruition at this moment in the life of the *Seventh Symphony*. After the poignant effort and frustration of m. 162–97, it culminates in a decisive fulfillment—both as a consistent pattern announced in the very first measures of this movement and as a significantly pervasive interval throughout the entire work—at the last, critical moments of harmonic emphasis. This completes the story of three tonalities in Beethoven's *Seventh Symphony*.

To "visualise" that work in terms of this inner structure; to see large portions of the resulting shapes at once, in a kind of birds-eye view that simplifies major contours and fits surface detail into its overall perspective; to relegate that awareness into the background (without ever losing the sense of it!) while work continues on further exploration, or on execution in performance; to summon at will whatever portions of that inner image may be relevant to the work at hand; that is as much part of the eventual *performance* of this symphony as anything it may require of the conductor on the podium.

If we could listen to Beethoven's A-major symphony with the ears of contemporaries conditioned by a century-old harmonic style, the confrontation of C major and F within the host tonality would certainly be more obvious than it is now, seen from our musical era. Attuned to a style in which the function of harmony was the basis of musical form, we should have had the advantage of sharing the composer's musical expectations. Beyond that, however, then as now, we should have encountered the same problem of reflecting Beethoven's wonderfully simple structure within the mass of subordinate detail throughout the symphony. For harmonic function is an *active* principle, and musical "structure" is a metaphor with which we describe something that is not only based upon movement in time, but on the relative attraction between musical elements which determine the rate of motion. What Beethoven created in his *Seventh Symphony* could best be described as a force field. The polarity of A, C, and F dominates this field. Tempo, dynamics, the distribution of climaxes and low points, even rhythmic patterns and melodic shapes serve to define, confront, and eventually resolve the threefold harmonic stress which shapes this large structure-in-motion.

Clearly the musical image in the conductor's mind which allows him to control this moving structure is vital to the successful exercise of his task on the podium. While it may be intensely personal, like all musical images we have examined, it should also be based on the simplest formula to express the overall design. Such a formula is attempted below. But it should be remembered that this is a compass rather than a map: as a means of orientation it points beyond itself; and the direction in which it points changes with our own changing location within the structure of the work, and according to the speed with which we move through any part of it.

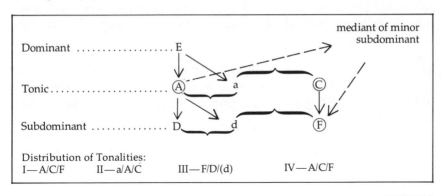

FIGURE 1

1. Memorize this design as a *graphic image*. Review the harmonic relations shown,
   a. with particular reference to the host tonality of A (e.g. tonic, dominant, subdominant, mediants);
   b. in terms of the three tonalities A, C, and F.
2. Make a detailed survey of the musical surface of Beethoven's *Seventh*, according to the outline in Chapter 2a. Keep a written record of every aspect bearing on No. 1 above. However, *do not limit your survey to tracing harmonic functions*. This is the time to *connect* your observations in this area with other musical clues or imaginal associations, as you find them, or as they occur to you spontaneously.

The harmonic construction of Beethoven's *Seventh Symphony* in the perspective of contemporary, early-nineteenth-century listening expectations and compositional practice, has been demonstrated in this order:

C major and F, prominently featured in the Introduction of an A-major symphony;
preliminary confirmation of the structural significance of this feature as we spotted appearances of these tonalities, at random, throughout the work (with D as an additional tonal center);
detailed analysis of symphony opening reveals complete preview of harmonic plot in first 10 measures;
representation of the structural design, in terms of harmonic stresses, by an easily remembered graphic image.

It is possible, of course, that quite different aspects of this work might stimulate the imagination of another conductor. It is unlikely, however, that, in any meaningful performance, the underlying structure determined by harmonic stresses can be left out of the planning and the pacing of the *Seventh*. And it would be quite inconceivable to expect any kind of effective articulation of the harmonic structure of this work, unless the plot of three tonalities, its exposition, unfolding, and resolution, engages the conductor's imagination to the point of real, personal involvement.

In itself, the outline of harmonic relationships represented by the diagram above is no more musically compelling than the chart of interlocking three-note cells of the trumpet call motto opening the first Promenade of Mussorgsky's *Pictures at an Exhibition*.* Both are intellectually stimulating. The process of creating a performance image of *Pictures*, as described, began with an analysis of the composer's employment of certain cells in certain kinds of variation. From there, the imagination was not simply *allowed* to contribute; it was systematically *employed*, with growing personal involvement. Involvement and identification may even precede empirical analysis; e.g. an answer to "why 1855?" might well have preceded (and enhanced) one's detailed comparison of "correspondences" between sections of Ravel's *La Valse*. The important thing is that a unique harmonic structure, melodic correspondences, a characteristic musical gesture (strong/weak), or any other point of contact be pervasive and likely to "stimulate the artist's tendency to vibrate."

Half a century after Beethoven's "tale of three tonalities," the *intervallic* motto F–A♭–F, in various transpositions and different harmonic settings, was to play a similarly unifying role in the *Third Symphony* of Brahms.**Listening expectations by then would no longer equate mus-

*P. 161.
**Cf. Chapter 8.

ical structure with harmonic functions alone: an increasingly rich palette of chromatic shadings was capable of reflecting very subtle expressive detail, *within* the structure. * Increasingly, however—and this is very important from our point of view as performers—this enhanced expressivity, together with the use of chord constructions which owed their sense of direction and tonality mostly to their cadential context, became its own musical purpose. Expressivity, not as a musical byproduct, but for the sake of a momentary, important effect, provided an independent thread of such moments within the musical fabric of large-scale works. At the beginning of our century, that thread of expressive moments *became* the structure in the work of some composers, and harmony a persuasive means of illustration.

The intervallic motto of Brahms's *Third*, its expressive significance varying according to different harmonic settings, was an example of what may be involved when "enhanced expressivity . . . serves its own musical purpose" within a large structure no longer determined by the exclusively musical, gravitational stress of harmonic events. Extensive and persuasive illustration is furnished in the work of Richard Wagner, particularly in the *Ring, Tristan, Die Meistersinger,* and *Parsifal.* Wagner himself insisted that a change of tonality should take place only when a change of mood justified it. Musical segments contained within such a harmonic field are given a special designation: "musico-poetic periods."† These periods, rather than "scenes," determine the organization of operatic acts in his mature work. Tonalities continue to inform musical structure, and harmonic function, though greatly enhanced in mobility and expressive refinement, still operates with the same concepts and conventions that applied during the preceding hundred years. And yet the difference is fundamental: musical structures whose shape was determined by internal, harmonic tension and resolution are *also* becoming the framework of expressive and descriptive, *extramusical* reference.

Wagner wrote for the theater. He was as greatly concerned with the word as he was with music. And he considered his staged musical drama, the "total work of art," capable of achieving depth of expression *and* precision of communication quite beyond the inherent capacities of any single one of the participating sister arts. In this immodest assertion he was probably justified—barring respective claims on behalf of some fellow composers or poets or dramatists not so preoccupied with the criterion of artistic totality. What concerns us here is a spinoff in terms of musical structure which, after more than a century and a half

---

* The use of harmony to illustrate expressive detail, *before* harmonic function became the arbiter of sonata forms in the mid-eighteenth century, played an equally important role (viz. Bach chorales).
† Wagner, *Opera and Drama,* Collected Works, vol. 4.

of primarily harmonic orientation, substituted a set of extramusical elements as essential components of musical construction.

The *leitmotif*, as the identifiable and completely mutable musical cell with a specifically ascribed literary or psychological content, is a concept which, in Wagner's hands, goes far toward insuring that the totality of his art is no idle boast. It fulfills two requirements: First, it provides unity within very complex patterns of the musical fabric during some twenty hours of opera. Second, it amplifies the unfolding drama on stage with a constant stream of commentary which grows more profound and more compelling with each new experience of his work. It also furnishes the chronological sequence of stage action with simultaneous glimpses of built-in recollection and foreknowledge.

Too much can be made of the "you can't tell the players without a scorecard" aspect of Wagner's leitmotifs. They do provide useful and sometimes essential orientation in his densely populated forest of Norse mythology. They also furnish a running gloss on the complexities of relentless fate that begins with a building fraud by the father of the gods, is compounded by incest, murder, and ritual suicide, and is resolved in universal destruction by fire and flood. Leitmotifs in Wagner's *Ring* are melodic fragments representing protagonists, moods, scenes past and future, as well as objects. They interact not only as musical labels with extramusical meanings, but as musically related shapes with "family resemblances" sometimes so close *that different harmonization of a single melodic interval may alter the significance of nearly identical materials.* Thus Wagner, having taken a decisive step away from harmonic stress as the sole arbiter of musical structure—a step away from the harmonic convention of the eighteenth and early nineteenth centuries—takes another step toward a musical concept that has dominated composition ever since: structures based on *nearly* identical materials.

One more step remained to be taken. As harmonic resources grew more sophisticated and the proportions of musical structures increased in size and complexity, additional means of giving significance to sound had to be found. In his last opera, *Parsifal*, Wagner undertook to give significance to time.

Parsifal is an opera about time in the same way that Beethoven's *Seventh* is a symphony about harmony. From the first dialogue we are made aware that the action we are witnessing in the present is conditioned by events of the past. In the course of that action, the past with its entire cast of characters emerges into the present, while time is suspended within the precincts of the Holy Grail. We are also given a good deal of verbal explanation and commentary during the first and last acts, which inevitably slows the action to a rather ritualistic, formal pace. By contrast, the middle act is theatrical enough to more than make up for the other two: the awakening of a centuries-old woman from a magic trance, a ballet of young enchantresses, a seduction scene, a miraculously aborted murder, and the instant transformation of a garden into a desert. Throughout all this, and throughout the two grand rituals of the outer acts, the leitmotifs relate what is seen to what is not seen, on another level of simultaneous experience.

How, then, is time past distinguished, musically, from present time? Or rapidly passing time of action from contemplative, narrative time; or the timelessness of a religious rite? The short answer is: through harmonic means.

The musical and dramatic structure of *Parsifal* is extraordinarily symmetrical. There are three acts,

each of which is divided into two halves;
each of which deals with different time references;
and while the outer acts function like exposition and recapitulation in
a very large sonata form, the middle one serves to develop and resolve
the dramatic situation.

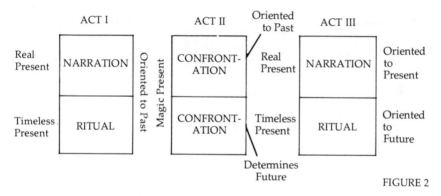

FIGURE 2

There are *five main characters,* all but one of whom exhibit two completely contrasting personalities.

Name	Background	Role
Gurnemanz	Chief servant of the Holy Grail	narrator
Kundry	She laughed at Christ's suffering	{ penitent temptress
Amfortas	Failed guardian of the Grail	{ king victim
Klingsor	Failed worshiper of the Grail	{ counter-king magician
Parsifal	Gains understanding through compassion	{ innocent fool redeemer/king

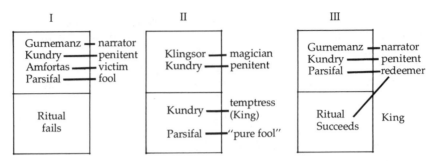

FIGURE 3

Even the *chorus* reflects the dualism to be resolved. It consists of the following:

Women—Flower Maidens
Men—Knights of the Grail
Boys—Pages and Acolytes of the Grail

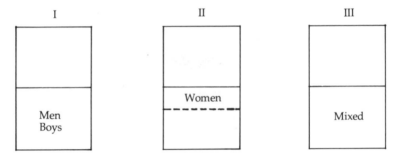

FIGURE 4

Harmonic structure articulates the dramatic form of *Parsifal*

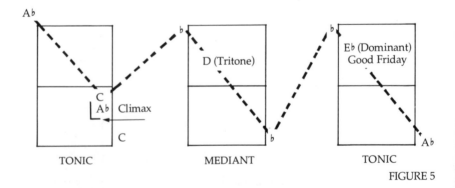

FIGURE 5

But there are *two further levels of harmonic structure* to be explored:

1. *Harmonic language:*
   Diatonic harmony to portray purity, simplicity, flirtation, service, and
   sacred office (Example 1a).
   Chromatic harmony to evoke confrontation, confusion, suffering, and
   sorcery (Example 1b).

EXAMPLE 1: Leitmotifs (*Parsifal*)

(a) *Grail*

Sacred Office

(b)

Heilandsklage   *suffering*

2. *Harmonic style:*
   Chordal writing, i.e. melody and bass with or without moving middle voices. No voice is independent of the melody. *Diatonic or
   chromatic harmony* results.
   Polyphonic writing, with truly independent melodic lines, results in
   chromatic harmony that is horizontally conditioned, vertically controlled.

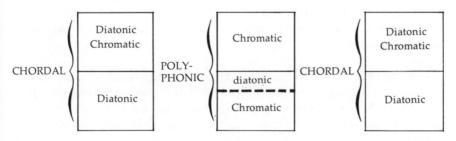

FIGURE 6

This chart corresponds to Figures 2 and 5.* By placing harmonic language, style, and suggested time together, we achieve the following, somewhat longer but more explicit, answer to the earlier questions about Wagner's musical means to distinguish different kinds of time and time settings:

Time/Quality of Presentation	Harmonic Language	Harmonic Style
Real present (narrative)	diatonic or chromatic	chordal
Timeless present (ritual)	diatonic	chordal
Magic present (confrontation)	chromatic	polyphonic

The use of leitmotifs is also affected by the employment of different harmonic means. In the first and last acts, the technique is much the same as it was in the *Ring,* and inasmuch as many motives refer to states of being associated with mystical traditions, they serve allusive purposes in their reflection of the past while they illustrate the feelings and reactions of participants in the present drama. The largely chordal style of composition favors the substitution of one motive for another when dramatic requirements are to be served. This, too, facilitates the frequent focus on things past in the narrative sections and the feeling of simultaneity of past and present in the ritual scenes.

In the central act of confrontation, however, the fact that many of the *Parsifal* motives are rhythmically and melodically more distinctive in outline than those of the *Ring* reduces the possibilities for convenient interchange and substitution in the truly polyphonic fabric of the Klingsor/Kundry and Kundry/Parsifal scenes. Here Wagner has achieved a true synthesis between melodic independence and harmonic control. The key is in the use of characteristic intervals, *both* for the constant change and modification among motivic materials and for the clear harmonic consensus of a highly chromatic, polyphonic style. This second act of *Parsifal* shall therefore serve us as the point in musical development when the logic of harmonic function and equally compelling methods of musical construction are in perfect balance. In this Wagnerian symbiosis of musical past and future, we can discern the powerful fulcrum upon which the old tradition turned, and new approaches became present facts.

With the capacity to extend tonal reference to the remotest harmonic regions—the harmonic outline of *Parsifal* is the "tale of tritone tonalities" A♭–D–A♭ —the operative stresses are equal on *both* sides of the tonality of furthest remove. *Harmonic function now does not translate into*

*P. 340.

movement, but into an equilibrium of contrary forces. And what happened here in terms of the dualism within a huge structure is to affect progressively smaller entities until, within the half-century following the composition of *Parsifal*, the smallest model of tension-to-be-resolved, the dissonance, will not necessarily suggest harmonic stress (and thus motion), but a degree of expressivity.

The implication for the conductor is this: harmonic function must be considered as variable and potentially uncertain as much of the other evidence on the musical surface that we have come to regard as composer's "instructions." Harmonic analysis as a tool to aid you in mastering a score is useful to the extent to which the meaning of harmonic function is determined in the context of all the musical evidence of the work in preparation. Identification of chord progressions in so-called tonal works has no more practical value for performance than the laborious classification of notes in a twelve-tone piece according to the permutations of the row.

The initial approach suggested in our chapters on the musical surface and the role of detail cannot be shortened or enhanced by "standard" harmonic analysis. There is no standard. Like musical shapes, harmonic functions have not only been employed differently by different composers, but were in fact extended and eventually redefined out of existence, as we have seen. The only measure of the effectiveness of harmonic functions is reflected in the works you will have before you.

However, as a lever with which to pry open the surface of a score, the harmonic evidence you examine is a most useful and flexible body of information, if you consider every score a unique case, and if your accumulated knowledge and experience in the field of harmony is applied to each new situation as you find it, and as it appeals to you.

PODIUM

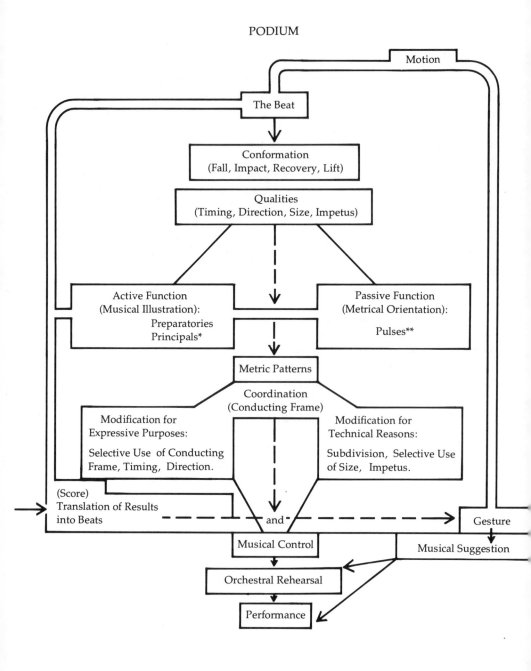

*Exception: *Series* of Principals: (*Passive* Function)   **Exception: *Accented* Pulse: (*Active* Function)

11

CONDUCTING: YIELDING CONTROL

This chapter addresses itself to special situations in which control over musical flow needs to be shared or yielded: conducting a concerto, a recitative, aleatoric music, or the live accompaniment of an electronic tape.

Y IELDING some control from the podium requires heightened control over your own beat, your own concentration, and your own judgment. Like a fly fisherman who has hooked his trout, the conductor determines the time and the circumstances when control is yielded or resumed. And like the fish at the end of the fishing line, the singer or instrumentalist who is given some temporary control enhances the occasion by participating freely within the limits permitted him or her. The thinner the line, the greater the sport; and the more scope must then be given the fish to contribute to the give and take of his own catching. Just so, the yielding of control to artists participating in your performance is a measure of your willingness to take risks in order to achieve a high order of shared ensemble.

This authoritarian description of the conductor's role in accompanying a soloist, pacing a recitative, or giving some scope for individual initiative to instrumentalists within the orchestra is essentially accurate, with only degrees of variation in practice. Never, under any circumstances, should yielding control over any part of a performance reach the point of yielding control over the momentum and the pacing of it. The time span and the degree of granting musical or dramatic initiative to a soloist or to a singer on stage are as much subject to the conductor's final judgment as any other decisions concerning the practical realization of a score. But there are five different kinds of musical conditions under which this judgment is exercised, and which may require differ-

345

ent technical skills in order to insure maintenance of fundamental control over the orchestra, while temporary control of musical detail is shared. The circumstances under which some control may be yielded occur as a result of

A. the personal factor, or
B. specific requirements of compositional style or intent.

The latter include conducting of concertos, recitatives, and some twentieth century works.

ACCOMPANIMENT OF A CONCERTO

One of the most important things to remember in connection with the rehearsal and performance of concertos is that the soloist is likely to present you with a composite of ideas, musical convictions, and solutions to technical problems based on far more extensive experience with the work than that of most conductors. This does not necessarily mean that, in a disagreement on tempo, phrasing, or articulation, the soloist's view should invariably prevail. But it does lend emphasis to the suggestion that, as far as possible, it is wise to explore potential differences before the first orchestra rehearsal, and to make an effort to accommodate the soloist's preferences if they can somehow be reconciled with one's own.

The extent of possible compromise depends a great deal on the work itself: the mature masterpieces of Brahms and Beethoven, for instance, represent a far greater musical commitment on the conductor's side than is the case with one of the Chopin piano concertos, in which the orchestra plays a modest and invariably subordinate role.

In this chapter we are mainly concerned with the technical side of accompanying a soloist, and from that point of view both Chopin concertos provide a great deal of opportunity for displaying proficiency and sensitivity in the most delicate aspect of yielding control: the kind that goes unnoticed when it is well done, but is the cause of friction and of frustrating rehearsal problems if the conductor is unable to allow the pianist considerable flexibility while maintaining firm control of the overall ensemble.

Firm control begins, as always, with a clear mental image of the music. One inviolate rule in preparing to conduct a concerto is: *learn the solo part.*

There is no way in which a conductor can follow his soloist and anticipate the requirements of the orchestra, unless he knows the solo part down to the minute detail of its decorative figuration. As we shall examine in more specific detail with the even greater freedom granted to singers in recitatives, "following" does not mean careful delineation of every tempo fluctuation with a corresponding subdivision, but being ready, and in the best position within the conducting frame, to signal the next orchestral beat without getting in the soloist's way.

Here is a very apposite comparison with the skillful fisherman who "plays" his fish without ever pulling hard enough on the rod to break the line. Until you have developed a practiced "feel" for the amount of additional movement necessary to allow for slight liberties in a given flow of tempo, you should remember that orchestral players have ears also, and that, especially with the standard concerto literature, this is a premium area of technical expertise in which Sir Adrian Boult's already quoted advice to younger colleagues is particularly valuable: "don't get in the musician's way."

Learn the solo part, follow the flow of fast notes, or, if in doubt, follow the bass. Whatever else you do, *be there when the soloist gets to the point of crucial ensemble requirements.*

Q. Which part of the beat is "there"?   A. *The center of the beat.**

The center of the beat is the best place from which to give a clear preparatory. The center of the beat is also the best place from which to give a clear, *small* preparatory. That becomes a consideration if the required preparatory is a shorter division of the measure than what you have been beating before, e.g. an important third beat in a 3/4 Allegro beaten in one, or the second quarter in ¢.

> Whenever the precise timing of a preparatory beat depends on the soloist's initiative, beats *prior* to that preparatory should be small, with minimum definition, and, above all, with minimum recovery and *no lift.* The last of these beats before the *precise preparatory* should terminate easily *near the center.*
>
> *N.B.:* Unless special emphasis is intended, the following principal should also be very small.

EXAMPLE 1: Chopin, *Concerto in E minor,* third movement

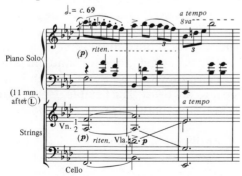

EXAMPLE 2: Chopin, *Concerto in E minor,* third movement

Example 1 is taken from the finale of Chopin's *Second Piano Concerto,* in e minor. Listen to a recording if possible. It is not too difficult to match the pianist's resumption of tempo in the third measure. You may find it surprisingly hard to match it with a *small* preparatory and an equally small downbeat. The passage is beaten in one until the second measure shown. The conductor will have paid special attention to the viola entrance (accented, but *piano*) on D♮. *He will not permit his downbeat to rise into a lift during the pianist's retard,* but will find his way to the *center and stay there,* without any indication of beats 2 or 3. *At the last moment,* he will treat the upbeat to the *a tempo* measure as a small, *isolated lift.**

The same principle applies in Example 2. While the score does not indicate a tempo fluctuation, the pianist is likely to make a slight retard following the E♭♭ accent in the right hand of the first measure. Instead of matching this delay with an extended upward lift, bend the recovery of the downbeat *back to center,* wait if necessary, and use a last-moment *isolated lift* for the preparatory to resumption of tempo in the second measure. The slight adjustment in the steady one-to-the-measure will hardly be noticed, if you do it well. It will certainly help the easy coordination between piano and accompanying strings whose music has no printed notice of a rubato. On the other hand, even a well timed, strong preparatory 3 would most certainly get in the way and impede the flow. Note that the second measure shown is, in terms of both harmony and thematic shape, an upbeat to the third. The flexible, isolated lift *into* the second measure is therefore anticipating a *preparatory* downbeat. (Now try it again.)

A general suggestion: until you have some experience in following a soloist while leading the orchestra, decide in advance what to listen for in the solo part and mark it in your score. Many soloists play very dif-

*Cf. pp. 47 and 247.

ferently in actual performance from what they may have led you to expect in rehearsal. While they may change, the notes should remain the same. Thus it may save some sudden anxiety if, at all times, you know what notes to follow in the solo part—and before long those notes will be in your mind, to be *anticipated* at your ease.

Recordings have made the preparation of concerto accompaniments much easier. If you have access to a library, listen to a variety of recorded performances well in advance of your first rehearsal, and note differences in your score. It is particularly helpful to know *where* to expect possible adjustments, even if you don't know *what* to expect until you meet with your soloist.

In terms of *yielding control*, we are stressing the problems of *following* a soloist. Needless to say, there are many instances in a concerto performance where the soloist should follow you. This too should be predetermined in your preparation of the score. If time permits, a run-through of the concerto is the best way of trying out the give-and-take of musical initiative. But if—as is unfortunately the case all too often—only parts of the concerto can be properly rehearsed, it is best to agree on those passages and connections with the soloist in advance. In that way the available rehearsal time may be devoted to an unhurried working out of the most difficult ensemble problems.*

CONDUCTING RECITATIVES

A very different approach is used in conducting recitatives. Here you are acting as coordinator of a performance depending heavily on someone else's temporary musical leadership. In the case of operatic recitatives this usually reflects a dramatic situation on stage. While there are limits to their discretionary powers, the final initiative rests with the singer, not the conductor. It is as vital to the dramatic success of an opera that the singer be fully conscious of this, as it is essential that the conductor remain ready for anything and command the technical resources to cope with the unexpected.

Conducting recitatives is probably the most demanding area of our craft in terms of technical command. Far from being a purely mechanical process of following stage action with appropriate signals to the orchestra, timing is of the utmost importance. A series of orchestral interjections that literally drive the vocal parts on stage before them can result in a mounting momentum of excitement, while the obvious dramatic initiative, from the audience's point of view, is clearly generated on stage. The least hesitation in giving these attacks in the pit can easily produce a leaden result, although the conductor in both cases would have kept orchestra and stage accurately together.

* For further suggestions on work with soloists, see p. 484.

It will be important for you to remember that in an accompanied operatic recitative the orchestra can *not* follow the stage action, as it can follow the performance of a concerto soloist. Sometimes there is text printed in the instrumental parts; but with translations, cuts, and the physical difficulty of hearing what is sung on stage from some positions in the pit, it is quite essential to assume that *all* communication with the orchestra is your responsibility. And all your communication is visual.

For the development of a secure and flexible technique of the beat, no better means of daily challenge and improvement could be imagined than a systematic review of the entire theory and practice of the beat, as presented earlier in this text, with the aid of some *recorded recitatives*. Learn the score, follow the rules below, and use as many different recordings of the same recitative as you can find. You cannot control the musical flow of a recording, but you can learn to cope with it.

Practice each set of recordings with different physical limitations, determined in advance. First imagine you are cueing to a highly elevated stage, while controlling an orchestra in the pit. You shall have to use the whole arm at times, but not always. Then pretend that you and the stage action are placed on the same level in performance. Now your beat, albeit clear, must be unobtrusive: you would choose to use the lower arm, wrist, and even the finger pivot (to mark the passage of silent measures), while meeting the intermittent requirement of dramatic illustration in the orchestral response. When one recorded performance becomes so familiar that it is predictable, try another.

The following rules should be memorized. They have been evolved through generations of trial and error. Once you have mastered the principles involved in their fairly simple application and practiced daily, with concentrated attention to the *dramatic effect of your timing*, your work on recitatives will produce results that may surprise you.

Now for the theory: the singers have taken off freely. After some measures you are to bring in the orchestra, *or part of it* (much more difficult, because the ones who are not playing must also know where you are).

> During "empty" measures of recitatives, *beat downbeats until the measure which contains the penultimate beat before the next instrumental entrance. Beat that measure in full, wait on beat before expected preparatory to signal attack, if you are ahead of singers.*

As to the preparatory beat, even the most neutral interjection of chords at odd moments during a recitative requires more specific preparation from the conductor than mere placement. In the special circumstances created by the technique of accompanying free recitatives which is described above, any entrance requiring expressive, metrically complicated, or necessarily sudden response from the orchestra calls for observance of additional precautions.

1. We *must be ahead of the singer*, particularly toward the end of a long silent period in the pit. While this will produce a little pause at the appointed place of reunion in the score, it will also

    a. focus attention;

    b. leave the singer free to the end;

    c. not be felt as a musical event in itself.

Any sudden rush to catch up, on the other hand, is bound to create an unintended sense of excitement, at best. If excitement is wanted, let it be produced on the singer's initiative or your own, not by default.

2. No matter where we wait in the final measure(s), it is absolutely essential that the center-of-the-beat rule be scrupulously observed. As we have seen in circumstances when the musical flow was under the conductor's complete control, this position gives us our best chance to attack when, where, and how we choose.

3. Marking the passage of time during the "silent" measures can be done in one of two ways: either by a recognizable but vague outline of the regular beat pattern (though often ahead of where the stage action is reflected in the measure-by-measure notation in the score); or, as already suggested, by giving unobtrusive first beats of measures as they go by, until we near the moment of orchestral reentry. We are more likely to choose the former in *brief*, albeit free, one- or two-measure interruptions of the musical flow. The latter is a more usual resort when there are a substantial number of measures to count before we assume the "alert," two-before-the attack position. In either case, the beat remains small, but the "ones" distinct.

The following two examples from Bach's *St. Matthew Passion* illustrate the basic principles of conducting a recitative. As we shall see, they also point the way to an expansion of the outlined rules, as would be the case with any other musical event depending for its intended effect, in part, on the performer's judgment and taste. Both examples combine the so-called *secco* recitative style (in which the conductor may or may not wish to undertake the keyboard accompaniment himself, while the continuo string part will follow his lead) with the accompanied (orchestral) recitative, which is conducted. Unlike singers in an opera, oratorio soloists stand still, usually close to the conductor, and while they must enjoy musical freedom comparable to that expected of their operatic counterparts, their is no dramatic "action" to contend with, and the few guidelines given above should suffice to secure a fluid ensemble between singer and orchestra.

In looking at Example 3, a few preliminary comments might help. Then, as already suggested, practice with many different recordings in order to review in a practical situation all you have learned and to *apply* it.

EXAMPLE 3: Bach, *St. Matthew Passion,* "Then answered Peter"

The cadence on the second and third beats in measure two of Example 3 should, for stylistic reasons, *follow* the completion of the Evangelist's "and said to Him." Thus, after giving the first and third beats of the previous measure, we wait on 4 (close to and slightly above the center of the beat). As the singer completes his line, give a slight (preparatory) 1 to introduce beats 2 and 3. If you are actually playing yourself, you can easily manage this with the right hand. Otherwise these would simply be cues for the keyboard player as well. After bringing in Peter on 4, *wait* on the following 1 in order to be in position for a fast, preparatory 2 to assure a firm, but freely arrived at 3 ("Thee"). The next measure is likely to be in a fairly even, moderately paced four, together with the singer. But although the continuo may not need much more than a slight nod on the cadence in beats 2 and 3 of m. 5, the orchestra will need a clear indication of the first beat of this same measure so that they know that the next entrance, in the sixth measure, will be theirs. Again, we wait for the Evangelist to complete his "Jesus said to him," before we bring in the bass F♯ on the first beat of that measure. For expressive reasons we shall take our time before allowing the strings to enter on the second beat, setting the slow, other-worldly pace of Jesus's reply. But then we must move very fast (if unobtrusively) through beats 3 and 4 of that measure, and 1 and 2 of the next. Thus we can be ahead of the singer, ready to anticipate a deliberate, soft, slowly prepared entrance on 4, independent of his handling of the third beat ("night"). We wait on the next 1, without forcing the singer to attack with us on that beat ("ere yet"). But the orchestra, having seen us mark the first beat of the measure, will be ready to follow our preparatory 2 into the chord change of 3. The next upbeat (4) must control the singer's entrance as well, so that "thou shalt thrice deny me" will be clearly and firmly in time with the conductor's beat. Now we can either close in tempo or, if we prefer, use a cutoff afterbeat 2 ("thrice") so that we have complete freedom for a very deliberate, preparatory 3—perhaps a little later than its "normal" pulse—to provide us with a final cadence in whatever tempo *we* choose.

The same technique will serve the Example 4, except that during the accompanied part of the recitative (from "I will smite"), the conductor should suddenly take full control of the faster tempo. He will relinquish it again after the subito piano before "But when I am raised again." Here, beginning with that third (*p*) beat, we move quickly toward the second beat of the next measure, taking special care *not* to encourage the singer to *follow* our faster tempo: we need to be there first, to wait. N.B. Why not wait on the first beat, according to the rule of "stop two beats before the next entrance"? Because in the slower tempo set by the singer meanwhile, we are now going to give a preparatory *eighth-note*

EXAMPLE 4: Bach, *St. Matthew Passion,* "And when they had sung"

beat (2+) and subdivide to the end. Needless to say, in view of the very measured character of the utterance, that subdivided beat shall control both singer and players from the moment it starts.

Even in these fairly simple examples we see illustrations of the give and take between conductor and soloist, although the initiative, as it is felt by the audience, should always *appear* to be held by the singer. The meaning of the word, its sometimes descriptive setting to which the music then contributes, must remain the determining force to lend conviction to the performance of recitatives, even in the unstaged setting of an oratorio. With the addition of dramatic action on stage, there is a good deal more to the lively management of recitatives, than the safe indication of continuity and a reassuring cue or two, for orchestra players. For this same dramatic content is not always within actual control of the conductor either. Nor is the logic which accounts for the speeding up or slowing down of passages in which few musicians play necessarily musical. To the extent that not only the timing, but also the quality of each subsequent entrance is unrelated to whatever has gone before, it becomes the conductor's sole responsibility to provide a visual substitute by way of clear and predictable signals to the orchestra.

This is the point at which we might, once more, review and practice our small but flexible repertory of beats. The almost unlimited number of combinations in which qualities and varieties of beats can be made to serve various musical functions is nowhere more impressively apparent than in the operatic recitative. Nor is true proficiency in the application of the beat better rewarded than in this visual transmission of musical signals, the causes of which many of the players can neither hear nor see for themselves. Stage events in operas of Mozart or Donizetti, Puccini or Strauss, generate their own momentum and singers, as actors, will react—in the very pacing of musical events—to dramatic, i.e. extramusical stimulation. Given good direction on stage and in the pit, the ease and conviction with which dramatic and musical logic merge in performance are bound to owe much to one man's flick of the wrist.

Summary: The Beat in Conducted Recitatives

Direction: Assume a free recitative measure in which the orchestra (or part of the orchestra) is expected to enter on the fourth beat. Needless to say, we shall have indicated the first beat either on time or in advance of the singer. Whether we shall now proceed gently to 2, wait if necessary, and then give a "normal," preparatory 3 in order to signal the entrance on 4, or whether we decide to describe a suitably vague outline of the entire measure, only to pounce on the last beat with contrasting precision, will be determined by our assessment of the dramatic situation, the orchestration, the length of the preceding period of orchestral inactivity and, rather importantly, by the players' familiarity with the work. But in all events, the *direction* of the fourth beat—toward the center and up, from a point of elevation depending on the intended impact—should allow us confidence with regard to the earlier choices, including the "wait on two and prepare on three" rule.

Size: As always, the smaller the better. But then, also as always, a small beat can pivot from the shoulder, the elbow, the wrist. Here again it is the musical nature of the attack and the dramatic context within which it is expected to fit that will be the determinant. If, for instance, after a long silence (measured by discreet first beats unless the opera is very familiar to all players) the whole orchestra is scored in a powerful tutti attack, just *after* rather than *on* a main beat, a slashing, surprise swipe with the full arm could be a lot more effective than the safe methods we have practiced. Only you, as the conductor, can make this decision. At the same time you should be fully conscious of the reasons why you are *not* doing something that is more clearly within the bounds of safety. But there are certainly moments when you may fling your arms wide, without warning, in a huge gesture defying any suggestion yet made in this book.

Impetus: Again, the musical and dramatic context must help you decide what is right. In particular, the nature of the attack will determine the impetus of its *preparation* (unless it is to be the kind of surprise we have just described, which cannot be employed too often anyway). The explicit connection within the recitative rules of wait-and-prepare place more emphasis on the beat preceding the actual attack. Brisk, *secco* chords warrant small, sharp preparations. A large preparatory, followed by a much smaller but vicious main beat may be just the thing to indicate "bite" from the orchestra pit without the sort of wave of sound that covers voices not because it is loud but because it is sustained. At the other end of the impetus spectrum, the recitative offers us plenty of opportunity to practice "mute" first beats, marked by very small pulses from the finger joints alone. These may merge gradually into an "accompanying pattern," increasing the beats in size but not in impetus or definition, so that the sung phrase is followed, without tempting any player into a premature attack. In such a case, however, it is important that, no matter how indistinct the outline of each measure is to be, first beats are unmistakable. Let the orchestra *see* the design by dipping below the horizontal axis at the start of each measure.

Timing: As we have already pointed out, it is up to the conductor to determine whether he condenses several measures by a number of fast first beats or "follows" the singer discreetly by an unobtrusive outline of the passing measures while the orchestra waits. Either way, it is essential that the orchestra is ready to play *before* the singer gets to the place of reunion. Secondly, if the music the orchestra plays during a recitative demands rapid changes of tempo, clear preparatories in the *new* tempo are called for if possible. In such cases the control of timing will rest with the conductor anyway. An important caveat: *in the event that something unforeseen happens, the musicians must be told to "trust the stick": follow the conductor.*

Any dramatic situation supporting the music is bound to add extra-musical perspective to the points of view from which we have already explored the musical surface (cf. Chapter 2). That this is particularly true of the operatic recitative is quite clear. Still, singers as well as conductors sometimes display an astonishing lack of curiosity about the general life situation in which the characters on stage are supposed to find themselves or about the setting in the story which motivates the action and interaction about to take place.

As the first-act finale of Mozart's *Magic Flute* opens (Example 5), the young hero, Tamino, emissary from the Queen of the Night, has been led by benevolent spirits to the gates of Sarastro's priestly realm. His quest is the rescue of beautiful Pamina, daughter of the Queen, from what were first described to him as the magician-ruler's evil clutches. In actual fact, Sarastro abounds in wisdom and good intentions, as do all his faithful followers (with one comic exception). At this stage of the plot's unfolding we are not yet aware of this, nor is Tamino. The spirits have now left him to his own devices with suitable exhortations concerning steadfastness, obedience, and silence. Virtuous Tamino reassures himself as to the righteousness of his mission to rescue beauty from the beast. That he and beauty are to be each other's reward has been established earlier in the act.

Thus we shall have a look at the annotated version of a very famous, difficult, and beautiful recitative. Careful analysis and frequent practice with different recordings will repay the effort, not only in the study of a musical masterpiece, but in the challenge to our technical proficiency with the beat.

The absence of intent to control musical events from the podium mandates the selection of beats that cannot be mistaken for active signals of when to play. It also requires careful judgment of the timing with which pulses or purposely indistinct principals record or anticipate the progress of these events. The final, pivotal wait at the point where musical initiative returns to the conductor, and the subsequent preparatory beat with which we resume full control, must be planned in advance, practised if necessary, *and executed in exactly the same way every time it is reached in rehearsal or performance.* For, unlike any other event we have described in the possible course of conducting an orchestra, this is a moment at which the very *function* of leadership is relinquished or reassumed. The technique, as we have seen, is not difficult to master; the point of transition must be clearly understandable to

EXAMPLE 5: Mozart, *The Magic Flute,* Finale to Act I

*The concept of "waiting" does not *necessarily* mean a full stop (although it can). Sometimes it just means getting there fast, and then, unnoticeably moving "into" the singer's free continuation.

*In absence of enough coaching time—or with some singers—"follow" means "lead."

*The backstage conductor of the chorus will follow *you.**

those who do the actual playing and, even more important, to those who are following the course of the music while they themselves are temporarily at rest.

The application of such a technique is by no means confined to accompanied recitatives of the eighteenth century. The famous violin solo in Richard Strauss's *Ein Heldenleben,* or a typical excerpt from Puccini's *La Rondine* (Example 6) are characteristic nineteenth-century examples. The latter, in particular, calls upon unobtrusive but well-practiced skills on the part of the conductor. The *Heldenleben* solo is well known to orchestra players, and a well-routined orchestra will be more familiar with its points of reentry than some conductors. But operas are long. Fast patter on stage cannot always be heard in the pit, and dramatic timing must be fluid.

In this excerpt we have the following situation on stage: Prunier, a fashionable poet-about-town, has been paying court to Lisette, a chambermaid. He persuades her to try for an acting career, which he will help promote. After a single, disastrous stage appearance, she is eager to resume her former duties; he, quite unable to cope with the affair while she was a "social equal," finds himself once more attracted to Lisette the chambermaid. He is granted a date after she finishes work.

EXAMPLE 6: Puccini, *La Rondine*, Act II

Measure 1 of Example 6 ends the normal beat with the cutoff of the upper strings on 3. Beginning with the second measure, the marking of first beats will suffice to identify the cutoff of the cellos in m. 4 and permit, at the same time, a fluid flow of conversation on stage, unhampered by control from the pit. After that, several things must be considered: the fermata in m. 8 should be placed for the benefit of the entire orchestra; the amusing turnabout of Prunier's announced intentions and apparent affections must be given the same freedom of stage timing as it would have in a play; and his matter-of-fact reacceptance by Lisette might produce a laugh in the audience, resulting in a necessary delay of Prunier's acknowledgment of the return to their old relationship, as well as the reentry of the strings (the placement of which must be clear to the rest of the orchestra). This may sound like a complex task, but it only requires a clear application of the principles we have already outlined and what old-time opera conductors used to call a "light wrist."

Given a thorough knowledge of what is being said on stage (the operatic equivalent of being well acquainted with every detail of the solo part in a concerto), here is one way in which we might go about the gradual relinquishing and reassumption of control in the *Rondine* excerpt. We shall continue with gentle pulses on every first beat until the fermata measure—more or less in time with the stage, but in no way inhibiting the flow of verbal interchange. The *wait* (which is bound to be exploited for some dramatic purpose by the stage direction) would naturally identify the fermata and the measure in which it occurs. (*N.B.* orchestral parts indicate large numbers of rest by their cumulative total; but landmarks like fermatas are allowed to interrupt that process and thus serve as a check before the counting starts afresh.) From now on we must be sure to get ahead of the stage, in order to be in position for the string attacks. Our goal is a "wait" on the third beat of m. 12. This will be distinguishable from the earlier fermata wait by the fact that we have given the two previous beats of that measure *in full*. Thus we shall have followed the fermata by three quick but unobtrusive "ones" (mm. 9, 10, and 11), followed by a fast but *directional* 1–2–3 of m. 12. The speed of these beats will make it clear that our beat is not related to what is being sung on stage, but is preparing an orchestral entrance. At the appropriate moment, a crisp 4–1 will bring in the first violins and violas in m. 13. With a steady beat from now on, and normal cues when necessary, succeeding attacks will follow our initiative once more. Even that large majority of players not involved in the reentry shown in our example *should be in no doubt about the place where the conductor reasserted full musical control.*

Some Twentieth-Century Applications

Music of the twentieth century introduced a special kind of give and take between players and their conductor. In the following example only the entrances and exits of certain groups of players are indicated. When they play is within the exclusive control of the conductor, as is the extent of their participation. What they choose to play—a choice offered in each case by the variable content of interchangeable "boxes" containing musical directions—is up to the player. But the *technique* of managing such problems from the podium is very much the same as that described above, in terms of eighteenth-century recitatives or the example from Puccini's *La Rondine*.

Helmut Lachenmann's *Introversion I* (Example 7) is written for clarinet, trumpet, harmonium, harp, double bass, and percussion. Our sample page of score (IIb) is in itself the result of choices already made by a performer, not the composer. We note, between each "staff" for each instrument, regular divisions of approximately ½ inch in length, corresponding in function to the equal divisions provided by conventional measures; the "boxes" labeled with capital letters may, in each case be interchanged as indicated. Similarly, the page itself, for any one player, may follow or be succeeded by one of several other possible pages; in effect, the score in this respect resembles a predetermined counterpoint so variously invertable, that the performer himself has the luxury of individual choice without risking the overall ensemble. The given limitations within each box might let him choose one of three instruments to play, but then commit him to the conditions which are also given in any one of the three cases. Since these conditions include precise instructions concerning rhythm and dynamics, as well as placement of events relative to a given framework (the "box" itself), the composer's "instructions" (cf. Chapter 2) are quite as specific, and must be as carefully observed, as those in more conventional music. The score itself will of course have to be arranged differently for each performance, in accordance with the predetermined choices in terms of sequence. The actual performance then still leaves some spontaneous decisions to the players.

For the conductor, such a score offers no new challenges in terms of technique. Our gestures and the control of events they represent are akin to what happens in an opera pit—not least because the players will not have the grid of counted measures to orient themselves within an established framework of time articulated by the conductor's beat. All the more reason why the conductor's *ear*, if not his technique as such, must accommodate itself to new demands. If he is to preside safely and successfully over the built-in uncertainties of such a score, his direction

EXAMPLE 7: Helmut Lachenmann, *Introversion I*

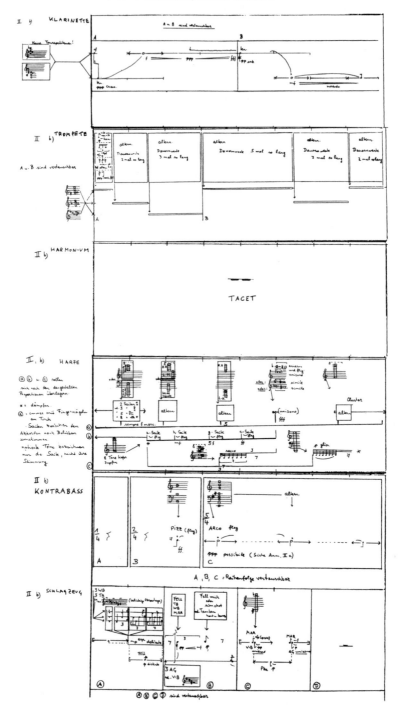

must be very clear. Overall musical continuity must at all times be clearly established in the conductor's mind, as his periodic resumption of control must be predictable by the players and executed with conviction.

Twentieth-century compositional practice may compound the problems already encountered in accompanying singers or instrumental soloists. The American composer Morris Cotel's *Piano Concerto* is prefaced by special instructions. The following excerpt is relevant to the musical example on p. 372:

Each score page takes about 10–15 seconds. The conductor gives the beat and each part goes as written.

For convenience the beats are numbered 0 through 5 with letters a through d. The conductor gives the number with his left hand (0 indicated by fist) and a, b, c, d with baton as in standard C [4/4] pattern—

$$a = \overset{\frown}{\downarrow}, \ b = \overset{\frown}{\leftarrow} \ , \ c = \overset{\frown}{\rightarrow} \ , \ d = \overset{\frown}{\uparrow} \ .$$

For example 0a through 0d would be done with the left hand clenched in a fist and the baton hand describing a C pattern with a 10—15 [second] fermata on each beat.

Example 8 illustrates how the beat is to be applied. Identified as "0a" (0 = fist; a = downbeat, according to the instructions above), the conductor extends his left hand, fist clenched, just before the piano reaches the page shown. With a suitable preparatory beat, as always, he will bring the stick *down* at the precise moment when the pianist comes to the quarter-note rest with which his line on this page begins (had the page been labeled 0b, the stick would have traveled to the left; 0c to the right; 0d upwards: always with clear preparatories *in the opposite direction*). Thus the pianist may complete each section in his own time, while the instrumentalists, improvising on their given notes, are kept informed on overall progress by conductor's signals in much the same way as an opera orchestra is apprised of its next entrance in an accompanied recitative.

In some conventionally notated scores, complexity itself may call for a decision on which aspects of the music are to be controlled from the podium, and which would then have to be left to the instrumentalists' initiative by default. The Coda of Elliott Carter's *Double Concerto for Harpsichord and Piano with two Chamber Orchestras* (see p. 373) requires such a choice. Here, as with all music, the decision ultimately depends on a personal factor; does the conductor prefer to control musical nuances, dynamics, accents, or would he rather facilitate the players' entrances and rhythmic accuracy?

Orchestra I, accompaning the Harpsichord, plays in a meter of 6/8, i.e., requires a beat of *two* to each measure; Orchestra II and the piano are in *three*. The conductor will either beat *two* with his left hand (for Orchestra I) and *three* with his right (for the other half of the group); or he may wish to maintain a strict beat of *three* in his right against which the first orchestra must coordinate its six eighth notes per measure.

EXAMPLE 8: Morris Cotel, *Piano Concerto*

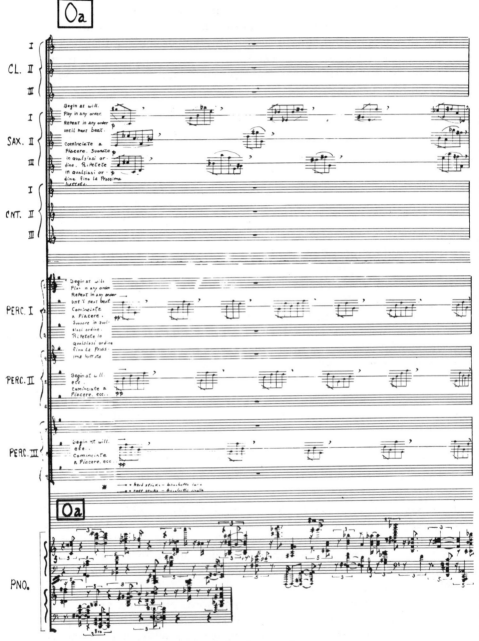

An accidental applies only to the note it directly precedes.
Le note senza accidenti davanti, si suonano naturale.

EXAMPLE 9: Elliott Carter, *Double Concerto for the Harpsichord and Piano*

Wherever the latter method lacks the strong pulse on the fourth eighth note which serves as a necessary second point of important metric reference in a measure (viz. all three measures in Example 9), the left hand could indicate it. At other times however, the left would be free to emphasize nuances, indicate entrances or secure balances in *either* orchestra. Under the first method, with each hand beating a different meter, all musical initiative must be left to the players. Good results can be achieved either way. The author's personal preference eventually led him to choose maximum metric clarity, two against three at all times, at the price of yielding some local musical control.

Electronic tape, fitted in with "live" instrumental music, often requires the additional use of a stopwatch in the left hand to synchronize the tape with variable control of the human element by the right. But not even modern technology is entirely fail-safe; and to add a lighter touch to what might otherwise be a rather forbidding section, the following is not only a true story, but an encouraging one as well. Precisely under the circumstances described—stopwatch in the left hand, baton in the right, and the calibrated graph of an electronic tape, with exact timings, in the middle of a score for large orchestra—the author was recording a work by Luigi Nono for the BBC in London. Although all the timings were scrupulously observed, both on the podium and, as an additional check, in the control booth, we could not get it right: one moment everything seemed to work together perfectly, but a few seconds later, everything went ever so slightly, but quite unaccountably, "out of synch." At last, a distinctly smug maintenance man revealed the answer. The district generators which serve the BBC Maida Vale Studios are provided with a booster mechanism which, every fifteen minutes, will slightly increase or reduce electrical power to the entire area, according to the amount actually used during the preceding time interval. The variation is small, much too small to affect ordinary electrical appliances. But ensemble requirements in our art are coordinated according to fractions of fractions of a second as a matter of course. The amusing occasion also demonstrated very powerfully how much precision and sensitivity to minute fluctuations of tempo we take for granted in the complexities of musical ensembles. We did solve the problem by fitting a recording into the slot between electrical power boosts. And we were most pleased with ourselves and with the art of music.

The Personal Factor

Observe any good conductor in action, and you will be able to analyze what he does according to the principles of beat and gesture you have begun to incorporate into your own work. Musical communication from the podium is based on a system of manual signals that remains unchanged in its essentials, no matter where or by whom orchestras are conducted. As a result, conductors as well as orchestral players are able to function efficiently from the first moment of rehearsal, even if they have never worked together before.

Yet one conductor's personal style of physical expression may vary so much from another's that their apparent differences will stand out more strikingly than their common code of meaningful movement. In fact, one need only think of a few celebrated virtuosos of the baton to realize that it would be virtually impossible to find a connection between style of movement (within the framework of generally accepted practice of the beat) and musical result. When you listen to recorded performances by a good orchestra, without knowing who is conducting, you cannot tell what kind of podium presence there was at the live event. Flamboyant or self-effacing, controlled or choreographic, whoever was conducting made the orchestra play *that* performance. But the *orchestra* did the playing, and it is the playing of the orchestra that is *heard*, in performance or on records. Well-schooled orchestras respond with precision to the *substance of musical direction* from the podium; the better the orchestra, however, the less it will reflect the conductor's *personal style* in giving such direction.

Temperament and physical predisposition play a part, but mostly as modifying factors of something equally fundamental in any conductor's identity as a practitioner of his craft. His attitude to *shared musical performance* reveals itself clearly in the degree of overt control he chooses to assert or yield in concert. Given the confidence of sufficient experience on the podium, a conductor's characteristic approach in this area would vary only little according to the relative expertise of his orchestra. A conductor to whom the orchestra is like a large keyboard for his exclusive use will certainly try to control every nuance of the music as if he were actually playing all the notes himself. Another might feel more comfortable in the role of coach to a well-drilled team: he will call the plays and the players will be encouraged to execute them as a team, with a degree of independent initiative. For such a conductor, the techniques of yielding control find their most rewarding application not only in the predictable circumstances of concerto accompaniment or operatic recitative, but in the normal give and take of every symphonic concert.

PART THREE

SCORE	PODIUM
The Image in Mind	*The Instrument*

The young conductor with a professional goal is addressed. Emphasis should now shift from structured teaching to a firmly committed learning process at the source: score and podium. These final pages are intended to provide background, some guidance, and perspective.

12

MUSIC AND MEMORY: TIME AS
RHYTHM

This chapter explores the practical implications of replacing the spatial concept of
shape, in the study of scores, with music's
own dimension, time. Score examined:
Mahler, *First Symphony*.

> to sing
> to lords and ladies of Byzantium
> of what is past, or passing, or to come.
> —YEATS

> Time passes at a rate which varies accord-
> ing to the inner disposition of the subject.
> —STRAVINSKY

INTRODUCTION: TIME AND THE ART OF MEMORY

Time is a dimension of everyday experience. Even what we perceive
in an instant, a flight of birds overhead, a group of railroad workers
glimpsed from the window of a fast-moving train, the fleeting impression of a familiar face in a crowd, must endure in time in order to be
experienced. The instant of perception itself has no extension in time,
yet seems to move irreversibly from past to future, from no longer to
not yet in time. Whether time really flows or whether our instant of
perception "moves" in a time dimension does not alter the nature of
our experience. One may refer usefully to the rising sun, knowing perfectly well that the sun does no such thing. A visual impression is nonetheless accurately observed.

The phenomenon of time has occupied a special place in the minds
of twentieth-century physicists, philosophers, and psychologists. It is
hardly surprising that, in the past fifty years, increasing interest has
centered on the role of time in music. Music not only takes place in
time, but it also deals with time, features varieties of time, is able to

repeat or reverse time, and, in the mind, is capable of reducing an extensive structure of used time to a single instant of concentrated experience. In our explorations of what lies beneath the surface of music we were selective: First we chose to examine musical shapes, the building blocks of larger structure. Then we considered the "gravitational force" of harmonic functions and substitute devices, musical and extramusical, which came to serve that purpose when the potent harmonic conventions of the eighteenth and nineteenth centuries became "traditional." The harmonic conventions were still in style, long after the absolute power of tonalities had given way to more egalitarian relationships, at first among chords, then among keys, and finally within serial structures. These last, stripped of all reference to traditional harmonic practice, might still involve a demonstrable tonal center; but this theoretical focus was not to be heard as such, nor was it of any particular use to us in managing the music, except as a metaphor of the structure of yet another, deeper layer beneath its surface—time.

Time lends depth and perspective to anticipation, experience, and remembering musical events. But music lends to time what only dreams, drugs, and waking fantasies provide, a turning *back* of the clock as a perfectly natural and acceptable function, among others. Who is to say which is real: the musical *déjà vu* in the recapitulation of a sonata, or the steady, simultaneous sweep of the second hand on one's wristwatch? Given the three interacting elements in any piece of music— the *mass* of musical shapes, the *momentum* of harmonic impulse or its equivalent, and the very pliable *dimension* of time—it is not difficult to understand why there is no such thing as a definitive performance of any work whatsoever; and why, far from expressing a somewhat liberal view on the subject, composer Roger Sessions is stating an obvious fact when he writes, "I am convinced that the performer is an essential element in the whole musical picture."

Less apparent, if hardly less important, is that the performer must carefully examine and recall not only the work he is to perform, but whatever essential element will distinguish his performance from all others. The results of his work in preparation of a score are likely to include as many of his own decisions on phrasing, balance, tempo, and overall pacing as details of the composer's instructions on which these decisions are based. *His success in making the most of this mixture depends on memory.*

In about 500 B.C., the Greek poet Simonides (whom the Romans called Melicus—the honey-tongued) was asked to deliver a festive eulogy at a banquet for the winner of the wrestling match at the Olympian Games. In his oration before the large gathering, Simonides made mention of the divine twins Castor and Pollux. When he concluded, he was told that two young men were waiting to see him in the forecourt of the house. No sooner had he stepped out of the entrance, when the entire building collapsed, crushing his unsuspecting audience beneath the weight of its fallen masonry. So quick and so total was this destruction, that the bodies of host and guests could not be identified. It was then that Simonides, assuming once more his earlier position within the now ruined banquet hall, was able to recall the faces of his entire audience from the direction in which he remembered them, and thus to provide names for the gruesomely mangled remains of his friends.

To succeeding generations, Simonides' grisly feat earned him the title of father of the *Art of Memory*, a now nearly forgotten system of instant recall developed in antiquity and highly regarded. From Aristotle and Cicero in Greece and Rome, to Aquinas and Bruno in the Middle Ages and the Renaissance, an extensive literature served the teaching of a craft of memory which only fell into neglect with the advent and increasing availability of printed books. Some of the technical information on this Art of Memory seems arcane today, but its principles agree with Simonides' alleged approach in first reconstructing the scene, and then the identity, of his late listening audience.

The Art of Memory dealt with 1) vivid visualization of *images*; 2) methodical distribution of images in *places*. Simonides visualized the remembered faces of his friends in placing these images at the locations where he had last seen them. Common to most schools of memory was the careful construction by every practitioner of his own *Theater of Memory*. Well-defined *places* on its imaginary stage served as repositories of *images*. The images stood for whatever was to be remembered, and the order of their placement helped to preserve their context as well as their identity for future recall. It was essential that one's theater of memory was always the same, and that one's mental path across its stage always followed a similar course. With growing familiarity and skill, the adept practitioner was able to add more and more places to store a wider range of information. The same set of locations, visited by the same imaginary route of reexamination, could serve the lifetime memory needs of orators, lawyers, and teachers.

Images were to be as striking and fantastic as possible. Summarizing an exposition of the kind of images likely to stick in one's memory, Cicero wrote:*

We ought then to set up images of a kind that can adhere longest in memory. And we shall do so if we establish similitudes as striking as possible; if we set up images that are not many or vague but active; if we assign to them exceptional beauty or singular ugliness; if we ornament some of them, as with crowns or purple cloaks, so that the similitude may be the more distinct to us; or if we

*Cicero, *De oratore*.

somehow disfigure them, as by introducing one stained with blood or soiled with mud or smeared with red paint, so that its form is more striking, or by assigning certain comic effects to our image, for that, too, will ensure our remembering them more readily.

The author had a student, a gifted young conductor, who seemed incapable of memorizing a score. He was conscientious, an almost compulsive worker, but even the most determined efforts produced little more than short-lived recollection of essentially useless theoretical information about a piece of music. In no way was he able to relate this to the results of his performance preparation of the score, or to any kind of musical continuity before an orchestra. Regretfully, one had to conclude that, for him, the use of the printed score, even during the crucial period of mapping out its performance, was to be preferred over his tortuous and inhibiting by-rote learning.

Then he discovered—quite by chance—the secret of active, exaggerated images which, at the time, was unknown to the author. He imagined the work as it would be performed by a make-believe orchestra. But it was a very strange assortment of players: a trumpet solo might be performed by a man leaping up on his chair; the harpist would have her head caught in the strings of her instrument; and the timpanist performed a little dance on his drums. From that day on, he learned his scores from memory with growing ease. He was able to recall more serious aspects of his analyses while he continued to indulge in outrageous fantasy images. And he clearly enjoyed the process. He had rediscovered a two-thousand-year-old technique, the "active images" of Cicero, and assigned them to his most natural theater of memory— the orchestra.

Images need not necessarily be representative of what is to be remembered. Their capability to trigger an instant association is important. A favorite example given in medieval texts was the cock crow which reminded Peter of Jesus's prediction of his betrayal. In Chapter 4a we indulged in a fantasy of images in connection with the Andante movement from Mozart's *Eine kleine Nachtmusik* which might well have struck you as extravagant. If you persisted nonetheless in following the text, you should now be in an excellent position to judge for yourself: try to recall the *images,* and you are likely to remember a surprising amount of *textual detail.* Not that the images *stood* for that detail—they were associated with it in your mind, as was the music we examined, the place in which you happened to be reading this book, and any number of thoughts, impressions, and conclusions which have become part of a composite memory pattern. A relatively brief glance at those pages will recall a lot more vivid detail, more quickly, than review of a more traditional analysis.

Memory: Images and Places

Images and places may be combined *as the basis of a memorizing technique.* As a preliminary to actual use in the preparation of scores, the two components of this approach had best be separated for the time being. Practicing as little as five minutes a day, seven days a week, and at the same hour, if possible, will produce surprisingly rapid results.

Images

The simplest way of memorizing a series of unrelated nouns is to string them together in combinations of twos, with a shifting image for each pair. Ian M. L. Hunter describes the system in his classic study.* The first four words in his chosen sequence are *sugar, daffodil, boat, tiger.*

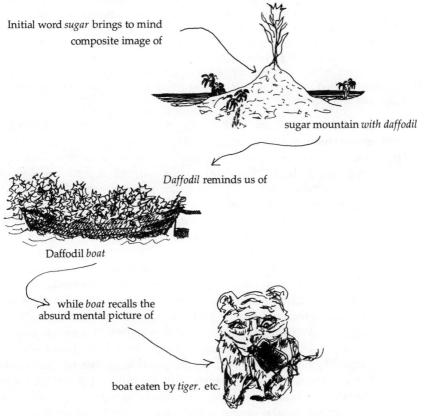

Initial word *sugar* brings to mind composite image of

sugar mountain *with daffodil*

Daffodil reminds us of

Daffodil *boat*

while *boat* recalls the absurd mental picture of

boat eaten by *tiger.* etc.

FIGURE 1: Word Sequence of *sugar—daffodil—boat—tiger*

*Ian M. L. Hunter, *Memory* (Penguin Books, 1957; rev. ed., 1964), p. 213.

The procedure is as follows: When the first word is heard, visualize sugar as vividly as possible. When the second word is heard, visualize daffodil. Then relate the imagined sugar and the imagined daffodil into one composite image which is as vivid, striking and fantastic as possible. For example, imagine a really gigantic daffodil, far more than life size, growing out of a mountain of granulated sugar, sucking up the sugar with relish, its trumpet and petals glistening with sugar crystals. This ridiculous, briefly imagined scene deals with the first and second words of the sequence. Now dismiss it from mind and deal similarly with the second and third words. Imagine daffodil and boat in fantastic conjunction. For example, a boat garlanded with bright yellow daffodils, filled with millions of daffodils, weighted down, groaning, and almost submerged by daffodils. Then dismiss this, and contrive a vivid composite imagining of boat and tiger. In short, the procedure is to deal with only two incoming words at any one time; relate these two words together into detailed imagining and combining the images together into a composite image which is detailed, far-fetched, exaggerated, and distinctive; when this composite image is achieved, dismiss it from your mind and make no subsequent attempt to recall it. When the time comes for recalling the sequence of words, the mnemonic must recall the first item of the sequence. He imagines this, sugar, and finds himself imagining the sugar-daffodil composite. This gives him the second item, daffodil, which prompts recall of the daffodil-boat composite, and so on. The brief but vividly detailed imaging of each fantastic composite suffices to lead him from each word to the next in succession. . . .

The exaggerated, comic combinations of image pairs recall the technique described by Cicero nearly 2000 years ago. But why images in the first place? The experience of the conducting student described on p. 382 turned out to be neither original nor isolated. A number of studies in our own century have supported the notion that *exclusive concern with intellectual and conceptual grasp* in the learning process *inhibits memorization,* and that giving *free rein to the imagination* from the start *will aid memory* and facilitate retention of large-scale structural concepts.*

Images, i.e. what we deposit in remembered places on a composite diagram of the composition in preparation, need not be visual. We have already worked through a large and complex work, Beethoven's *Seventh Symphony,* in which the imaginary protagonists were three tonalities— A, C, and F.** With music of the Classical period, harmonic relationships and departures from accustomed practice (e.g. Introduction to Beethoven's *First Symphony†*) may well provide the memorable context which the imagination can furnish with meaningful detail. But whatever the fabric of our concentrated overview of a work, it is really essential that the total mental image is vivid and instantly accessible.

---

*Readers wishing to pursue this aspect of memorization and to learn more about work being done in this field are referred to the bibliography at the end of this book.
**Cf. p. 329.   †Cf. p. 326.

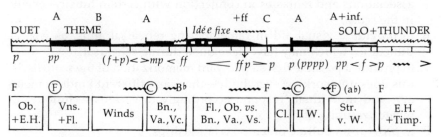

FIGURE 2: Berlioz, *Fantastic Symphony*, third movement

Figure 2 shows a time chart prepared by a student of very strong intellectual gifts whose approach to music so strongly favored the analytical side that suggestions involving the use of metaphoric imagery met with great resistance. Instead he invented for himself an elaborate sort of a diagram which not only illustrated relative time spans within the structure of a movement, but provided a graphic shorthand picture of thematic events, dynamics, key relationships, and orchestration. Most interesting, however, is his attempt to outline the waxing and waning of affective intensity. The line just above the calibrated base represents the emotional continuity of the third movement of Berlioz's *Fantastic Symphony*. A glance at the parallel dynamic ranges shows that the two comprise quite different series of events—as, in turn, they are independent of the thickness of texture in the orchestration (bottom line). On the other hand, there is a kind of very loose symmetry in the emotional range of intensity throughout this piece. Beginning and ending in a diffuse, overall mood, it indeed has a striking shape—over and above the inherent musical structure—which is the intended experience of the work in emotional terms. Certainly a remarkable structure into which to fit memorized events: a series of "places" to provide light, shade, and background to whatever will furnish them.

Time charts serve several purposes:
1. To provide a concentrated, visual summary of large works, so that the succession of musical events may be seen from selective points of view (e.g. harmonic, dynamic, associative, etc.);
2. to provide a framework showing the proportional distribution of certain musical events over the entire length of the piece;
3. to provide a kind of "aerial photograph" of the musical surface which may suggest features which are not apparent at "ground level";
4. to provide an alternative approach to interpretative analysis of works in which more conventional methods have failed to yield useful information, or when the results of conventional methods seem ambiguous;

5. to provide a framework for remembering spontaneous, extramusical associations and fantasies in connection with certain musical events in the score;
6. to provide a visual aid in remembering rehearsal aims, as well as difficulties which may have developed during rehearsal;
7. to provide a possible first step toward memorization of the score itself; this does not work for everybody—there are different kinds of memory, and individuals respond accordingly to various techniques of memorization;
8. to provide an outline of tempo relationships.

The basic ingredient of a time chart is a straight line, evenly callibrated to mark the number of measures involved. The more compact the image is to be, the larger the number of measures represented by the space between marks. If more detail is desired, the number of measures represented by each space must be smaller. While it is possible to draw a time chart with one measure for each space, the "aerial" perspective suggested in item 3 above would be lost. In a time chart, as much of a score as possible should be taken in at a single glance. Detail is important, but the advantage of a simultaneous view of an entire movement or work is lost if you have to turn a great many pages.

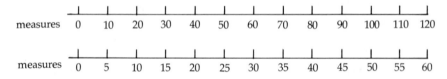

| measures | 0 | 10 | 20 | 30 | 40 | 50 | 60 | 70 | 80 | 90 | 100 | 110 | 120 |

| measures | 0 | 5 | 10 | 15 | 20 | 25 | 30 | 35 | 40 | 45 | 50 | 55 | 60 |

FIGURE 3: Calibrated Base Lines

Above and below the base line representing continuity of time may be placed remarks, graphs, or even pictures, depending on one's purpose in drawing the chart. Have that purpose clearly in mind so that the chart may reflect areas you have decided to explore. It is *not* a good idea to mix functions to be recorded on any one line or graph. A time chart tends to impress itself on the mind as a pictorial image. If one's memory is of the "photographic" sort (and, like absolute pitch, memory is quite trainable), we can even search a memory image much as we would examine an actual page. Therefore, the information with which we have "programmed" each line should be as consistent within itself as possible, or we run the very real risk of retrieving a confusing "printout."

When we furnish places with images of whatever sort, we supply the total memory picture with a unique contribution of our own. What is to be stored in memory is not only information in proper order (sugar—daffodil—boat—tiger) but perhaps the performance of an orchestral work, with all the nuances, rubatos, underlined contrasts, or subdued melodic exchanges with which a conductor would not only represent the musical surface of a score, but have to plan, organize, and remember *his own decisions and discoveries,* in great detail.

The young conductor whose time chart of Berlioz we showed was learning the *Fantastic Symphony* for the first time. As a working conductor,* he will have to rework and rethink his original mapping out of the slow movement. But the chance to feel again the fluctuating intensities he had once plotted so sensitively should provide him with a starting point. Being able to review his originally planned performance at a glance, without laborious reconstruction in time, will also assist him in recapturing the marvelous contradictions between the obvious rise and fall of dynamic level and thickness of orchestration in the score, and the searing intensity of a single line of solo music as he perceived it. What ideas, associations, and feelings *we* inject into a planned performance must be stored in memory and preserved for future development as much as any other aspect of musical preparation.

A well-drawn time chart usually deals with several aspects of a piece at once, requiring several lines or, better still, a combination of lines, remarks, and graphs. The drawing of time charts in itself is an excellent discipline, for it imposes the need to make choices even while we learn a score. In the process we learn something about ourselves as performers. Decisions concerning the actual performance must be made before we mount the podium for our first rehearsal, of course. A time chart can reflect those only to the extent to which we have involved our intelligence, our feelings, and our imagination in the preparation. But we begin by selecting our points of musical reference. These will be aspects of the music about which we care, and in determining what these are we had best be as personal and imaginative as possible. Let it be clearly understood: we are not yet making interpretive decisions; we are establishing points of departure from which to begin the work.

IMAGES, PLACES, AND MEMORY

There is a very curious story about Mahler which Bruno Walter tells in his little book about his teacher and friend.** Mahler, at the conclusion of the opening movement of his *First,* "saw Beethoven before him, breaking out into peals of laughter and running off." As Walter points out, the laughing Beethoven has really nothing to do with the experi-

---

* At the time of this writing, he is music director of his own orchestra.
** Bruno Walter, *Gustav Mahler* (New York: Knopf, 1958), p. 125.

ences out of which, by Mahler's own account, the *First Symphony* arose. But as a spontaneous image, experienced presumably by the conductor Mahler in preparation of, or even during, a performance of his work, it could hardly be more memorable, and to illustrate the sort of image to which we have referred in this chapter, we could not wish for a better example.

"How this music poured forth from me," marveled Mahler in a letter to friend Fritz Loehr, "like white water from a mountain stream!" Can we, in hoping to recapture the essence of his score, try for less? The excitement is not suddenly added in the concert hall. It begins in our study and includes whatever we bring to the transfer of music from page to memory. We shall have plenty of occasion to observe in later examples that the time-honored active images "that move the soul" are more than aids to memory. In the experience of many conductors, such images arise from apparently autonomous recesses of the mind while our conscious attention is focused on more mundane aspects of the score. Once in focus, however, they are hard to forget. At this time, we will attempt to give a detailed example of how the principle of places and images might be applied to memorizing a large and complicated piece of music.

Implied in the principle of places and images is a general overview of the work before memorization begins. We should be familiar with the entire "street," or have some notion of the whole "theater of memory," before we place our images. And, as we already pointed out in connection with the study of the musical surface, any available information on the composer's thought and life circumstance at the time of composition will furnish a little perspective while we collect observable data.

This much of the personal background of Mahler's *First Symphony* is history: he was young when he wrote it (middle to late twenties); he'd had two unhappy love affairs and, by his own account, wrote them into the symphony and out of his system (his *Wayfarer Songs*, on his own texts, are quoted in the materials of the symphony, with the relevant lines as implied commentary); the autobiographical intent is amplified in later references by the composer (e.g. the opening of the Finale as "expression of a deeply wounded heart"); he was much involved in the romantic worlds of early nineteenth-century literary figures like Paul Friedrich Richter and E. T. A. Hoffmann; and the work's original title (later withdrawn, as were the subtitles to the original five movements) was that of a novel (c. 1800) by Jean Paul, *The Titan*. For general flavor, and as an introduction to the ambiance of Mahler's *First*, that should suffice.

In exploring the surface of this music, we shall have discovered an extraordinary unity of thematic material. Behind the facade of horn calls, trumpet fanfares, bird noises, and folk melodies, the melodic outlines fall into two main categories based on the intervals of a fourth and of a second respectively. Mahler's *Wayfarer Songs,* which appear to have served the composer as a kind of study or preview for the big work in the way Wagner's *Wesendonk Songs* (also the peroration for a lost love) were intended as reconnaissance into *Tristan* territory, begin with two motives:

EXAMPLE 1

Thinly disguised, this melody reappears in the fantastic funeral march of the symphony:

EXAMPLE 2

The central position in that melancholy movement is occupied by a literal quote from the last of the *Wayfarer Songs,* reminiscent in mood and text of that earlier wanderer singing of betrayed love in Schubert's *Winterreise:*

EXAMPLE 3

And the forward motion of the piece comes almost to a stop with this haunting evocation of the opening words of the same song:

EXAMPLE 4

Clearly, Mahler's own text for his *Wayfarer Songs,* flowing out of the fresh pain of personal experience, can be taken as a sure guide to the mood of the symphony, while the close relationship of the thematic material will permit an easy reference as we develop it.

Armed, as it were, with the composer's own commentary on the extramusical intent of his symphony, we would be foolish not to take advantage of the opportunity he has provided. The very opening of the symphony's exposition ([4], fourth measure) appears as a direct quote of the second *Wayfarer Song*, in the same key (D major), and with the low strings assuming the vocal line:

EXAMPLE 5

Tempo indications (symphony—*sehr gemächlich*, vs. song—*in gemächlicher Bewegung*) would have the symphony movement slower at this stage, a hunch which is confirmed almost at once, when the continuation of the symphony text skips (four after 5) to a section of the song which is indeed slower than its opening speed (second measure of [14], *Wayfarer Song 2*). Then, at [8] of the symphony (having also reached a faster tempo by this time), we go back to the very beginning of *Wayfarer Song 2* ([9]) and quote extensively almost to the end, the sad little *Abgesang* of pain, in the face of so much beauty and joy of living. Where the song ends, the symphony only begins—that seems to be the composer's clearly compelling reason to alter the sequence of quotation in two movements otherwise so similar. At the same time it supplies further support for the text's relevance to the symphony's message. Since, in the preparation of a performance, we would certainly have become familiar with the text by now, and since it is relevant, we shall quote it here in full:*

Through the field I took my way, dewdrops hung on grass and tree,
Said the merry finch to me: "Fine bright day? So good morning!
Good morning! Is this world not fresh and gay? Fresh and gay?
Sing! Sing! Everything! All the world is glad in May!"

On the fields the bluebells sway, merrily their heads they swing,
Sounding bells which gently ring, gently ring, sing to me their
Morning lay: "Is this world not fresh and gay? Fresh and gay?
So ring! Ring, ring! Everything! All the world is glad in May! Heigho!"

Sunshine spreading over all, filling all the world with light—
Sparkling rays make sounds and colors all so bright! Bird and flower,
Large and small! "Happy day! Happy day! Is this world not fresh and gay?
So good day, yes good day: World so gay!"

*Translation: Edition Eulenburg, Redlich, 1959.

Then comes the melancholy afterthought:

> *Will my happiness return? Will my happiness return?*
> *No! No! Well I know: For this one gift my heart must yearn.*

The music for this is *not* quoted in the opening movement of the symphony. Instead it culminates in the hyperbolical exuberance that stimulated the composer's odd vision of the laughing Beethoven—running off.

As the following examples show, the materials for this symphony are very closely interrelated. In this instance, all the cited melodic and thematic fragments have been traced to the opening theme of the exposition (first movement)—also the beginning of the second *Wayfarer Song*. In a way, this apparently extraordinary economy of thematic construction is the natural consequence of the composer's already well developed *Varianten* technique.* The choice, therefore, of *Frère Jacques* in the third movement, is as much testimony to a tough-minded composer's skill in manipulating musical materials as it is the possibly conscious reference by a romantic young man whose brother had committed suicide not long before, and who, himself in a painful life situation, might have given thought to the solace of such sleep. It cannot be said that Mahler necessarily derived all his musical building blocks from the first complete thematic statement in the exposition of this opening movement. Nor would this be of more than passing interest to the serious performer. Very important, however, and clearly demonstrable, is the basic uniformity of all his building blocks, in view of the even more striking consistency with which these are employed to achieve structural *and* expressive unity. (See Example 6, p. 392)

As has been stated, these building blocks fall into two categories: those featuring the interval of a fourth and those based primarily on a progression of seconds. These basic intervallic contours govern melodic forms of "his-and-hers" variety—whether by conscious design or intuitive association is not our concern. In the event, the themes and motives dominated by fourths tend to suggest the hero's experience of the symphony's drama; the seconds recall his lost love.

Figure 4, like the musical surface of a score, represents flexible suggestions as well as hard evidence, "instructions" as well as "facts," for the formation of a performance image of this music. Mahler's own text for his *Songs of a Wayfarer,* and his use of the same musical materials in the *First Symphony*, establish the central role of a young man who has an experience. The likeness of the lady's face, or indeed her identity, might well vary in the imagination of the performer. Identification may be in the first person or the third. But the nature of the experience is to be part of the performance image in either case.

*Cf. Theodor W. Adorno, *Mahler* (Bibliothek Suhrcamp), Chapter 5.

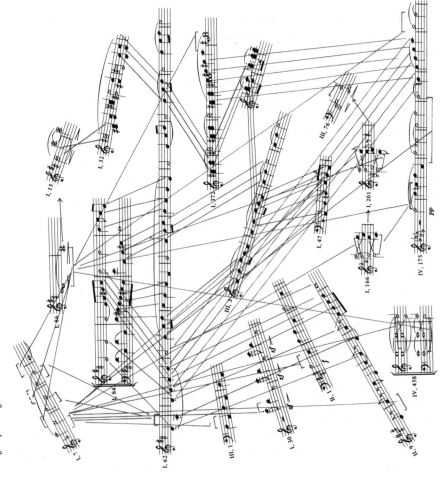

EXAMPLE 6: *Mahler Symphony No. 1*

FIGURE 4

The same is true of other specific allusions in the work: for any conductor who has actually spent some sunny mornings walking across fields, the remembered scene may become associated with the young man's pain at the thought of his sweetheart's wedding to another. But the prescribed image could well consist of an imagined field and a personal memory of lost love, jealous rage, and a melancholy vision of two blue eyes. The component parts of the image are "facts"; the settings and, as we shall see, the course of events suggested by the music are "instructions." Both are established by the composer. Only the latter leave a margin of personal identification to the imagination of the performer.

A course of events suggested by the music would resemble our conposite sketch a little. Discontinuous, overlapping musical references that repeat or anticipate descriptive fragments of a story already known in its entirety are more like parts of a dream. They do not come in the order of happenings in a play. For all that they determine the quality of ordinary *clock time* in performance, musical events, with or without extramusical reference, take place in *musical time*. Debussy spoke of "rhythmicized time."

Time charts are convenient, spatial projections of rhythmicized time. But they are useful only to the extent of our conscious and imaginative inclusion, on the chart or firmly in mind, of associative qualities which appear relevant to performance of the music. Thus, the way in which melodic components of a phrase may be progressively shortened might suggest excitement, anxiety, or whatever, *even within a very small musical shape*. That is a function of rhythmicized time, comparable, if perhaps more subjective, to the function of harmony in the Classical convention.

In the case of large structures like Mahler's *First*, two-dimensional representation on a chart must include specific, musical evidence of whatever generates inner participation. It will be seen that feeling and fantasy in which such participation is reflected have an inner logic that follows multidirectional paths of musical time much more easily than the chronological model of events from which their sequence of presentation seems to depart. In the same way, while abstract analysis as such is neither memorable nor useful in performance, it may provide the framework for a variety of coexistant images whose musical sequence differs from our accustomed experience of time.

The idea of a performance image, in fact, is conceivable only on the assumption that musical events do not merely overlap, repeat, or double back upon one another, but may be perceived in the mind all at once, in one moment of intense concentration. At the same time, a performance image becomes more memorable the more distinctively the musical or associative vents are conceived by the performer as part of the musical structure, i.e. the framework within which they are to "determine the quality of ordinary clock time in performance." The larger and the more complex the structure, the more essential becomes our intimate exploration of its rhythm of time, the way in which intended musical experience is to be furnished in imagination.

The way in which the images in our sketch reflect Mahler's intentions is fairly obvious. How the events formerly described in his *Songs of a Wayfarer* are comprised within a large symphonic structure is quite another matter.

The arrow is my own visual symbol for an elemental *breakthrough* of dammed up feeling, *at m. 352 in the first movement and at m. 623 in the last.* Let us take these two equivalent *places* in the symphony as points of departure in *placing images.* Being analogous in materials, they are also a fine example of musical events, separated by a substantial span of listening time, but *contemporaneous in terms of one's awareness of them in time and memory.* In order to make this clear, we shall try to retrace a possible approach.

The "breakthrough" is a fanfare, first in B♭, later in tonic D, on an A pedal point. Introduced at the very beginning of the work (*pp* in the weakest clarinet register and again in the offstage trumpets), it is preceded by descending fourths, one of two very important intervals in the symphony. That interval sequence (D–A–F–C–D–B♭), over the A pedal point, contains *both* the thematic elements of the work: the fourths and the second (B♭ against the underlying A—resolved *upward,* not into A for the time being).

Example 7

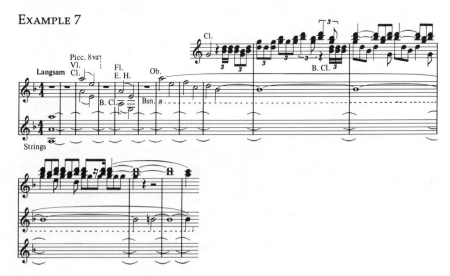

In Beethoven's *Seventh Symphony*, the introduction of C major right at the beginning yields a clue to performance. The comparable incongruity of a Bb fanfare over A at the start of the Mahler *First* does not entitle us to similar expectations of a musical style based on harmonic expectations and frustrations. *But the tension of Bb–A remains apparent.* That something special is being suggested is underlined (almost tritely, at first) by the use of a fanfare in itself. This is stunningly confirmed when that fanfare bursts full force into the melancholy discourse of the development section. In terms of anything that went before, this breakthrough into the tonic is so hugely out of proportion that neither the harmonic return nor the structural formula of a recapitulation (which significantly does not take place) would seem sufficient justification. *The breakthrough itself has been elevated to a structural principle.* That this is taking place under cover of an inner program will help us in adapting image to structure (i.e. place).

The effect of the breakthrough in the first movement is negative. It inhibits the orderly conclusion of the movement along conventional formal patterns, suggesting something "behind" the music, and that of course is what extramusical programs do. Adorno has a marvelous way of placing this hidden content *before* the beginning of the music. "Thus might a youngster be wakened from sleep, at five in the morning, by the awareness of an overwhelming sound swooping upon him, just recalled in the second between sleep and consciousness, but with a lasting anticipation of its return never again to be forgotten."* *Then* the piece begins. The "action" of the symphony, in the composer's own words, is a description and development of being as it is experienced by the protagonist—himself. The breakthrough, when it returns at the end, has a liberating effect.

These two "places," early and late in the huge work, and nearly identical in text, are not related to each other or to any other structural joint in the music by anything rational in terms of music theory. Therefore, the whole fabric, surveyed in conventional analysis of its surface, must be reexamined in terms that will *include* these special moments.—Images.

Preceding the fanfares are a series of descending seconds, at the top of the score and in the bass, repeated over and over again with increasing pressure. These seconds appear prominently and thematically throughout the symphony (e.g. the expressive but still ambiguous two-chord motive introduced in m. 166 at the very reflective opening of the first-movement development, or in the anguished string passages demonstrating the emotional state of "a deeply wounded heart" in the Finale). But we meet this important interval first in the ninth measure

*Adorno, p. 12.

of the first movement when, instead of the expected fall of a fourth from
D to A, the melodic flow stops on B♭ instead, creating the minor-second
tension B♭–A with the pedal point, and triggering the first appearance
of what is to be the breakthrough fanfare. In the *Wayfarer Songs*, the
significance of the descending minor second is not difficult to find: it
dominates the third song (the only one dealing with uninhibited outbursts of anguish) and is set to the words *Oh Weh!*—oh grief! We know
that this grief is for a lost love. Here, in part, is some of the support for
the author's already mentioned "his-and-hers" interpretation of the
intervallic significance of fourths and seconds throughout the symphony: The emotional complication which snags the quiet descent of
the protagonist's fourths right at the beginning starts with that B♭
(against the lower A); and the consistency of this programmatic use of
the interval is not only fascinating to trace but sticks in the mind, which
is our present objective.

N.B.: Genuine images can be an odd and unpredictable lot. It takes a
little practice and a lot of conviction not to feel self-conscious about
them. In the case of Mahler's *First*—the only instance of its kind in the
other's own experience—they were not only seen but heard. And when,
in the first movement, for instance, the hero and his girl burst into song
(Example 8),* one is understandably, if quite wrongly, apt to be
squeamish about having overheard the duet. The question of whether
Mahler himself might have had some *secret* lyrics in mind for certain
melodic fragments (in addition to the corresponding words of the *Wayfarer Songs*) is quite irrelevant. We are concerned with memorable
images. And having connected the falling minor second with the outcry
"Oh Weh!" of the third song—and applied that, not unreasonably, to
the cry of a wounded heart with which the last movement begins—who
is to say that the two-chord motive mentioned earlier (p. 392) may not
have been intended to carry the sweet burden of a beloved name?

EXAMPLE 8

"Go with me, go with me............"

Provided such charades do not interfere with one's concept of the
music, it is easy to see how they can be enormously useful in fixing the
music firmly in the mind. It can also be seen how parallel passages, like
the two breakthrough sections we discussed, can actually be experienced side by side, and savored for their difference—not only for tex-

*It should be clearly understood, of course, that this little duet in thirds is the author's aural fantasy,
and does not have any textual reference to Mahler's words for the *Wayfarer Songs*. In the quotes that
follow, Mahler's text is always referred to in the original German.

tual discrepancies, but for all the divergent emotional freight and momentum that we must assign to them.

Our two parallel breakthrough passages are cases in point. The first one is followed by the triumphant return of a horn call which made its first appearance early in the introspective development section. At that stage the opening movement had seemed to turn inward and this horn passage (prominently featuring the interval of the fourth) marked the dreamlike reemergence of tonic D major. As if that had been a mysterious preview, it now shines over the sunlit orchestral landscape and leads into an apotheosis of "Go with me" and the almost hysterical, if euphoric, laughter with which the movement concludes—in a cascade of fourths!

She went, but she did not stay with him. The second breakthrough passage follows the painful healing process of the wounded heart and sets off the glowing final statement of a brass figure (also featuring fourths, but upward) which is derived from the only really new thematic material in the finale, and (in this performer's view) has played a kind of determined get-well role throughout. This leads to the ultimate return and triumph of the very opening sequence of fourths in the symphony, often referred to as the "And He shall reign forever" theme because of the reminiscence to the "Halleluja Chorus" of Handel's *Messiah*. Be that as it may, our hero now stands confidently on his own feet, where we shall leave him for now.

The graphs on p. 399 provide a sense of the inner connection between the breakthrough passages in the first and last movements and furnish the user with a most convenient set of "places" for personal images.

Graphic representations cannot justify the choice of a particular *performance image* any more than accuracy of harmonic analyses may be proven by a diagram. What may be demonstrated, however, is the extent to which, in either case, the results contribute to a memorable overall concept of the work, based on the reflected inner logic of a particular premise.

In our case, watching the "breakthrough" passages and their nearly identical introductions in the first and last movements of Mahler's *First Symphony* provides a pair of remarkable similar outlines. In the Figure 5 diagrams, musical references to the protagonists's remembered experiences are charted below the callibrated time line. Their intensity is reflected in the changing distance from this assumed level of conscious, present experience. The struggle of the "wounded heart from Hell to Heaven" is represented variously above that line. The dreamy first movement is shown as an incomplete version of the finale, lacking the initial strength of its painful acceptance of the here and now. The breakthrough, albeit identical in preparation and release, fails to bring the first movement to a satisfactory conclusion, succeeds in the last.

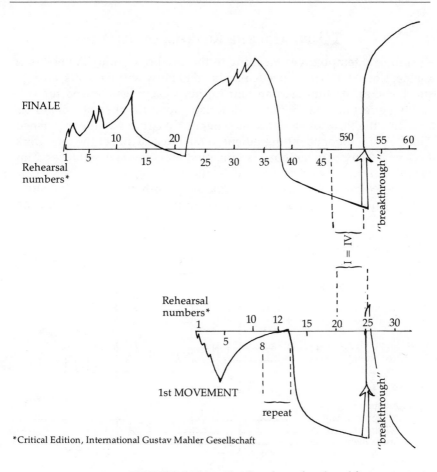

FIGURE 5: Mahler, *First Symphony,* fourth and first movements

In a score securely memorized to the point of "owning," its interior connecting routes become much more than a convenient means of comparing parallel passages. Furnished with meaningful metaphor, it enables us to *experience the structure* of a large work (e.g. Mahler's *First*) not only intellectually, but as an independent part of the actual musical display. The score comes to life. We may then organize and balance the moving moments, conscious of the changing musical flow on which they ride. The flow itself, the rate of its apparent motion as it passes, is a significant element in the "aerial" overview of a musical structure. The determination of a relative rate of flow, to serve each musical moment according to its present requirements, to enhance present experience with the memory of former thrust, and to balance these in terms of later needs, is the conductor's exclusive responsibility.

TEMPO AND THE RHYTHM OF TIME

In music, tempo gives meaning to the rhythm of time. A Beethoven theme, slowed down or speeded up beyond fairly narrow limits, changes its character. Brahms was an heir to this legacy: we showed the controlling effect of a harmonic characteristic upon the thematic materials, and thus the flow, of an entire movement.* Wagner was the watershed. Time, as an independent ingredient in the musical mix of the total work, became a factor of conscious manipulation for expressive purposes. Thus *the role of tempo was changed,* and is still changing.

The chart that follows deals *exclusively* with tempo relationships, without reference to their actual distribution within the performance

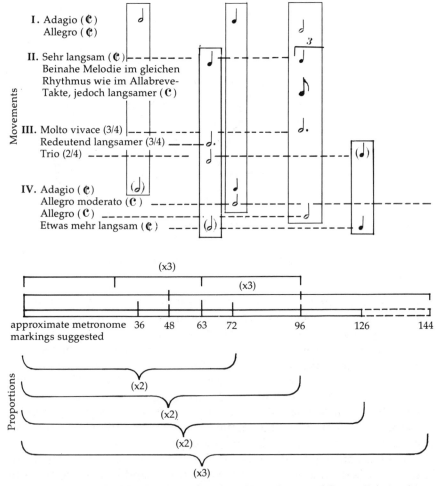

FIGURE 6: Bruckner, *Symphony No. 5,* Suggested Tempo Relationships

time of a very long and complex work, Bruckner's *Fifth Symphony*. Bruckner is astride the Wagnerian watershed. His thematic material and development is almost Beethovenian in design; his harmonic language pays homage to Wagner, but serves symphonic construction instead of dramatic and psychological theater. Wagner's approach was based on harmonic ambiguity and thematic transformation; Bruckner's on varieties of time—linear time, stratified time, time that moves, or time that seems to stand still. The common denominator is tempo, the one component of music which Wagner stretched but did not transform. Bruckner did.

As may be seen from the diagram, all pulses and beats in this performance of Bruckner's *Fifth* can be reduced to metronome speeds of 36, 48, 96, and 126 (with an additional ♩ = 144 where a ♩ = 72 is beaten in four). These speeds, in turn, fall almost perfectly into multiples of two and three in relation to each other. The main action of each movement, listed in the left-hand column with the composer's verbal tempo indications, are taken at the metronomic speeds shown on the horizontal scale. Notes *not* in brackets indicate the actual beat; bracketed notes relate this, where necessary, to the time signature.

EXAMPLE 9

Bruckner himself determines the *ratio* of the tempo relationships within the slow movement. If the triplet quarter note in Example 10= 96, the plain quarters will become ♩ = c. 64. The composer's famous two-against-three rhythm was much talked about when such metric cross-relations were more unusual than they are today. Correspondences suggested in our chart strike a rather contemporary note, even in an age when the concept of metric modulation has become almost commonplace.

The very titles of many contemporary compositions suggest an active preoccupation with time *as such:* Stockhausen, *Zeitmasse* (Time Signatures); Penderecki, *Dimensionen der Zeit und der Stille* (Dimensions of Time and Silence). Alois Zimmerman speaks of the "spherical shape of time," an imaginary time/space in which past, present, and future coexist. On the basis of what has been said about roaming back and forth over the musical surface in our minds and imagination such ideas should have a familiar ring for us by now.

Elliott Carter recalls his own discovery of the role of time in music, in words which suggest both the wonder and the opportunity.*

Around 1944, I suddenly realized that . . . people had always been consciously concerned with only this or that peculiar local rhythmic pattern or sound texture or novel harmony and had forgotten that the really interesting thing about music is the time of it—how it goes along . . . All the materials of music have to be considered in relation to their projection in time, of course, I mean not visually measured "clock-time," but the medium through which (or the way in which) we perceive, understand, and experience events. Music deals with this experimental kind of time.

Suggested Assignments: Time Charts

	Suggested Components of Charts:
1. Tchaikovsky, *Symphony No. 4*	formal structure tonalities tempos *N.B.:* These are melodic and rhythmic resemblances among all thematic materials in this work. It would be worth your while to explore these, and to plot them along the *structure* line of your chart.
2. Bruckner, *Symphony No. 5,* second movement	formal structure tonalities tempos *N.B.:* Use the metronome markings in this chapter. Distribute along chart. Indicate nodal points where the *beat* changes, and note whether tempo becomes faster, slower, remains the same.
3. Debussy, *Prelude to "The Afternoon of a Faun"*	tempos plot likenesses of materials *N.B.:* This piece is a Nijinsky ballet after the poem "The Afternoon of a Faun," by Mallarmé. *Plot:* The Faun awakes from

*Allen Edwards, *Flawed Words and Stubborn Sounds, a Conversation with Elliott Carter* (W. W. Norton, 1971), p. 90.

slumber on a warm summer afternoon. Nymphs come to bathe in the nearby lake. The Faun makes advances to one of them, but is rebuffed. He remains alone, agitated and confused. At last, he returns to his afternoon sleep.

Plot "scenario" of images. Memorize that plot, with musical references.

4. Ravel, *La Valse*

Devise *two parallel time lines:* from opening to 54, and from 54 to the end.
Notate all rehearsal numbers.
Indicate main divisions of structure (the waltzes).
Connect waltzes on first time line with corresponding ones on the second one below, with lines.
Number materials in introduction.
Notate all tempo markings and assign approximate metronomic speeds at these points.
Construct a tempo line for *La Valse* (speeds on left margin, rising from slowest to fastest).

N.B.: Study your chart. Add whatever lines may reflect your further interest in this work. After each day's review, *read* through the score, trying to visualize chart. Check the chart as soon as you are not certain of your memory. This is particularly important in connection with the tempo line. Test your memory, without scores or chart, beginning at different parts of the work each time.

The more time charts you draw, the better you will understand the selective process which goes into this exercise and the more imaginative you will become in choosing promising time lines. A useful time line must serve the *basic function of a time chart:* to condense its subject so that it may be taken in at a glance. The four scores above will serve as practical examples for the application of the beat (Chapter 7). Construction of time charts, like all other aspects of the preparation of a score must be based on a prior survey of the musical surface. But you may wish to do a time chart *sketch* while you are engaged in such a survey. Additional time lines may suggest themselves to you as a result.

13

Perspectives:
The View from Our Century

> For the living performer, music of the past acquires fresh meaning in the perspective of his own time, and from the work of composers who created that perspective. Scores of Bartók, Debussy, Ives, Ruggles, Schoenberg, Stravinsky, and Varèse.

> Alas, our theory is too poor for experience.
> —ALBERT EINSTEIN

> No, no! Experience is too rich for our theory.
> —NIELS BOHR

THE RISK OF NEW MUSIC

A distinguished man of the theater, director Peter Brook of the Royal Shakespeare Company, wrote how, on a visit to New York, he stood one morning

in the Museum of Modern Art looking at the people swarming in for one dollar admission. Almost every one of them had the lively head and the individual look of a good audience—using the simple personal standard of an audience for whom one would like to do plays. In New York, potentially, there is one of the best audiences in the world. Unfortunately, it seldom goes to the theater. . . . It is the audience, year after year, that has been forced to elevate simple fallible men into highly priced experts because, as when a collector buys an expensive work, he cannot afford to take the risk alone: the tradition of the expert valuers of art, like Duveen, has reached the box office line. So the circle is closed; not only the artist, but also the audience, have their protection men—and most of the curious, nonconforming individuals stay away. This situation is not unique to New York.*

*Peter Brook, *The Empty Space* (Pelican Books, 1972), p.

404

The problem of presenting the music of our time is comparable to the wistfully described situation in the theater, but worse. A new play, favorably received by the "experts," may well be a financial success. In the orchestral world, where good box office means minimum annual deficit, even success must meet the criterion of being affordable. It would be foolish to ignore the conductor's responsibility in this area while insisting on his duty to serve the music of living composers. When loss is inevitable, there is a moral and professional imperative to make it worthwhile.

Much of what has become standard repertory had a poor reception in its day. But the rejection of new music by a majority of devoted concertgoers *because* it is new—is new. It would be very difficult to avoid the conclusion that as performers, teachers, musical administrators, and managers, we have done a bad job. Whether by default, through ignorance or arrogance, we have deprived the composer and his potential audience of a two-way communication beweeen live creator and live listener, which served music in a variety of social settings over the years.

Of all the many arguments for the need to play the music of our time, the most compelling from a performer's point of view is that it has to be the music we are best suited to perform. The heritage entrusted to us reaches far into the past, in an uninterrupted flow of treasured works. That stream of music continues into our time, and it would be senseless to pretend that we should enter it at any place except the bank on which we stand. But it would be even sillier to do so without some knowledge of the footing and the current.

Mr. Brook makes his point, and his judgment applies to conductors no less than to the "protection men" of the art world. Since the audience has elevated us "simple fallible men into highly priced experts," we should be serving our own interests if we tried to become less fallible and more expert in the most conspicuous area of taking risks—the new music.

Why should this be so? Because, like musicians before us, we cannot safely ignore a single link with a past whose heritage we claim. Compelling performances can evoke something of that past, but artists and audiences of today may recreate and experience what is performed only in the here and now. An informed sense of musical perspective on the part of the performer must include conscious awareness of his own vantage point. Such awareness, for us as conductors, needs to be developed at our usual source—the score.

FUNCTIONS OF NEW MUSIC

You are now at the point where your most immediate and absorbing task will be to build your repertory. Clearly this should involve more than the number of works you may have played, listened to often, or even the scores of your favorite composers with whose musical language you are familiar and comfortable. Methodical examination of the surface on the one hand, and free-wheeling personal involvement with a number of scores to be mastered on the other, may soon lead to your discovery of an "odd" detail in one, or to your asking the kind of very lucky, simple questions that become points of departure toward productive, personal involvement for which no listening or playing familiarity can compensate.

In preceding chapters we have examined some general approaches. The microcosm of individual musical shapes, larger structures created by stresses of a harmonic force field, or the even longer rhythm of time itself, as it is articulated and directed in a particular work under study, provide promising avenues of exploration beneath the musical surface, until the privileged moment when personal involvement and identification begin to generate their own momentum. This is the moment when the paths of critical study and creative performance intersect, particularly welcome with scores of the so-called standard repertory in which familiarity tends to make cowards of us all. But there cannot be the slightest doubt that thorough knowledge as well as intimate identification with this basic literature is absolutely essential for any young conductor preparing for a professional career. And, yes, the "short list" of required repertory is quite long.

But there is one more problem: the further back one tries to reach into the musical past, the more difficult becomes the achievment of a sense of personal participation and of its likely reflection in performance. Music being a participatory art, every performer needs to find, for himself and for the listener, that proportion of past, present, composer, and self which will suddenly make one care and experience the music in performance with something more than conditioned recognition. Thus we are to assemble a personal repertory. But where to begin?

Some suggestions are made in this chapter. Perspective from a twentieth-century vantage point will add a personal sense of depth and identification to your view of earlier music and of music closer to your own time.

In some ways it is *easier* to establish perspective and ask questions about music of our day, provided you avoid the trap of confusing method with musical meaning. In a letter to his brother-in-law Rudolf Kolisch, leader of the Kolisch String Quartet, Schoenberg wrote in 1932: "I can't utter too many warnings against overrating these analyses, since they only lead to what I have always been dead set against: seeing how it was *done*; whereas I have always helped people to see: what it *is!*"*

---

*Arnold Schoenberg, *Letters*, ed. Erwin Stein (London: Faber, 1964), p. 164.

ROOTS

In the following pages we shall look at scores from the first third of our century. The work of a few composers during that period provides us with guidelines for the new music of the present and a fresh perspective on the music of the past. Contemporaries Schoenberg and Ives (both born in 1874), Carl Ruggles (1876), Bartók (1881), Stravinsky (1882,) and Varèse (1885) have more in common than a birthdate within the decade of Wagner's *Parsifal* (first performance 1882). The characteristics their work shares (i.e. what it *is*) far outweigh the differences of compositional method (how their music was *made*) that sometimes divided their disciples so violently. But it was in the music of an older composer, Debussy (1862), that most of the elements may be found that inform the compositional practice of the other six. Viewed together, the music of these seven composers points to a new consensus on the state of the art. For us as performers, this new sense of musical identity provides a strong point of departure, not only in dealing with music of our own time, but also with works too far removed from us in time to permit exclusive viewing from a perspective appropriate to their own day.

All but one of the works listed below represent an early fully characteristic contribution by a young composer. *Jeux,* last and supreme among Debussy's orchestral works, is the achievement of a mature master. Significantly, the fact that Schoenberg's compositional method ("how it was *made*") was yet to undergo its celebrated sea change to the so-called twelve-tone technique, or that on the other hand the parameters of Bartók's musical language were already fully established, is irrelevant to the conclusion that within six years on either side of World War I (because of "what these works *are*"), a body of music changed contemporary awareness of all the literature that went before and was to come. The works appear in the order of their composition. Together, they represent the roots of the new music of our century.

Schoenberg	*First Chamber Symphony*	1906
Ives	*The Unanswered Question*	1908
Bartók	*Allegro barbaro*	1911
Debussy	*Jeux*	1912
Stravinsky	*Le Sacre du printemps* (The Rite of Spring)	1913
Varèse	*Octandre*	1923
Ruggles	*Men and Mountains*	1924

It is fitting that Schoenberg's *First Chamber Symphony* should head the list. Schoenberg, who seems fated to remain the popular symbol of "atonal," "twelve-tonal," everything-but-tonal "modern" composers, was in fact the heir to a musical tradition based on functional harmony as the conceptual key to musical structure. His *Harmonielehre* (1911), a comprehensive review of traditional harmony, was followed, late in his life by another textbook, significantly titled *Structural Functions of Harmony* (English translation published posthumously in 1954). These books are a page-by-page testimony to the musical roots of a composer whose attempts to find substitutes for harmonic function as the determinant of musical structure bear witness to a cast of mind that mourned the loss of a logical, unified, and beautiful order of musical thought.

Unlike Debussy, whose work reflects his pleasure in freeing himself from the restrictions of what he considered an alien system of musical reference, Schoenberg never denied his roots. But, much as he felt at home with an approach to composition in which ever more complex harmonic phenomena are incorporated into the traditional system of functional harmony, his early interest in whole-tone scales, chords built on fourths, and the accelerating use of serial elements as cohesive elements within the musical structure forced him to *construct* alternative frameworks to accommodate his materials.

Schoenberg's five-movement *First Chamber Symphony* is a fine example of his skill in incorporating whole-tone scales and chords built on fourths into a grand structural design within the conceptual framework of the harmonic function. Even more striking is his *Second Chamber Symphony*, begun in the same year, laid aside, and completed some thirty years later in the *same* harmonic language in which it was begun. The end of this two-movement work is a most eloquent tribute by the mature composer to his musical roots and a stunning demonstration of his undiminished skill in the use of the grammar and syntax of a musical idiom he had so long denied himself.

Why? The answer to that question may help us not only to gain some insight and perspective into Schoenberg's work, but also into the music of our own time and the music that went before. The question is not unlike "Why C major?" in the Introduction to the Beethoven *Seventh:** the answer will be more important in terms of a much wider frame of reference than the one in which it was raised. We shall try our hand at exploring a work by Schoenberg, which was written three years after the *First Chamber Symphony* and has defied formal analysis—his monodrama *Erwartung*.

SCHOENBERG, *ERWARTUNG*

It is said that when Verdi first managed to get a look at Wagner's *Tristan* score—around which an almost mystical air of controversy had

*Cf. p. 328.

been created—he was astonished that it was, in fact, a score. *Erwartung* is a score as well. Thus there is no reason to depart from the pattern of study already suggested. If our method of organizing the musical surface (cf. Chapter 2a) may have seemed a little pedantic when applied to Beethoven or Brahms, this is the occasion to prove its worth. The score of *Erwartung* is an enigma, not only to young conductors learning their craft. If our approach can produce some answers (where we are not even sure of the questions), it may also lead us to questions with regard to scores about which we may think we have all the answers.

The mapping of the *Erwartung* surface, following the outline in chapter 2, is reproduced in full. With succeeding examples only a few hints are given, but the reader should go through the *whole* process, pencil in hand. Promising features for future consideration (i.e. Group D, which tends to come up out of sequence) are to be marked at once. We shall use the symbol (#) in the margin.

I. *Initial Survey*

A1: *Composer.* Quite a lot has been said about Arnold Schoenberg. We are therefore beginning our survey with certain expectations. He composed this in 1909.

A2: *Title. Erwartung* is the German for "Expectation." A monodrama is "a theatrical entertainment in which there is only one character."*

A3: *Tempo* varies. Leafing through the score may leave us with the (correct) first impression that *the frequent tempo changes reflect the affective quality of the text,* in very small sections. In fact, even this preliminary scanning of the music shows us that it seems to *consist* of a string of very brief sections, played without pause. We make a note to look (**#**) into the matter of program (D4) implied by this treatment of the text.

A4: *Instrumentation* is huge, including a large number of strings. A second glance through the score, however, shows us that rarely, if ever, are all those forces used at the same time. This makes for a constantly changing chamber-music texture (D1). *N.B.:* Here is an extra benefit in (**#**) being methodical about surveying the musical surface: an excuse to go through the score several times, from several points of view, even before actual study begins. Many young conductors are surprised to find how much of what they have looked at, with a special purpose in mind, sticks in their memory (cf. Chapter 12).

A5: *Key signature.* None. There are a great many accidentals. Our outline in Chapter 2a said: Key signature (*or Other*). We make a note that the nature of this "other" will bear looking into. (**#**)

A6: *Meter.* Changes are not quite as frequent as tempo changes: Almost always together with change of metronome markings but not

*J. A. Cuddon, *A Dictionary of Literary Criticism* (Doubleday, 1977).

(**#**) the reverse. Note: Is change of meter therefore an even more significant indication of section limits?

   A7: *Special notes:* Yes.

    1. Metronome markings are only approximate.

    2. Detailed instructions on trills, grace notes, harp harmonics.

    3. ⊓ *Haupststimme* (principal line), ⊓ *Nebenstimme* (secondary line).

    4. All else is accompaniment (!).

    5. Unless otherwise noted, voice is always ⊓.

   N.B.: At the end of section A in our sample outline, Chapter 2a, we advised a frequent, silent "reading" of the score. Obviously, this would require phenomenal powers of inner hearing and imagination in this piece. You could astonish yourself: Try. Start with the text—translations are available on record covers. Be sure you fit each German word to its proper English equivalent. Whether this makes sense in terms of English syntax does not matter at all—write it into the score as it comes, feel the more suggestive words, and observe their surrounding instrumental colors, textures, closely or widely spread chords, contrasting rhythmic patterns, and dynamics. Finally, without forcing yourself, try to hear pitches.

   One of the most provocative, courageous, and perfectly true statements Charles Rosen makes in his Schoenberg book is that

> pitch can no longer be given the central position in the hierarchy of musical elements. . . . In the third piece of *Pierrot Lunaire,* for example, the clarinet part could be transposed a half-step up or down while the other instruments remain at the correct pitch, and (although some effect would be lost) the music would still make sense; but if the dynamics are not respected, the music becomes totally absurd and makes no sense at all.*

Thus, you may establish a few "bridgeheads" on the shore of this music from which, always in the inner imagination, you can fan out over additional musical territory. You will indeed begin to hear something, and your bridgeheads should become useful points of orientation when you view the score as a whole.

   B1: *Structural joints.* The dramatic changes are marked, and the text itself falls into groupings within these. Indicate preliminary decisions, as suggested.

(**#**) B2: *Correspondences.* None! This in itself is of tremendous importance. File it away for special reference under D, Joker in the pack.

   B3: *Key changes* must await further study of A5; but not likely.

   B4: *Other.* Already covered by several previous discoveries, but there may be more. Meanwhile we shall move on.

---

*Charles Rosen, *Schoenberg* (London, Fontana, 1976), pp. 58–59.

B5: *Rehearsal numbers.* Score is simply numbered by measures. As we have already noted, the sections are small enough to make manageable subdivisions without the artificial use of numbers.

C1: *Periods and phrases.* Determined by the text, as we have seen. This provides an easy and natural opportunity to come to grips with the small, sectional segments into which the music seems to devolve, *as per our # at* A3, A4, A6.

C2: The sections under C1 were so short that in almost all instances C2 requires no further subdivision.

C3: *Instrumentation.* Much of the work has already been done by the composer. H⁻ and N⁻ clarify contrapuntal priorities aside from the vocal line. Some special indications remain to be sorted out (e.g. a solo violin passage in the first violins, and marked if, at this early stage, it seems noteworthy).

D1: *Texture* has already impressed us by its chamber-music character, within the huge palette of available instrumental timbres. We may have noted some very sparse places (pick out three of these, right now, and memorize text and texture as best you can) and some very dense ones (the loudest: "It is he!" m. 153; but getting denser and denser at the end: "Oh, are you there . . . , I searched.").

Since the voice always leads, this might be a good time to go through the whole work again following the vocal line, the words, the word value and meaning, *and* noting the surrounding texture. You will probably be impressed with the improvement in your comprehension of the work. It should begin to sound for you.

D2 and D3: *Shapes and rhythm* change constantly. They are part of a score consisting of endless detail, shifting, forming, and reforming as required by the program.

D4: *Program.* As we have already determined, this is of controlling (**#**) importance.

II. *Follow-up on Notes*

The first note we made, at A3, concerned frequent changes of tempo, related to word meaning and illustration of text, and resulting in a string of very brief, dissimilar sections following each other without pause (except where a pause is part of the expressive illustration itself, e.g. m. 158).

The second (A4) amplifies the first. In examining instrumentation we found that small instrumental groups in constantly changing combinations are only occasionally offset by the use of full tutti. These changes nearly always occur in support of A3. Thus text, tempo, and a fluctuating variety of chamber-music textures form a connected, well-delineated, and continually evolving series of short, expressive statements.

The third reminder (A5: Key signature or Other), suggests a more speculative area of observation. In the absence of Key signatures we must inquire into the nature of the "other." The short answer, that there are no keys and few if any tonal references, is not helpful. The harmonic background of *Erwartung*, or its absence, has been the subject of much critical comment. Where are we to look for possible enlightenment? The composer's textbook on harmony (1911) would seem the more obvious a point of departure, as none of the published analyses known to the author (Craft, Goehr, Perle, Rosen) make much, if anything, of it.*

Generally, in the use of chords consisting of six notes or more, a tendency to extenuate the dissonance by wide spacing of the individual tones will be apparent. That this results in an extenuation is obvious. For thus the model of what dissonances really are, i.e. far removed overtones, is agreeably simulated. In this sense the following example from my monodrama *Erwartung* can be understood:

Schoenberg's
Example 340

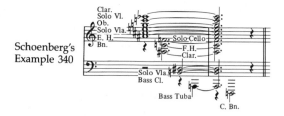

This chord consists of eleven tones. But the delicate instrumentation, and the fact that the dissonances are so spread out, account for the gentle effect of this sonority. And perhaps something else: The individual groups are spelled in such a way that one could easily trace them back to earlier forms of resolution. I believe, for example, that the ear expects the first entrance to be resolved as follows:

Schoenberg's
Example 341

That this does not in fact happen should matter as little as when simple harmonies are not resolved. The second chord may be understood in connection with a resolution (342a), plus the chord resolved above (341), superimposed as in 342c: an addition of two chords that have a seventh chord in common which, by virtue of two different bass notes, become two different ninth chords.

But such a derivation will not always work, and tracing it back to earlier (harmonic) usage will not always succeed; or only with the benefit of a very

---

*Arnold Schoenberg, *Harmonielehre*, 3rd ed. (Universal Edition, 1922), pp. 502–503 (my transl.).

Schoenberg's
Example 342

flexible interpretation. *For on another occasion I write such a chord in much closer position.* (Italics added.)

Perhaps the last two sentences are, for us, the most significant: While Schoenberg, in the context of theoretical analysis in his textbook on harmony, does suggest the tracing back of this chordal event to harmonic usage of an earlier period, he immediately limits this application as far as his work at that time is concerned, and refers to the existance of a different use (*not* widely spaced, i.e. *not* gentle in intent) within the same composition. After this effective disclaimer of harmonic derivation in terms of function (even "with the benefit of a very flexible interpretation") there remains only the expressive intent of the chord he describes (widely spaced dissonance / gentleness) and, by inference, the opposite intent with a closer spelling. Again, it is not the "how was it made," but the "what it is" which we must look for.

Schoenberg does not specify the place in *Erwartung* where this event occurs, but we can find it in m. 382 and 383. The full sentence which these two measures conclude reads: "Oh, I did curse you . . . but (even) your pity made me happy . . ." (here comes m. 382): "*I believed, and was glad. . . .*" Most clearly a discordant yet tender statement—the expressive value of the text, and the intended feeling / reaction on the part of the listener, determined the choosing of such a chord, quite aside from the possible rationalization of its construction in terms of music theory. We have the composer's word for it.

The fourth note we made, A6, registered frequent changes of meter, nearly always accompanying changes of tempo intended to reflect changes in the text or the mood. Thus we have yet another gauge with which to define the expressive intent of the small sections which form the multifaceted surface of this score.

B2 comes as no surprise now: There are no "correspondences," no references of thematic or motivic relations and recognizable returns in the work. There is no formal structure in the generally accepted sense of eighteenth- and nineteenth-century musical architecture. The love scene, second act, of *Tristan* (albeit "through-composed") is a sonata, and Strauss's *Don Quixote*, program music par excellence, is a set of variations. *Erwartung*, expressionistic musical setting of an unfolding dramatic sequel, has *no* "structural" foundations in terms of motivic or thematic development.

For some, however, *Erwartung* demonstrates "correspondences" of another sort, which seem so important with regard to placing this score into perspective of the composer's total opus, that a very brief summary follows herewith. British composer Alexander Goehr and his late father Walter, conductor and one-time composition student of Schoenberg, coauthored an essay on *Development of the Twelve-Note System.** An analysis of *Erwartung* as the pivotal point in Schoenberg's own development as a composer occupies a central place in this persuasive presentation. According to this analysis, there *is* an overall shape, a pitch-oriented structure, which "enabled the composer to differentiate between sections which return to their starting-point and those which move away from it."

The analysis turns upon Schoenberg's employment of quasi-tonic–dominant notes C♯ and G♯. Not only do these define the beginning and end of the work, but "practically all important structural notes, the notes which begin and end all phrases, are C sharp and its neighbour notes."

The orchestral introduction of four bars makes a clear movement from G sharp to C sharp (quasi-dominant / tonic). It is repeated in a contracted form, this time moving to the leading note (C natural-B sharp); the soprano enters for the first time on C sharp. The first scene, as it were in closed form, is clearly founded on a structure in which the notes C sharp and G sharp are predominant. . . . The second half commences from G sharp (the first note of bar 273 and 274) and moves up to the B flat of bar 313, cadencing back to G sharp at bar 317, just before the extraordinary bars where the voice sings the words "*Oh, der Mond schwankt* . . ." The final solution comes in the contrabassoon's C sharp in the middle of bar 425, introduced most characteristically by the last melodic phrase of the opera. The voice, which had taken the G sharp (quasi-dominant) at bar 424, continues in 425 to the last utterance and reaches by a tritonous step the G sharp, slightly later than the C sharp bass has been established by the bassoon.

The Goehrs' conclusion, quoted in advance, that we have here a pitch-oriented structure replacing familiar forms based on harmonic functions, points clearly in the direction of Schoenberg's development, and that of a very important movement in twentieth-century composition to come. In the context of what may be useful in preparation of a performance, the reader must determine whether or not to pursue this particular set of "correspondences" throughout the score, in the hope of finding yet another promising avenue of descent beneath the surface of *Erwartung*.

Finally, with regard to D6, it would seem almost redundant to bring up the matter of program yet again, except that every indication has pointed in its direction as the arbiter of fluctuations in the stream of consecutive detail. All sections follow one another, and differ from each

*In *European Music in the Twentieth Century*, ed. Howard Hartog (Pelican Books, 1961), Chapter 4.

other, as the meaning and mood of the text and the drama evolve, move, suggest, and control. Having already mapped out the scenes, transformations, and dramatic episodes (B1), it remains to put them into overall dramatic context: The sinister search for the woman's lover, the discovery of his body, and her feverish conversation with the corpse—a tempestuous and tender inner repossession of the dead.

Work on *Erwartung* completed along these lines will have given us a chance to get acquainted with the score, but in terms of preparation for performance we still have a long way to go. This is the point at which we would do well to make a conscious effort at memorization. Following the technique of "images and places,"* and concentrating on the vocal line with its suggestive text, we should try to learn it, sentence by sentence, as if we were to sing it ourselves. If necessary, each singing phrase should be played slowly and repeatedly on the piano until it is remembered. The H and N in the instrumental characterization are then examined and, in the context of the verbal expression, the instrumentation, dynamic nuance, and general texture incorporated into a memorable image. Whether it is more effective to proceed slowly from beginning to end, or to select, on the basis of the initial survey, certain characteristic segments throughout the work with which to start, is a matter of individual choice. But in either case, each small phrase, once learned, must be securely and memorably placed within the "theater of memory," the emerging, overall dramatic image of the work.

We have not found out why Schoenberg felt the need to leave the conceptual framework of functional harmony. Perhaps the most promising lead is the suggestion that, with the continuing prominence of the pitches C♯ and G♯, a tonal framework was inferred.** Schoenberg had deep roots in the tonal tradition. By leaving it for the sake of a musical language whose main characteristics are varieties of expressive dissonances, he has also rejected structural determinacy. We shall leave it there, for now.

IVES, *THE UNANSWERED QUESTION*

The Unanswered Question of Charles Ives (1908) is a remarkably forward-looking little piece, practically a compendium of compositional techniques and concepts of the twentieth century, barely begun. There is spatial separation of the two ensembles (strings and flutes) and the trumpet soloist; different speeds and improvisatory sections occur simultaneously; polyrhythms are forced forward over virtually stand-

*See p. 383.
**See p. 414.

still rhythms; dissonant polytonality all but effaces tonal reference over slowly pulsing, diatonic progressions; and these separate, antipodean ensembles flank a questing solo line which goads the one to travesty while the other remains aloof.

In order to hear this work in imagination, it is best to examine its three components separately at first. The very slow string harmonies ("Impervious Eternity") are not difficult to manage, but they must become firmly and naturally established in the inner ear if we are not to lose the sense of them when the trumpet ("Perennial Question") is added, and when, at last, we shall try to imagine the "Fighting Answers," as Ives called the flute ensemble, as well.

While in *The Unanswered Question* the use of two conductors makes good sense (enhancing the aleatoric aspect of the flute frenzy), other Ives scores are better off with overall control in the hands of one person (e.g. *Fourth of July, Fourth Symphony*). Consolidation of barlines in the score and careful rehearsal of resulting isorhythms are more likely to solve the problem than dividing the leadership for purely technical reasons. As long as we remember that it is easier to play three against two than the other way around, five, seven, or eleven, against whatever even beat will not present much more of a problem with orchestras today. Again, as always, it is essential that the conductor *hear* the simultaneous meters and rhythms in his mind before he can expect to control them from the podium. Facing on p. 417 is a characteristic example (and yet another Ives anticipation—in 1915—of the much later common usage of what Elliott Carter first referred to as "metric modulation").

The orchestra is divided into the small ensemble which begins this movement and a much larger group, gradually to join later on. The small orchestra must be able to see the conductors beat, although they may be placed far away. Conducting them in slow four, we shall soon monitor the horn player's departure from our beat pattern (he has it cued in the part and, while it sounds complicated, it is a problem best left for the player to solve without "extra" beats from the podium). The key to the approaching transition is the solo bass part. Ives allows player and conductor to "settle in" for a few measures of 6 (Bass) against 4 (beat). Then comes a small accelerando for everyone; and at the lower string entrance of the large orchestra the speed of the *6-pulse* in the bass becomes the *4-beat* of the conductor, for the cellos.

Some years ago, the author was invited to participate in a panel discussion on the music of Charles Ives, sponsored by the Music Critics Association at the Berkshire Music Festival at Tanglewood. The discussion turned almost at once to the odd question of whether it mattered if, in Ives's music, extremely difficult passages were sometimes played inaccurately. Having played quite a few Ives scores with quite a few

EXAMPLE 1: Ives, *Orchestral Set No. 2*, third movement, opening measures

orchestras and, alas, with varying degrees of instrumental accuracy, the author was able to report that Ives's music, if played correctly, sounds better. The question is not as academic as it may seem. At the climax of *The Fourth of July*, for instance, when two village bands are being heard simultaneously, there is such a buzz of cacophanous sound that, almost invariably, the hard-pressed double basses will ask, "Does it matter?". It does.

BARTÓK, *MUSIC FOR STRINGS, PERCUSSION AND CELESTA*

Three years after Ives's *Unanswered Question*, in 1911, the year of *Petrushka*, Bartók wrote his aptly named *Allegro barbaro* for piano and the opera *Bluebeard's Castle*. In the *Allegro*, with its elemental vitality and its folklore flavor, the thirty-year-old composer's musical language appears fully developed, declaring itself with an unmistakable temper that marked his works for the rest of his life.

Like Schoenberg, he took as his point of departure the weakening force of the harmonic function in Western music of the late nineteenth and early twentieth centuries. Unlike his Viennese contemporary, Bartók did not pursue the path of harmonic self-destruction, which eventually led the Second Viennese School to an abandonment of tonality itself. Rather, he began his own search by grafting branches of Western musical tradition onto a much older stock, the folk music of Hungary, Rumania, Slovakia, and the Near East, in which he believed he discovered a different sense and use of tonality and melodic structure. For ten years he spent most of his working time traveling throughout remote rural areas, in order to record, in many volumes of carefully classified manuscript, the idiomatic musical heritage of Eastern Europe.

The use of folk music, national or exotic, is not new in Western music. From Mahler to Britten, from Dvořák to Ives, genuine or fabricated, it has infused much of the symphonic music written around the turn of the century and beyond. Bartók chose a different route. He began with native materials; and he made some startling discoveries.

Before continuing with a brief outline of Bartók's musical system (and what he constructed for himself, as a composer, was nothing less than a complete, absolutely self-contained, system), the reader is urged to undertake a methodical survey of the musical surface of a major Bartók work. One of the finest examples of his virtuosity in merging organizational control of materials with marvelous musical spontaneity is his *Music for Strings, Percussion and Celesta*. Once this has been worked through, as outlined in our second chapter, it will be useful to fill in some gaps, or even to reconsider certain findings, in light of the information to follow. Then each conductor must determine to what use he might put this new perspective, in order to make a performance of Bartók's masterpiece his own.

"We follow nature in composition," wrote Bartók. But even the fact that he had evolved a method to integrate technical and structural elements of his craft according to a single principle, let alone its relationship to natural laws, became general knowledge in the West only with the publication in London of Ernö Lendvai's first book in 1971.*

Bartók's musical language was rooted in two strong but not particularly compatible aspects of his personality as a composer: his almost clinical fastidiousness and absorption in constructional detail, and his lifelong, equally absorbing fascination with the folk music of his country. Bartók's system of musical composition remained unremarked while he lived. But to us as performers, it matters not only in terms of how his music was *made*, but for what it *is*.

What impressed Bartók in particular was persuasive evidence that certain "natural" scale formations and their harmonic consequences conformed to mathematical principles formulated by the ancient Chaldeans some 2000 years before the Greeks applied them to architecture and their visual arts: *the laws of the Golden Section*. At the harmonic crossroads in the development of art-music in our own culture, this evidence from his folkloristic studies struck him with its practical implications as an alternative structural principle in his work: "Every art has the right to strike roots in the art of a previous age; it not only has the right but it must stem from it," Ernö Lendvai quotes the composer at the beginning of his book on Bartók's compositional techniques.** Accordingly, new tonal principles and the proportions of old formal structures were carefully and very systematically applied to an advanced and very personal style of composition by a twentieth-century composer who found his roots in the folk music of his people preserved over millenia of time.

The Axis System

Lendvai situates Bartók's tonal system in the familiar circle of fifths. Taking C as tonic (T), he stipulates a pair of *flanking* subdominants and dominants. Then, moving clockwise to (parallel) tonic A etc., he achieves the circle of respective tonics, subdominants, and dominants shown in Figure 1. Connecting the four tonics subdominants and dominants are intersecting axes. The resulting system of harmonic reference is called the *Axis System*.

While traditional harmonic functions *within* any tonic key and its dominant and subdominant regions are maintained, the *axes* connect-

*Ernö Lendvai, *Béla Bartók, An Analysis of his Music* (London: Kahn & Averill, 1971).
**Ibid., p. 1.

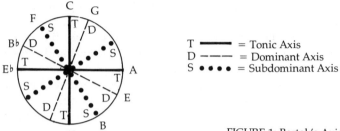

T ——— = Tonic Axis
D - - - - = Dominant Axis
S • • • • = Subdominant Axis

FIGURE 1: Bartok's Axis System

ing these regions represent additional, strong inner relationships among keys not considered particularly close in terms of conventional harmonic practice. The furthest of them of all was the tonal center directly opposite in the circle of fifths. Now it is being moved into most favored place: *The tritone is the key toward which and from which the gravity of harmonic force functions in Bartók's mature works.* Here is how this new relationship of old "opposites," the Axis System, is reflected in his *Music for Strings, Percussion and Celesta:*

Movement	Beginning	Middle	End
I	A	E♭ (*m.* 56)	A
II	C	F♯ (*m.* 263)	C
III	F♯	C (*m.* 46)	F♯
IV	A	E♭ (*m.* 83)	A

For further analysis of Bartók's consistent exploitation of the voice-leading potential in this important tritone relationship (e.g. a rather characteristic kind of deceptive cadence, as well as tritone-related chords* which may *assume* dominant or subdominant relationships) the reader is referred to Lendvai's book.** For "how it was made" is fascinating indeed. But for our own purpose we must further explore "what it is."

The Golden Section and Fibonacci Numbers

Bartók's formal structures are based on the *principle of the Golden Section.* In geometry, the Golden Section is determined by *dividing the total length of a line* so that *the larger segment is the geometric mean between the overall distance and the smaller part. The value of the larger section is .618.* These proportions can be expressed in numerical values of any kind, of course. In *Music for Strings, Percussions and Celesta,* for instance, the first movement has 89 measures. Its Golden Section (89 × 618) is 55. The

---

*On pp. 342–43, we observed that the tonal structure of Wagner's *Parsifal* spanned a tritone. Bartók's stipulation of this relationship—the most strained in Western harmony—as his harmonic norm takes on added significance in the light of his conscious break with Western tradition.
**Lendvai, *op. cit.*, pp. 12–16.

Golden Section of 55 is 34. The climactic E♭ (see table above) follows measure 55, and initiates a return to the tonic A in 34 measures. Expressed in sequence—34, 55, 89—these numbers form part of a series in which the sum of each two consecutive ones equals the next. This series, *the Fibonacci series*—2, 3, 5, 8, 13, 21, 34, 55, 89 . . . approximates in whole numbers the irrational numbers of the Golden Section.*

Bartók's *Allegro barbaro* (1911), with its pounding F♯-minor pulses over 3, 5, 8, or 13 measures is a powerful example of his fascination with the Golden Section, an unmistakable influence which informed his later work completely.** If we divide the first 55 measures of the opening movement of *Music for Strings, Percussion and Celesta* further into the preceding Fibonacci numbers 34 and 21, we discover that mutes are removed at m. 34. Instrumentation is used consistently to amplify Bartók's constructional detail: In the second movement, the bass drum supports each entrance of "axis" keys E♭–F♯–A–C during the development. But the most astonishing of all examples cited by Lendvai (p. 29) is once more a structural application. The following graph reflects the Golden Section symmetries in the third movement. The numbers represent metric units of 4/4 (with the occasional 3/2, thus= 1½ units).

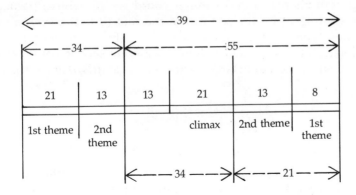

FIGURE 2

Fibonacci Chords and Intervals

Lendvai distinguishes between Bartók's *"chromatic" system* of harmonic and melodic structures (in which chord and interval relationships are based on Golden Section and Fibonacci proportions), and the

---

, *Fibonacci, a thirteenth-century natural philosopher of Pisa, is said to have discovered the series while breeding rabbits. He calculated that if every pair of animals produced one new pair in the second month of their lives and if all new rabbits were given one month to work out the system, the number of pairs should increase monthly by 2–3–5–8–13–21– i.e. in a series in which each digit equals the sum of the two preceding.

**Ibid., p. 27.

"diatonic" system based on the overtone scale. According to the former, intervals are determined by counting half steps (hence "chromatic"):

> 2 = major second
> 3 = minor third
> 5 = perfect fifth
> 8 = minor sixth
> 13 = augmented octave

The numbers conform to Fibonacci (e.g. $8 = 3 + 5$; *not* $4 + 4$ or $7 + 1$). The system is very strict and strictly observed. Major thirds and major sixths, being incongruous to the Golden Section series, not only have little melodic use, but are carefully placed in the spelling of triads: major third *below* the fundamental note (making a minor sixth interval), minor third *above*. Thus the chords acquire the proportion 8:5:3.

EXAMPLE 2

Merging both chords, a major-minor chord results which, particularly when completed by the seventh of the root (B flat) becomes the most common type of chord in Bartók's music (Ex. 2, c). As a prototype it is referred to as an "alpha chord", different sections of it being designated by the succeeding Greek letters beta, gamma, delta, epsilon.

EXAMPLE 3

How these chords work in Bartók's music, in connection with the Axis System, is the subject of further analysis in Lendvai's book.

The "diatonic" system, including the overtone scale and "acoustic" chords (also built on the natural overtone series) is an *inversion* of the Golden Section intervals: It produces intervals *excluded* by the laws of Golden Section and Fibonacci numbers.*

EXAMPLE 4

*Ibid., p. 67.

Bartók, *Music for Strings, Percussion, and Celesta,* fourth movement

Chord formations may be based on either the chromatic or the diatonic system, and consist of intervals contained in one or their inversion in the other (e.g. perfect fourth or minor sixth—chromatic; inverted: perfect fifth or major third—diatonic). A scale model built on a 1:2 succession of half steps (chromatic)*

EXAMPLE 5

can , among others, make major / minor chords, sevenths, as well as merge into a model built on 1:5.**

EXAMPLE 6

The 1:2 model also makes up notes of the "axis" (cf. above).†

EXAMPLE 7

Metric applications of Fibonacci numbers abound (the opening of *Music for Strings, Percussion and Celesta* is an example of 2, 3, 5, 8 groupings and subdivisions), and result in systematic exploitation of the possibilities in juxtaposing odd and even meters, strong and weak phrase endings interchanging when a theme returns, or even-metered measures in odd rhythms coming back as odd meters in even rhythms.

---

* Ibid., p. 57.
** Ibid., p. 57.
† Ibid., p. 55.

Lendvai points out that Fibonacci numbers abound in nature. "For instance the sunflower has 34 petals and its spirals have the values of 21, 55, 89, 144. It is interesting to note that the Golden Section is always associated only with organic matter and is quite foreign to the inorganic world."

Bartók was extraordinarily reticent about technical aspects of his craft. Ironically, perhaps, while the highly communicative Schoenberg was destined to become the archetypal theoretician among twentieth-century composers, Bartók acquired an equally limiting popular label of rhapsodist, colorist, folk melodist. In the case of both composers the descriptions are accurate, but so incomplete as to be misleading. Not least in lending perspective and depth to the conductor's inner image of *Music for Strings, Percussion and Celesta,* the *Violin Concerto,* or the *Miraculous Mandarin,* is that, far from "going native," Bartók drew from the music of Eastern Europe (and indeed the Near East) something which occupied a central position in his musical imagination as well as his technical concepts as a composer. Unlike some French impressionists, for instance, who also used melodic elements inherent in much of this material (e.g. pentatonic and whole-tone scales), Bartók abstracted principles from the indigenous and idiomatic music of his country which became part of his language as a Western composer, and found that he had stumbled upon the foundations of very old artistic concepts never before applied to musical composition.

Not that Bartók's determination to achieve such a synthesis should have come as a surprise. In an autobiographical sketch (1921) he wrote:

It became clear that the old scales, no longer used in our art music, had not lost their viability after all. Their application also made possible new harmonic combinations. This treatment of the diatonic series led to liberation from the ossified major / minor scale, and consequently to *the completely free availability of every single tone in our chromatic twelve-tone system.* (Italics added.)

This had no reference, of course, to Schoenberg's first use of a twelve-tone row construction in his *Piano Suite,* Op. 25 (composition of which was begun in the same year, but not completed until 1923).

Even with only this sketchy outline of Bartók's system to guide you, review your survey of the surface of *Music for Strings, Percussion and Celesta.* Likely changes may appear in Group A4 and 6, Group B1, 2, 3, and 4, Group C3, and Group D1, 2, and 3.

In comparing these results with our earlier outlines of works by Schoenberg and Ives, it should become even more evident that not only harmonic functions, but even elements of structure once entirely determined by harmonic conventions of Western music since the eighteenth century can no longer be taken for granted in the twentieth. The basic significance of this to performance and to preparing a score for performance should emerge even more powerfully when we examine two works by Debussy and Stravinsky, *Jeux* and *The Rite of Spring*. This profound change leading to the music of our own day, and also inescapably affecting our view of music of the past, will encompass not only melodic, harmonic, and rhythmic elements of structure, but the use of time itself.

DEBUSSY, *JEUX*

You should begin, as before, with a methodical survey of the surface of Debussy's *Jeux*. Under A1, this might include Pierre Boulez's simple statement of fact, "Since the flute of *Faun* and the English horn of *Nuages* music has breathed differently," Igor Stravinsky's declaration, in *Answers to 34 Questions*, that the man to whom he owed most as a composer was Debussy, and Monsieur Croche's description of his own music (and *Jeux* in particular): "One thinks of a legendary tree whose buds all suddenly open." We shall return to Debussy's metaphor when we begin to wrestle with the problems posed by his *Poème Dansé* and its "constant variation" of similar but different materials, its "vegetative" inexactness of quasi-organic musical unfolding, in Group B of our outline.

For now, a little more background: Lady Ottoline Morrell, patroness of an intellectual and artistic circle in London known as the Bloomsbury Set recalls the following scene as her guests Nijinsky and Bakst (scenic designer for several Diaghilev ballets, including *Faun* and *Jeux*) were leaving her house one afternoon: "Duncan Grant and some others were playing tennis in Bedford Square garden* . . . [Nijinsky and Bakst] were so entranced by the tall trees against the houses and the figures flitting about playing tennis that they exclaimed with delight 'Quel décor!' "** Thus the scene of *Jeux* was born, and Bakst's stage design shows the flat fronts of London Regency row houses in back of the park rather than the roofs of French villas one might have expected.

Jeux is the first ballet in sports costume, but the game of tennis is in itself "décor" for the amorous involvements of a young man with two girls in search of a lost tennis ball among the trees surrounding the (offstage) court. Diaghilev, according to Nijinsky, had thought about choreographing the work for three male dancers, but was prevailed upon not to use a further "décor" of homosexual flirtation. The original scenario preserved in the piano score of *Jeux* is shown on pp. 426–27 along a time line of the work. Do transfer it to your score.

Constant variation, a melodic unfolding in which musical shapes emerge from those which went before and merge into the next, hardly

---

*Many London squares still enclose private gardens and little parks, reserved for the use of residents.

**Richard Buckle, *Nijinsky* (N.Y.: Simon and Schuster, 1971), p. 258.

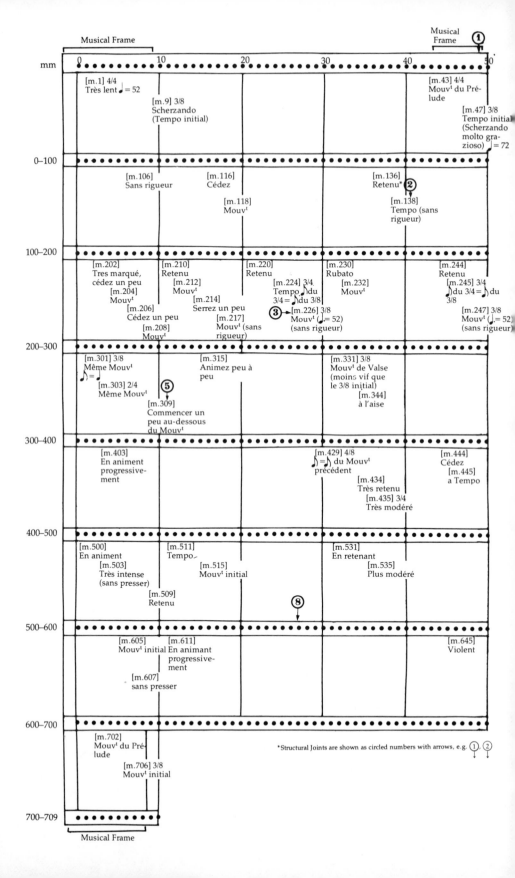

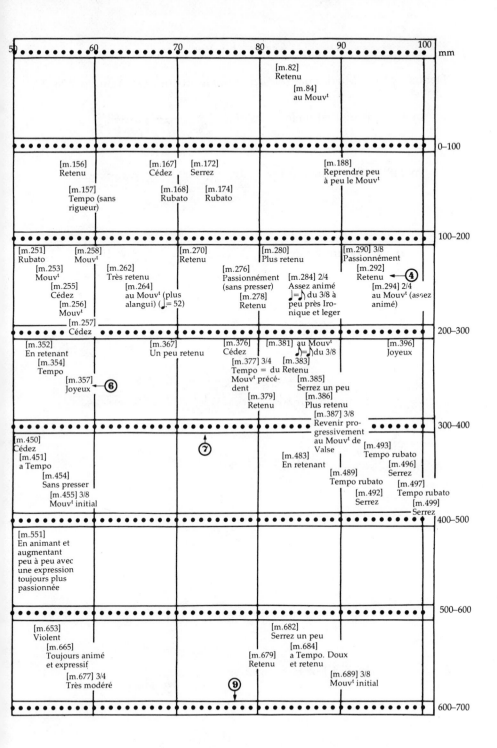

FIGURE 3: Debussy, *Jeux*, tempo markings and structural joints.

Debussy, *Jeux:* Music cues for Structural Joints indicated on pp. 426–27.

1. m.49:   Principal melodic matrix

2. m.138:   Rhythmic motive

3. m.157:   Variation of
             rhythmic motive

4. m.226:   Variation of rhythmic motive

5. m.309:   Exploitation of 3rd
             in melodic matrix

6. m.357:   *Joyeux*

7. m.473:   Melodic matrix

8. m.535:   Tritone
             melody

9. m.611:   Quasi RI of Horn motive

10. m.677:   Melodic matrix

ever coalescing into phrases, periods, or "themes," presents us with a vast raiment of motivic "leaves," much the same in general appearance yet different from each other in countless little "inexactnesses." This is indeed Debussy's "legendary tree," with its vegetative profusion of evolving materials.

EXAMPLE 8*

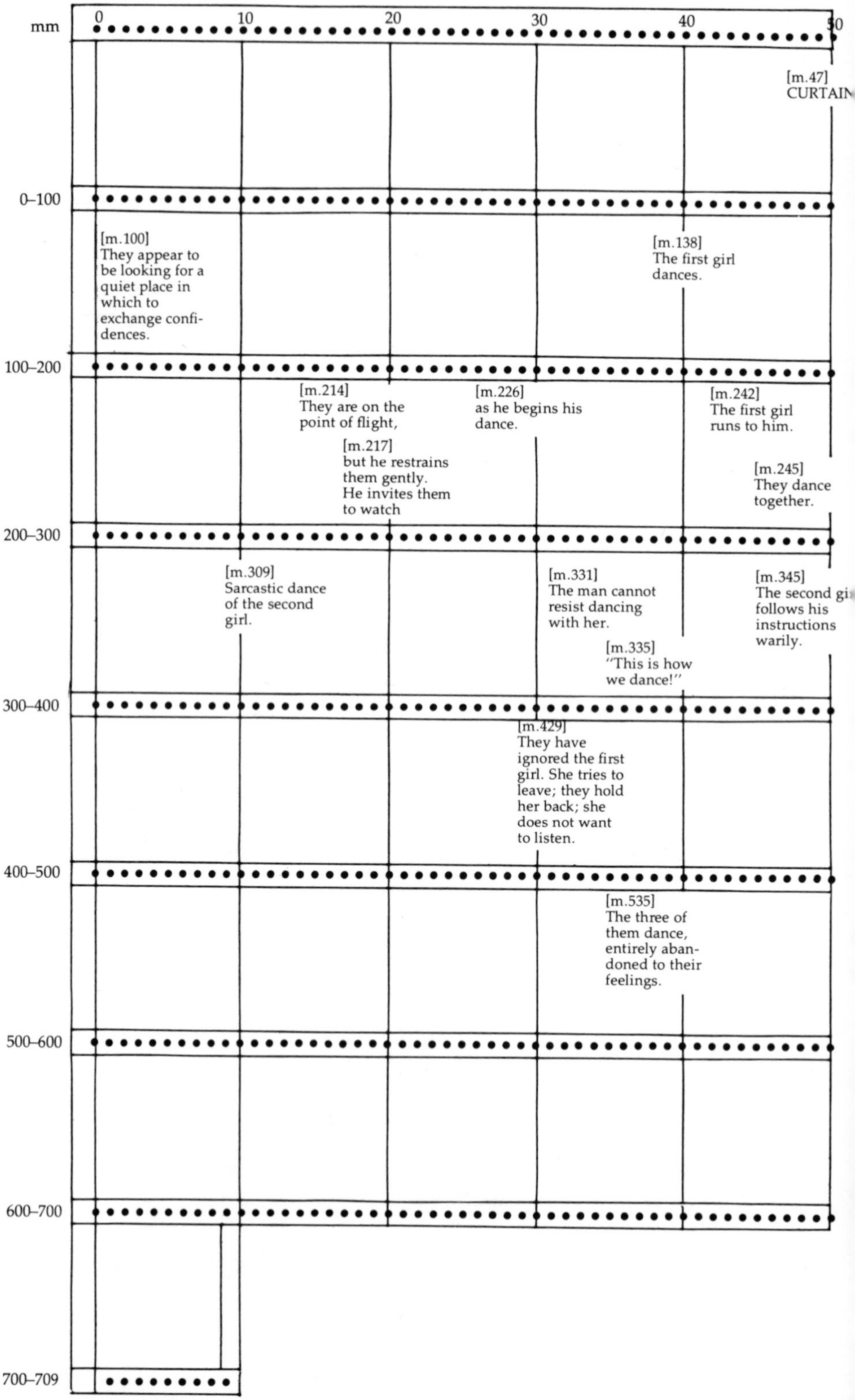

mm	0	10	20	30	40	50

[m.47]
CURTAIN

0–100

[m.100]
They appear to
be looking for a
quiet place in
which to
exchange confi-
dences.

[m.138]
The first girl
dances.

100–200

[m.214]
They are on the
point of flight,

[m.226]
as he begins his
dance.

[m.242]
The first girl
runs to him.

[m.217]
but he restrains
them gently.
He invites them
to watch

[m.245]
They dance
together.

200–300

[m.309]
Sarcastic dance
of the second
girl.

[m.331]
The man cannot
resist dancing
with her.

[m.345]
The second gi
follows his
instructions
warily.

[m.335]
"This is how
we dance!"

300–400

[m.429]
They have
ignored the first
girl. She tries to
leave; they hold
her back; she
does not want
to listen.

400–500

[m.535]
The three of
them dance,
entirely aban-
doned to their
feelings.

500–600

600–700

700–709

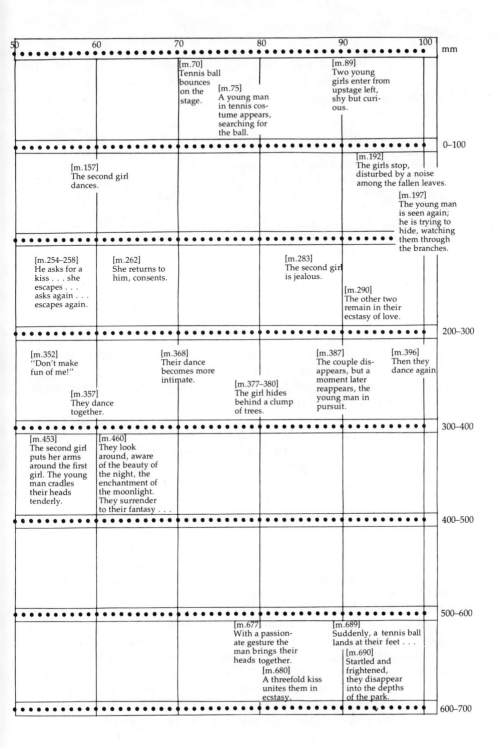

FIGURE 4: Debussy, *Jeux*, stage directions according to two-piano score

In terms of "how it was made," Eimert's analysis of *Jeux* is still the classic. His impressive table of "leaves" from Debussy's magic tree is reproduced in Example 8.

He writes:

The three-line scheme picks out only "inexact" steps in diastematic (melodic) movement; the intervals can be major or minor seconds or thirds, and scale-like movements go to make up the ornamental waveline; of these, the two waltz melodies 6/340 and 6/566, when reduced to the scale, are identical with the wave itself, and give rise to the smaller wave 7/387, a rolling figure which is extremely prominent by its crescendo and accelerando, and which later sets the waltz tempo going again. Lines 10 and 14 show the form of wave-movement culminating in the third, with many variants that go as far as the "inversion" in 13/365 or the isolated third-formation 12/82, which, among the powdery sounds surrounding it, emerges as a melodic interval-event of the most wonderful kind: melody reduced to two notes.*

Not that this helps us much in organizing *Jeux* in our memory image. The old outline, or at least Group B, seems to have lost its usefulness. Harmonic functions play no part in determining the structure of this work; there is continual evolution instead of form; the choreographic instructions we have marked on our time line may serve as points of orientation, but we need musical landmarks as well. However, when everything looks nearly the same, whatever is really different becomes memorable. With almost every melodic fragment consisting of stepwise, wavelike progressions (sometimes stretched a little by the "inexact" larger interval of a third in place of major or minor seconds), we find three instances of prominently featured fourths, and one phrase opening based on the tritone.

The first of these, an E♭ horn call—*joyeux*—at m. 357 (and again at m. 396), consists of three eighth notes spaced at intervals of a second and a fourth, and features, in outline, the fifth above E♭. In both instances it signals the Pas de Deux between the tennis player and the second girl. We shall mark it on our chart. At m. 611, starting the final accelerando into *violent*, we find a three-eighth-note retrograde inversion of this figure, also encompassing an octave. We mark this as well. And we add a reminder for the plain inversion of the *joyeux* figure at m. 473. These are the motifs featuring the fourth. At the beginning of the Pas de Trois, leading off with the tritone A♭–D, and including several more versions of the three-eighth-note figure enclosing a second and a fourth, we mark what Eimert rightly calls the most remarkable of the lines in *Jeux*. He sees in it circular formations akin to Webern's mirror series— the more striking, in terms of "how was it made," for its position at the opening of a final "stretto" in a work which in every way is constructed

---

*Ibid., p. 14.

in the opposite fashion to Webern's tightly controlled, closed structures. What concerns us, in terms of "what does it do," is the powerful contrast—on whatever level—which makes this line a landmark in this work. As we then review the pattern of motivic exceptions to the wave pattern of most of the "leaves" of *Jeux*, we find that we have noted on our time line these important moments of the choreography:

1. the man's Pas de Deux with the second girl (mm. 357/396);
2. the sudden awareness, by all three, of the beauty of the night (m. 473);
3. the beginning of the Pas de Trois (m. 535);
4. and the start of the violent abandon in its climax (m. 611).

Clearly, Debussy furnished his garlanded wreath of motivic "leaves" with connecting blossoms at important turns in the choreographic plot. We are thus encouraged to mark other turning points in the stage directions as Structural Joints (Group B).

What about the first half, the dance of the first girl, for instance? This time, perhaps because we are looking for it, it is the metric displacement (m. 137) of three against ♪ ♪ | ♪ ♪ | ♪ ♪ | ♫. | following a remarkable eight-measure rhythmic introduction of 3 against 4 against 5. With an eye for correspondences—now that we may get back to our outline after all—we find that rhythm again throughout the final Pas de Trois (mark it!), culminating in the metric collisions of the two places marked *Violent*, and the 2–3–4–6–8 metric cluster before the climax on m. 677. The unison motive of this climax is an augmentation of the melodic matrix (m. 49) sounded when the curtain first opened. Then there is the man's solo (m. 226): a rhythmic variation of the first girl's solo (m. 138), and an indication that "constant variation" produces metric as well as melodic variety among similar but unlike foliage. The *pas de deux* which follows (m. 245) provides yet another example. Figure 4 shows other structural joints and illustrates how the resulting divisions of the work correspond perfectly to the choreographic directions. For good measure we now frame the entire work between the whole-tone measures of its opening and close, and we have an outline which should hold in our memory.

Further perspectives are to be gained by charting *dynamics* and *orchestral texture*. Either might be represented by drawing a freehand series of waves across your time chart: as in performance, judgment is bound to be subjective but should meet the printed evidence. Debussy's large orchestra almost never plays a tutti, but presents the music in a constantly changing series of chamber-music combinations. Here is yet another form of constant variation: instrumentation that is almost the same as before, but not exactly (e.g., mm. 226 and 247). It is also worth noting that the loudest places and the softest are not necessarily the most / least lavishly orchestrated.

This sense of unidirectional flow of time is created at a price: changes of actual pace are so carefully masked by a continuous pulse that one might fear the result to be perceived as a single, albeit undulating, tempo. That this does not indeed happen raises once again the most important issue of a difference between "how it was made" and "what is it," the latter being essentially a matter of listener's perception.

In the case of *Jeux* a great deal of planning will have to go into the extent of tempo fluctuations. Another glance at Figure 5 impresses us with the great profusion of fluctuations within each tempo zone, and with the invariable care with which the merging of one zone into another is hidden behind reevaluations of metric values: ♪ = ♩ , or ♪ du 3/8 = ♪ du 3/4. The significance of such transformations is not merely local. Only two metronomic numbers are given throughout: 52 and 72. But *"au mouvement"* at m. 226 means ♩. = 52 (*sans rigueur* indeed), as compared with ♩. = 72 of the original 3/8 *tempo initial*. Both motivic and choreographic identity would indicate m. 138 as the most favorable moment at which the slower tempo ought to be introduced. To achieve that, the *Retenu* at m. 136 (only in piano score) is not sufficient. It corresponds to another at m. 82, and offers no musical justification *to the listener* for more than a slight hesitation. There is, however, an earlier marking of *Sans rigueur* (m. 106) which offers just such an opportunity, albeit no specific change of tempo is indicated in the score. But the music allows an even more substantial slowing down than the required ♩. = 52. Beginning with a generous ♪ = c. 104 (i.e. ♩ = quasi 52), and allowing a slight *Cédez* at m. 116, the "return" to ♩. = 52 at m. 118 will *seem* like a return to *Mouvement* while actually very much slower than the *Tempo initial*. And the music is enhanced throughout. There can be little doubt that the composer intended such "liberties." The style of adjusting tempos so that certain tempo changes may become true metric modulations must of course be observed throughout the entire score.

A careful reading of tempo markings will reveal other instances where apparent inexactness of metronomic reference almost certainly suggests not merely sanction, but expectation of calculated liberties at appropriate moments in performance. The profusion of changes, retards, accelerandos and rubatos, some written out in metric values, some noted as directions, and some apparently left to the performer's taste and ingenuity, are perhaps the most obvious indications of the wavelike free flow of this work in time, without suggested perspectives of structural reference within the enclosing frame of prelude and postlude.

The absence of time reversed, of a sense of recognition and return within a closed musical structure while, at the same time, much of what is new appears familiar because it *is* an inexact repetition, should help us to understand how, after Debussy, "music breathed differently." Time flows in one direction only. In the works of Debussy's maturity, musical time becomes as irreversible as ontological time. There are benchmarks along the musical surface we have traced on our chart, to be sure, but the motion of musical flow is without a sense of return.

Not least among consequences of exploring works in which repetitions are replaced by reminiscences—a very different experience, in music as it is in life—should be a heightened awareness of opportunities to emphasize *reversible* time in the performance of older music. The closed structures of the "classics" do require tighter control of their design today than might have been necessary when the multidirectional force field of harmonic functions was taken for granted by composer and listener alike, and when, as a result, performers' indulgences in "loving detail" were less apt to blur one's sense of that design. Much of the new music, on the other hand, has its only intended impact in performance at the constantly moving intersection with the listening "now." This is the music requiring most careful emphasis on every passing moment of Debussy's "rhythmicized time."

STRAVINSKY, *THE RITE OF SPRING*

By comparison, even so daunting a work as Stravinsky's *Rite of Spring* might seem easier to approach. We shall map its surface:

Group A: You will have quite a bit of information about the composer, both general and as far as your own tastes and interests are concerned, and we have said a good deal about the state of music before World War I (*The Rite* was completed in 1913). Debussy and Stravinsky not only knew each other in Paris at the time, but were on friendly terms and took a lively interest in each other's work. They are said to have played parts of *Rite,* four hands at the piano, since composition began in 1910—the period also of the writing of *Jeux.*

Group B: Unlike *Jeux,* however, *Rite* falls into place before our eyes with deceptive ease. Titles, double bars, and key signatures provide us with clear, large divisions. The main movements of the ballet appear to be simple formal structures. Even Stravinsky's once "scandalous" harmonic usage reveals itself as layered chord formations with unmistakable reference to tonal centers. Most often, harmonic territory of tonic, dominant, and subdominant is suggested, albeit without necessarily following the classical pattern of their functional relationship. Harmonic *movement,* in fact, is sometimes at a standstill.

(*Group D.*) Instead, ostinato basses, on or around the root, emphasize the tonic while vertical, chordal structures with neighboring notes of melodic or ornamental meaning piled on top merely emphasize the static, tonal foundation.

Group C: Much more complex is the matter of periods and phrases. The work grows more intricate as we come to examine its smaller and smallest components. Rhythmic structures of great sophistication are distributed at apparent random over rigid metric foundations, while the barline, the downbeat, our conductorial reference of last resort, more often than not has no inherent musical relevance whatever. Some suggestions may be of help.

Pierre Boulez, whose classic analysis of *Rite* (*Stravinsky demeure**) provides the serious student with a definitive guide to "how it was made" (an English translation has been published as part of *Notes of an Apprenticeship,* unfortunately not always clear or even accurate), speaks of isorhythmic structures and, elsewhere,** of "rhythmic cells from which a structure is developed which comes close to African and Indian rhythms." The emphasis should be on the word *Structure,* for as with Bartók's use of folk music, Stravinsky's debt to the fourteenth-century theorist of Ars nova, Philippe de Vitry, to Guillaume de Machaut, or to ethnic music of North Africa is not so much decorative or coloristic, like that of other composers at the time, but provides a startling advance into an area of compositional technique from which he himself soon retreated (but which his great contemporary, if late starter, Varèse, reached by a different route—and surpassed).

EXAMPLE 9

**Musique Russe,* Vol. 1 (Presses Universitaires de France, 1953).
***Contrepoint,* Vol. 6 (1949).

Group D: The independence of recurring and often complex rhythmic patterns within apparently unrelated metrical, harmonic, and even melodic structures is the glory of Stravinsky's *Rite of Spring*. Six hundred years after Machaut, rhythm remained the least developed element in Western music. Yet the first appearance of isorhythmic music in Europe antedated even Ars nova by nearly another five hundred years: the forbidden fruit of contact with the rich Islamic culture during the Moorish occupation of southern Spain. In essence, that tradition has survived in the folk music of North Africa and the Near East. Example 9, a Tunisian song with rhythmic accompaniment, will tell us something about Stravinsky's use of rhythmic "cells" in *Rite*.*

The simple, flowing melodic line in the upper staff is accompanied by a sequence of two different drum patterns, which are articulated by strictly prescribed alternations of loud and soft attacks. In modern metric notation, pattern *a* might be written:

$$\frac{3}{4} \, \text{♩.} \, | \, \text{♩.} \, | \, \text{♩} \, | \, \frac{2}{4} \, \text{♩} \, | \, +$$

and patterns *b* and b_1 :

$$\frac{3}{4} \, \text{♫♫♫} \, | \, \frac{2}{4} \, \text{♩} \, \text{♫} \, | \, \frac{3}{4} \, \text{♪♫♫} \, |+$$

Although equal in length (sixteen ♪ units), both patterns are clearly distinguishable by their different character: the first moving gently in values of ♩ , ♩. , and ♩ , the second in a more excited grouping of ♪, ♪ , and ♩ . Both patterns remain constant in themselves, while they are repeated independently of the melodic phrases they accompany; and, as single-pitched designs of loud and soft, they become recognizable, rhythmic punctuations of passing time. By their contrasting character they divide this passage of time into clearly defined, equal lengths. They are "rhythmicized time."

This simple concept shall now serve to amplify one of the not so simple constructions of Stravinsky's *Rite,* the Finale to Part I, *Dance of the Earth (Danse de la Terre).* (See pp. 438ff.) First, however, as always, we must take a look at the musical surface.

We can see at a glance that this movement is a binary structure in which, at the end, both parts are pressed into one another. Since space will afford us no more than an illustration of Stravinsky's reduction of small musical shapes to rhythmic groupings of their smallest values, we shall confine ourselves to the first, expository part (24 measures). The reader can continue his own exploration and is urged to refer to the Boulez analysis.

*Grove's Dictionary of Music and Musicians, 3rd ed., Vol. 3, p. 577.

EXAMPLE 10: Stravinsky, *The Rite of Spring, Dance of the Earth,* rehearsal numbers 72 to 74

Fl. picc. 1 2
Fl. gr. 1 2
Fl. alto
Ob. 1 2 3 4
C. ing.
Cl. picc. in Re
Cl. in Sib 1 2
Cl. bas. in Sib 1 2
Fag. 1 2 3
C. Fag. 1 2
Cor. in Fa 1 2 3 4 5 6 8
Solo (cuivrez)
fassai
f stacc.
Tr. picc. in Re
Tr. in Do 1 2 3 4
Trbn. 1 2 3
Timp.
G. C.
Tam-t.
p sub.
Vl. I
gliss.
Vl. II
Vle.
Vc.
Cb.

SURFACE INFORMATION

Rehearsal
Numbers:

72		Prestissimo in three, ♩ = 168
		No key signature
		Whole orchestra to be in use, assignments *en bloc*
upbeat to 3 after 72 (also: 2–1 before 73)	(*a*)	Strings (except Bass) gliss. G–E Horns 4, 6, 8, Fl, Cl. Bn, C-major arpeggio with F♯ introducing chord pattern (*a*¹)
3 after 72	(*b*)	Bass, Timpani C, F♯ pedal Bass, Horns 1, 2, 3, 5, Bn, C. Bn whole-tone ostinato F♯–C (later: C–E)
3–5 after 72 (also: 3–4 after 73)	(*a*¹)	Same instruments as *a;* *un*arpeggiated chord patterns of C-major triad with tritone F♯ Same, different rhythm
3 before, to 2 after 73	(*a*²)	Same instruments as *a;* unarpeggiated chord patterns of D-major triad with quintuplet/triplet arabesque from D-major with tri- tone G♯
4 after 73	(*c*)	Horns 6, 8 introduction of triplet figure E♭–B♭, which is to dominate middle section (from 75)

Organizing the C + tritone chord patterns above in a one-line notation of their respective rhythmic shapes, like the drum accompaniment
to the Tunisian song of Example 9, we shall find symmetrical sequences:

EXAMPLE 11

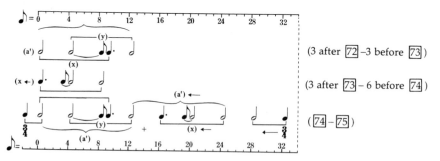

Metric reference is 2/4, in contrast to the 3/4 ostinato figure (*b*). Example 11 is based on a time line callibrated in eighth notes. Brackets indicate rhythmic elements.

The basic rhythmic shape (a') is introduced 3 measures after 72. It
includes two partial units: x — $4 + 5 + 3$ eighth notes, and overlapping

y—$5 + 3 + 4$. In the third measure of $\boxed{73}$ the retrograde of x is used. When the C + tritone chords reappear ($\boxed{74}$–$\boxed{75}$), a ♩ unit precedes a' or a ♩ + ♩ unit = 3/4 precedes y. In the former reading, the retrograde of a' overlaps on the final ♩ of a', followed by the retrograde of the opening 3/4; or, according to the second reading, x follows y, again with the retrograde of the opening 3/4 to close. Either way, the 2/4 of the chord pattern and the 3/4 of the ostinato figure it interrupts are reconciled by the addition of the beginning and ending (♩+♩) and its retrograde ♩+♩.

The D chords (a^2) appear as part of a melodic arabesque in thirds, featuring *their* tritone at the top, on the second beat of their entering measure (3 before $\boxed{73}$). Fractions of this arabesque reappear later (5–4 before $\boxed{74}$, also 2 before $\boxed{74}$), reintroducing the C + tritone chord in its original, arpeggio / glissando form (a). As at the beginning of the movement, a is followed by a quarter rest, i.e. an eighth-note value of 4.

As common denominator of smallest values we may now use the quarter. When the glissando element (a) no longer appears, the succeeding quarter rest will continue to be counted as one pulse (4 before $\boxed{74}$). Similarly, the D arabesque may appear in the form of a single chord (1 before $\boxed{73}$).

In Figure 5 below, the D-chord element (a^2) is represented by the actual rhythmic values as they appear in the score and a shaded rectangle extending over its cumulative duration in quarters, along the time line. The C + tritone arpeggio is shown as an arrow pointed upwards and to the right. Together with a succeeding quarter rest, this compound element (a) *accumulates tension.* When only the quarter rest appears (2nd of $\boxed{73}$, 5th–4th before $\boxed{74}$), the suggestion of gathered tension is still strong. Tension mounts most strongly in the pile-up of a elements during the three last measures before $\boxed{74}$. Element b, the ostinato bass progression of three ascending whole steps shown below the time line, remains constant in tension (as does a^2).

N.B.: These diagrams of "rhythmicized time" are intended to suggest that interpretive decisions, e.g. the variable application of tension, may be taken on quite novel grounds (rhythmic momentum instead of harmonic function in this case), albeit in equally careful observance of evidence in the score.

This analytical sketch on p. 444 is only the beginning. The triplet element introduced in the fourth measure of $\boxed{73}$ will dominate the second section of *Dance of the Earth* in various groupings, featuring its interval of a downward fourth. As already mentioned, the ostinato bass will be expanded to include the next three notes of its rising whole-note scale and will also feature different combinations of its six-beat and three-beat versions. There will be a last element of sixteenth-note cells. With the return of the first section, cumulative rhythmic tensions, together

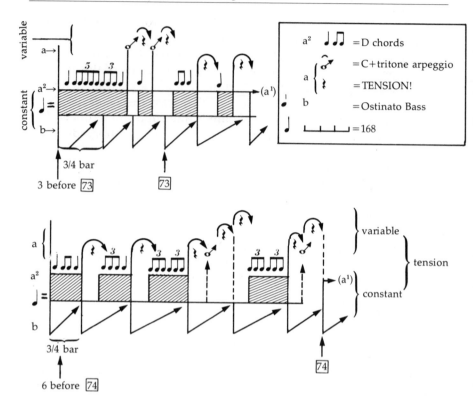

FIGURE 5

with an accretion of harmonic and melodic elements—the extended, rising bass ostinato, falling fourths, persisting pedal points, and repeating
chord patterns, all emphasizing or aiming at C—a final consummation
is powerfully prepared. It is achieved on the final pulse of the piece.

VARÈSE, *DÉSERTS*

The image of Varèse as rebel and loner is a popular commonplace in
musical circles. That this iconoclast was a builder as well, as ruthless in
condemning his own work when it no longer satisfied his vision, is so
much taken for granted that it is overlooked. His youthful *Bourgogne*
(1907) was the only score to survive a fire that destroyed his manu-
scripts in 1922. He himself destroyed it later on. Yet his stated objective
in writing that score sounded much like that of the mature Varèse of
Ionisation, as he describes it in an interview with Gunther Schuller:

I was trying to approximate the kind of inner, microscopic life you find in certain chemical solutions, or through the filtering of light. . . . I was not influ-

enced by (older) composers as much as by natural objects and physical phenomena. As a child, I was tremendously impressed by the qualities and character of the granite I found in Burgundy, where I often visited my grandfather. . . . Then there was the old Romanesque architecture in that part of France . . . In 1905, when I composed *Rhapsodie Romaine*, I was thinking of Romanesque architecture, not Rome! I wanted to find a way to project in music the concept of calculated or controlled gravitation, how one element pushing on the other stabilizes the whole structure, thus using the material elements at the same time in opposition to and in support of one another. . . . [Later works] reflect a greater refinement of my earlier conceptions. I also became increasingly interested in internal rhythmic and metric relationships, as in *Ionisation* [1933; but then] I had an obsession: a new instrument that would free music from the tempered system. . . . To me, working with electronic music is composing with living sounds, paradoxical though that may appear. . . . But I want to be *in* the material, part of the acoustical vibration, so to speak.*

Déserts (1954) consists of four instrumental sections framing three electronic interpolations. The genesis of this work, its title, and how it was cast in its present shape provide another perspective. The author was to have conducted the first performance in New York (1953). Varèse had not yet completed work on the electronic portions, but the instrumental sections were finished. How did one learn this music, which broke a silence of many years within Varèse's opus and, for the first time, posed the problem of pitting the performance of instrumental music against electronic sounds, presumably as the result of some conscious calculation on the composer's part? Taking my cue from the title, I asked Varèse if what he had intended was a musical setting of "inner deserts," deserts of the mind and soul, against the awesome, inanimate deserts of interstellar space and the still fresh horrors of reported atomic deserts where cities had been: instruments played by musicians vs. an electronic tape played by a machine. Varèse was delighted and said, "Follow your instinct about what the music *is*, don't worry any more than you have to about how I put it together, and play it like any other kind of score! You are right about those deserts. I like that. I like that very much."

That performance never took place, because the musicians' union would not allow it. I never knew their reason—perhaps it was the juxtaposition of live and what they considered "canned" music. Hermann Scherchen gave the premiere in France, in 1954, and, according to the Paris *Express*, "it was the finest scandal this auditorium built by Perret has known since that night in 1913 when Monteux conducted the first performance of *Le Sacre du Printemps*." Five years later, the author performed *Déserts* at the Stratford Festival. The instrumentalists laughed

---

*Gunther Schuller, "Conversation with Varèse," in *Perspectives on American Composers*, ed. Benjamin Boretz and Edward T. Cone (W.W. Norton, 1971), pp. 35–37.

as hysterically at the electronic sections as the audience. After the first performance in London, in 1966 (!), one paper reported that the noise of feet rushing to the exits at times almost drowned out the noisy score. But the audience gave Varèse a standing ovation at the conclusion. And the survivors at our London Promenade Concert of 1966 finally cheered that score in the Royal Albert Hall. It is hard not to react, one way or another, when music really takes charge. My notes to a Boston performance said:

One may be certain that music will always appear in new ways; that many of these ways will be shocking at first; that the shock will wear off (it always has); and that great works will survive—neither because they were once shocking, nor in spite of it. But in order to live, these works must not only be heard but listened to; not only be performed but reacted to; not only be witnessed but experienced.

Another perspective, but what does it reveal? Two things: the need to *react* to all works one intends to perform (e.g. the *idea* of "deserts") and to expect a reaction in turn; and the need to sort out the apparently incomprehensible with whatever tools one has at hand. The first touches the very roots of musical performance itself. Varèse's long-time champion and sensitive biographer, Fernand Ouelette, put it this way in a description of *Density 21.5* (dedicated by Varèse to Georges Barrère, the title referring to the specific gravity of the flutist's new platinum instrument):

For me, *Density 21.5* is one long cry. Only *Déserts* (or *Etude pour Espace*) was later to attain this same tragic intensity. *Density 21.5* achieves such purity that we can truly qualify it as Mozartian, even though the conception of song that animates it is at antipodes of Mozart's. For this is truly a song-cry. In Mozart, the cry is a piercing explosion within the song, but in Varèse it becomes the very substance of the song: it makes the song possible. Mozart begins from the song and allows it to explode into a cry. Varèse begins from the cry and transmutes it into either song or silence. In Mozart, the tension is a peak; in Varèse, silence is an abyss that cleaves the tension like a crevasse. The moments of relaxation are to him what tension was for Mozart. These are two conceptions of tragedy. But Varèse's, like Webern's, is certainly more in conformity with an age of Nazi concentration camps, thermo-nuclear bombs, and interminable and savage civil wars.*

Varèse had this to say about Debussy: "In *Jeux*, we find a higher state of tension than in any work before it." That was said in 1953, the year of *Déserts*. Ten years later, the author gave the first performance of *Jeux* in Boston since its unveiling by the Boston Symphony forty years before. The *Boston Globe* commented on that time-lag, and then justified it on the grounds that *Jeux* was, after all, only a warmed-over second serving

*Fernand Ouelette, *Edgard Varèse* (Orion Press, 1968), p. 135.

of Debussy "favorites," "a pastiche of clichés from his more popular (thus deserving) earlier works." But Varèse had seen something of "what it *is*," because he looked at the music from where *he* was.

Assignment

Conduct your own examination of Varèse's *Octandre.*

The object of this exercise is to deal with materials which, to a larger degree than any of the foregoing, will not yield useful information in response to performance analysis based on nineteenth-century compositional practices. Observe the following sequence in working through this score:

A. Complete the usual survey of the musical surface of *Octandre.*

B. Study the following statements on Varèse's music:

1. "Timbres are extensions of the total sonority; they articulate it and accentuate it."

    —Gilles Tremblay, *Les Sons en Movement, Liberté* 59, Vol. 5

2. "One key to a comprehension of Varèse's music is the fact that he is more interested in finding a note that will sound in a certain way in a certain instrument . . . than he is in just what position the note occupies in the harmony."

    —Henry Cowell, in Ouelette, *Edgard Varèse*

3. "Besides the harmony of notes which with Varèse is somewhat secondary, there is also a harmony of tone qualities . . . More important than the chord itself is the harmony resultant from tone qualities of the instruments owing to . . . his particular scoring."

    —Cowell, ibid.

4. "To me orchestration is an essential part of the structure of the work . . . Variations in the intensity of certain tones of the compounds modify the structure of the masses and planes."

    —Varèse, ibid.

5. "Rhythm is the element in music which not only gives life to a work but holds it together."

    —Varèse, ibid.

6. "The phrase, generally composed of disjunct notes, moves constantly from one register to the other and allows itself to be attracted by . . . pivot-notes . . . either by changing its timbre and color or not, by means of different instrumentations."

    —François Morel, *La Conscience du son et de l'espace, Liberté* 59, Vol. 5

7. "One finds that dynamic nuances on the same note, or repeated tones, often take the place of melody."

    —Cowell, in Ouelette, *Edgard Varèse*

8. "Varèse was one of the first composers to employ dynamics as an internal formal element."
                              —Robert Craft, in *Musical America*, June 1962

C. Work through *Octandre* according to the guidelines above.

Note your observations, e.g. repetitions of notes

> abrupt changes of register
> characteristic use of timbre
> melodic emphasis on 4-note cell

As you will have discovered, this work divides quite naturally into sections (Group B). Proceed through each section separately, then reconsider your results in terms of the whole. Two more quotes:

9. "Calculated or controlled gravitation, how one element pushing on the other stabilizes the whole structure, thus using the material elements at the same time in opposition and in support of one another."
                              —Schuller, "Conversation with Varèse"
10. "Form is the result of his expression."
—François Morel, *La Conscience du son et de l'espace, Liberté* 59, Vol. 5

Varèse used the term *density* in connection with the particular sound quality of an instrument. He identified individual densities by assigning to an instrument special, often extreme registers or, in some of his later works, a particular, easily recognizable rhythm. As the work unfolds, the listener becomes aware of very slow, gradual changes like a natural process—crystallization:*

> Crystal form itself is a *resultant* (the very word I have always used in reference to musical form) rather than a primary attribute. Crystal form is the consequence of the intersection of attractive and repulsive forces and the ordered packing of the atom.**

In conceiving of structure as "the consequence of the intersection of attractive and repulsive forces," we are reminded of the Classical style,

---

*Crystallization, is a process of unorganic nature. Cf. the earlier section on Bartók's music and the laws of organic nature, pp. 423–24.
**Varèse, "The Liberation of Sound," in *Perspectives on American Composers*.

resulting from the interaction of *harmonic* stresses. The gravitational field of a score dominated by opposing harmonic forces extends both forward and backward in time. But reference to the chief tonality controls the direction of musical time and may as convincingly require a return to the point of origin as lend its weight to the forward momentum into a final resolution. A Classical score is "programmed" by the harmonic events which support passing and future musical happenings in performance, as the composer intended. This was the music of closed forms.

But when there is no recognizable reference, or when the process of musical unfolding seems more potent than recognizable references (timbres, pitches, instrumental registers), then *unidirectional time* in which music is experienced becomes the structure. In Debussy's own definition, music has become "rhythmicized time."

Thus it becomes perfectly clear that "how the music was made" not only determines "what it is," but also establishes a perspective that allows us to see what older works "are." Adorno speaks of Wagner's maintaining, "even in his mature works, with all their riches of orchestral imagination, a resolute adherence to academic four-part writing."* But within a conceptual framework of melodic indicators that may change their (extramusical) meaning according to their placement within this harmonic context, and as a result of harmonic events which acquire special significance because of their coincidence with such moments of dramatic interchanges of *musical* meaning, "what seemed so old became so new," in the words of Hans Sachs of *Die Meistersinger*. Such things, concludes Adorno, "become completely understandable only in the light of the most advanced methods of employing the materials of contemporary music."**

Eimert says much the same at the end of his essay on *Jeux*, while referring the reader to Debussy himself:

The subtle novelty of *Jeux* lies not in its construction, but in *time*, the pre-constructive, true element of music, which has only today become theoretically accessible. "Music," says Debussy, "possesses timbre and flowing tempi," and he adds that it is "a very young art, both in its resources and also in respect of its appreciation." *To appreciate* Jeux, *one must be familiar with the resources of present-day composition.* They are methods of musical time, not introduced as ornament or colour but engendered from within the work itself—this is the eminently new thing about it.† (Italics added.)

The chart on p. 451 shows the distribution of some characteristics common to some of the works we have discussed in this chapter. The following observations should help to establish musical ground shared

*Theodor W. Adorno, *Versuch über Wagner* (Suhrkamp, 1952), pp. 64–65.
**Ibid., p. 20.
†Eimert, p. 20.

by these composers and to suggest the framework of a new musical convention which influences our musical awareness as performers and our musical expectations as listeners.* "Since the flute of Debussy's *Faun*, music has begun to breathe differently."

1. None of the characteristics appear in isolation, i.e. only in the work of one single composer.
2. None are representative of compositional practice of the Classical or Romantic periods.
3. The distribution of these characteristics differs with each composer.
4. Only in Varèse's music do we find all of the characteristics. This is not altogether surprising, since *Déserts* is the only post–World War II work discussed. The generation of composers active in the 1950s included others who would have received equally full marks in all categories (e.g. Messiaen, Stockhausen).

One or more of categories III, IV, and VII are checked for every composer on the list except Stravinsky. As we have seen, these affect the new sense of unilinear, irreversible time, and thus the very basis of how we experience music. This is the most important effect of "how it was made" on what it is.

The chart reflects the author's perspective on music of our time. Another conductor might add to it or modify it. To this extent, however, it offers yet another approach to what lies beneath the musical surface of *any* work in preparation for performance.

What is perspective but the necessarily unique view of something seen from a particular vantage point? While most music of the past shares characteristics with music of our time, the main value of a new point of view is the bold relief in which *differences* are revealed. The absence of structural and thematic correspondences in *Erwartung* is an important feature of that work. But even more important is the realization that structural and thematic correspondences are not inevitable attributes of all music (any more than is the observance of harmonic conventions of the "common practice" period) and must therefore be clearly demonstrated in performance wherever they exist. Even where thematic resemblances of the musical materials involve constant evolution of original thematic substance, as in *Jeux*, the significance of delineating shapes that retain their identity, in older music, is enhanced. Indeterminancy of harmonic function, metric disorientation due to layered rhythms, reductive use of dissonance of purely expressive purposes: all these relatively new aspects offer unsuspected insight into music in

*Cf. p. 406.

COMMON PREMISE: WEAKENED STRUCTURAL FUNCTION OF HARMONY EMANCIPATION OF DISSONANCE FROM CHORDAL DEPENDENCE.

		Schoenberg	Bartók	Ives	Debussy	Stravinsky	Varèse
I	Absence of traditional harmonic functions	✓			✓		✓
II	Pitch-oriented structures (nonfunctional)	✓				✓	✓
III	Continuously evolving materials		✓		✓		✓
IV	No significant structural correspondences	✓					✓
V	polyrhythms, isorhythms, simultaneous speeds			✓	✓	✓	✓
VI	Emphasis on smallest components of thematic materials		✓		✓	✓	✓
VII	Indeterminacy other than any above		✓	✓	✓		✓
VIII	Spatial separation of sound sources			✓			✓

N.B. The characteristics checked off refer only to works examined in this chapter.

which these facets may have become too familiar or too obvious for us to notice or to care.

Learn the following works of the standard literature, *examining their scores for characteristics opposite to those found* in the chart above. They will acquire new meaning when these are *not* taken for granted, but presented from the musical perspective of our century.

Bach	B-minor Suite
Beethoven	Symphony No. 8
Mendelssohn	*Hebrides Overture*
Berlioz	*Fantastic Symphony*
Schumann	*Manfred Overture*
Brahms	Symphony No. 2

Assignment

In addition to the usual survey of their musical surface, check these scores for the *absence* of twentieth-century characteristics listed on the chart above. Be ready for some surprises.

The Beethoven symphony, for example, shows every musical attribute listed except categories I, III, and VII. For a pitch-oriented structure, the powerful series of sixteen consecutive rising fourths in the finale (mm. 120–43) would have been remarkable in the Schoenberg Chamber Symphony that began with these intervals. The careful spatial separation of each pair of pitches from the preceding and following fourths is matched by the overall metric independence of this elemental invasion of harmonic and rhythmic texture, within which it will dominate as awesomely as the conductor may allow. In the absence of characteristics other than pitch and duration, the shrinking time values within the series contribute to a sense of increasing momentum. In a final contraction (mm. 144–47) half notes are echoed by quarters in the winds, brass, and timpani across the back perimeter of the stage, and propel the music into a frenzied pedal point of alternating C♯ and D, the remains of a thematic pattern of major and minor seconds that followed each pair of fourths like the tail of a comet. When all sense of harmonic reference has been swept aside, the main theme is triumphantly reestablished— in the wrong key.

We have been here before, when we examined the Introduction to Beethoven's Symphony No. 1.* At that time we approached what lay beneath the musical surface of the work from the consensus of a harmonic convention well established *before* the time of composition. In the present case we attempted an approach from the vantage point of our own century.

What this means, and what balance may be struck between these two approaches, needs to be established by you, in your own work. At the very least, it means that with each perceived shift of emphasis in musical composition, the performer is offered remarkable opportunities of fresh insights into familiar works. Wagner's imperative "make it new!" addresses itself as much to you as to the composer, provided you maintain a true perspective from the muscial awareness of your own time, and are willing to go forward with it.

"What are those of the known but to ascend and enter the Unknown?" Walt Whitman's words, set by Carl Ruggles as his motto above the score to *Portals*, serves us well at this point. We have covered a fair amount of known ground in this chapter, and suggested directions in which to

*See p. 219.

find the knowable. Our unknown lies not in contemporary techniques of composition, but in conscious application of twentieth-century musical perspectives *forward* to very recent works and *backward* to the so-called standard musical repertory. What was proposed at the beginning of this book should now be open to view from different angles: that there is no point in trying to duplicate even the finest performances on record, but a constant necessity to rethink "old" music in fresh terms.

For a number of reasons, *Portals* is a very good score for you to explore and learn on your own at this point. There is nothing in it which requires special information on compositional theory, but also nothing in the "known" of compositional theories that would likely be much help to you in trying to "ascend and enter into the Unknown" of this score. With a systematic working-through according to our outline, and the help of your own fantasy, you will have to do the best you can—or any of us can. *Portals* is a very special score. It is written for twelve-part string orchestra, juxtaposing two thematic groups, through two climaxes until—the Unknown?

We have come full circle. Our working assumption that music of the past gains meaning and vitality from an informed viewpoint based on our musical present is well supported by evidence in the musical literature itself. Its application to the learning process promises to be more than a dialectical alternative to "starting with the classics." And its reflection in the concert hall, by giving the listener the benefit of musical continuity from today into the past, need not be justified only by the moral imperative of serving the cause of living composers.

Symphonic music does not remain safely refrigerated in some cold storage compartment of our memory. It becomes part of us and part of our experience with it, whether we are aware of it or not. Continuing reexamination of your own musical values and concepts, with an open mind on form, structure, harmony, or any other musical element that depends on interpretive insight for its actual manifestation in time, is your best guarantee that what is bound to be unique in your performance will also represent something of the essential quality in the music.

It is in this sense that every conductor's repertory is personal and that his performances of any work will be a synthesis of what *he* is and what *it* is. It is only natural that this should reflect an awareness of contemporary musical perspectives, for, as Varèse put it, "to be modern is to be natural, an interpreter of the spirit of your own time."

14

PLAYERS AND ORCHESTRAS

*The live cast that is to represent each staff
in the orchestral score is introduced,
individually and as part of an ensemble.*

ORCHESTRAS are remarkably similar to one another in their collective outlook. Leaving aside all considerations of proficiency, reputation, budgetary classification, or collective experience, a vital common denominator remains that any conductor, neophyte or superstar, will ignore at his peril: orchestral players are engaged in a love affair with their *instruments*—an affair which may be spectacularly successful in the case of some, or ill-starred from the start for others. This is an area of such complete personal absorption that a conductor's most penetrating insights into the subtler points of a score will pale to insignificance, in the players' eyes, should he fail to relate this to the actual sound they produce and the way in which their contributions are matched to achieve the final result in a performance.

Where to begin? With so many different points of view, based on such diverse problems encountered by players of various instruments that have little in common, what general classification will help us to separate overall attitudes and expectations, so that we may begin to recognize and eventually anticipate problems which we shall be expected to control?

Like other groups of people who must act together for a very intricate purpose, orchestras are divided into leaders and followers. While all leaders (the conductor included) must at times follow another leader, the followers are carefully conditioned in the arts of catching and matching some one else's lead. So ingrained is this separate function that there is no special stigma attached to it. A string player in the section who insists on his own way of bowing after his principal's indications have been made clear is as useless to the group as a wind player who, at the appropriate moment in a score, will not take the lead as unchallenged soloist under the conductor's guidance. This, then, from the podium, is the primary division of orchestral players' functions, as individuals and as a whole. All their art and effort is directed either to developing a flexible technique permitting almost instant response to frequently changing group demands, or to cultivating an individual sound and musical identity which can always be identified and enjoyed as a special contribution of one artist. Of course, there are in-between situations: the greatest solo trumpeter must know how to blend in to the brass sound of his section in a tutti; the most virtuoso timpanist needs to gauge a gradual crescendo so that it supports, not drowns, the rising wave of sound in the strings. But there is a basic difference: *Strings perform as a uniform source of sonority; all others are potential soloists.*

What about the concertmaster, or the section principals and first-desk players of strings? They play solos, adjust bowings to fit different conductors' often radically different ways with the same music, and watch each other like individual chamber-music players so that cello phrasing is reflected in the violins or violas, and each section follows, desk by desk, the leads and responses given and received in the course of an emerging interpretation. But their background as players and their orientation as principals are the result of long conditioning as musical contributors without overt individuality; and this sets even the leadership of the strings apart from their colleagues in other sections. At their finest, such players are able to instill something in any good string section that only two or three wind or brass sections in the world can approach: A true *style* of producing their collective sound that can be identified by the listener, that distinguishes "their" string sound from that of other orchestras, and that sensible guest conductors will reckon with.

That string players never listen is a popular canard in orchestra circles. Unfair though this is, it may contain an important kernel of truth. Like any good team, the string section of an orchestra is fully absorbed in its own give and take; and the very fact that individuality is suppressed diminishes the player's personal sense of involvement in the musical dialogue of the winds, for instance. To this extent, strings depend more heavily on the conductor's shaping of a phrase, adjusting of dynamic nuances, or even control of intonation, than other players in the orchestra. But what resources of sound, and of variety of sound, they can offer, if the conductor asks! Theirs is a neat arrangement of naturally divided skills: left hand for pitch, right arm for sound. And while undue variety on the left usually contributes to their oddly besetting sin of playing sharp and sharper at the top (is it because the natural overtones are closer together up there?), many a string rehearsal—and an enthralled section—could happily spend its loving attention on those rich resources of the right arm. To a large extent, phrasing, nuance, and sound itself are functions of the bow and bowings. Conductors who are not string players should let the concertmaster solve those problems; but one who can suggest a convincing, if not necessarily obvious, bowing solution to a difficult phrasing will have won instant respect.

There is another aspect of the string player's background that must be mentioned here, and that conductors with no experience as violinists, violists, or cellists will do well to remember: the music student playing a string instrument is more likely to think of himself as a soloist, while his colleagues studying wind, brass, or percussion instruments are consciously preparing themselves for an orchestral career. The situation has changed since the author's conservatory days, when a gifted violinist did have a chance to succeed as a recitalist and concerto soloist, supplementing that income with "a little teaching." Todays prospective teacher is likely to be a prospective orchestral musician as well, and he knows it. But his student days are nonetheless occupied with the string literature—sonatas, concertos, chamber music—all of which will make him a better musician as an individual.

A string player's training does not encompass his eventual role as member of a team in which his musical judgment must be sublimated to the collective achievement. Paradoxically, his fellow student playing the oboe, and practicing orchestral excerpts from the moment he can read them, will have a good deal more freedom as interpreter of his orchestral solos when he lands an orchestra job. But for most violinists, and particularly the most sensitive among them, the discipline of being a section player is painful at first. For the love affair with that fiddle still goes on in the player's heart; ask him what kind of violin he plays, or the make of his bow, and he will quickly accord you the benefit of the doubt as a possibly sentient being, even though a conductor.

Once the shock of being only a small cog in the elaborate gear of a string section has worn off, and the importance of being indistinguishable from the other cogs in one's particular wheel has sunk in, the violinist, violist, or cellist has the full advantage of his solo training: While his function is to conform, his mind and his trained musical perception enable him to follow the "action." And the constant challenge of new directions from the podium in familiar pieces involve him more closely in the why and wherefore of an interpretation than most of his colleagues in other parts of the orchestra. Add to this the sometimes forgotten fact that in much of the standard orchestral repertory the strings have the most continuous playing assignment, and their lot is not such a bad one after all.

String sections have a curiously consistent makeup in most orchestras. At the front, and on the outside, are the best players. In the back are the young ones—nearly as good, not as experienced, eager; sometimes difficult. And in between there is likely to be (depending on the orchestra's contract) a concentration of older players who have not advanced from the back into the front desks. They are among the most experienced, and often the most impatient when it comes to rerehearsing a work they know well. Unless the conductor has the musical authority and the personal persuasion to insure at least their acquiescence while tempos, bowings, and fingerings are adjusted, trouble is likely to arise from that quarter. Because of the numbers involved, this situation applies mainly to the violins—usually about three times the number of violas or cellos, and therefore a more clearly noticeable stratification of elite / solid, middle ground / young, new. It is probably accurate to say that the quality of an orchestra's string section is equivalent to that of the "middle group" of its violins. Only the handful of our very best orchestras can boast of nearly uniform quality. One of the great concert masters of our time, Joseph Silverstein of the Boston Symphony, complained rightly that "it takes only one to play between the notes." Lesser orchestras and concertmasters, as well as nearly every conductor who travels, must face the need of hiding, inspiring, or terrifying a good many more players than that one, in order to achieve an acceptable performance without noise "between the notes."

Two string players share a stand and a folder of music for each program. Unlike wind and brass players sitting side by side, the strings depend on their stand partners for small but important services in order to function efficiently. Since in much of the repertory a violinist plays without stop, someone has to turn the pages. In order to avoid a breakdown of continuity, it is customary for the player on the inside of each stand to take care of the task. Less rigidly ritualized is the responsibility for making and erasing markings. The more experienced of the two will undertake this, but it is important that *somebody* does. Nothing is more destructive to section discipline than bowings that are still not uniform once a passage has been rehearsed and established. In the end, either the conductor or his concertmaster will have to make an issue of something which reduces the rehearsal to something less than it should be, and the professional relationship to that of a schoolmaster with an unruly class. Good rehearsals may well depend on a lot of erasing and careful marking. Suggestions by an imaginative and fastidious conductor will require that much of his particular phrasing be spelled out in appropriate bowings, and sometimes fingerings. The eventual result may be greatly helped by verbal reminders of his musical decisions.

A final word about the concertmaster: He or she is the conductor's principal liaison to the string section, and his relationship with this player will determine his relationship with all others. Clearly such a relationship should rest on mutual respect, and such respect, in order to be effective, must not only exist but be *seen* to exist. Even conductors with impeccable credentials as string players in their own right are well advised to defer to their concertmaster on matters of bowings or, if they feel strongly, to discuss their differences away from the rehearsal.

String players are private persons as well, among the most private in the orchestra. Perhaps because they do not ever emerge as individuals in concert, they are the great hobbyists, the gardeners, and the nucleus of the poker-playing crowd in most orchestras. As one member of the fraternity put it to the author, "We are the most normal guys in the orchestra. Except for talent, you can't tell us from suburban commuters anywhere."

Talent *and practicing*. From concertmaster to rawest recruit, there are no days off for any of them. The technical proficiency expected of today's orchestral musician is based on many years of daily conditioning; and instrumentalists—more and more of whom are now working on 52-week contracts each year—cannot afford the luxury of "spring training" which seems sufficient to keep major sports teams in shape. The professional discipline reflected in this way of life is ingrained from childhood, nurtured through the distractions of adolescence, brought into clear focus during conservatory years, and continued by successful job placements over dozens of competitors. Orchestral rehearsal time is so precious that little of it can be spent on the learning of notes. The most cynical and difficult orchestral musician will not excuse a colleague who does not measure up to the standards of playing ability in the orchestra itself. What may seem to other members of the orchestra "the most normal guys" could be considered, especially by conductors, the most extraordinarily motivated and devoted musicians.

Double-bass players alone among the strings do not have to go through a period of adjustment to the fact that the symphony orchestra is their natural professional habitat. While there are some exceptions, a solo career is not something the average bassist has ever seriously considered. His whole background as student and young professional does not differ in orientation and early effort from that of a brass player. He will practice the bass solo literature (which with modern playing standards includes a good deal of cello music), but he knows that his future is likely to lie with the orchestral excerpts with which he will audition some day. Conductors, on the other hand (and some very experienced professionals among them), often fail to recognize the crucial function of the bass section within an orchestra: together with tuba and bassoons, the double basses provide the bass of the *music* most of the time, and thus hold the key to the vexing problem of intonation. Orchestras tune to the oboe, but they will *play* in tune to the bass line. The best players know that, and it is part of the conductor's job to school the others and, if necessary, himself, to listen from the bass up.

The magic words *listening* and *intonation* bring us to the wind section. Both subjects are of great concern to good players and can become sources of frustration, anger, and near paranoia among the winds. Each wind player is responsible for every note he plays and for the way it relates, at that moment, to other notes in the orchestra. If a chord is out of tune, it is impossible for *anyone* to sound in tune.

Given adequate facility on his instrument, the wind player has a life-long, absorbing concern with four aspects of his craft: articulation, sound, phrasing, and intonation. While all these are general problems of performance for any musician, and of equal concern to a string player, the nature of a wind player's role in the orchestra make his contribution more individually conspicuous to conductors. At the same time, his own preferences in these areas of musical performance will influence his initial response to direction more significantly than that of his string counterparts. Add to this that the instrument he plays is not as uniformly voiced as a violin, and that the general timbres of woodwind instruments are far less homogeneous within the whole section than those of the strings, and one can quite easily appreciate the difference in approach and attitude demanded of both player and conductor.

Take articulation: even the most basic expectation by any condutor, with any orchestra, will include wind attacks that are clean, i.e. coincide precisely with those of other participants in the chord of which they are a part. (*N.B.* Simultaneous *releases*, alas, are too often part of that cloudy middle ground of chance which, albeit within technical reach of any group, is permitted, by carelessness on the podium, to mar many a potentially fine performance.) These are virtues to be taken for granted with most orchestras under a competent conductor. Whether that attack, however, should have the sharp, sibilant articulation of the consonant "t," or the more resonant, percussive quality of "d," is a matter of decision. Most experienced sections, having played together over the years, will prefer one or the other as a matter of style, and favor its use unless otherwise directed. It is what happens between tutti attacks that concerns the solo player. The variety of articulation possible within a single phrase, the consummate skill required to meet the dictates of speed and score as laid down by the man on the podium, are an expected part of a wind player's daily challenge. Conductors who appear indifferent to this consideraton or clumsy in their suggestions may expect a rough ride from the wind section.

There are many aspects of the always fascinating problem of sound which are particularly vexing to wind players. As we have already said, the timbre of each wind instrument is different and distinct from the others. The composer has taken this into account, and will have written for the oboe with its particular sonority and resonance in mind. To make

the sound of all oboes match the others in the section, and to determine
whether, within possible limits, that sound should be dark or bright,
is one part of orchestral training. Naturally, as a guest conductor, one
is not likely to attempt upsetting the clear preference and conditioning
of a disciplined section. But with more frequent contact, any orchestra
will begin to look for guidance from the podium, if only through an
occasional suggestion. The less disciplined the section, the more such
hints are likely to be appreciated, for many good players spend their
working days in frustrated attempts to improve matters which could
more easily be mended by clear directives from the person in charge.

Almost any player will put everything he has into the performance of
a solo phrase, even at rehearsal. Given a good relationship with the
conductor, he may welcome a suggestion on its shaping or articulation.
But to criticize his sound is to humiliate him in front of his colleagues.
The utmost tact is required, and the most transparent circumlocution
will be appreciated.

More than tact is required of the conductor when it comes to the
phrasing of solo passages. Here he becomes truly the coach, the one
whose ideas on *how* the music is to be executed, its shape, its shading,
the relative prominence of certain strands in the musical fabric, are to
be realized as faithfully as possible. So many variables go into the shaping of a phrase—tempo, overall style of a particular performance, the
way the preceding phrase was played—that both player and conductor
must be flexible and perceptive. Endless care and prodigious concern
with detail go into each successful execution of an important phrase.
The soloist must emerge from the surrounding ensemble and submerge
in the end; he must carry the musical burden of being the temporary
focus of attention but match the sound and the dynamic framework
within which he makes his contribution; and he knows, his colleagues
know, and the conductor should know, that every detail of his phrase,
from articulation to the right amount of rubato, will affect what is to
come and reflect what went before. Small wonder that the subject tends
to become almost an obsession with good wind players. They place
their self-respect as artists, and sometimes their jobs, on the line.

Far less fluid, but at least equally difficult to manage, is the matter of
woodwind intonation. Wind players have a real problem here, and they
know it. Given some encouragement, they will try to do something about
it, but the question of who should do what is not always easy to determine. It takes not only a good ear, but also experience, to supply a valid
answer from the podium—little hand signals, up or down, are usually
all that time and the continuity of a rehearsal permit; but these signals
must be directed at the right person, and they must be accurate! Wind
instruments are not built "in tune." By judicious lengthening or short-
ening of the instrument's barrel, the tube which determines the dis-

tance between the source of vibration and the exits for the vibrating column of air, the overall tuning of a wind instrument can be adjusted. The pitch of each note can then be "lipped" up or down while the player performs. This is necessary, not only to play in tune with others, but to accommodate certain built-in intonation flaws within each instrument.

Speaking very generally, the flute plays flat in its lower octave, sharp on top. Oboe and bassoon have the same problem to a lesser extent. The clarinet is designed with a slightly sharp bottom register in order to allow the twelfths to be in tune. All winds tend to sharpen in crescendos, and rising room temperature (as well as the warming of the instrument itself as the player's breath continues to flow through it) will also raise the pitch quite perceptibly. All these factors engage a player's attention, but even the best and most experienced controls only his own pitch. Careful tuning at the beginning of each session of a rehearsal helps. But the already mentioned rising of the pitch as the instruments warm up can amount to a quarter tone in some cases, less in others. As a passing note of further confusion, strings contract (i.e. rise in pitch) with *cold*. Good intonation is relative, and good wind sections are trained, by good conductors, to relate their pitch to the bass. Overall orientation, therefore, is from the bassoons to the double basses, with all harmonic happenings built upon that platform. Young conductors can practice the kind of ear training most neglected in our music schools by listening to all performances, their own as well as those of other orchestras with jaundiced ears. It is barely a beginning to say that a certain chord is out of tune; it is the beginning of a skill which perhaps more than any other will win any orchestra's respect when one learns to identify a source of bad intonation, and eventually to know, in an instant, whether one's left hand should make a suggestion to that player to adjust upward or down. Like solfeggio, it is a knack more congenial to some than to others. But it is an essential ability for any conductor, and it can be developed with consistent practice.

French horn players are in a class by themselves. Like woodwind players, they have important solos. Like the brass, they strive for a coherent sound as a group. Unlike either, they tend to have problems of attack (the embarrassing burbling sound which mars many a beautifully executed solo) whenever concentration on embouchure wavers for a moment. From the conductor's point of view, the function perhaps most often neglected in the horn section is a matching of basic tone qualities between woodwinds and horns. This includes a reasonable adaptation not only of volume, but also of sound quality. Obviously this basic quality may vary from composer to composer, and between various styles, in such characteristics as a brighter or a richer, darker sound. And the question of vibrato must be resolved in terms of the whole group, albeit with proper allowances for instrumental differences: Vibrato applied on a scale appropriate to a bassoon would make a French horn sound like a badly played saxophone. As in other aspects of conducting, it is more a matter of discovering, supporting, and blending strengths within the orchestra than of the arbitrary pursuit of preconceived notions. But notions, and their judicious and logical pursuit, are nonetheless one of the more acceptable reasons for having a conductor, from the players' point of view. And, also from their point of view, some of these notions should be concerned with aspects of performance which are constantly in the forefront of their daily efforts. Matching tone qualities, articulation, intonation, and phrasing are close to woodwind and horn players' hearts. A conductor who can really cope with these problems and make the section sound better is more likely to enlist cooperation—and get it—when it comes to realizing musical objectives which may seem more esoteric to the orchestra.

Sound is the operative word with the brass. One might well paraphrase Sir Thomas Beecham's description of his countrymen by stating that what brass players enjoy about music is the kind of noise it makes. The emphasis here should be equally divided between noise and a certain kind of noise, for although a fine brass section will concede nothing to the winds when it comes to establishing "their" particular quality of sound, they are nonetheless conscious of the fact that theirs is the powerhouse of the orchestra. Secure in that knowledge, most brass sections will be content to "speak softly and carry a big stick." But somewhere, sometime in an evening of performance, they would like to shine in their full glory of golden sound.

There are many areas of characteristic performance quality which the brass section shares with the strings, all based on the fact that during long stretches of the music brass players will play a collectively supporting role in which the overall sound should be as uniform as possible. At other times, important solo passages will make demands on the brass which are more akin to what we have described as the normal role of the winds. There is one aspect of playing in the brass section of an orchestra in which an extramusical problem combines with an instrumental difficulty to the frequent, mutual exasperation of player and conductor: In virtually all seating arrangements of modern symphony orchestras the brass is placed at the furthest distance on stage from the man on the podium. Add to that the fact that the trombone and tuba naturally "speak" slowly, and the frequent time lag in entrances of the low brass—clearly a function of these two disadvantages—is only part of a more general difficulty. No matter how well disciplined within itself, or how splendidly responsive to the sweeping gesture, it is hard to fit the brass section into the very precise clockwork of a complex orchestral ensemble without constant vigilance that *internal section discipline* does not become *separate discipline* within the orchestra. Better to sacrifice some of the sweep and conductorial choreography which admittedly tempts us all at the very moments when the players have greater need to listen than to watch. And the brass, like the back stands of strings, tend to be more responsive to the conductor's eyes on them than to the theatrical threat of an outflung arm.

But the problem of communicating at that distance is real. A sotto voce remark to the first oboe will carry over an orchestral tutti, but whatever may need to be said to the brass means a shout or a halt in the rehearsal. Being shouted at, dramatically pointed at, or the cause of repeated interruptions of the rehearsal is bound to affect a fine section like pulling the reins too hard, too often, to control a good horse.

The brass section of a fine orchestra knows its strength, its maximum collective sound both in terms of balance and of the hall in which it usually performs. A wise conductor will determine almost at once whether he is getting full "concert" sound, whether the section is pacing itself carefully in a work they do not yet know, or whether he is being tested for his expertise as a "pacer" himself. For his role vis-à-vis the brass has something in common with that of a good athletic coach: The physical strain of rehearsing a work with heavy brass orchestration is always a factor to be reckoned with. The best coach, in the eyes of the section, is one who can lead them through the entire sequence from first rehearsal through performance with pacing that will not require artificial scaling down of their playing in order to keep them in shape for the performance. The strain on lips, wind, back, and stomach muscles must be tested at some stage, if the work is a new one to the orchestra, or the conductor's particular demands are likely to impose new pressures on the section which can only be tried in a full "run" of the work. But in the vast majority of cases a setting of the levels, and a careful rehearsal of important solos and connections within the ensemble, should achieve better results than repeated readings at full blast. More of this in our chapter on rehearsal.

The brass section, like the woodwinds, is bound to have its stars. With the physical distance between podium and brass in mind, we are particularly well advised to treat key players in that section with the visible respect and consideration they deserve. All our communications being very public, both parties are interested in an amicable exchange. But in a test of mutual rancour, any popular brass player, choosing his moment for a necessarily loud and intentionally embarrassing question, is in a strong position. And whatever the merits of a particular incident may be, a conductor's previously insensitive and perhaps amateurish treatment of the brass as players will have its effect on the whole orchestra.

All of which is even more true of the percussion. From a rather subsidiary role in most symphonic scores even a century ago, the scope of

instruments used, and the skill expected of the performers, has grown
enormously. What distinguishes the percussion player, in this respect,
from other instrumentalists in the orchestra, is the fact that, with some
allowances for specialization, every percussionist plays all percussion
instruments. The knack of producing an even pianissimo roll on the
snare drum, or carefully graduated cymbal strokes in a crescendo from
very soft to very loud, or a reliable thumb roll on the tambourine, require
consistent practice. The pyrotechnics expected on keyboard percussion
instruments, from the xylophone to the marimba, extends routinely over
the borderline of virtuoso performance; and the choice of mallets alone
is a bewildering matter into which the less-than-expert conductor should
enter with the same caution he would use in discussing oboe reeds.
While not every percussion player aspires to the position of timpanist
(the only member of the section who will rarely alternate on other
instruments), every timpanist is likely to have begun his career as a section player. Like most instrumentalists, percussion players are as much
involved with the instruments they play as with the playing itself. Unlike
other orchestra members, many of them also become designers and
builders of percussion instruments. Since many modern scores demand
unusual manipulation and carefully planned distribution of whichever
instruments are assigned, prerehearsal conferences between percussion
players and conductor are more common than with other sections. Even
in older scores, the sound of a triangle or the size of cymbals must be
predetermined to enable the player to produce the desired effect. Again,
as with the brass, all communication during rehearsal is conducted at a
distance and is, by nature, a public event witnessed by a bored (or
worse: enthralled) orchestra.

Harpists complain that most conductors know very little about their
instrument, and they are right. Their lot is not improved by the additional fact that most composers (including Wagner and Strauss, according to Carlos Salzedo) require sympathetic translation of the harp parts
into something more idiomatic to the instrument. Sight reading on the
harp is virtually impossible, since an often complicated game plan of
pedaling must be laid out in advance, so that the right strings are available on the needed succession of pitches. In this area, harpists throughout the world seem to work on the courteous principle that they will
not bother the conductor unless he bothers them.

Professional orchestras are organized in two ways: According to their
musical function, and in relation to the job interests of the musicians.
The first is shared by student and amateur orchestras as well, and various adaptations of the second sometimes are adopted by nonprofessional or semiprofessional organizations. Naturally, it is the first which
concerns us most in the context of our study; but the job orientation of

the musician, and in particular its effect on working arrangements within the orchestra, must also be dealt with.

Musically, orchestras all over the world are set up on a system of delegated authority throughout their sections. The string section, being the largest in number and composed of players of four kinds of string instruments divided into five sections (two violin sections, viola, cello, and bass), is headed by a violinist with overall responsibility for the entire group, the concertmaster. We have already touched on his role, and shall return to this subject in the following chapter dealing with some specific aspects of the working relationship between conductor and members of the orchestra.

Leaders of all other sections, including strings other than the first violin, are called principals. Titles of associate principal, coprincipal, or, in the case of the first violins, assistant concertmaster, are either ceremonial, or (when they do affect the contractual arrangements with the musician) may mean a nearly interchangeable position with that of the first principals, depending on the sections' musical and numerical strength and, if possible, on the conductor's judgment. This last, conditional reservation falls under the second of the organizational schemes mentioned above and allows us a little glimpse into areas where the two may indeed overlap.

While it is the conductor's privilege to address himself to any member of the orchestra and to expect instant cooperation, it is very bad form to go over the head of any section principal in remarks or suggestions which are not intended to correct a fault on the part of the addressed player *alone*. A string player in the back of the section may well be taken to task if his bowing varies from that of the whole group. But the conductor should not engage in a discussion of this overall bowing without deferring courteously and publicly to the section principal and, if appropriate, the concertmaster. As with all conventions, actual use depends to a great extent on specific circumstances. It is to be expected, for instance, that in case of a discrepancy in printed articulation between the first and second trumpet, the principal will ask the conductor about his preference. But if players and conductors have worked together repeatedly and are sufficiently comfortable with each other, there is no reason whatever why ceremony should not be discarded in these little ways, provided we keep a wary eye out for signs of trouble. Experienced orchestral players will be watching us in the same spirit.

The orchestra is represented by committee which, as elected representatives of the whole group, deal with matters of mutual concern—usually not directly with the conductor, but with the personnel manager (also an orchestra member, but appointed by management). This is part of the second area of organization within an orchestra, the one which concerns the musicians' interests as employees. Contrary to general misconception, only a relatively small part of this concern has to do with wages, or with the union contract which is printed and distributed to each member of the orchestra when it is negotiated. Musicians are certainly as interested in the safeguards bearing on their livelihood as any other wage earners. But their motivation is probably a great deal stronger when it comes to insuring the quality of their joint product. As many of the strictly enforced rules have to do with musicians' duties and responsibilities as are designed to protect their job security. Inevitably, there comes a point where the two concerns may be in conflict. But it is fair to say that orchestral players have a collective stake in the manufacture, selection, marketing, and sales of a quality product. Their very real concern is less esoteric than what they suspect the conductor's to be; and any conductor must be prepared to meet the *players'* standards of quality before he may count on the full cooperation of his orchestra.

A few additional words concerning the musicians' personal and professional aspirations: their hopes are not only determined by the conditions within the orchestra and the proficiency and expertise of their conductor. They know well that their fortunes are bound up with the state of our profession, and that conditions over which neither they nor management have any control determine their economic and professional future. There are two assurances which any young musician would like to have: reasonable job security, once he has been accepted in an orchestra, and a reasonable chance at promotion within the field itself. Almost all orchestral contracts with the musicians' union have standard, industry-wide protection clauses which, following a period of probation, go far towards meeting a player's requirements for job security. Upward mobility is another matter. Unless he has had the good fortune to gain admission to one of the top orchestras at a very young age, his chances for significant improvement of his status depend on his passing an audition for a vacancy in one of the next-higher-ranked orchestras. A second oboist will certainly have the chance to audition for the post of principal, should that vacancy occur within his own organization. He is not likely to get it. The job will probably go to an applicant from outside with experience as first oboe in an orchestra of comparable standing, or it might be given to a second oboist from a substantially superior orchestra. In order to get into that queue, the young player must leave his hard-won post as soon as possible, for there is yet another fact of professional life with which he must reckon: as an unspoken but nonetheless real condition of employment with top orchestras, age plays an important part. The great orchestras rarely engage new members over the age of thirty-five. Statistically, the average age of recruits is very far below that. Even if a young player's ambition will be well satisfied with an eventual principal post in an orchestra just below world class, he must either be prodigy enough to convince the auditioning conductor and orchestra committee of his outstanding merits practically fresh out of school (and this does indeed happen, even in top orchestras); or he must acquire a fine service record in a very fine orchestra, early enough, to compete with hopes of success for the first desk of an orchestra just below that in reputation and budget. The resulting turnover among younger and gifted players in most orchestras is a matter of major concern to the conductor responsible for the orchestra's training and stability. Here, as in the more self-evident areas of instrumental performance we discussed earlier, it is in his own as well as the orchestra's interest that the conductor respect the point of view of his best and most valuable players—not as a bid for personal popularity, but as part of a realistic policy in achieving his artistic goals.

Clearly, conductor and orchestra may pursue their common objective in separate ways and from different points of departure. A small autobiographical example from a rehearsal of Mahler's *First Symphony*, may illustrate the point. When we came to the famous double-bass solo at the beginning of the mock funeral march, the principal bass player made it sound as smooth and rich as if it were played by a first-class solo cellist. Knowing what years of work and what pride of artistry would have gone into achieving such a performance, the author said nothing in rehearsal. Had it been technically conceivable, in Mahler's time, to produce such lushness of sound in that register of the double bass, he would most certainly have chosen another instrument to begin the march. Having known the player during several years of work as guest conductor with his orchestra, the author shared his views with him at intermission. It came as no surprise that this fine musician quite agreed with him and thanked him, of course, for not pressing the point in front of his colleagues. He added wistfully: "If only Mahler had written a second bass solo in this symphony! As it is, most of the audience would think that's my sound, if I played it your way." With mutual expressions of sympathetic appreciation the matter was dropped. But it was with a warm thrill of real admiration, on the night of performance, that one's unbelieving ears registered the whining sounds of a thin, straining bass solo; and one's eyes and heart rejoiced in the sight of that marvelous artist's great beaming face.

Under less positive circumstances, with a less-established performer in a lesser orchestra, there might not have been a mutually satisfactory solution. One might have insisted right away—and lost something else. It is for the conductor to decide; and in his musical judgment he must not only weigh the extent and limitations of what is possible on the instruments, but the legitimate point of view of the musicians who play them. This is where theory leaves off and conducting begins.

15

ORCHESTRA AND CONDUCTOR

A working relationship is described, as
well as some of the working conditions
under which partly divergent interests
serve a common artistic goal.

THE orchestra as a musical instrument is subject to social change.
Its members, its conductors, and its audience live in a wider world and
are as affected by changing conditions and attitudes within this wider
world as are schools, places of business, and institutions of government. Naturally, these changes of attitude and expectations must be
reflected in the changing attitudes and expectations of young conductors in training. Fortunately, students in their daily contacts with the
real world of part-time employment and auditions for summer jobs tend
to be more aware of a new sense of partnership between orchestra and
conductor than some of their teachers. We shall try to outline some of
the major areas of change in the orchestra–conductor relationship, always
remembering that while there has been some modification in the forms
and customs of behavior at rehearsals, the conductor's overall function
has remained the same.

At the outset, it is important to note that almost nothing in the relationship between conductor and orchestra is new in itself. Many conductors, for many years, have enjoyed the positive and flexible approach
which recognizes the orchestra's participatory role not only as a social
right but as a musical asset. What is new is that, whether he realizes it
or not, the "maestro" is dead. And since it was just this part of the
conductor's image that received the widest publicity during past
decades, we might well begin by examining the *stereotype of the conductor* as an absolute, irrational, and terrifying authority figure. By
almost exact inversion, this should give us a remarkably strong start on
our way to understanding what orchestras look for and what, in recog-

nizing their reasonable expectations, we should be prepared to give them.

Orchestras of world class employ some of the foremost intrumentalists of our time. Even major orchestras of the second rank can usually boast a majority of outstanding players, and standards of proficiency and expertise rise with every audition. For every vacancy there are many applicants. For every choice among finalists there are likely to be half a dozen overqualified alternates. As a group, the modern symphony orchestra has its equivalent in professional expertise among the medical teams of great hospitals or the star-studded rosters of major sports teams.

Enter the conductor. Even in a guest appearance with an orchestra, he *has very real powers*. No matter how expert the solo horn, how uniform in bowing style the strings, how carefully blended the brass, all this remains true only with the concurrence of the person on the podium. He can demand that the principal hornist prove himself yet again in new phrasings, ask for radical changes in the amount of bow used by the violinists, and upset the balance of trumpets and trombones. Giving him the benefit of much doubt, all concerned will work very hard until results are achieved that may compare in quality of sound with what was available before the person on the podium demanded these changes. The final product may well justify the upheaval; but if the maestro added his own sense of impatience to the proceedings before his aims were clear, he will surely have carved another notch in the orchestra's scoreboard of irrational behavior up front. If, on the other hand, he went to great lengths in explaining his objectives, he would have been damned as a professorial bore. And if, in the end, it were to have appeared that his changes served only some purposes of conductorial self-assertion, he would have lost the orchestra's cooperation.

"All of us do our best just to make you look good!" was a retort by an angry player at a very uncomfortable rehearsal under one of the author's more aggressive students. The remark, though rarely quite true, should be engraved on every conducting stand—perhaps together with another by the concertmaster of a great orchestra: "We'll play well for any one, better than he deserves, as long as he doesn't come on strong."

Any performer's effectiveness is measured in terms of performance. There are intelligent instrumentalists of adequate technical proficiency and preparation who somehow fail to communicate in concert. There are others whose actual playing ability is far surpassed by their powerful and effective projection to an audience. There are singers endowed with a vocal prowess so gloriously persuasive that the sensual pleasure in listening to beautifully produced sounds can outweigh musical flaws and indifferent preparation. And there are also brilliant and conscientious musicians with fleet fingers and moving insights who play too many wrong notes. In all cases the moment of truth is what the audience hears. With conductors, on the other hand, there is the question of what rehearsals are like, a question that can have a telling effect on the performance. There is an essential difference between the cumulative effect of practice sessions on a solo performer's recital and the results of rehearsal achievements, musical and personal, in terms of orchestral concerts. The orchestra itself and the conductor's relationship with it make the difference. Any good orchestra can raise a reasonably good job on the podium to greater heights in performance; or, failing a productive rapport, may also fail to translate into musical reality the conductor's more subtle interpretive insights. Much of the give and take between conductor and orchestra is determined, directly or indirectly, at rehearsal. Thus the rehearsal situation, more than the concert itself, is the ideal and exclusive setting for us to examine orchestra–conductor relationships.

It cannot be emphasized strongly enough that very little of this has to do with an orchestra's personal *likes* or *dislikes* of the person on the podium. Conducting is not a popularity contest. While a pleasant mediocrity is likely to be afforded a competent performance by supportive players, a demanding taskmaster may infuse the results of even painful rehearsals with just that inspired responsiveness in concert that can only be had at the price of making everyone strain to grasp what lies beyond the comfortable reach of all. But while the margin of safety may thus be wider for the indulgent tyro on the podium than for an equivalent individual performer, the risk for the conductor who has inflicted some discomfort in order to achieve a real performance is greater: if, in the test of performance, he should *fail* to justify that remembered rehearsal pain, the orchestra is more than likely to close ranks against him in retaliation for his (real or assumed) responsibility for *their* failure. So much for the hazards of leadership—but we are getting ahead of our story.

Successful musicians are clock watchers in the very best sense of the word. From childhood, the value of the weekly lesson-hour has been impressed on them. With growing experience in the good use of practice time, they have learned that time is precious, and efficient use of time brings rewards. Years before most of their contemporaries in other walks of life would learn that "time is money," they had to manage their time in order to achieve what money cannot buy—a good bow-arm, a secure embouchure, a soft, even snare-drum roll. Disciplined use of practice time had to be taken for granted by every member of the orchestra, long before he or she passed the audition.

It is strange, therefore, that many gifted and well-meaning young conductors approach an orchestra rehearsal as if it were a class for students who had to be "turned on." To say that an orchestra's first collective rehearsal requirement is that its time not be wasted (no matter how amusingly) would be a very safe statement. Playing time is working time; rehearsal time is working time, precious and limited. They have all learned to make good use of working time, and a good conductor is one who, in rehearsal, is able to show them how to use it to even better advantage. In the end, it is a matter of instinct, judgment, and experience—whether to "play through" or to "clean," whether to give a little time to every part of a program or to concentrate on important sections and connections. There are no safe rules. A veteran conductor will sometimes risk leaving some passages to chance in order to concentrate on shaping and identifying a few features important to the performance. If he miscalculates, he will lose the orchestra's confidence; but if, after having carefully judged the tolerances of mounting anxiety, he is successful, the unspoken verdict of "well steered" can transform courtesy to an honored guest into the rough affection of fellow veterans.

Nowhere do the interests of orchestra and management go more clearly hand in hand than in their common appreciation of a conductor who can make good use of rehearsal time. Time is money in the commercial orchestral world; and a conductor who produces reliable results with efficiency on the podium and without fuss, in the minimum number of rehearsals, is a great man to all concerned, always provided that the product in performance does not show the ravages of time lacking for its achievements—which is where our task becomes very complicated.

Whenever possible, some overall rehearsal objectives should be planned in advance. Since there are so many imponderables, our plans cannot be rigid—in fact, they must be reviewed and adjusted constantly, not only after the end of each rehearsal, but while the session is still in progress. With a framework of rehearsal sequence in mind, we shall then be in conscious charge of the concert preparation at all times. A relaxed sense of control contributes to that quiet working atmosphere which is far more productive in the long run than the most spectacular series of diverting mini-demonstrations from the podium. The occasional unexpected departure from predictable routine will then be the more effective.

The first thing to determine, and to post for the orchestra's benefit, is the general rehearsal order up to the concert. There are any number of theoretical objections to committing oneself to a definite sequence of works to be rehearsed, in advance; and the more specific the announced order (i.e. just what is to be rehearsed at what time), the more anxious some conductors seem to become. Actually the chances of having to change the posted list are not very great. There are only so many hours of rehearsal in which to rehearse so much music. Error of judgment involving all of the second half of a rehearsal, say, are rare. And in the event, changes can be announced, of course.

How do we start? Take the sum of available minutes of rehearsal, and

the individual total minutes of playing time for each work on the program; assign an anticipated proportion of minutes of rehearsal time to
each work; and distribute this rehearsal time in various dosages
throughout the available rehearsal dates. You will be guided by considerations of the relative difficulty of the music, the orchestra's familiarity
with some of the works, your own intended emphasis on certain aspects
of these works in performance, as well as such possible further demonstration of your regard for the players' convenience as will be determined by the orchestration: There is no point in beginning with a score
for large orchestra, making a third of the wind and brass wait throughout the following rehearsal of a Classical symphony, and ending with
an orchestration similar to the one with which you began. The strengths
and weaknesses of the orchestra, as far as you know them, are also a
major factor in determining the rehearsal order. Some very experienced
orchestras have little occasion to read new music and are not very good
at it. Or a work on your program may have been played recently under
a very good, or very bad conductor—always a tricky situation, but at
least the notes should be there. Or, most delicate of cases, the orchestra
may consider a piece, or even a composer's whole opus, their special
property. Finding himself trapped in such a situation (for only the un-
knowing, the unwary, or the very great would actually have chosen to
be in it), the rehearsal order would either reflect the conductor's intention to rehearse the work as little as he dares, hoping that the orchestra
will appreciate the implied compliment and give their all in performance; or it will signal the conductor's brave and / or very foolish determination to make that piece, with that orchestra, his very own, and his
intention to devote extra time in the undoing of what are likely to be
beloved "traditions." In either case, we find a very real illustration of
the use of a posted rehearsal order as the first genuine and significant
contact between conductor and orchestra. Finally, there is the matter of
soloists who usually arrive for, and sometimes monopolize, the better
part of the dress rehearsal—not as bad an arrangement as it may seem,
since, by that time, the less the other rehearsed pieces are "performed"
once more, the more spontaneous and exciting their eventual performance is likely to be.

It is at this stage also, while we plot rehearsals and the relative portions of rehearsal time to be allotted to each work on our program, that
we must rely upon whatever our preparatory work beneath the musical
surface has impressed most strongly on our minds. Given comparable
conditions, for instance, and a good orchestra to work with, a rehearsal
schedule including Beethoven's *Seventh Symphony* would necessitate
long, uninterrupted stretches reflecting the waves of interaction between
our three protagonist keys,* and alerting the orchestra to whatever means

*Cf. p. 327.

we shall employ to illustrate that drama in performance. On the other hand, the significant shapes we found in the Poco allegretto movement of Brahms's *Third** or in Ravel's *La Valse*** would have to be worked out in more detailed rehearsals, provided for in the preliminary, posted plan. In none of these cases would we "explain" anything to the orchestra, in so many words; but we should carefully weigh the necessary time we are likely to need in establishing our particular plans for these scores by way of gesture (cf. Chapter 7), direct suggestion, and repetition.

Aside from the published rehearsal schedule, we shall try to establish a far more elaborate preliminary plan in our own minds. This unpublished estimate of anticipated progress, unlike the posted rehearsal order, is subject to constant change and revision as its goals are achieved either sooner or later than we thought, or as unexpected, overriding problems must be resolved. It is essentially a strategic battle plan according to which certain clearly defined objectives are to be realized in whatever preliminary order of priorities we may have determined. Adjustments, additions, or reductions in time spent on various details will depend on the situations encountered in rehearsal. The *general* outline tells us (and the participating orchestra) where we are in relation to where we intended to be when it was posted. Our *personal* "computer print-out" charts our course, checks our progress against objectives, and helps us determine what to do next.

Let us suppose that we are to conduct a program consisting of Mozart's *Symphony No. 32* in G (*Italian Overture*, 9 minutes), the Chopin *Piano Concerto in E minor* (33 minutes), and, after intermission, William Schuman's *New England Triptych* and Ravel's *La Valse* (ca. 13 minutes each). We shall also assume that the orchestra is a good one, but not one of the world's top twenty. The soloist will be of the first rank, experienced and pleasant to work with. Available rehearsal time: Four 2½-hour sessions, i.e. a total of ten rehearsal hours, including the dress. Our first step will be to assign 71 minutes of musical playing time in adequate proportions to the total of rehearsal time at our disposal. We begin by determining the minimum we think necessary for each work.

STEP I

Mozart (9')	—	75'	(1¼ hours)
Chopin (33') Orchestra only	—	45' ⎫	(2 hours)
With soloist	—	75' ⎭	
Schuman (13') Strings only	—	60' ⎫	(2¼ hours)
Tutti	—	75' ⎭	
Rehearsal Intermissions	—	4 × 15'	(1 hour)
Ravel (13') Balance remaining	—	210'	(3½ hours)
			(10 hours)

*Cf. pp. 257ff. **P. 76.

Even though *La Valse* (unless the orchestra knows it very well) will probably require most of the rehearsal time, the 3½ hours now remaining for Ravel seem excessive in proportion to the suggested minimum anticipated for the other works. A second tally brings the relationship more closely into line:

Mozart	—		1½ hours
Chopin	—	(same)	2 hours
Schuman	—	60'⎫ 90'⎭	2½ hours
Rehearsal Intermissions	—	(same)	1 hour
Ravel	—		3 hours
			10 hours

Our next step will be to distribute the total time available for each work in some productive manner over the four rehearsal periods. The pianist is expected only for the dress rehearsal. We therefore begin by assigning the first half of that session to him, thus allowing for an emergency extension of the time allotted to him (into the second half of the dress rehearsal). As we shall see, some flexibility with regard to the other pieces is reserved in the event that this extension should not be needed after all.

STEP II

Orchestration determines pairing of

Mozart (2202—2200—Timp.—Str.) with
Chopin (2222—4210—Timp.—Str.)

and of

Schuman (3342—4331—Timp., Perc.—Str.) with
Ravel (3333—4331—Timp., Perc., 2 Hps.—Str.)

In view of the fact that Schuman has some passages in the first and last movements which could very profitably be rehearsed by strings alone, and a middle movement for strings, oboe, bassoon, and drum, this score also could be rehearsed with the two works on the first half of the program. The following rehearsal plan would then suggest itself:

Rehearsal I Ravel	—	1¼ hours	(of 3)
Intermission			
Schuman			
	—	¼	(of 1)
	—	½	(of 2½)
	strings only, excerpts of 1st movement and Finale.		
Mozart	—	½	(of 1½)

Rehearsal II Ravel	—	1¼	(2½ of 3)
Intermission			
Schuman			
	—	¼	(½ of 1)
	—	½	(1 of 2½)

strings, oboe, bassoon, and drum for slow movement; repeat Rehearsal I excerpts, *strings only*.

Mozart	—	½	(1 of 1½)
Rehearsal III Schuman	—	¾	(1¾ of 2½)
Ravel			
Intermission			
Chopin			
	—	½	(3 of 3)
	—	¼	(¾ of 1)
	—	¾	(of 2)

Orchestral balances in tuttis (difficult!)

Mozart	—	¼	(1¼ of 1½)
Rehearsal IV Chopin	—	1¼	(2 of 2)
Intermission			
Schuman			
Reserve			

with pianist

	—	¼	(1 of 1)
	—	½	(2¼ of 2½)
	—	½	

The dress rehearsal (IV) is flexible. The reserve item could be used for the concerto, if necessary. On the other hand, the concerto may require less than the full first part of the rehearsal. Thus, key passages in Schuman and Ravel could be reviewed (a run-through of either work, on the day of performance, would not be advisable) or the Mozart symphony read and cleaned once more. *N.B.* An orchestra given the chance to take a little time off at the end of the dress rehearsal is likely to show its appreciation at the concert.

Step three, then, is posting a general rehearsal order based on the rehearsal plan. *N.B.* The second halves of Rehearsals I and II should be reversed, as mentioned above, if the full string section is used for the Mozart symphony.

STEP III

ORDER OF REHEARSAL
Rehearsal I   Ravel
                 Intermission
                 Schuman (strings only)
                 Mozart

Rehearsal II	Ravel
	Intermission
	Schuman (strings, oboe, bassoon, drum only)
	Mozart
Rehearsal III	Schuman
	Ravel
	Intermission
	Chopin
	Mozart
Rehearsal IV (Dress)	Chopin
	Intermission
	Schuman
	Ravel
	Mozart

The wording of the dress rehearsal order is such that all needed players would be available at whatever time any of the works following the concerto should be played, without further announcements.

A conductor's first audience is the orchestra. His performance for them is not confined to music, but includes his walk, his talk, his interest and concern in everything to do with upcoming concerts and their preparation. The rehearsal is a quickened kind of mirror in which orchestra and conductor see each other and react each to the other's image.

Rehearsals begin with the tuning of the orchestra, with the oboe A given at the ritual request of the concertmaster. This does not require the conductor's participation—in fact, many conductors insist that the orchestra be tuned before they mount the rostrum. But for some it can be a first declaration of their particular priorities in performance. If really playing in tune is to be a special feature of a rehearsal, or if the conductor should wish to impress his special concern with intonation upon an orchestra, then he may well wish to begin by enlarging on the tuning ceremony. The story is still told about the guest conductor of the New York Philharmonic who spent the first full hour of rehearsal tuning that famous orchestra. Needless to say, a hundred pairs of ears will inevitably become alert to the intonation problems of their peers and to the accuracy of the conductor's reactions. If he passes the test, he will have achieved at least grudging respect. If his judgment, however, was in the least debatable, he will have lost almost irretrievable ground and been considered presumptuous as well. But if he can sustain an initial impression as a conductor with ears, who did not mind putting his own image in the balance from the start, he may find himself music director of the orchestra he has thus impressed as guest—as happened to that conductor in New York.

First in our order of rehearsal is Ravel's *La Valse*. What the orchestra should now see—and hear—right away is an uninterrupted run-through. The subtle shapes of certain phrases which concerned us in an earlier chapter (cf. Musical Shapes, p. 255), the difficult ensemble problems and balances with which we shall have to deal throughout this music, should not worry us just now. First priority goes to the orchestra's initial impression of how we intend to play and pace this work, and what we beat, when, in order to manage various effects, rubatos, and climaxes.

It must be remembered, of course, that there are no rules of rehearsal to which there are not also exceptions; and that what applies to a normal rehearsal with a fine orchestra might be virtually impossible with a lesser group (although, again as a general rule only, an orchestra should not attempt to play what it cannot read, after a fashion at least, at sight); or what does indeed apply for a first rehearsal of a public concert might be inappropriate at a recording session, when common sense would argue for getting one section of the piece "into the can" before attempting the next. There are even national characteristics in the working habits and expectations of orchestras which, in this case, range from the English preference for "bashing through at first go," no matter what, to a fastidious passion for detail in German radio orchestras even during a first reading. Still, the fact remains that any orchestra would rather play than be interrupted, and that, at the beginning of a rehearsal series, it is helpful to develop a sense of orchestra and conductor playing together, before they each become involved in the other's unfolding detail.

At the conclusion of this run-through, we shall clear up any apparent misunderstandings about the beat (e.g. where do we "go into three" or "back to one," etc.). On the whole it is best to assume that one's beat is sufficiently clear to speak for itself, without further commentary. But in a work as rapidly and repeatedly changing in pace, and therefore in pattern, as *La Valse*, there is no onus in settling remaining questions. After that, it will be important to show that, far from finding the rough results of the reading satisfactory, we intend to "clean" the performance measure for measure, if necessary, before attempting another run-through. We shall have had a particularly tricky section in mind beforehand, and would now proceed to a very detailed, and even fussy, rehearsal, with special demands to be met by the maximum number of players. Right notes, rhythms, ensemble, musical shapes, and general balance—in a limited number of measures somewhere in the middle of the piece—should keep us occupied until intermission.

Schuman is next. Strings only. There are some difficult, high unison passages for the violins in all three movements, but it is the fugato of the first which really justifies a sectional rehearsal. The atmosphere will be a very different one from that of the first half. We shall have established whatever basic working relationship we are to have for the present. And the very fact of our having reduced the orchestra makes this half seem more like a practice session now than an orchestral rehearsal, more intimate and more businesslike.

This time we shall not start from the top or demonstrate the work as a whole. We have already chosen to specialize; and m. 153, the beginning of the fugato, is destined to conjure up a number of special rehearsal recollections in the players' minds when it finally appears in performance.

EXAMPLE 1: Schuman, *New England Triptych*, first movement, string passage, mm. 153–73

The difficulties of this passage are compounded by the very fast tempo. Until the notes fit comfortably under every one's fingers, it will be helpful to try it at a slower speed. But from the start we shall insist on the *sempre p*, about which the orchestra is likely to hear a good deal more, and which must last for fully forty measures. Fast and very soft must be the total impression. The initial entrances—cello, viola, first violin, second violin—are capriciously displaced, yet must sound neither sweaty nor strained as tag ends of the tune are tossed and caught between section and section. Something is bound to happen now which, as an example of conductor–orchestra interaction, shall serve as an excellent demonstration to remember. It is very simple and quite important: Because of the speed and displacement of the first entrances, we are going to look at the players of the sections being cued, of course (and remember: look at *someone*, preferably at the *back* of the section). At this rehearsal, while cues are still vital in themselves, this will be a matter of practical necessity, even with an experienced reading orchestra. If somebody happens to "play between the notes," sing the entire passage and, again, look at the sections (same person) which are supposed to enter. As the orchestra gains familiarity, we need cue no longer. In fact, we need not look either—but we shall. This is an instance of player and conductor being conditioned, during rehearsal, to take note of each other at certain points in performance. There are many different sorts of places where it may happen; our example is only a most obvious one. Another would be the beginning of an important solo, though it may well be that we will take note of the possibly tricky *accompaniment* of the solo. But there need be no particular rationale to it at all: a section which caused a stop in rehearsal, a funny mistake, a memorable comment (perhaps from a player)—any place at all at which eyes met and remembered. A repeated instance of the same eye contact in rehearsal will condition reflex in performance. If it should feel appropriate, a little smile, or a cautioningly raised eyebrow will recall and confirm a shared instant and will make for a heightened sense of participation for all concerned. Sometimes, in going over a score in one's mind just before performance time, it is useful to recall the exchanged glances and their associations along the route of memory—where, with whom? Places and images!*

There will not be time, at this rehearsal, to do more than the fugato and perhaps some of the high unisons in this movement and the finale. We shall leave the middle movement for the next session, to be rehearsed with its three solo instruments. But if the orchestra has shown signs of intonation trouble today, we shall make a mental note to be on special alert at the unison-octave tutti passage at mm. 39–42 in the second

---

*Cf. Time and Memory, p. 383.

movement. This quiet note taking *before* action is called for, but in reasonable anticipation of what the future is likely to hold, will become an important part of your professional equipment as you gain experience and control. And now we should try to let the orchestra earn a sense of accomplishment by managing a final, *a tempo* run-through of the fugato—perhaps announce also that all future rehearsals will begin with this particular little virtuoso excerpt—and turn to Mozart.

This may be the moment to make a real demonstration of tuning and playing in tune. Since new players will join the remaining strings (i.e. the winds), a fresh A will be given. The opening of the symphony, with its unison tutti attack, should allow us to continue this line of emphasis beyond the actual tuning itself. Likely as not, the strings will be a little sharp, the winds not warmed up. Be sure that you're right; and if you are, make an issue of it now. Politely, maybe even a little apologetically, but make it, if it is to be made.

The Mozart rehearsal itself, during this last half hour, should be a pleasure. This is no longer a sectional practice session, nor the first contact with a very large virtuoso vehicle for orchestra, but probably the work every player has looked forward to. Start rehearsing. The opening gesture of a rock-hard, unison rhythmic "motto" with its declamatory and repeated ending is worlds away from its pleading continuation in the strings. Set that, and if it goes well, play on perhaps to the extraordinary long phrase in the middle section. With its preliminary shaping, the rehearsal will probably have come to an end, and everyone should now be left with a sense of beautiful things to come.

It is obviously impossible to predetermine what may happen at any rehearsal, and what we have described is fiction, but possible: the "idea" of a first rehearsal which one might well bring to the occasion as a point of departure. As in a game of chess, it is possible only to generalize about opening moves in a rehearsal sequence and about some "end plays" at the dress. What happens in between depends on a great many imponderables—the quality of the orchestra and the distribution of its strongest and weakest elements; the general morale of the players and their individual willingness to participate; the past relationship one may have developed with the orchestra and with some of its key members; to say nothing of even less predictable or constant factors from the heating or air-conditioning in the hall on any given morning or the nearness of union contract negotiations, to the popularity of one's predecessor a week ago. In all this we have tacitly assumed a situation in which the conductor has taken on a guest assignment with an orchestra new to him, at least from the perspective of the podium. Much of what determines professional success depends on one's ability to sustain the test of such situations, and the young conductor will certainly begin his career in this capacity.

Situations which would call for a radically different approach (e.g. continuing work with an orchestra of one's own or a series of commercial recording sessions) would probably involve an experienced conductor after some years of developing his own style. Pioneer situations with an orchestra less capable than that which we stipulated would not really call for a basically different approach, just for more available time in the follow-up. Such organizations, depending at least in part on nonprofessional membership, must rehearse in the evenings. And most players who work at their regular occupations during the day cannot afford more than one or two nights each week for orchestral rehearsals. Aside from reading and playing ability, which, collectively, would probably be on a less proficient level than was the case with our ficticious group above, the hiatus between rehearsals would call for more repetition of ground covered the week before, so that, for various reasons, the primary difference should be an increased number of rehearsals. The opening rehearsal itself, however (barring reading problems which, as we have said, would have mitigated against our choice of program in the first place), could probably have been planned and conducted, with good results, along the lines we described.

The second rehearsal often means trouble, often because a fine beginning was not followed by a measurable improvement. Whatever initial good will and mutual curiosity benefited the first rehearsal may have been spent for the time being. The pressure of imminent performance, on the other hand, is not yet in evidence. Momentum will therefore depend very much on whatever force we may be able to exert effectively from the rostrum. Second rehearsals, at least at the start, should match the more sober mood of the occasion. Conductors as well as the orchestra want to see solid results now. Technical problems must be solved rather than identified, and at least one major work on the program should be well on its way to being "finished." In our sequence, we are scheduled to devote the first half again to Ravel. Instead of starting with another run-through (without having thus far established our own musical demands except in one or two isolated instances toward the end of yesterday's rehearsal) we might do well to begin at the return of the Introduction (rehearsal number 54). Most of the material involving the intricate shapes that we discussed earlier will reappear in what is to follow; and the altered orchestration in the long Coda should give us a chance to work on the most difficult parts of the work first. When we have pushed through to the end, a request to start from the very beginning will suggest the possibility of another run-through before intermission. But unless the orchestra knows the work well and is now able to make adjustments to corresponding passages in the Exposition, on the basis of what has been rehearsed thus far, we would be well advised to begin a detailed working through of the opening as though it were indeed music which, by now, they *should* play better. If intermission time finds the orchestra a little discouraged by relentless insistence on detail, so be it. As we said: Conducting is not a popularity contest, and rehearsals are not occasions for demonstrating one's ability to "turn on" most participants most of the time. We have a definite objective, limited time in which to achieve it, and a professional mandate we must discharge. If necessary we must generate the pressure this will require. Provided we do not go too far, we shall have a lot of time left in which to ease the temporary burden.

Temporary relief may be granted after intermission in any event. A trial run of the first-movement fugato is likely to yield a surprisingly positive impression, either at first go or, if necessary, in an immediate repeat. The presence today of three players who were not at yesterday's workout (the three soloists for the slow movement) as a symbolic audience for this achievement is a plus. A sign of approval, depending on the conductor's personal style in such matters, may also be in order if things have really gone well. Otherwise a tough recapitulation of work on that section, as well as on yesterday's high unison passages, is essential. It is now or never. The slow movement will be enjoyed the more. Most of the actual rehearsing of it will probably be spent on intonation at the big unison place we already mentioned, the phrasing of the string orchestra canon to follow, and—for the first time in this rehearsal sequence—the achievement of a really rich, homogenous string sound (from the bass up!) at the *subito forte* passage (m. 163) toward the end. Proper sticks used by the drum, and the depth of the instrument to be used, could have been checked at intermission time. The wind solos, if appropriate, may receive a sign of appreciation—nothing else. Whatever problems might have been in evidence today will be worked on, for certain, by the wind players before the next rehearsal. They are likely to involve different reeds anyway. In any case, tomorrow will be better.

The concluding Mozart rehearsal will emphasize the "life is earnest" character of today's session in general. Details of bowing, phrasing, and articulation must be settled. A complete run-through is not necessary, and could be counterproductive. There may even be string passages which could do with a baleful injunction to practice. (*N.B.* This, however, should be employed only if the conductor's relationship to the players is comparable to that of a *maestro* in the literal meaning of the Italian word, i.e. teacher. If his professional standing and experience do not match the orchestra's reputation in the field, the general reaction is bound to be very negative, especially if the comment was deserved.)

Our third rehearsal features two novelties: A first full-orchestra rehearsal of Schuman and the tutti rehearsal (without soloist) of the piano concerto. With the strings now in fairly good condition, particularly in the difficult first movement, the addition of winds, brass, and percussion should see the work well into its final phase of preparation today. The brass will already have some notion of our ideas on section sound (light or dark, strident or mellow, brassy powerhouse or golden reserve) from the climactic moments of the Ravel score. Now it will have its chance to swagger and shine without being allowed to overpower the strings in shared passages. It will be important, by the way, that our consideration of their physical strain (e.g. following m. 225 in the opening movement) is balanced by the knowledge that—if the dress rehearsal is to be on the day of the concert—today is the last chance to play the work, full force and with repetitions of the loud passages, before it is heard in actual performance. The major part of the rehearsal's first part is therefore given over to the Schuman. The winds will enjoy the finale in particular (it is easier than it sounds), and the timpanist is likely to present us with his big cadenza leading into our string fugato with his most practiced virtuosity. In fact, one's guess would be that it will all come together now so quickly and so well that we might be tempted to neglect the prophylactic virtues of repetition. Several times over, for the difficult sections at speed, will pay off handsomely in the end.

For *La Valse*, today should be considered the dress rehearsal. Whatever weaknesses the run-through will reveal can be "cleaned," and a mental scoreboard can be started for use in actual dress rehearsal allocation of leftover time. Unlike the *Triptych* (which is to have another careful but understated recapitulation in any case), the Ravel score may go well enough so that the most profitable action with regard to it at dress rehearsal would be to leave it alone. A little productive nervousness on the players' part might then be just what is wanted to give it that extra momentum in performance. With this in mind, we must be very sure to pay meticulous attention to details today.

The same could be true of the Mozart symphony when we get to it later. Although in its case there is no consideration of physical strain before performance, the playing may well come into its own today, so that, given an otherwise tight dress rehearsal schedule (and with a soloist on the program it could go either way), we might be able to dispense with a final warm-up reading. Still, and for no very compelling reason the author could inject into this entirely conjectural situation, it would "feel" best to give this lovely piece at least a "standby reservation" for the last quarter hour of the forthcoming dress rehearsal. Certainly it would then be well in mind and better in hand when it opens the evening's concert.

The closer we come to the performance the more apparent will be our concern with the choices in the use of remaining rehearsal time. Throughout this third rehearsal the thought of ensuring flexibility for the dress has accompanied almost every decision. Freedom of choice in our initial planning has gradually given way to an awareness of the narrowing funnel of remaining time through which we must arrive at the concert. A partially predictable performance is emerging as we work. The one remaining unknown, and a major reason for safeguarding flexibility in the allocation of time for the final rehearsal, is the soloist.

A chapter in itself could be devoted to the soloist–conductor working relationship. In a way the soloist has an enormous advantage over the conductor. He is by definition a "visiting fireman," a guest; he is by trade a superb instrumentalist, and thus assured of a very direct appeal to the players; and, no less important, he is a privileged person on stage without being in authority; in fact, he is a counterbalance to the authority figure on the podium. These days, even small orchestras engage big soloists. And for the young conductor there is the additional handicap that most soloists with whom he is likely to work may enjoy a wider reputation than his own. Thus, in addition to presenting problems of strictly musical compatibility and collaboration, the appearance of the soloist at the end of a rehearsal sequence affects the conductor's own relationship with the orchestra in some subtle ways. It is up to us to let this change be in our favor.

The soloist appears at a crucial moment during the preparation period of a concert. Much of the work has been done; the orientation to the podium has been achieved; the performance is nearly upon us. Enter a new force. Everything depends on the conductor's familiarity with that force. With growing experience, this is bound to become a diminishing problem. For the comparative newcomer to the podium, however, it is as important to "learn" the soloist before rehearsal as it is to learn his solo part. Some notion of the soloist's approach to the scheduled concerto, through a recording, a tape, or even by "talking through" the score for a few minutes before the rehearsal will help establish tempos, articulation, and some phrases in the first orchestral tutti which should bear some resemblance to the soloist's way with them.

In the case of our piano concerto we have the additonal problem of rather indifferent orchestral writing, when the orchestra has something to play. The young Chopin was clearly not very interested in providing more than a frame for his sparkling piano score. It is unfortunately necessary to adjust the frame a bit so that it balances not only the melodic flow of the solos, but also provides something like the nuances and careful shadings available to the pianist, when the burden of musical discourse is shifted to the orchestra alone. Nothing is likely to reassure our soloist more quickly than tuttis which are rhythmically crisp, full of clear musical shapes, and flexibly balanced. If we have been able to allow for our pianist's particular tempos and phrasing, so much the better. And some early warning of just how freely he intends to apply rubatos and ritards in general should enable us to "change gears" safely in terms of our beat which, in this work, must be accomplished with the same easy confidence and virtuosity that is expected of the pianist.

Back to the context in which this subject is being raised: our relationship with the orchestra. More important than our basic musical agreement and compatibility with the soloist's performance is our demonstrated ability to signal flexible and supportive changes to match the constant flow of tempo and phrasing in the piano part. Because of the orchestra's musically subordinate role in this score, the match of ensemble depends on the soloist's initiative and our ability to follow. In our chapter on the Yielding of Control we chose examples from the E-minor Concerto for this very reason.* The beat must be so flexible, the patterns so clear, that without verbal explanations a constant flow of rubato *initiated by someone else* can be instantly transmitted. As was pointed out at that time, it is essential that the conductor be very familiar with every note of the piano part. Not only his ears, but his eyes will have to be with the pianist more than with anyone else on stage. Balancing and flexible matching of tempo and dynamics could occupy most of our scheduled time at the dress rehearsal; hence our great care in the earlier session to leave a maximum of possible choices for the dress. In any event, the major part of this last rehearsal should be available; and the more clearly apparent a lack of strain and pressure will be to the orchestra, the more willing and productive should be its vital participation in a complex and sensitive exercise in ensemble playing.

Ensemble playing, the key objective in orchestral performance, puts into professional perspective the gradual social and psychological changes which have affected the orchestra's relationship with its conductor. Like other authority figures, from admirals to college presidents, conductors have had to reassess their role in terms of these changes. And as sailors are no longer flogged in the fleet and students are exclusively on the receiving end of one-way educational direction, so orchestras play a more participatory role these days in their own development as an instrument and in an ongoing evaluation of the person to whom this instrument is entrusted in performance. Whatever the respective consequences of social change may be in running the navy or university, in our case the results are highly productive. Music being a participatory art, the feeling of give and take which has entered the relationship between orchestra and conductor at many levels, has brought with it a new opportunity to enliven the basis of orchestral performance. There is little doubt that playing standards have greatly

*Cf. pp. 347ff.

improved within the past generation. Increased technical proficiency of our young players and the competitive pressures under which they are expected to develop have had a positive effect on the general level of orchestral performance. But it cannot be denied that there is a tough, new spirit, particularly among young orchestras, which finds many more members actively and critically listening and evaluating than was the case even within the author's own memory of his early orchestral experience. And if, as in the imaginary rehearsal sequence above, every musical decision also becomes a conscious tactical move in terms of the orchestra, it seems a small price to pay for the kind of musical participation one associates more often with the performance of chamber music.

There is, of course, another large area of a conductor's relationship with an orchestra which lies outside his professional responsibility. In order to protect his primary, artistic function and authority on the podium, this relationship is carefully defined within the general structure of the orchestral organization, and the young conductor is well advised to acquaint himself with its few general principles (and taboos). On the whole, although they may seem restrictive, they really work to his advantage.

While the conductor is responsible for the artistic "product" of the orchestral association, *it is the manager to whom all matters concerning the musicians' employment are referred*. Like the conductor, the manager is an employee of the association, responsible to the conductor's employer—be that a board, a government functionary, or any other group or person in authority. It is essential that the manager be neither the conductor's subordinate nor his superior. Under a good working relationship between conductor and manager, a natural division of function funnels matters of orchestral concern into separate channels for solution.

The orchestra in turn is organized along similarly dualistic lines. As we said,* it is usually represented by an elected committee which concerns itself with matters ranging from individual complaints to collective bargaining at contract negotiation time. On the other hand, the orchestra's personnel manager, appointed and paid by management, but under most agreements with the musicians' union a playing member of the orchestra, represents the employers's *and* the conductor's concerns in consultations with his peers. In the best situations, this key figure is as valuable to the orchestra as he is to management and to the conductor.

Specific ramifications of this general structure may vary greatly from one orchestra to another. As a general rule, however, it is fair to say

---

*Orchestration and Orchestra, p. 465ff.

that it is a very serious mistake for any conductor, particularly the young and experienced person, to enter into discussions with members of the orchestra on subjects other than those subject to his own musical authority. This is a hard lesson to learn and an important principle to remember from the start.

Conversely, the many off-the-podium decisions which do fall within the conductor's scope must be made, communicated, and carried out with the least possible delay. This is where a good personnel manager is invaluable, for as with any tightly knit group of workers who see each other almost daily, members of an orchestra are more easily upset over relatively minor matters of administrative detail than with problems involving major policy decisions. We have discussed one example of this, the posting of an up-to-date rehearsal schedule. More ill will may be generated by neglect of this weekly task than by conducting one really poor rehearsal. Orchestral players, it must be said once more, are employed musicians, not animated illustrations from an orchestration text, and their daily welfare and comforts are important to them.

Matters of bowings, chronic intonation problems in one particular section, and choices of cymbals, triangles, and mallets are among the endless concerns to be shared with concertmaster, section principals, and individual musicians. They not only care about the matter under discussion, but they enjoy talking about music, and the more informal contact there is between conductor and player, the better. Not the least advantage in establishing this kind of relationship is that close touch is maintained with what the politicians call the grass roots of potential support. And, like it or not, a job which includes daily contact with the same group of people is political. Just because the conductor's function on the podium is somewhat ritualistic in the eyes of most beholders, a healthy counterbalance of being senior musician but, on many occasions, only first among equals, can be an enormous help in the hands of a skillful leader.

Personal styles differ, as much in the management of daily contacts as in one's manner on the podium. Easy and casual assumption of authority could be one person's special gift, as strictly maintained discipline and distance may be another's. What we have shown as a substantially changed relationship between orchestra and conductor today may be the most reasonable development to one conductor or a continual irritant to another. Most conductors enjoy being liked and are prepared to go to some lengths to achieve this happy state. And quite rightly too: an orchestra will respond better to someone they enjoy having up on the box. But, to paraphrase cellist, Felix Salmond's commencement topic in addressing a Juilliard graduating class long ago ("you can't play espressivo all the time"), you can't be popular all the time. Perhaps the surest way to lose the musicians' confidence is to bid obviously for popularity at any price with that constant, tiresome display of talent, charm, and wit which is both familiar and offensive to most players. The orchestra does not want a pal on the podium, or an entertainer, or a child prodigy: It wants an artist. Artists come in all ages. Maestro means teacher. Some things never change.

16

ORCHESTRA PLUS

This chapter is devoted to the dance, chorus, and opera, three areas of conducting in which musical forces are added to the orchestra under the conductor's direction, and in which he shares authority in the preparation of a performance.

ON the podium, the conductor is in charge. He may share control, to an extent, with a concerto soloist, as we have already observed. With a responsive orchestra, and particularly with musically aggressive principals, initiative can also be yielded temporarily to certain players in the group, while the conductor coordinates and balances the accompanying ensemble. With an effective management of the beat, many moments of freedom may be delegated to shape a phrase or to provide a sense of individual exchange within an orchestral performance.

But there can never be a question of ultimate authority. The reason for the maintenance of absolute control from the podium is to be found in the nature of the score: what the orchestra is expected to play exceeds the mechanical reproduction of data and instructions transferred from the conductor's score to the orchestral parts. The realization of this musical composite, painstakingly assembled in the conductor's mind, increasingly becomes a one-man show, long before its final result has been communicated in rehearsal. What will be heard in performance is the unique blend of musical evidence and its transformation in one person's mind. When the orchestra plays, that person needs to be in control.

This happy conclusion loses some of its force when a performance has more than one responsible leader. There is a large body of musical literature in which the central, creative role is divided, and in which effective realization, by either side, must depend on personal accomodation before and during rehearsal. This situation arises whenever words or movement carry a major share of the effect in performance, i.e., in works for chorus and orchestra, the dance, and opera.

In each of these media, at least one person other than the conductor will have been making decisions affecting the orchestra's contribution long before the actual collaboration really begins. The choral director, the choreographer, and the stage director of an opera are authority figures with whom the orchestral conductor must come to terms in joint productions. A clear grasp of the function and professional concern of the conductor's opposite number and a realistic appreciation of the areas of mutual support are essential starting points if inevitable confrontations on matters of mutual artistic concern are not to degenerate into petty bickering.

Music for the Dance

Nothing in Purcell's music to *The Gordian Knot Untied* could prepare one for the unforgettable experience of seeing José Limon dance the *Moor's Pavane* to it. But neither could Limon and his choreographer Doris Humphrey have told the story of Othello with anything like the drama and conviction of this dance, without those Purcell strings in the pit. And those strings need a conductor.

That conducting for the dance is an inferior assignment is one of many canards about our profession. Only an inferior conductor will make a danced production of *Petrushka* sound inferior to a concert performance. To perform Adolphe Adam's deceptively simple score to *Giselle* in a way that will lend support to the dancers and achieve a sense of dramatic unity as the story unfolds, is a task worthy of any fine professional on the podium. But what the dance does require, in addition to all the seasoned virtues of conductors in the concert hall, is a feeling for movement.

First of all, this means a highly developed sense of tempo. As singers depend on their available length of breath, dancers can only function within a framework of tempos in which certain physical motions are possible. It takes a man a very definite time span to leap as high and as far as he can. His skill, his muscles, and gravity determine the result. A slightly faster tempo would literally leave him "up in the air." Or a tempo that is too slow for an Adagio is bound to ruin a pas de deux, even with a pair of world-class dancers. The ability to recall a very narrow range of tempos suitable for a particular section of the choreography is part of what it takes to be a conductor for the dance (and one of the reasons why the discipline of working for ballet is excellent training for young conductors). The ability to sense when a certain dancer, on a certain occasion, might be able to manage a slightly faster or slower tempo because he appears "up" for it goes beyond basic requirements.

But conductors with a genuine feeling for movement develop an uncanny instinct and an almost physical empathy with the dancers on stage.

Most dancers are highly musical, if not always musically literate. They often count steps rather than beats per measure, or beats as they relate to movement. The story of a celebrated American choreographer who commissioned a new work "in three," but rejected the music because it did not go ♩ ♩ ♩ , is a true one.

The reason for such misunderstandings is that dancers and musicians do not listen to music in the same way, and that a very simple metric pattern may quite literally be heard as the beat of a different drum by one who must create *an inner image of movement*. In collaboration with a choreographer, the conductor deals with a fellow artist whose approach to the performance is not unlike his own, but whose premise is different. The forces under the choreographer's control, moreover, are independent of the conductor's authority and traditionally far more rigidly disciplined than any orchestra. Since the functions of stage and pit are interdependent, their respective leaders can only hope to achieve a rewarding performance on the basis of artistic accommodation on every possible level.

It is easy to understand why the conductor should involve himself at an early stage of planning, long before musical rehearsals begin. If the score is especially commissioned for the occasion (almost all of Martha Graham's repertory had music written for her), the choreographer is bound to welcome as much input from the person responsible for that side of the production as possible. With standard repertory, however, most choreographers use recordings while creating the dance and afterwards. It is very much to the conductor's interest to help choose that recording, for it will be played while the work is being mounted on the company, until its surface is little more than scratches, and until the dancers need no longer "follow" it, but are able to anticipate its every change of tempo and musical gesture. By the time the orchestra is assembled in the pit, the resources of live sound can certainly add a great deal to the basic framework around which the choreography was designed. But it may no longer change it, even for persuasive musical reasons.

Dancers tend to be among the most unassuming, indefatigable, and highly motivated performing artists. They are totally absorbed in their work, have little small talk, take class until the day they retire, and are chronically underpaid. For the conductor, they are ideal performance partners, as long as he remembers that they are not a species of underdeveloped musician, but artists with their own values, their own set of references, and their own requirements for successful performance. This understanding, and some flexibility in sharing decisions affecting both stage and orchestra, are basic to the kind of collaboration in the theater of which the dance offers the least complex example.

Music with Text

Words have meaning. Grouped into sentences, words are useful for providing precise descriptions, expressing wishes and feelings, or establishing a conceptual context in which abstract ideas may be understood. Words are specific. Properly used, they are a means of conveying accurate information, but they lend themselves as readily to confuse, withold, or even controvert meaning. In all, being our most common form of communication, words are nearly as much a part of everyone's daily experience as the natural sights and sounds of the world around us.

By the same token, a special setting is required to lift the experience of words above its commonplace role in our daily environment. Poetry and music provide such a setting, often in combination. It is important that we keep this in mind, because, almost invariably, the role of music in such a case is to enhance the meaning and the significance of the word, not the reverse. Whatever else, this meaning must be clear to the listener. Not only must the word be part of a carefully balanced musical texture like any other component of the ensemble, it must be *understood*.

Most conductors and vocal coaches begin singing rehearsals by having the words spoken in rhythm. Some attention is given to diction at this stage (particularly if this involves pronunciation of words in a foreign language), but as some vowels require modification according to the tessitura in which they are to be sung, much of this must await a later stage of coaching.*

Words that are sung are musically amplified. Therefore it is not only important that the listener understand their meaning, but that the singer be fully aware of the relative weight to be given to each word, so that meaning and musical context complement each other. Even taxing coloratura passages, like those in the Queen of the Night arias, or the Mad Scene from *Lucia*, contain key words which need to be heard and understood if the dramatic situation in the opera is not to be entirely abandoned for the sake of vocal acrobatics.

But the most vexing problem for most symphonic conductors in the early stages of working with singers seems to be bound up in a curious

---

*In this connection, it must also be said that some coaches lay primary stress on vocal production, even in early rehearsals of an unfamiliar work. Contrary to the above, it is their view that works for voice require beautiful singing above all, some sacrifices of verbal clarity notwithstanding. The difference is one of degree, albeit hotly contested at times. Certainly a good case can be made for the fact that often repeated, well-known words (e.g. in a liturgical text) may be taken for granted. But in general, the requirement to sing intelligibly rarely precludes singing beautifully, as well. Robert Schumann gave excellent advice to young conductors: "You can learn a great deal from singers, but don't believe everything they say."

paradox: familiarity in the use of words and experience in the performance of music does *not*, in itself, prepare one for the use of words in the performance of music! Daily experience with the spoken word fails to alert us to the fact that singers have to breathe, and should do so at musically appropriate places in the score. Understandably, singers are not sympathetic to a conductor who fusses with bowings in the first violin section while they are forced to struggle for breath without any signs of concern from the podium. For conductors who, like the author, happen to be string players, extensive work with singers is the best remedy for this widely shared failing. In the words of a great French conductor and teacher of conductors, "it is a musical handicap that the violin bow doesn't have to breathe."*

Since, more often than not, a musical setting will lengthen some syllables of the text, more breath will be required to sing than to recite the words. Add to this the infrastructure of melodic phrases and periods, and the assumption that the singer will breathe according to imagined punctuation of a written text becomes unrealistic. Musical embellishment to enhance meaning adds yet another problem:

EXAMPLE 1: Bach, *St. Matthew Passion*, "Then answered Peter" (Evangelist)

In this example, the word *wept* is melodically enhanced to suggest bitter weeping. As it happens, in this case there is no need to breathe differently than the sense and punctuation of the two phrases would require: "and he went out" (comma—i.e. breath) "and wept bitterly."

*Statement by Jean Morel in addressing the orchestra of the Juilliard School where he conducted from 1947 to 1973.

EXAMPLE 2: Mennin, *Voices,* No. 5—"Stark Madness" (Emily Dickenson)

Much sense_ the stark-est mad - - ness, stark-est mad - ness, mad - - ness.

But in this setting, very similar in expressive and descriptive intent, the singer would certainly have to breathe more often than if he were to speak the words of the poem. If you will try to read aloud "much sense the stark madness, madness, madness," observing the dynamic indications but not the note values or an approximation of the pitches, you should easily be able to do it all in one breath. Try using three breaths, as the singer must, and the effect would be quite unnatural.

The point to remember is that the effect of words combined with music does not result in merely adding the characteristics of one to the other, but *in an entirely different mode of expression.*

CHORUS

Before turning to the most complex collaborative enterprise in the theater, the opera, it will be helpful to consider one other event in which authority over large forces is shared. Like opera, music for chorus and orchestra requires awareness and understanding of singers and singing. The opera house as training ground for young conductors, and choral societies as a significant part of the civic musical scene, have given way to the symphony orchestra as the main focus of musical life in our day. The following brief outline of what is special about working with chorus is intended for the symphonic conductor who, from time to time, has occasion to use a chorus.

As with the dance, ultimate success in working with a chorus depends on genuine cooperation with the person who prepared the group for their first rehearsal with orchestra. The fact that, unlike choreography, choral preparation is based on the same musical score used by the orchestral conductor, should not disguise differences in approach, in technical objectives, and in response to direction from the podium. These differences set choral singing as distinctly apart from orchestral practice, as the requirements of either differ from those of the dance.

Symphonic Conductor's Brief Guide to the Chorus

A: *The Instrument*

1. Some of the best choruses are amateur choruses. Their members are not paid, and few if any of them are likely to be trained singers. In any fine chorus, however, all members are trained *choral* singers.
2. There are radically *different approaches to choral singing*. At one extreme is the notion that clear projection of words and musical reflection of their meaning are the prime reasons for having words with music in the first place; at the other is the production of a consistent kind of sound which becomes a hallmark for the group. Most choral conductors profess an active interest in both aims, but will nonetheless lean very distinctly toward one or the other ideal of good choral singing.
3. *Diction* is the vehicle of clearly projected verbal meaning. In its simplest form, the theory of diction is:
   a. *vowels* are for sound,
   b. *consonants* are for meaning.

   Accordingly, syllables are sustained, on their *vowels*, over the full value of the note(s) on which they are sung. *Consonants* separating one syllable from another are carefully placed, either
   a. *on* the metric pulse with which the next syllable begins:

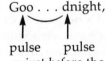

   b. or *just before* the following pulse:

   The second vowel sound of a diphthong is treated as a consonant: "smiling" is sung smah . . . iling, or smah . . . iling.

$$\uparrow \qquad \uparrow \qquad \uparrow \qquad \uparrow$$

   pulse   pulse   pulse   pulse

   The choice is up to the choral director, but a well-enforced decision is essential for the sake of unanimously pronounced consonants and diphthongs. The second method requires more collective concentration and practice, but is particularly well suited to the frequent separation of syllables in English. The former, almost instantly achievable even by indifferently schooled choirs, is preferable for the natural legato of the Italian language. *N.B.* Latin texts are usually sung with

Italian pronunciation in the United States, and with classical Latin diction in Europe (e.g. *magnum* = mahnyoom [U.S.] vs. mahgnoom [Europe]).

Diction is a complex and vitally important part of singing. The reader is urged to consult one of a number of excellent texts.*

4. Good choral sound is a subject on which choral directors disagree. There would be a consensus, however, on the fact that the sound of one well-trained chorus may differ greatly from that of another. Differences are the result of both technical and aesthetic choices on the part of the person training the choir. The former reflect a method of vocal production, voice placement, and projection; the latter concern personal preferences with regard to unanimously produced colors of vowel sounds.

   a. Some choral conductors refuse to accept singers with large voices, for fear they will "stick out." Choral training will emphasize a strictly defined upper limit of dynamic level and specify an appropriate range of softer levels below. The dynamic framework will be small, but beautifully articulated. Every singer will command the prescribed range without strain. Much attention will be lavished on smooth transitions between pitch levels and on changing registers without changes in sound quality. The overall balance of voices must always reflect the ideal uniform vocal style, of which a well-articulated dynamic range and even registers are a part. Individual voices must never stand out, and a noticeable vibrato anywhere is even less acceptable than wrong notes. At almost any cost, this kind of chorus will achieve and maintain a beautiful but undramatic sound.

   b. Vowel sounds may vary greatly in everyday speech, and in regional dialects only familiarity with local usage could equate what sounds like *pack* or *pork* with the word *park*. Good choir singing demands identical shading of all vowels, as determined by their choir director. One of the most difficult tasks for any group of singers is to produce uniform vowel sounds in unison passages. Some choir directors incorporate a personal signal system for "lighter" or "darker" into their repertory of conducting gestures, and are thus able to control the color of sound even in performance. The further forward a sung vowel is produced, the brighter it will sound (mouth wide, teeth bared); the further back (with a well-rounded opening of the lips), the darker its shading will be. Active movement of mouth and lips is an important factor in the achievement

---

*The most widely used text for English diction is Madeleine Marshall, *The Singer's Manual of English Diction* (Schirmer, 1953).

of well-projected choral singing. The more voices participate in articulating the same words and sounds, the more the result is likely to be blurred. For this reason, uniform timing of consonants, uniform coloring of vowels, and, in high registers, uniform modification of vowels* contributes to a compelling sense of common purpose in choral performance.

5. *Intonation and breathing* are related problems in choral singing. While faulty intonation and musically awkward breathing places are obvious to orchestral conductors as well as to their choral counterparts, the fact is that most choirs sing better in tune for their own director than for an instrument-oriented maestro whose conducting does not "breathe" with them. Singers support the sound they produce with the diaphragm, and proper control of available breath affects every aspect of that sound, including its pitch. This does not mean, of course, that spacing of phrases by proper breathing should be ignored, or that intonation does not also depend on listening.

B: *Working with Chorus*

A great many decisions with regard to performance will have been made long before the chorus becomes available for rehearsal with orchestra. The orchestral conductor's personal preference in any of the categories we have mentioned is most effectively expressed in his *choice* of the chorus itself. There is little he can do to change fundamental habits of singing during his preparation for a joint performance; and even partial success in the effort would not only affect his working relationship with the choral director but, more than likely, the morale of the chorus as well. There remains, however, a large area of musical responsibility in which his judgment is needed and his active participation expected.

1. *Size of the chorus.* As with the number of strings used in orchestral works of different periods, the size of the chorus should reflect the requirements of the music. Not only historical performance practice, but also considerations of musical and verbal texture often militate against the use of massive forces just because they are available. Determination of numbers in such a case becomes the conductor's first, decisive interpretive act. That this cannot always be accomplished was demonstrated some years ago by the citizens of Huddersfield in England, home of the Huddersfield Chorale and of a

---

*In the high register of any voice, the bright vowels in particular must be modified to avoid their sounding unpleasantly shrill. The word *green*, for instance, would be sung with rounder lips than usual, and might sound rather like its German equivalent *gruen*.

rich choir tradition. After the guest appearance of a celebrated, small group of singers and instrumentalists in Handel's *Messiah*, the audience, who liked their Handel big and lush, stoned the departing BBC buses.

2. *Seating* varies according to requirements. Most choruses place sopranos and altos in front, men in the back. If the tenor section is small, it may occupy the center of the back rows, with basses on either side. If space permits, it is a good idea to maintain seating of the chorus behind the orchestra so that sections are in the same relative position to each other as in earlier piano rehearsals. Choristers will stand whenever they sing.

3. *The warm-up* is a set of vocal exercises designed to limber up the chorus at the beginning of every rehearsal. Scale fragments and arpeggios are sung on a variety of syllables and transposed throughout the practicable range of the voices. Some choruses use this time for intonation practice as well. Others enjoy being whipped into an emotional frenzy at the end of warm-ups that resemble shouting matches between choir director and singers. Unless they wish to demonstrate expertise in the field, orchestra conductors should leave this ritual to a choral person. *Caveat:* Most professional choruses do *not* warm up. Members will resent it.

4. *Balance* between chorus and orchestra should favor the chorus. Even with excellent choral diction, words may get lost in a thick orchestral texture. Thus it is not volume alone that may inhibit understanding, but also a dense instrumental fabric. On the other hand, there is little point in employing an orchestra if its overall sound is to remain an undifferentiated trickle ranging from *piano* to *mezzo piano*. Among the techniques useful in achieving the illusion of a large dynamic range are the following:

   a. If the orchestral texture involves melodic lines, the contrast between solo (even though this may be the entire cello section) and the rest of the orchestra should be greater than usual. The melodic line could be played at normal dynamic level, or very nearly so; the rest of the orchestra very much softer. The chorus should have a good chance to be heard, but the orchestral contribution would change as leading melodic lines are exchanged between solo instruments. This should be carefully planned in advance and adjusted in rehearsal.

   b. In passages dominated by forceful, sustained orchestral entrances (particularly in the brass), overall reduction of instrumental volume will result in loss of musical vitality. An excellent remedy is the so-called *opera forte*. This is an attack of almost normal strength that is instantly reduced to a lower level of volume over which the chorus can be heard. The illusion of a powerful orchestra is striking, if the conductor will exercise care in avoiding two problems: the sudden reduction of volume must *not* sound like a forte-piano (forte–meno forte is required); and a forte-diminuendo effect must be strenuously avoided. The lesser dynamic level must be reached at once, and sustained in full.

5. *Attacks and releases* must be given to a chorus far more consistently than is necessary with an orchestra. There is a world of difference between the needs of singers in sustaining a long note and the self-sufficient way in which a well-schooled brass section will manage its long chords. Choruses are far more dependent, but also more immediately responsive to direct manipulation from the podium than their orchestral counterparts.

6. *Singing response* in general is more visceral than what conductors would expect from instrumentalists. Orchestras resent the cheer-leading type of conductor; choruses thrive on a constant flow of encouragement, running commentary, and funny remarks. Orchestral players are impressed by efficient use of rehearsal time, even at the price of pressure from the podium; choristers love a dramatic show, even though the point illustrated could have been made in one brief sentence. At a chorus rehearsal, Robert Shaw wanted a more savage enunciation of the word *crucifixus*. After explaining how unpleasant it was to be nailed to a cross, he began to shout words to the chorus which they had to shout back: "cross—cross, crucified—crucified," etc., then in other languages: "Kreuz—Kreuz, croix—croix," until the point had been made not only intellectually, but emotionally and physically as well. The choral impact on *crucifixus* after that was unforgettable. On the other hand, it is possible to put an orchestra through a tough rehearsal at which the conductor is resented, and nonetheless achieve a performance that shows the benefit of a measure of ruthlessness. With a chorus, the same approach would be absolutely fatal.

7. *Physical limitations* are very real. The human voice is a fragile instrument compared to a trombone, but trombonists know a good deal more about the care of their horn than the average choral singer about his vocal chords. Not only unproductive fatigue, but real damage may be caused by thoughtless overrehearsing of taxing choral passages. On the other hand, the habit of "marking" (singing with less than full voice) should be permitted only at the conductor's discretion. The orchestra's time is precious, balance is an ever-present problem, and untrained voices are likely to be hurt by unaccustomed use. The same applies to the otherwise excellent idea of speaking texts in rhythm before they are sung: this exercise is a lot

harder on the voice than singing the same words.

8. *A special approach,* well planned and carefully executed, will engage the interest of a chorus. This might involve frequent references to the color of certain vowel sounds; or one might create some excitement about words (Kreuz / croix / cross); or, if there is room on stage, the distribution of voices can be completely "mixed up," so that a soprano would find herself surrounded by two contraltos and a bass, and a tenor by women only. Such "games" are more suitable for early rehearsals with piano (at least some of which the orchestral conductor should attend), and can have wonderful consequences in terms of cooperation and morale as well as of a genuine stirring of the imagination.

9. *Choral directors* are the traditional underdogs in the pecking order of conductors. Acknowledge them, and you will gain a valuable ally as well as the sympathy of the chorus.

10. Allow your singers to sit down every once in a while in rehearsal, and be sure to indicate the ups and downs of the chorus in performance.

Conducting Opera

The production of an opera is a collaborative tour-de-force. When combining orchestral, vocal, and theatrical forces, preparation problems will be compounded by the need to coordinate the requirements of all three areas. Leafing through an opera program book one might well be astonished that the production staff often outnumbers the singers on stage in the way ground maintenance outnumbers the flight crew of a jet liner.

It is essential to have some notion of the mechanics of preparing an opera for performance before the artistic problems can be understood. The chart below shows the forces available to those in charge of an operatic production and the timing of their effective involvement. In small companies producing a limited annual series of operas for a few performances at a time, each member of the staff assumes more than one particular responsibility. In a large repertory house, where new productions are constantly added to a revolving staple of established ones (which need to be kept intact), the numbers are larger. *But the functions listed below are all essential and must be carried out in roughly the prescribed order.*

A brief description of these functions should help to clarify the various areas of participation in the preparation of an operatic production.

OPERA: PRODUCTION STAFF AND PRODUCTION SEQUENCE

CONDUCTOR	*DIRECTOR*	*SCENIC DESIGNER* *COSTUME DESIGNER* *LIGHTING DESIGNER*

Cast
Chorus
Orchestra
Dancers
	Staff:
	  Assistant(s)
	  Stage Manager
	  Production Manager	

Staff: Assistant(s)
  Coaches
  Chorus Master
  Ballet Master
	Cast & Dancers
	Stage Personnel:
	  Carpenters
	  Electricians
	  Crew
	Backstage staff:
	  Wardrobe & Wigs
	  Makeup
	  Properties
		Resident or Outside
		Staff

I → PLANNING − − − − − − → PLANNING − − − − − − → PLANNING

II → COACHING—CHOREOGRAPHY*   − − − − − − − → DESIGNING
    Individual   Sets
    Ensemble   Costumes
    Chorus
    Dance

III → COACHING (continued)   BLOCKING   − − − → BUILDING
     READING REHEARSALS (Piano)   Individual   Sets
                                  Ensemble   Costumes
                                  Chorus**   − − − − → DESIGNING
                                  Dance*   Lights

IV → STAGED REHEARSALS   STAGED REHEARSALS − − → INSTALLING
         (Piano)†   (Piano)†   Sets

                     (NO BOOKS)   − − − − → FITTING
V → ORCHESTRA REHEARSALS   Costumes
      Orchestra alone
      Sitzproben

VI → STAGE REHEARSALS − → STAGE REHEARSALS − → STAGE REHEARSALS
                            Cast
                            Chorus   − − − − → TECHNICAL REHEARSALS
                            Orchestra   Lights
                            Dancers   Cues

VII → DRESS REHEARSAL − − → DRESS REHEARSAL − − → DRESS REHEARSAL
Run-through with Costumes, Wigs, Makeup, Lights, Cues, and Curtain Calls

VIII → PERFORMANCE − − → PERFORMANCE − − → PERFORMANCE

---

*Conductor's and Director's involvement depends on extent to which singing cast is involved.
** As above. Interaction between Solo Cast, Chorus, and/or Dancers means shared responsibility.
† Not necessarily on stage but in equivalent rehearsal space; individual scenes, whole acts.

The cast is specified, in most operatic scores, according to the vocal range of each role. Actual selection of singers involves additional considerations. Foremost among musical qualifications are the timbre and quality of voices. On that basis, the general categories of soprano, alto, tenor, and bass are further defined by such descriptive adjectives as "lyric" for light, supple voices in the high range, or "dramatic" for their big, powerful equivalents. Descriptive nouns, e.g. coloratura (a voice, usually soprano, capable of "coloring" the highest register with virtuosic vocal pyrotechnics); Heldentenor (German for the "heroic" tenor voice needed for some Wagnerian roles); or Verdi baritone (a male singer with a large intermediate range between tenor and bass and a ringing quality in the upper range of his voice, as required for certain baritone roles in Verdi's operas), are usually self-explanatory. But finding the right voice to suit a particular role is a task in which even outstanding musical ability is no substitute for experience. Success or failure of an opera production may well depend on selection of a fine cast. Whether the choice is made by audition or engaging a number of "name" singers, young conductors are well advised to share the process, if not the responsibility, with some of their colleagues on the production team.

The stage director, usually present at auditions, will be only too glad to offer suggestions. He is likely to have had a good deal of experience with singers, but at the same time his judgment will be based on some extramusical considerations as well: the singer's general appearance, how he or she moves on stage or projects an image of the character.

The head coach of an opera company can be relied upon to combine experience with a musical bias. He is a most suitable person to consult, as long as it is clearly understood that final determination will be made by the conductor. Authority in a collaborative enterprise is enhanced by the confidence of those over whom it must be exercised. Willingness to seek advice, an ability to listen, and a capacity to make firm decisions are attractive qualities in the eyes of the conductor's prospective team.

Coach and cast are apt to develop an empathy during a production which is never approached in even the most successful working relationship between conductor and singers. The maestro, no matter how pleasant and capable he may be, is everyone's boss. The coach, as most singers perceive their musical mentor, "is just for me." Some conductors like to coach, at least in the later stages of musical preparation. If they do it well, so much the better. Aside from a good knowledge of the voice and singing, proficiency at the piano is essential. But there is more, and here are some very basic suggestions:

1. Simplify. Play what the singer may expect to hear of the orchestra, not what you hope to achieve in terms of instrumental display in the pit.
2. Be prepared to play or sing the singer's own line whenever such a reminder may save an untimely interruption. Later, explore the difficulty in detail and work out the passage until it is secure.
3. "Voce pianissimo, parole fortissimo": Toscanini's wonderfully succinct request for soft singing with clearly projected diction should be repeated many times in every coaching session.
4. Play the piano softly as well, and remember that an orchestra does not have a sostenuto pedal.

The chorus master of an opera company does not share the same exclusive working relationship with the music director as the choir director with the symphonic conductor. Since the chorus, like all singers on stage, must serve two masters, continued communication is even more important in opera than in a concert performance. If the work calls for a real acting chorus, and especially if crowd scenes require supers or dancers, the chorus master, ballet master, *and* stage director must understand at what points in the score the conductor considers it essential that the singing cast have an unimpeded view of the beat. That such a basic requirement may even affect the scenic design can be vouched for by any conductor who lost visual contact with an ensemble on stage because an essential piece of scenery blocked the view of some members of the group.

There is much to be said for the school of staging which maintains that the audience must never be aware of singers on stage actually looking at the conductor. It spoils the illusion. Closed circuit television screens showing the conductor are placed in various hidden locations around the stage, so that the cast may follow direction from the pit while the visible focus of attention remains wherever the dramatic situation requires. *This does not work with an acting chorus.* A firm, well-directed cue from the pit will point in the *wrong* direction from the monitor screen, depending on the relative position of the viewer. In these cases the chorus master must be somewhere in the wings, visible to the chorus, and conducting as *he* follows the monitor. At best the result will be mechanically accurate. The flow of excitement which many crowd scenes could generate must be curbed for the sake of caution. Such problems and many more can best be solved by avoiding them altogether. Extensive and detailed planning sessions between conductor and stage director will not only alert both "field commanders" to potential traps, but may well yield unexpected, creative opportunity.

Conductors' assistants must be able to function as substitutes for the music director in any capacity. Obviously, they are expected to be completely familiar with the score. It is the conductor's responsibility to insure that they are completely familiar with his artistic plans in general. In a relationship which is defined by mutual respect and trust, it is best for the conductor to offer some evidence of his own confidence in his staff. Popularity, though enjoyable and sometimes helpful, is not a viable objective in itself. Competence is expected; a capacity of sharing hard work will be admired. But for his leadership to be effective as the pressures of production increase, the conductor must be *seen* to care—first for the product itself, and then for his personal staff.

The stage director's staff is larger and its functions more complex than those on the musical side of an opera production. The technical aspects of providing the cast with working stage setting, and of transforming that cast into a convincing theater ensemble, appropriately dressed, lit, and made up, is rigidly dependent on a succession of carefully met deadlines of which the performance itself is but the final event.

The production manager coordinates logistics and keeps track of the budget. Unlike the general manager of a symphony orchestra, however, he is not in a position either to initiate or to control any of the decisions that affect either side of his responsibilities. Instead, he collects information on rehearsal requirements, contract bids, delivery dates of materials, and estimates on labor costs. He serves two very visible masters, conductor and stage director, and acts as their liaison with the management of the company. Since he is not actually seen to "do" anything, and yet must frequently deny requests, the production manager is an easy target for conductors on the rampage. That this is unfair may occur to the maestro after a few minutes' reflection or after a lengthy series of adverse experiences in opera which seemed to bear no relation to the excellence of his musical contribution. Production managers are only too glad to work with you. They are not employed to work *for* you.

The stage manager, on the other hand, enjoys high visibility and is seen to "do" almost everything on stage except sing. As people and props begin to converge on stage, bringing with them their problems and their requirements for attention and time, active responsibility devolves on the person who supervised the installment of sets and will give the "ready" signal on opening night which sends the conductor into the pit. In the end, the stage manager is in virtual control of everything and everybody on and around the stage. He will have absorbed all but the musical functions of stage initiative, including the lighting and stage cues at performance time. To this end, the entire stage personnel is under his direction throughout the production period.

Functions of the remainder of the stage director's staff shown on our chart are self-explanatory, as are the roles of scenic, lighting, and costume designer. The conductor is likely to have been introduced to the last three, but will not have any professional contact with them except through the stage director. This exclusion is quite as it should be, of course, but it adds to the feeling of most opera conductors that, when they first take over a full rehearsal, every one on stage seems to work for the other man. That impression may well extend to the cast as well.

The lower part of the chart, showing the sequence of tasks to be accomplished in preparation of performance, also points up the sources of two potential difficulties: the timing of each step depends on the accomplishment of previous assignments; and contact between conductor and stage director is not naturally continuous during very important periods of preparation.

The importance of overall timing in the production schedule is evident at a glance. Step IV, for instance, staged rehearsals with piano, can be undertaken only after the singers involved have had musical coaching in the scenes to be rehearsed, have taken part in reading rehearsals to get used to the flow of ensemble, and know the blocking* (i.e. have accomplished their objectives in steps II and III). In order to undertake step VI, on-stage rehearsals with orchestra, major pieces of scenery affecting the action (e.g. platforms, doorways etc.) should be in place, the orchestra should have had its own rehearsals and Sitzproben** with the cast, and the cast should have memorized their parts (rehearsal "without books"). The closer to opening night, the more complex the collaborative effort of mounting the production becomes.†

It would be a great mistake for any conductor to undertake the musical preparation of an opera, believing that knowledge of his craft and genuine willingness to respect the point of view of his colleague on the staging side alone will assure problem-free, successful rehearsals. Even master strategists are likely to find themselves in an adversary position unless they become fully acquainted with each other's stratagems while there is still time to reach an accommodation. The boxes on our chart

---

*Blocking is the technical term used to describe the staging equivalent of musical coaching. Blocking is the stage director's instruction.

**German for "sitting-down rehearsals" with orchestra; i.e. the cast sits down and sings as in a concert performance of the opera.

†It should be noted that the chart represents a schematic and simplified outline. Not only does every production require its particular solution to its combination of problems in preparation for performance, but the successive steps to be accomplished are never as neatly divided as those shown. In an opera consisting of a given number of separate scenes, for instance, there would be no need to coach and block them all before the first staged run-through of some of them. Nonetheless, the sequence illustrated in the chart holds true for whatever *part* is to be taken to its next step in the preparation.

around steps II, III, and V in the music column and step III in staging, indicate areas of preparation in which work on either side is expected to proceed independently. This means that between step I, general planning, and step IV, the first staged rehearsals, there is no built-in opportunity to compare notes on what singers are being taught.

Chances of being taken by surprise at a point when conductor or stage director may have to reverse decisions before the assembled cast are far greater for the conductor. The director has the musical score to work with, and most directors know the score very well. The staging, on the other hand, is created completely afresh for each new production, and it is to the conductor's own interest that he acquaint himself with the concrete details of a staging concept he will have discussed only in general terms before production began. It is not true that most conductors would prefer singers to stand still most of the time and stage directors would have them in motion all of the time. But stage rehearsals are not suitable occasions for public debate. And debates are not the best means to achieve a necessary compromise.

The problem is compounded by a conductor who leaves most of his own rehearsals prior to Sitzproben to his musical staff. He will take charge of his first stage rehearsal like a guest in his own house, and not only his coaches and assistants, but the director and his staff will be closer to the singers than he. Any changes he then suggests might be received as criticism of what has been achieved, and resented regardless of their merit. Even if other commitments preclude regular attendance throughout the entire period of preparation, at least one concentrated stretch of involvement during the early stages of coaching and blocking will establish a working relationship whose benefits later on will more than repay the small investment of time.

But the single most important factor in assuring artistic cooperation between music and stage is a mutual willingness to talk through the opera, in detail, while conductor and director are planning the performance from their respective points of view. If, for the conductor, "talking through" involves a lot of listening, so much the better. In performance he will control the musical flow as well as the timing on stage, and the more he understands of the dramatic concept the more successfully will he be able to supply the musical energy, passion, and poetry which can make opera something more than a play with musical accompaniment. This transformation, in its widest sense, is the *score* part of opera. Everything else we have discussed thus far was part of communicating the results to performers, i.e. *podium*.

Earlier in this chapter we observed that music, like poetry, has the power to raise the experience of words above their commonplace acceptance as part of our daily environment. In the drama, selective use of poetry can intensify the poignancy of certain situations by directing a set of images at the audience with the penetrative precision of a laser beam.

The dying John of Gaunt, in Shakespeare's *Richard II,* hopes the young king might heed his last counsel because "they say the tongues of dying men enforce attention like deep harmony." And like deep harmony *our* attention is enforced:

> *The setting sun, and music at the close,*
> *As the last taste of sweets, is sweetest last,*
> *Writ in remembrance more than things long past.*

The role of music in opera is comparable and continuous. "We must always rely on the music," says Edward Cone, "as our guide toward an understanding of the *composer's conception of the text*"* (italics added). Why the composer's conception, rather than the stage director's or that of any other authority on the drama? Was Verdi's conception of Shakespeare's *Othello* definitive, or Alban Berg's tightening of George Buechner's dramatic fragment *Wozzeck* dramatically superior? The answer must be an unequivocal "yes" as far as the operatic result is concerned. As Joseph Kerman put it, "only a great symphonist could have written *Don Giovanni.*"** And with this rather unconventional statement in mind we should be able to train our sights on the central problem of collaboration between stage director and opera conductor: music not only provides an emotional context within which the drama on stage gains in depth and intensity of feeling, *music imposes upon the continuity of dramatic events its own directing force of structure.*

"The coincidence of musical and dramatic events is the glory of Mozart's operatic style," writes Charles Rosen.† "In fact, no description of sonata form can be given that will fit the Haydn quartets but not the majority of forms in a Mozart opera."‡ The second statement becomes the more remarkable in light of the first: Mozart's evident inability to write music without its own formal logic failed to diminish the exegetical power with which this same music supports the drama and the psychological nuance on stage. The conductor who, once more in Roger Sessions' words, must try to fulfill his "essential role in the whole thing" is bound to discover that this "whole thing" requires an *a priori* accommodation with his *Doppelgänger* of the stage—not to satisfy respective artistic egos, but to meet twin conditions inherent in the work.

Composers of opera have expressed strong views on the subject of that accommodation. "The poet must take his inspiration from the

*Edward T. Cone, "The Old Man's Toys: Verdi's Last Operas," in *Perspectives USA,* No. 6, Winter 1954, pp. 114–33.
**Joseph Kerman, *Opera as Drama* (Knopf, 1956), p. 76.
†Charles Rosen, *The Classical Style* (Norton, 1972), p. 309.
‡‡Ibid., p. 296.

musician,'' wrote Wagner in 1857.* ''He must construct his drama with
a single-minded regard for the specifically musical intentions of the
composer.'' Nevertheless, he allows that while ''feelings may well be
aroused by musical means, these means are not sufficient to identify
the exact nature'' of feelings. What sounds contradictory in Wagner's
writing is superbly resolved in the dialectic of *Tristan*, the opera which
was soon to follow. Tristan has no words to explain his betrayal of King
Marke, but while he stands mute, we hear the love potion *music* with
which the opera began. The second act ends with the attempted suicide
of a flawed hero, helpless under the spell of feelings that are eloquently
expressed by Wagner's music. But Tristan's great moment is yet to come.
Waking from unconsciousness to tortured self-reproach, the dying man
finds release at the peak of his delirium when he finds his own answer
to King Marke's question. This time the *word* is needed to clarify the
catharsis, and permit the peaceful vision of Isolde that follows. Tristan
has to find those words which are the dramatic turning point of the
opera. The magic curse of his life becomes personal triumph and fulfillment in death as he sings: ''the dreadful potion that consigned me to
torture, I myself, I was the one who brewed it. From father's bane and
mother's sorrow, from tears of love, from laughter and crying, from
bliss and misfortune, *I* culled the poisons in that drink. Draught that I
brewed and savored with delight, dreadful draught be cursed! Cursed
he who stirred that draught!''

EXAMPLE 3: Wagner, *Tristan und Isolde*, Act III

''Ich selbst hab' ihn gebraut!'' On the very *words* with which the spell
is broken, Wagner the *composer* introduces a new and powerful musical
motive (Example 3) which dominates the frenzy of purgation and mor-
tification that follows. And when Tristan wakes once more, it is to a
serene vision of Isolde. We recognize the music from the love duet of
the second act. But the melodic outline repeated in the horns, pianissimo—più pianissimo, is now revealed as a prefiguration of the violent

*Richard Wagner, *Musik and Drama*.

exclamation with which the spell was broken, and of the peace which has transformed the image of love.

EXAMPLE 4: Wagner, *Tristan und Isolde*, Act III

The drama is in the music: is this the ultimate convergence of two modes of expression in Tristan? By no means. But it may be one of those rare moments in opera when a dramatic experience itself can be transformed from something to be witnessed to something in which we participate

on a very personal level. In no way could that be negotiated during the
busy rehearsal schedule that is represented by the chart on p. 501. Nor
could the *musical* consequences of the dramatic interpretation above be
justified, say in staged piano rehearsals, to a director who, quite possibly, might have arrived at a very different way of looking at this scene
and might now be at the same disadvantage of not having communicated soon enough. The predictable consequence of mutual frustration,
multiplied by the length of the entire opera, and aggravated by everyday production pressures, is unfortunately the rule rather more often
than the exception in the preparation of opera.

But, you may say, how many conductors get the chance to take part
in a new production of Tristan? Fair enough. The example was chosen
because it represents one of the great moments in opera, because there
is only one singer under discussion (Tristan's faithful Kurvenal is present only as a lookout for the ship that is to bring Isolde, and to worry
about his master's failing health); and because it was written by a master at the height of his powers (composers who require our help to mask
their shortcomings represent another kind of problem). But above all,
what distinguishes the "score" aspect of the delirium scene of *Tristan*
from that of other scenes in other operas is its relevance to the subject
under discussion: the preparation of opera, as a collaborative effort,
from the point of view of a conductor whose experience has been largely
in the concert hall. We were able to outline the timing and the mechanics of operatic production rather quickly. Collaboration with a stage
director, the mutual assimilation by two experts of views expressed by
an informed amateur in their own, respective field of expertise, is vital.
It is also difficult because, as we have seen, there is no clear determination of the way in which decisions by one may affect the other, except
as the unique and one-time-only result of accommodations reached.
That, and not costume design or anecdotes about the cast, should be
the subject of preproduction planning.

Compare the mounting flow of musical passion that supports the sec-
ond-act love scene of *Tristan* with the fountain scene of Debussy's *Pelléas et Mélisande*. In the very measure in which they declare their love,
the orchestra, which has been playing forte–crescendo, stops playing
altogether! Then in silence:

   Pelléas: *"Je t'aime"*
Mélisande: *"Je t'aime aussi . . ."*
   Pelléas: *"Oh! qu'as-tu dit, Mélisande! Je ne l'ai presque pas entendu! . . .*
French Horn entrance *piano/diminuendo/pianissimo.* Strings *pianissimo.*

"I have made use, quite spontaneously, of a medium which I think
has rarely been used, that of *silence,* as an expressive element which is

perhaps the only way in which the emotion of a phrase can be conveyed," wrote Debussy.*

Who controls silence—the conductor? the director? If the former, are the rests between softly spoken entrances to be strictly observed? Is the tempo to be continuous? If the latter, how much control will really be exercised over a singer who, in fact, has now become an actor singing in the pauses of a musical framework?

Pelléas: "*Tu m'aimes? tu m'aimes aussi? . . . Depuis quand m'aimes-tu?*"
Mélisande: "*Depuis toujours . . .*"

The words are sung, always in low register, always softly, in the silence separating pianissimo orchestral entrances. The rhythm is noted very exactly, in eighths, sixteenths, triplets. But the timing: "Since when have you loved me?" Would Mélisande answer in strict tempo "since always"? A director's decision. Only, on the downbeat following shy "toujours," the composer writes *Très retenu*, surely in invitation for a slow preparatory upbeat, or at the least an opportunity to stretch the last quarter, on the syllable touj*ours*. A *conductor's* decision.

"Functional harmony gave little opportunity of arriving at a real understanding of the essential part played by the time factor. It is only since the most recent developments in music that it has been possible to appreciate the important part played by *tempo.*"** Very much a conductor's decision, but it involves a style of acting as well. Too deliberate a preparatory beat would be bound to exaggerate the perceived gesture of the acting response: *director* again. No universal solutions.

Artistic collaboration requires above all intuitive anticipation of another artist's response. Whether initiative is shared between a conductor and his soloist in a concerto, or with a dancer whose body determines the limitation of his timing, or with the principal oboist for the brief span of an orchestral solo, *ultimate* collaboration must sense what the occasion allows and the artistic framework can sustain. In opera, *collaboration between conductor and director aims at eventual, shared initiative in performance between conductor and cast.* Rather than diminish the importance of close contact between the two artistic heads of an operatic production throughout the period of preparation, this circumstance alone suggests a visibly constructive working relationship. An orchestra is not an animated orchestration book, but a large group of instrumentalists who, under skilled direction, may function as a responsive musical ensemble. No singer can give a convincing performance in opera unless the result of coaching and directing is a firm conviction that everything was done for his or her benefit, an undivided effort to per-

*Letter of Debussy to Chausson, October 2, 1893 (from *Debussy, Impressionism and Symbolism*, by Stefan Jarocinski, translated by Rollo Myers, London: Eulenburg Books, 1976, pp. 151–52).
**Stefan Jarocinski, p. 140.

mit the character on stage to act and react, to sing and to feel and to make the audience care. The director's active function ceases when the curtain goes up for performance. His technical responsibilities are carried out by his staff, headed by the stage manager. Artistic decisions are realized by singers and orchestra, directed by the conductor. So it turns out that, in the end, it is not the *podium* part of opera that is shared by two masters, but all aspects of *score* throughout the entire period of preparation.

In the case of opera, "orchestra plus" becomes "orchestra merged," and the conductor's function that of a conduit. The great emphasis Wagner placed on the orchestra's role in opera was an emphasis of *score*, of composition, concept, and preparation. For *performance* he built himself an opera house in which neither the orchestra nor the man of the podium were visible to the audience. Edward J. Dent, in his classic introduction to opera, puts it into words. "The more I frequent opera, the more keenly I am interested in the work itself and its presentation as a whole, and the more indifferent I become to its individual parts. I should always prefer not to see the orchestra at all, and certainly not the conductor. . . ."*

*Edward J. Dent, *Opera* (Penguin Books 1940), p. 26.

CONCLUSION

A UNIQUE WAY OF BEING A MUSICIAN

Skills of score and podium may be employed in a wide variety of professional capacities, and false notions of an elitist calling should not be allowed to place limitations on learning or restrictions on who is to learn.

FIGURE 1

TOWARD the end of our introductory chapter, you saw this drawing of a mountain landscape. You were asked to imagine a person ascending the central peak from the lower left, climbing to the top, and descending on the right. You had to determine, first of all, whether the scene was observed from a distance, in which case the climbing figure would have remained small and barely defined throughout, or whether

513

the scene was witnessed from somewhere near the top of the central peak, a helicopter, perhaps, in which case the figure should have appeared to grow larger and more distinct as it approached.

The assumption of an observer was an essential factor in this exercise, and the observer's angle and perspective affected the observation. Throughout this book you were that observer, and what you learned revealed itself to you in the perspective of your own point of view. But as a conductor, you yourself are going to be "an essential element in the whole musical picture," a moving figure, observed.

Thus, in the context of these concluding remarks, our first illustration takes on a new and different meaning. Appropriately, the initial instructions are also the same: you must determine the point of observation, the perspective from which the moving figure that is yourself should be observed. Only this will not be an exercise any longer, but a unique way of being a musician.

To paraphrase the old conundrum "if a tree falls in the forest, but there is none to hear, did it make a sound?", the answer, as far as the conducting profession is concerned, is "no." In order to function, conductors need a cocreative audience, in whose eyes they are an essential element *in whatever part* of the "whole musical picture" they are best able to be an essential element.

The decision is not entirely yours, of course; though to the extent that it is a matter of choice, that choice belongs to no one else. To determine a professional environment in which you would wish to be essential requires a very difficult reorientation: during the course of study, as in the preparation of a score, you are your own subject of main concern, doubt, or approval. In performance, or in your future professional life, you will have to function as a provider. Whether or not your audience approves of your performance, regardless of its merits, is something you must live with. That a particular professional environment may or may not prove congenial, regardless of your merits, is something you must reckon with. Meanwhile it is important that you begin to look at yourself, as a conductor, from any provisional vantage point of professional perspective you wish—as long as it is outside yourself, looking in.

Here is the final manifestation of the two-sidedness of our conducting coin, *score* and *podium*. Score demands single-minded, concentrated, and artistically uncompromising involvement deep within yourself. Podium stands for the outward professional condition, without which there would be no artistic outlet. If solid musical accomplishments are the test of a conductor's success on one side of the coin, equally high accomplishments are expected of him in his coping with a complex professional environment, on the other.

You are the ultimate judge of your own achievement in terms of everything relating to the transformation of a score into your most vivid musical image. You will also have to accept the inexorable fact of professional life, that your success or failure in the podium aspects of your career will always be subject to the judgment of others.

This simple but tremendously important discovery—that there are two, often conflicting, sources of control over any conductor's career—will do more for you than provide perspective. It should go a long way toward clarifying career goals, in terms other than opportunity. Beginning with the tough part, the prospect of lifelong submission to the judgment of others, let us take the most impressionable, albeit powerful of judges as an example: the audience. Which audience?

In the broadest sense, concertgoers are audience, but so are members of the orchestra, colleagues, critics, students, benefactors and employers, symphony board members and advertisers. All these have the power to judge, to reward, to hurt, or to jeopardize your career. A working conductor accepts the reality of that power as a condition of his professional existence and lives with it as a factor of every single decision he makes, from the choice of his programs to the extent of a retard.

Or take a different source of judgment: the employer. Symphony boards are employers of conductors, as are government functionaries, ruling committees of self-employed orchestras, conservatory directors and college presidents, church authorities and public school systems. Keeping in mind the other side of the coin—your own valuation of musical merit and artistic morality is an uneasy companion to whatever ability you will develop to "manage" judging situations—with what kind of employer could you or could you not see yourself negotiating a concert program involving clearly perceived risk of public failure?

More often than not you will be choosing, in effect, a combination of the above. The music director of an orchestra is answerable not only to his symphony board, but to the individuals and organizations on whose support the orchestra depends. A free-lance conductor has more employers than any other: as guest, he will wish to be reengaged by American orchestras (boards), European opera houses and radio networks (government civil servants), European orchestras (self-governing: orchestra committees), etc. Conductors in school situations must take the risk involved within a fiscal framework which, unlike all others, is not primarily designed to support and promote musical performances. Few incumbents would describe employment as teacher / conductors as a sheltered kind of existence.

Later in your career, judgment of a less tangible but all the more powerful nature will have attached itself to your name: you are a terrifying disciplinarian; you are an understanding and effective orchestra trainer, but a boring performer; you give exciting concerts (thanks to superb efforts on the part of the orchestra), but you don't know how to rehearse; you change your mind about tempos; you are not kind to soloists; you don't know how to play Mozart . . .

Now that is one side of it. It's all true, but of course that's not all there is. There *are* two sides of the conducting coin, and survival in the profession is possible—even exhilarating—because judgment from without is balanced by forces within, which can be as potent and powerful as you make them. The score side of conducting has an ally in the podium camp: you.

A standing ovation at the end of a concert is hard to argue with, even by less than enthusiastic members of the symphony board's finance committee. And although, inevitably, this would only mean the substitution of spontaneous approval by an enthusiastic audience, for cooler assessments of your worth in the light of a drop in annual subscriptions, the *dynamics* are an important element: in a profession that provides you with high visibility, evident success in one area tends to balance inevitable setbacks in others. Unpopular conductors may draw audiences, controversial program makers attract foundation grants. But the rate of "burnout" is high—sooner or later most conductors are fired.

"The only medal music directors can look forward to from their board of directors is the Order of the Purple Behind," quipped Erich Leinsdorf on leaving the Boston Symphony in order "to do better work under more reasonable circumstances." The history of great orchestras shows many examples of the termination of highly successful tenures—New York under Barbirolli and Mitropoulos, Boston under Muck, Philadelphia under Stokowski, to say nothing of Vienna under Mahler—which certainly did not reflect on the abilities of the departing maestro. In all cases, the orchestras disliked the conductors, but in only one of the above was this a factor: the Vienna Philharmonic, one of the first orchestras to enjoy autonomy in selecting its conductors, voted not to renew Gustav Mahler's contract after three brilliant but stormy years, and engaged an amenable mediocrity instead.*

On June 8, 1978, the *New York Sunday Times,* in its business section, published an article of extraordinary pertinence to our subject. Under the headline "What Are the Chances of Being Fired?", Carl W. Menk, president of Boyden Associates, Inc., an international executive recruiting organization, set out causes, remedies, and some conclusions concerning the wasteful turnover among well-qualified executives employed in senior positions in America. In its two-sentence, bold-print quote from the article, the *Times* features this statement as a summary: "Before

---

*Under their agreement with the city of Vienna, the Philharmonic, as the official *opera* orchestra, had the privilege nonetheless to play under Mahler, director of the *Hofoper,* for another seven years.

an executive takes a job, he'd do well to take a hard look. The company's style may not be his." Substitute the word conductor for executive, and orchestra for company, and there is much to learn from Mr. Menk's report.

The orchestral field is nowhere more wasteful of available resources than in the filling and maintaining of conducting posts with well-qualified professionals. But conductors themselves are never so negligent of their own best interests than in *choosing and preserving a job for which they are really suited,* one which is right for them in terms of personality and interest as well as professional strengths and weaknesses. With the mixture of musical morality, personal specialization, and sense of opportunity which marks many of our professional decisions (and thus affects our image from an employer's point of view), it is very difficult to illustrate the importance of "audiences" in the abstract. The very close analogy with a field in which a young conductor's sense of musical mission, or fear of personal limitation, are not directly involved, should make the following excerpts* the more helpful by way of illustration.

Outplacement counselors claim most of their assignments involve competent executives who lost their jobs because of personal incompatibility, political infighting, or corporate reorganization. [Conductor vs. board]

Of all major reasons for terminating a competent manager [viz: conductor], problems arising from interpersonal relationships is by far No. 1 on the list.

I recall one outstanding production executive whose emotional involvement with the product he helped design eventually propelled him out of his job. He held the title of Vice President—Operations for a medium-sized electronics company that was extremely marketing-oriented.

His product was technically superior from an engineering point of view, but testing indicated the market place was not yet ready to accept it. The vice president refused to accept the market place's verdict when it was conveyed to him by the marketing vice president, a formidable power in the company.

"It wasn't long before the two were avowed enemies and the marketing vice president eventually triumphed. Any business person can cite similar situations where personal factors resulted in dismissal of an effective executive." [Conductor vs. audience or manager]

The moral of the story is not only that in a market-oriented organization, the product-responsible executive (i.e. the conductor) must be flexible to survive; the more immediate conclusion for us should be that unless such flexibility is a price he is *willing to pay,* and pay many times again, he must choose a different "company style" in the first place.

*New York Times, June 8, 1978.

Boards of directors charged with fiscal responsibility for symphony orchestras are made up, to an increasing extent, of successful executives in the business community. Their judgment of a conductor's merits will be closely bound up with their own experience in the corridors of power and the executive suites of corporations and companies where to be effective involves an intricate mix of informed concessions. The most vibrant acclaim of a conductor's achievements on the music page of the morning paper cannot be a viable alternative for a poor year-end audit on the orchestra's books. And even with high marks on both counts, continuous conflicts within an orchestra's leadership, in which personalities often masquerade as issues, may in the long run "finger" the conductor as the most expendable member of the team.

As there are different kinds of audiences, so there are different kinds of conductors. And while, with combinations and overlappings of the former, large if not altogether homogeneous groups of potential listeners can be brought together to support such an expensive and complex undertaking as the modern symphony orchestra, the young conductor must bear in mind that whatever his special interest and musical preference, his will be a very wide mandate of musical responsibility. Of course, it makes sense to acknowledge, as early as may be, one's real limitations. There are those who truly cannot think of themselves as future teachers and as a consequence should be aware that an academic base (i.e. not only college orchestras, but the many borderline ensembles which combine community, professional, and school forces) will not be a likely start for them. There are those who are not proficient performers on any orchestral instrument. They must exclude from their consideration the well-established path to the podium via an orchestral chair. The nonpianist is not likely to find his first job in an opera company. Young conductors without experience or interest in vocal training will probably miss out on the many choral conducting posts which offer opportunities to engage an orchestra at least once or twice a year. These are negative but practical considerations which lend perspective to one's beginnings and expectations.

But there is also the opposite way of looking at preferences and aptitudes in terms of one's future. An interest in teaching may well mean contact with a university audience, with the possible freedom to perform repertory which even subscription audiences in large cities would only occasionally tolerate. An expert instrumentalist may well find a specialized opening in the many-sided activities of his orchestra which may serve the purposes of his employers as well as his own: Arthur Fiedler started as a violist in the Boston Symphony. Conductor-pianists with operatic interests who invest some of their student time in a thorough study of the repertoire—and some voice lessons—have an excellent chance of making the time-honored transition from coach to conductor at a fairly young age. But as diverse audiences are most effective in support of an orchestra if they can be combined into a single, potent force, so should the entire potential of any young conductor be developed and groomed for a future which will offer its opportunities in a sequence he is yet to learn.

A conductor's finest and most atypical audience consists of his own students. Unlike any other, the audience of "his" young conductors is less interested in his performance than in him, less inclined to accept their own experience of his work on the merits of the effect, than on the extent to which method and approach may appear to have proved useful in achieving such an effect. Why, therefore, "finest audience"?

Perhaps because any teacher / conductor (and *none* should assume that role unless he has been, in his own right and for many years, a conductor / conductor) sees something of himself in his students. Perhaps because his own continual search, that part of any performer's life which makes him an artist, is still an unquestioned aspect of the student conductor's attitude to music itself. And most certainly because this audience asks questions which might never have occurred to him. To that extent it is also his best and most exacting teacher.

We have left out what is in effect our first, most faithful and ever-present audience—ourselves. That this is not merely the physical self who stands on the podium, but includes the person who surveyed the musical surface of the score, explored beneath, memorized, gave free reign to his fantasy, and disciplined his final choices before he proved, discarded, or amplified them in rehearsal, will be understood by anyone who has followed our encounters with score and podium throughout this book. It also includes the self that serves a belief—in a musical cause, a composer, or a particular way of presenting music. We cannot escape from this person and, in his audience role, he may be more critical, encouraging, disappointed, or proud than any of the others out there. He may also decide for whom this particular performance is being played: someone "in the house," someone remembered, some one he never knew—the composer perhaps.

The conductor as listener has occupied us in several chapters of our presentation. The performer as his own audience at the concert adds a further dimension to that: Audiences are served, better or worse than they expect. Audiences have preferences, limits of attention span, reactions, and, above all, a sense of something happening here and now. Listening to an actual musical performance is a rite, a consciously designed escape from our confining sense of clock time, a participatory witnessing of an event which includes the score, the stage, and everyone in the house. Any performer knows the feeling of being part of all that, of receiving as he gives, of judging as he submits to judgment, of being a focus for what he directs.

The indivisibility of music and the ultimate impossibility of distinguishing between what had already been created, what is being recreated, and what is being achieved for this time only find their equivalent mystery in who performs and who listens: We all do both as we listen, never more than while we perform. This is also the point in anyone's development as an artist at which he really begins to learn and the point at which a textbook must end.

INDEX